BUILDING
CONSTRUCTION
ILLUSTRATED

BUILDING CONSTRUCTION ILLUSTRATED

Francis D.K. Ching
Registered Architect
Instructor of Architecture
Ohio University

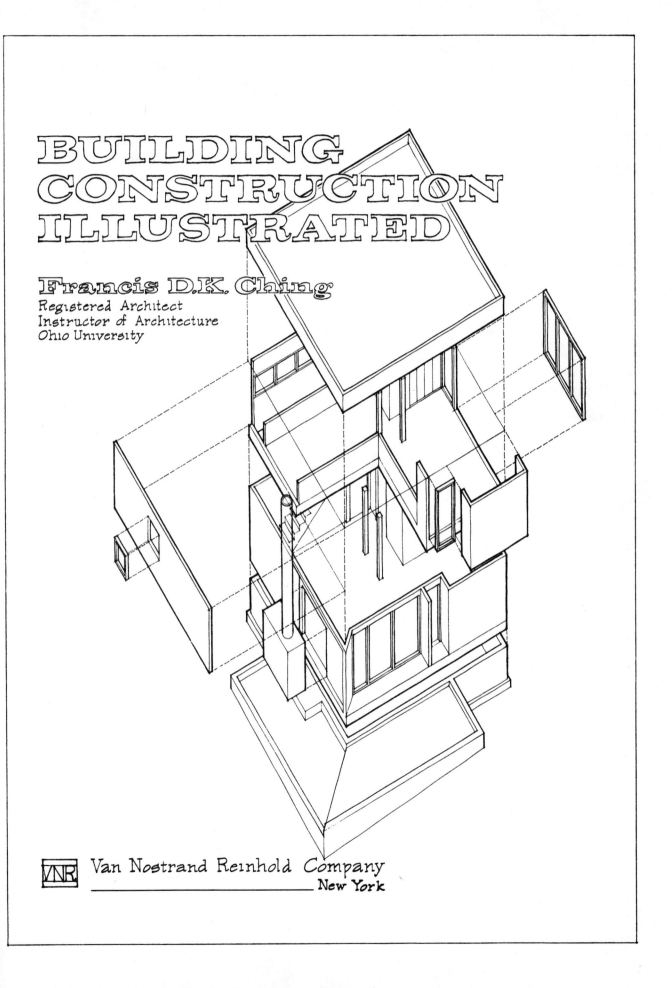

VNR Van Nostrand Reinhold Company
New York

I wish to thank Christopher Krupp, Paul Laseau, Michael Scarmack, Richard Schultz, and Thomas Truax for their help in the production of this work.

Special thanks go to Forrest Wilson for his invaluable help and encouragement.

This book is dedicated to the students and faculty of the School of Architecture at Ohio University (1972-75) for their dedication and enthusiasm for the study of architecture as a fine art.

Manufactured in the United States of America

Published by Van Nostrand Reinhold Company Inc.
135 West 50th Street, New York, NY 10020

Van Nostrand Reinhold Company Limited
Molly Millars Lane
Wokingham, Berkshire, RG11 2PY, England

Van Nostrand Reinhold
480 Latrobe Street
Melbourne, Victoria 3000, Australia

Macmillan of Canada
Division of Gage Publishing Limited
164 Commander Boulevard
Agincourt, Ontario M1S 3C7, Canada

15

Library of Congress Cataloging in Publication Data

Ching, Francis D.K.
    Building construction illustrated

    Bibliography: p.
    Includes index.
    1. Building   2. House construction. I. Ti-
tle.
TH 146. C52   690   75-28203
ISBN 0-442-21532-0 Paper

ISBN 0-442-21533-9 Cloth

PREFACE

This illustrated guide to building construction is intended to acquaint the beginning student of architecture and laymen interested in the principles of building construction with an overview of how the major components of a building fit together and the rationale behind their construction. It is the intent to present as clearly as possible the implications of the choice of structural system and building material on the final building form, and how this choice affects the overall building image in terms of physical dimension, solid/void relationships, fenestration patterns, color, texture, and the building's relationship to its site.

The information presented in this handbook is broken down according to a building's major components, starting with a look at the building site and the factors that should be considered before deciding on a building's location and orientation. Following this is a brief description of the physical building and its major components, and how they relate to one another. Each succeeding chapter then discusses a major system or component according to structural geometry and type of building material, from how each component is constructed to how each interfaces with adjoining components. The last chapter and the appendix provides reference information on building materials and space planning. The bibliography lists sources which, if one is interested in pursuing a subject further, will provide more in-depth information.

It would be nearly impossible to cover all building materials, all construction techniques, under all conditions. But the building systems presented here should be applicable to most normal residential and light construction situations encountered today, and provide a useful context to which the various aspects of building design and construction can be related. The building components themselves are described in terms of their end use. Their specific form, quality, capabilities, and availability will vary according to manufacturer and locale. Always follow the manufacturer's instructions in the use of a material.

Since the visual imagery of the potential building form is implicitly a very important element in the consideration of the material presented, information is conveyed primarily through graphic illustrations. Pure data, raw information, changes with the times just as building materials and construction techniques change with the improvements being made today. What does not change is the underlying rationale behind the construction of a building. That is what is intended to be presented here.

On the following page are listed basic factors and considerations which may be applied to almost any building material or component system to test its appropriateness or applicability to a given design or construction situation.

Since we are currently in the process of converting to the metric system of measurement, metric equivalents are given throughout this book to acquaint the reader with the system and to enable him to begin to build up a mental image of this new set of dimensional values.

Metric equivalents are given according to the following conventions:

- all whole numbers in parentheses indicate millimeters
  - all equivalents are to the nearest whole millimeter
  - all linear dimensions, both nominal and actual are directly converted
    eg. a nominal 2"x4" is converted to (51x102) although its actual 1½"x3½"
    dimensions would be converted to (38x89)
- all numbers expressed to three decimal places indicate meters
  - note that (3048)(mm) = (3.048) meters
- in all other cases, the metric unit of measurement is specified

* see A·0/0 for metric conversion factors

The information in this book can be categorized according to the following factors:

MATERIALS
- structural properties (see STRUCTURE below)
- form and dimensional characteristics
- visual properties: color, pattern, texture
- durability: resistance to · physical abrasion and wear
                           · the elements: sun, wind, rain
                           · corrosion caused by moisture or chemical action
- finish and maintenance requirements
- physical properties of: · weight and density
                          · thermal expansion and conductivity
                          · permeability
                          · fire-resistance
                          · acoustical value
- method of manufacture and supply

STRUCTURE
- form and geometry: linear, planar, volumetric
- foundation, bearing, and support requirements
- forces and stresses to be resolved:
    · type   compressive, tensile, shear
    · direction   vertical (downward or uplift), lateral, angled
    · magnitude   uniformly distributed or concentrated
    · duration   type of load: dead, live, wind, impact, earthquake, moving
- materials used: · strength
                  · stiffness or rigidity
                  · elasticity
- type of connections required: · butt, lap, or interlocking
                                · joints flush or articulated by reveals or offsets
- structural requirements for cantilevers, suspended construction and openings

CONSTRUCTION
- number and size of the pieces to be assembled
- modular implications, if any
- connections and joints: method of fastening required
                          · mechanical (nails, screws, bolts, rivets, clips)
                          · welded
                          · adhesives
- equipment and tools required
- place of assembly: on-site or at the factory
- standardization of parts and prefabrication: where required or advantageous
- erection process: work coordination, erection time, workmanship requirements

THE CONSTRUCTION ASSEMBLY
- control of the flow of: · heat   - thermal conductivity, resistance, reflectivity
                                    - thermal expansion characteristics
                          · air   - infiltration and ventilation
                          · water - vapor: condensation control
                                    - liquid: permeability
                                            : waterproofing/dampproofing requirements
                                    - ice and snow protection
- fire-resistance and acoustical ratings
- form and overall construction depth or width
- accomodation of mechanical equipment, distribution, and supply systems

GENERAL FACTORS
- safety, comfort, health, and sanitation requirements
- suitability and cost (initial and maintenance)
- compliance with applicable building codes

CONTENTS

BUILDING CONSTRUCTION ILLUSTRATED

THE BUILDING SITE

Before one begins to design and construct a building, one should carefully consider the implications of its proposed physical context, the building site. Its geographical location, topography, climate, orientation, and peripheral conditions should influence the overall building form, its orientation and relationship to the ground plane, and its interior space design and layout. These factors affect the choice of a building's structural system, and its materials and construction. The correct siting of a building can also help to control natural light, heat, view, noise, and other environmental elements by providing the building and its occupants with access to desirable elements and absorbing or shielding the building from those elements which may be undesirable.

GEOGRAPHICAL FACTORS:

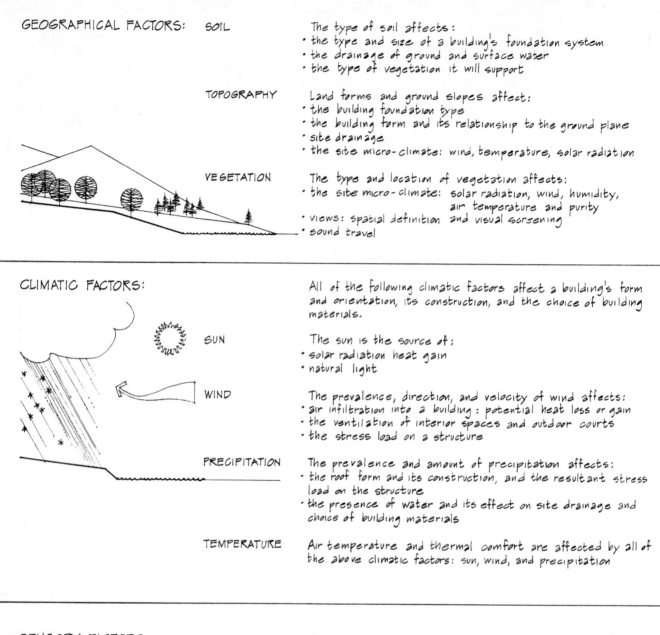

SOIL

The type of soil affects:
- the type and size of a building's foundation system
- the drainage of ground and surface water
- the type of vegetation it will support

TOPOGRAPHY

Land forms and ground slopes affect:
- the building foundation type
- the building form and its relationship to the ground plane
- site drainage
- the site micro-climate: wind, temperature, solar radiation

VEGETATION

The type and location of vegetation affects:
- the site micro-climate: solar radiation, wind, humidity, air temperature and purity
- views: spatial definition and visual screening
- sound travel

CLIMATIC FACTORS:

All of the following climatic factors affect a building's form and orientation, its construction, and the choice of building materials.

SUN

The sun is the source of:
- solar radiation heat gain
- natural light

WIND

The prevalence, direction, and velocity of wind affects:
- air infiltration into a building: potential heat loss or gain
- the ventilation of interior spaces and outdoor courts
- the stress load on a structure

PRECIPITATION

The prevalence and amount of precipitation affects:
- the roof form and its construction, and the resultant stress load on the structure
- the presence of water and its effect on site drainage and choice of building materials

TEMPERATURE

Air temperature and thermal comfort are affected by all of the above climatic factors: sun, wind, and precipitation

SENSORY FACTORS:

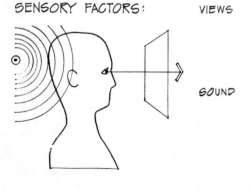

VIEWS

The consideration of desirable and undesirable view will help determine:
- the building form and orientation
- the building's fenestration (door and window openings)
- the type of vegetation used in landscaping

SOUND

The level, quality, and source of sound affects:
- the distribution and orientation of the building mass
- the choice of building materials and their construction
- the type of sound control methods employed

Practically all buildings depend on soil for their ultimate support. Their structural integrity depends on the soil type and its strength under loading.

A soil's strength under loading is dependent on its resistance to shear, a function of its internal friction and cohesion. The measure of a soil's strength is its compressibility or bearing capacity in pounds per square foot. (see table below)

A foundation and footing system must distribute a building's loads over an area large enough in such a way that the resultant unit load on the soil is uniform under all portions of the structure and does not exceed the soil's load bearing capacity. While there are few if any problems with high load bearing soils, poor soils may dictate the type of foundation system and load distribution pattern to be used for a building and therefore it's ultimate form. In extreme cases, unstable soils may render a site unbuildable unless an elaborately engineered and expensive foundation system is designed. (see 3·2/3)

In cold climates, the freezing and subsequent thawing of soil may cause ground heaving and place stress on a building's foundation system and structure. The extent of this frost action depends on the soil type and the site's region. In any case, a building's footings should be placed below the site's frost line.

A soil's drainage qualities should be taken into account to ensure that both surface and ground water is properly channeled away from the building structure to avoid:
- deterioration of a soil's load bearing capacity
- possible leakage of water into a building's interior
- harmful effects of moisture on a building's materials

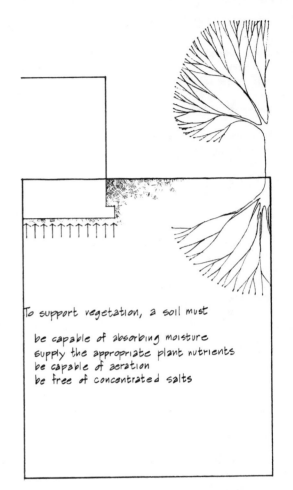

To support vegetation, a soil must

- be capable of absorbing moisture
- supply the appropriate plant nutrients
- be capable of aeration
- be free of concentrated salts

The following table contains generalized information for reference only. Most soils are in fact a combination of different soil types. Refer to local building codes and usage for allowable bearing capacities of the soils in the site's region. When in doubt or when there are unusual loading conditions, it is best to have a soil engineer perform soil borings and tests.

SOIL TYPE	SOIL BEARING CAPACITY	FROST ACTION	DRAIN
compact, partially cemented gravel or sand; well graded with little or no fines	20,000 lbs/ft² (97 640) kg/m²	none	excellent
compact gravel; gravel and sand mixture	12,000 (58 584)	none	excellent
course, compact sand; loose gravel; hard, dry, clay	8000 (39 056)	slight	fair to good
course, loose sand; fine, compact sand; loose sand and gravel mixture	6000 (29 292)	slight	fair to good
fine, loose sand; dry, stiff clay	4000 (19 528)	high	fair to poor
soft clay; soft, broken shale	2000 (9 764)	high	poor
organic soils	unsuitable for foundations		

(1 lb/ft² = 4.882 kg/m²)

The presence of water, the variation in particle size, and the stratification of the soil bed are all important factors in determining the load bearing capacity of a soil bed.

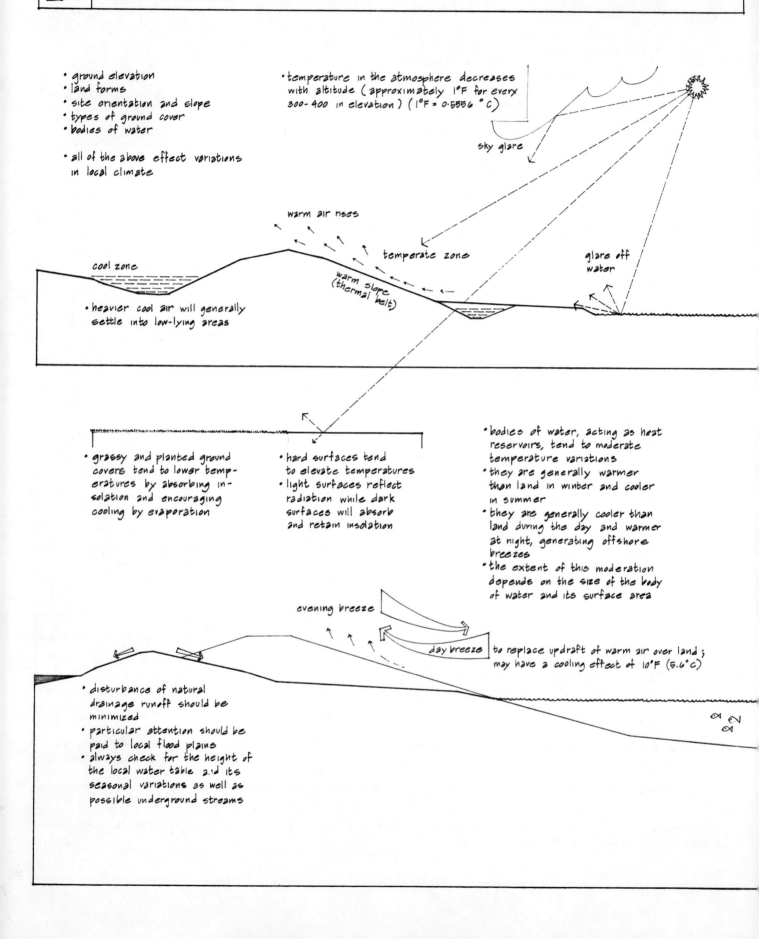

- ground elevation
- land forms
- site orientation and slope
- types of ground cover
- bodies of water

- all of the above effect variations in local climate

- temperature in the atmosphere decreases with altitude (approximately 1°F for every 300-400 in elevation) (1°F = 0.5556 °C)

sky glare

warm air rises

cool zone

temperate zone

glare off water

warm slope (thermal belt)

- heavier cool air will generally settle into low-lying areas

- grassy and planted ground covers tend to lower temperatures by absorbing insolation and encouraging cooling by evaporation

- hard surfaces tend to elevate temperatures
- light surfaces reflect radiation while dark surfaces will absorb and retain insolation

- bodies of water, acting as heat reservoirs, tend to moderate temperature variations
- they are generally warmer than land in winter and cooler in summer
- they are generally cooler than land during the day and warmer at night, generating offshore breezes
- the extent of this moderation depends on the size of the body of water and its surface area

evening breeze

day breeze to replace updraft of warm air over land; may have a cooling effect of 10°F (5.6°C)

- disturbance of natural drainage runoff should be minimized
- particular attention should be paid to local flood plains
- always check for the height of the local water table and its seasonal variations as well as possible underground streams

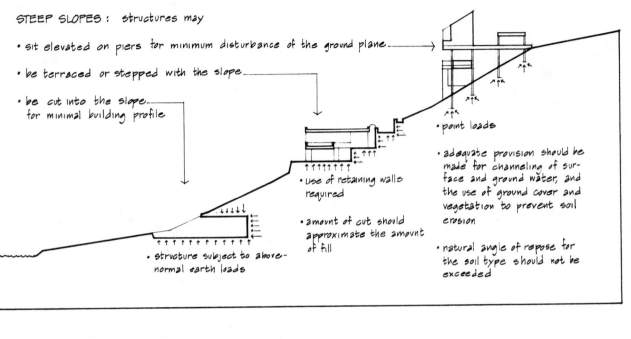

STEEP SLOPES: structures may

• sit elevated on piers for minimum disturbance of the ground plane.

• be terraced or stepped with the slope.

• be cut into the slope. for minimal building profile

• use of retaining walls required

• amount of cut should approximate the amount of fill

• structure subject to above-normal earth loads

• point loads

• adequate provision should be made for channeling of surface and ground water, and the use of ground cover and vegetation to prevent soil erosion

• natural angle of repose for the soil type should not be exceeded

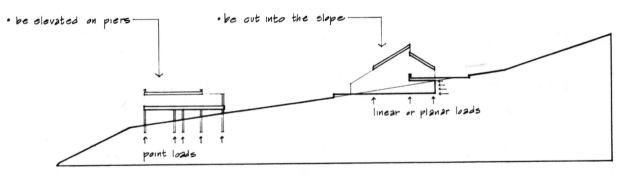

MODERATE SLOPES: structures may

• be elevated on piers

• be cut into the slope

• linear or planar loads

• point loads

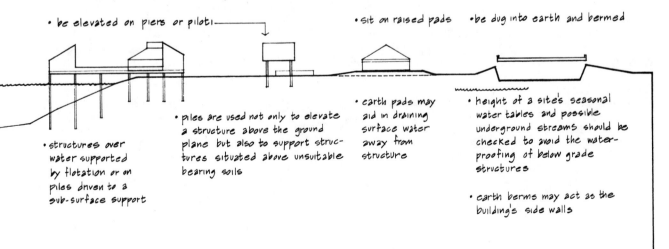

FLAT SLOPES: structures may

• be elevated on piers or piloti

• sit on raised pads

• be dug into earth and bermed

• structures over water supported by flotation or on piles driven to a sub-surface support

• piles are used not only to elevate a structure above the ground plane but also to support structures situated above unsuitable bearing soils

• earth pads may aid in draining surface water away from structure

• height of a site's seasonal water tables and possible underground streams should be checked to avoid the waterproofing of below grade structures

• earth berms may act as the building's side walls

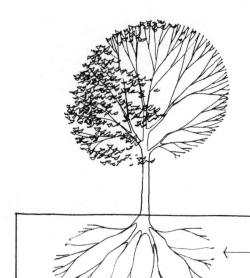

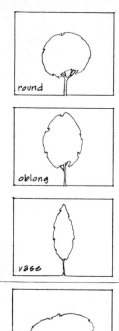

round

oblong

vase

horizontal oblong

Factors to consider in the selection and use of trees in landscaping include:

- overall form, density, and color of the foliage
- potential height and spread
- speed or rate of growth
- size and depth of the root structure
- soil, water, sunlight, air and temperature
- requirements

- trees planted too close to a building may disrupt the building's foundation system with their root structure
- similarly, a tree's root structure may interfere with underground mechanical and plumbing lines

- the manner in which trees and plant life adapt their form to climate hints at ways buildings might do the same

Grass and vegetation ground covers:

- tend to reduce temperatures by absorbing insolation and encouraging cooling by their evaporation process
- aid in stabilizing soils and preventing erosion
- increase a soil's permeability to air and water

- similarly, vines can reduce the heat transmission through a wall exposed to the sun in warm weather by providing it with shade and cooling the immediate environment by evaporation

Trees affect the immediate environment of a building by:

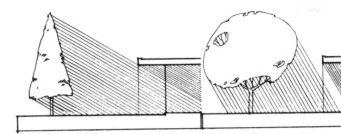

• providing shade
 the amount of shade depends on the tree's
  · orientation to the sun
  · proximity to the building
  · shape, spread and height
  · density of foliage and branch structure

• trees are best located to shade buildings from the southeast and southwest when the morning and late afternoon sun has a low altitude and casts long shadows
• south-facing overhangs provide more efficient shading during mid-day period when the sun is high and casts short shadows

  · deciduous trees provide shade and glare protection during the summer and let solar radiation (as well as glare) through during the winter
  · evergreens provide shade throughout the year and helps reduce snow glare during the winter

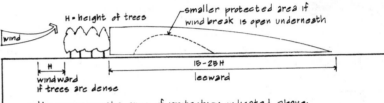

• reducing sky, ground, and snow glare (see above)

• providing wind protection
  · foliage reduces wind blown dust
  · evergreens provide effective wind breaks during the winter and reduces building heat losses

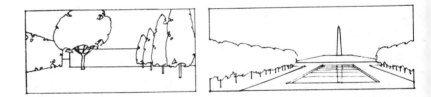

• the approximate area of protection indicated above depends on the height and density of the trees, and wind velocity
• the protection provided is primarily a reduction in wind velocity producing an area of relative calm

• absorbing solar radiation and cooling by their evaporation process

• filtering the air and wind-blown dust in the immediate environment

• aiding in soil stabilization, increasing its permeability to water and air, and preventing soil erosion

• defining space and directing views

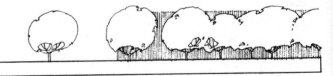

• providing visual screening and privacy

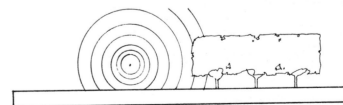

• reducing air-borne sound

A building's location, orientation, and form should attempt to take advantage of the sun's thermal, hygienic, and psychological benefits.

Solar radiation, a primary source of heat gain, may or may not be beneficial, depending on the building site's climatic region. (see table below) The control of solar radiation is the critical factor. The sun's rays should be allowed to penetrate and be absorbed by a building when beneficial and blocked when undesirable. (see facing page for solar shading devices) If solar energy is to be taken advantage of as a power source, the orientation of a building's surface may become even more important. (* see 11·24)

As the source of natural light, the sun affects the layout and orientation of interior spaces and the size and placement of their window openings. (* see also 11·21)

The sun's path through the sky varies with the seasons and a site's latitude. Its altitude and bearing angle range should be determined before calculating solar heat gain and shading devices for a specific site.

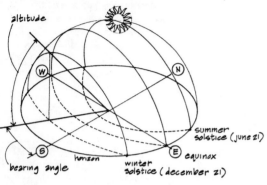

altitude
W
N
summer solstice (june 21)
S
E equinox
bearing angle
horizon
winter solstice (december 21)

The table below pertains primarily to isolated buildings. The information presented should be considered along with other contextural and programmitic requirements.

In determining a building's form, location, and orientation, the objective should be to maintain a balance between underheated periods when solar radiation is beneficial and overheated periods when radiation should be avoided. The long face of a building should normally face south if possible. East and west exposures are generally warmer in summer and cooler in winter than south, southeast, or southwest exposures.

OPTIMUM SHAPE	LOCATION	GENERAL OBJECTIVES	ORIENTATION
low temperatures encourage minimizing of form's surface area		**COOL REGIONS** · increase solar radiation heat absorption · reduce radiation, conduction, and evaporation heat loss · provide wind protection	
temperate climate allows considerable along the east-west axis		**TEMPERATE REGIONS** · solar heat gain should be balanced with shade protection on a seasonal basis · wind: air movement desirable during hot periods; should be blocked during cold periods	
closed forms; building mass enclosing cool air ponds desirable		**HOT-ARID REGIONS** · reduce solar radiation and conduction heat gain · promote cooling by evaporation (using water and planting) · shading desirable	
form may be freely elongated along the east-west axis to minimize east and west exposure		**HOT-HUMID REGIONS** · reduce solar radiation heat gain · utilize wind to promote cooling by evaporation · shading desirable	

Shading devices shield a building's surfaces and interior spaces from solar radiation. Their effectiveness depends on their location, orientation and form. Exterior shading devices are more efficient those located within a building's walls since they intercept the sun's radiation before it can reach the building's surface.

Below are illustrated some basic types of solar shading devices. Their orientation, form, materials, and construction may vary to suit specific situations. The visual properties of exterior shading devices (spatial character, composition, rhythm, color, light and shadow patterns) contribute much toward a building's appearance.

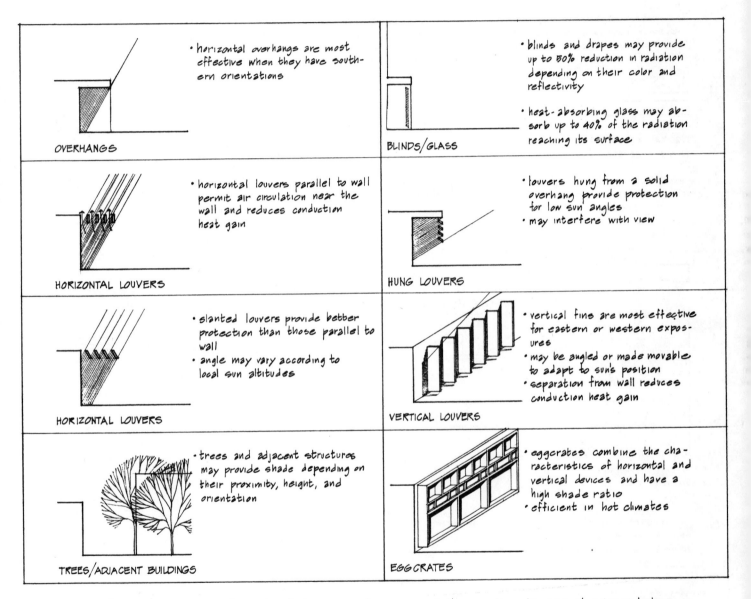

OVERHANGS

• horizontal overhangs are most effective when they have southern orientations

BLINDS/GLASS

• blinds and drapes may provide up to 50% reduction in radiation depending on their color and reflectivity

• heat-absorbing glass may absorb up to 40% of the radiation reaching its surface

HORIZONTAL LOUVERS

• horizontal louvers parallel to wall permit air circulation near the wall and reduces conduction heat gain

HUNG LOUVERS

• louvers hung from a solid overhang provide protection for low sun angles
• may interfere with view

HORIZONTAL LOUVERS

• slanted louvers provide better protection than those parallel to wall
• angle may vary according to local sun altitudes

VERTICAL LOUVERS

• vertical fins are most effective for eastern or western exposures
• may be angled or made movable to adapt to sun's position
• separation from wall reduces conduction heat gain

TREES/ADJACENT BUILDINGS

• trees and adjacent structures may provide shade depending on their proximity, height, and orientation

EGGCRATES

• eggcrates combine the characteristics of horizontal and vertical devices and have a high shade ratio
• efficient in hot climates

Since a building's exterior walls and roof planes are its primary sheltering elements against solar radiation, the materials used in their construction should be considered in terms of their reflectivity and thermal conductivity. A material's reflectivity depends on its color and texture. Light colors and smooth surfaces tend to reflect more radiation than dark, textured ones. Effective insulating materials usually incorporate captured dead air space. Massive materials such as masonry absorbs and stores heat for a period of time, thus delaying heat transmission. (see 8·14/15)

Wind prevalence, velocity, temperature, and direction are important site considerations in all climatic regions. During hot periods, wind-induced ventilation is desirable for cooling by evaporation. During cold periods, wind should be blocked or avoided to reduce air infiltration into a building and lower heat losses.

The seasonal and daily variations in the wind should be considered in evaluating its potential effect on a building. In temperate climates, for example, where ventilation is desirable during the summer and wind protection is required during the winter, the wind normally changes directions on a seasonal basis and can be controlled to achieve both of the above objectives.

The protection afforded by wind breaks is primarily a reduction in wind velocity. The extent of the area of relative calm created by a windbreak depends on its height, density, form, orientation to the wind, and wind velocity. Wind breaks may be in the form of earth berms, trees, or structures.

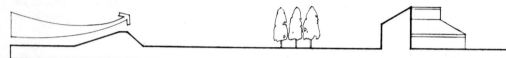

Natural ventilation in buildings is generated by differences in air pressure as well as temperature. The air flow patterns generated by these forces is affected more by building geometry than by air speed.

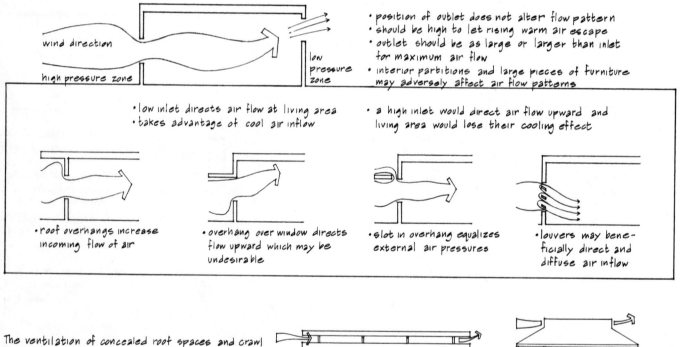

wind direction

high pressure zone

low pressure zone

- position of outlet does not alter flow pattern
- should be high to let rising warm air escape
- outlet should be as large or larger than inlet for maximum air flow
- interior partitions and large pieces of furniture may adversely affect air flow patterns

- low inlet directs air flow at living area
- takes advantage of cool air inflow

- a high inlet would direct air flow upward and living area would lose their cooling effect

- roof overhangs increase incoming flow of air

- overhang over window directs flow upward which may be undesirable

- slot in overhang equalizes external air pressures

- louvers may beneficially direct and diffuse air inflow

The ventilation of concealed roof spaces and crawl spaces can help control condensation during cold periods and reduce heat gain in hot periods.

Wind causes lateral loads on structures and induces uplift forces on flat roofs, on pitched roofs with slopes up to 7:12, and on leeward slopes of roofs with slopes above 7:12.

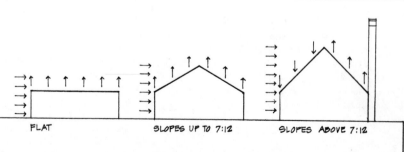

FLAT   SLOPES UP TO 7:12   SLOPES ABOVE 7:12

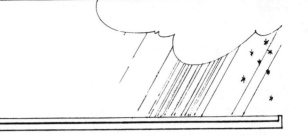

 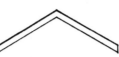

- steep sloped roofs have fast runoff and shed rain, snow, and ice easily

- moderately sloped roofs have easy runoff

- flat roofs require either interior roof drains or scuppers along their perimeters
  water-cooled roofs used in hot arid climates hold rainwater and must support above-normal roof loads
  in cold climates, flat roofs are subject to heavy snow loads; layer of snow can act as additional insulation

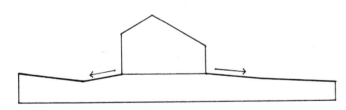

- overhangs protect a building's wall surface from both sun and rain and their weathering effects

- damp or waterproofing is required for below grade spaces when ground water is present
- ground water should be drained down and away from a structure's foundation to a natural outfall or drywell

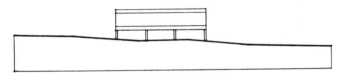

- natural surface drainage patterns are least disturbed by lifting a structure off the ground plane with piers

- always slope the ground plane away from a building to avoid water leakage problems
- to prevent soil erosion, protective ground cover should be provided for swales with grades over 3% and ground slopes with grades over 33%

- minimum grade for planted ground cover areas: 2% (3% recommended)

- minimum grade for paved areas: 0.5% (1% recommended)

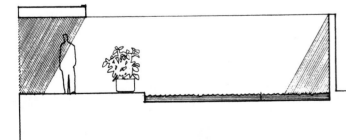

- bodies of water tend to moderate temperature variations and temper their immediate environment
- in hot arid climates, even small bodies of water are desirable both psychologically and physically for their evaporative cooling effect
- protection from reflected glare must be provided

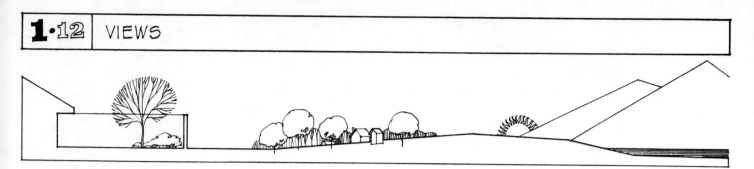

A building's window openings should be positioned and oriented not only to satisfy natural light and ventilation requirements but also to frame desirable views. Depending on a site's context, these views may be close in to the building, or they may be a short distance away or long range in nature. Desirable views may even be non-existent in which case they may be created.

Windows may be cut into a wall in various ways depending on the nature of the view and how it is to been framed and seen.

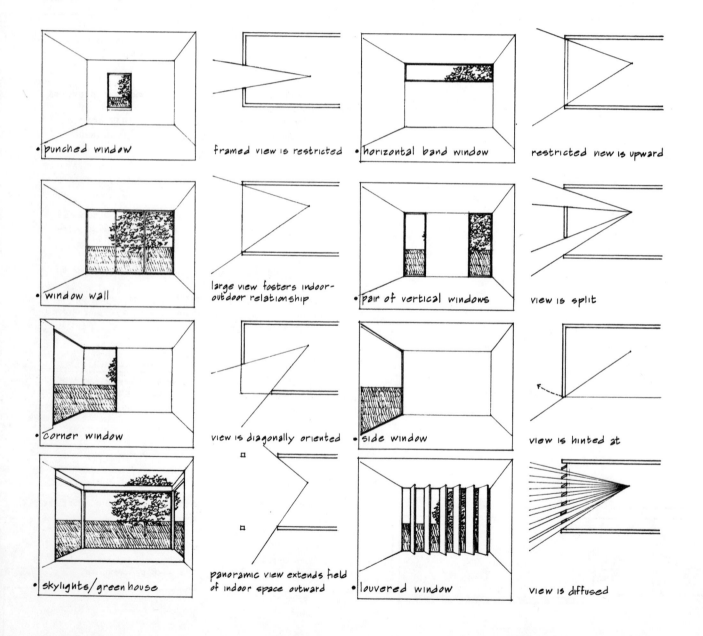

• punched window — framed view is restricted

• horizontal band window — restricted view is upward

• window wall — large view fosters indoor-outdoor relationship

• pair of vertical windows — view is split

• corner window — view is diagonally oriented

• side window — view is hinted at

• skylights/green house — panoramic view extends field of indoor space outward

• louvered window — view is diffused

Sound requires a source and a path. Undesirable exterior sounds or noise are caused primarily by cars, aircraft, and other machinery. The sound energy they generate travels through the air outward from the source in all directions in a continuously extending wave. This sound energy lessens in intensity as it disperses over a wider area.

The first consideration in reducing the impact of exterior noise is one of distance, locating a building as far from the noise source as possible. When this is not possible because of a small, restricted site, then the interior spaces of a building may be screened from the noise source by:

• physical mass such as earth berms

• building zones where noise can be tolerated: ie. mechanical, service, and utility areas

• the exterior walls and roof are a building's primary barriers against external noise transmission into its interior; door and window openings are the weak spots in these barriers and should therefore be oriented away from the noise source if possible.

• landscaping elements:
• dense tree plantings may have a screening effect on noise
• planted ground cover areas are preferable to hard, non-absorbent surfaces

Exterior courtyard spaces should be acoustically treated as rooms.
* see A·12

THE BUILDING

This chapter illustrates a building as the physical embodiment of a number of necessarily related, coordinated and integrated systems, and provides a context for the following chapters, each of which takes a major building component, illustrates its construction in various materials, and how it interfaces with other components. Included in this chapter is a brief introduction to building structure and the illustration of how the choice of a structural system may affect the final form of a building.

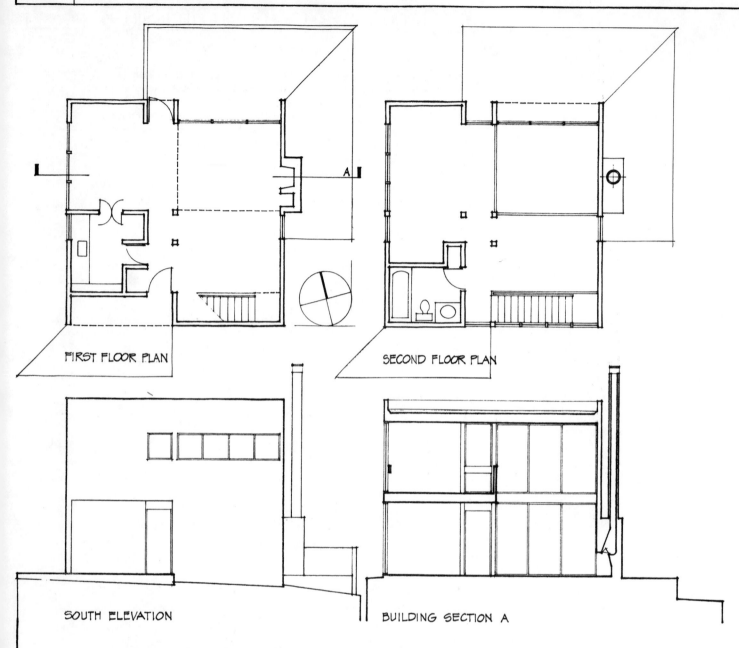

FIRST FLOOR PLAN

SECOND FLOOR PLAN

SOUTH ELEVATION

BUILDING SECTION A

The site plan is a view looking straight down at a building illustrating its location and orientation on a plot of land and providing information about the site's topography, landscaping, utilities and sitework.

The floor plan is a view looking straight down after a horizontal plane is cut approximately 4' (1·210) above the floor and the top piece removed. It illustrates the size, form, and relationships between the spaces of a building measured horizontally as well as the thickness and construction of the vertical space-defining elements (walls, columns, door and window openings).

The building section is a horizontal view of a building after a vertical plane is cut through significant spaces of a building and the front piece removed. Like the floor plan, it also illustrates the size, form, and relationships between the spaces of a building but measured horizontally (in one dimension) and vertically. Although the building section illustrates primarily the thickness and construction of horizontal (floors and roofs) and vertical (wall) elements, it may also include exterior and interior wall elevations.

Architectural drawing is the graphic language of building. They visually convey the design form (as in the case of presentation drawings) and the instructions necessary for the construction of the design (as in the case of "working drawings"). The following is a brief explanation of the major types of architectural drawing according to your point of view.

Most people associate architectural drawings with "blueprints" or construction drawings. For the most part construction or "working" drawings consist of orthographic views of a building (as briefly explained and illustrated below and on the preceding page). These are also called multi-view drawings since a series of related views is required to understand the overall three-dimensional form of the design and its constituent parts. The main advantage of this type of drawing and the reason why it is used for the construction of buildings is that building elements are seen in true size (to scale), shape, and orientation when viewed from a perpendicular aspect. Orthographic drawing's main disadvantage is its inherent ambiguity in the definition of depth or the third dimension. For this reason reliance on conventions and symbols is necessary for the description and understanding of what is drawn.

All drawing is convention utilizing varying degrees of abstraction. The type of drawing that comes closest to communicating three-dimensional form as we naturally perceive it is an accurately drawn perspective. Its pictorial value however cannot be taken advantage of in construction drawings since elements within the perspective are foreshortened and cannot be scaled. A type of drawing that combines the pictorial value of a perspective and the scaleability of orthographic drawings is the axonometric. For this reason, whenever possible, graphic information throughout this book is presented via axonometric drawing.

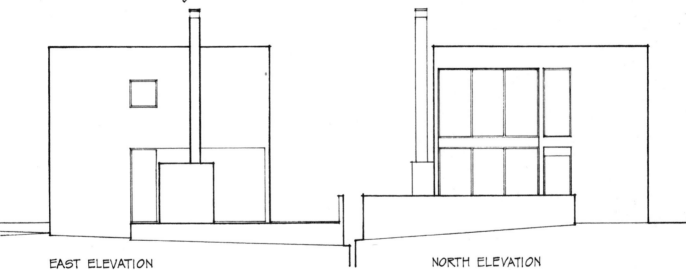

EAST ELEVATION   NORTH ELEVATION

Building elevations are horizontal views of a building's exterior usually taken from a point of view perpendicular to the building's primary vertical surfaces illustrating the size, shape, and material of the exterior surfaces as well as the size, proportion, and nature of the openings within them.

These orthographic drawing types (plan, section, elevation) are used to portray not only whole building forms but also the form and construction of a building's components (ie. wall sections, window sections, cabinet details, etc.)

plan of door jamb

isometric of door jamb

section through wood joist floor system

isometric of wood joist floor system

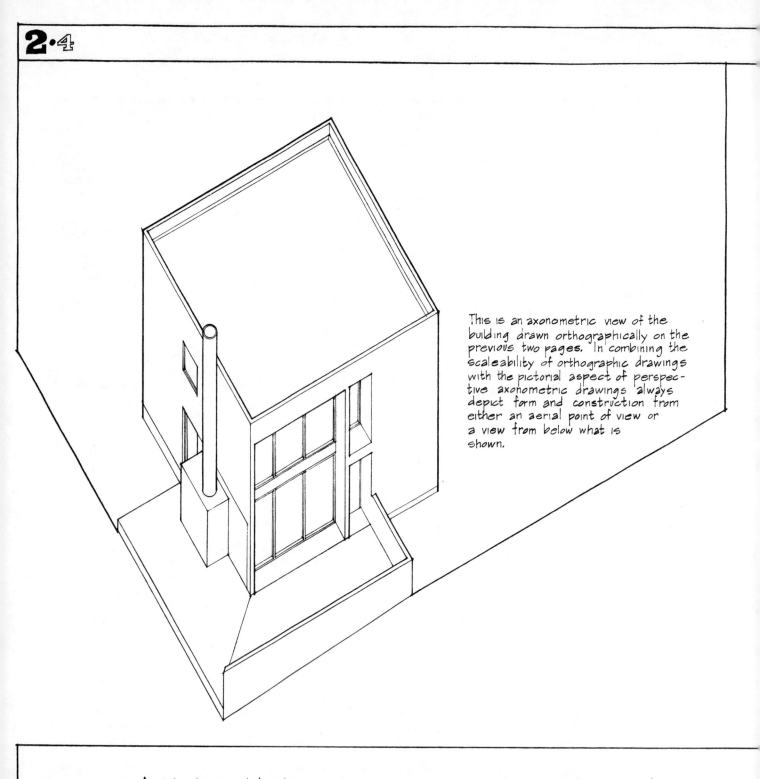

This is an axonometric view of the building drawn orthographically on the previous two pages. In combining the scaleability of orthographic drawings with the pictorial aspect of perspective axonometric drawings always depict form and construction from either an aerial point of view or a view from below what is shown.

Architecture and building construction are not necessarily one and the same. An understanding of how the various component systems of a building fit together, how they must be compatible and integrated with one another, is necessary during both the design and construction of a building. This understanding, however, enables one to build architecture but does not guarantee it. A working knowledge of building construction is only one of several critical factors in the execution of architecture.

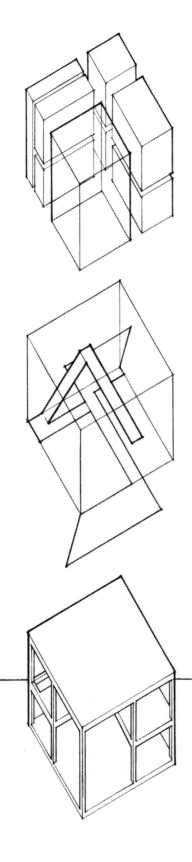

When we speak of architecture as the art of building we must consider conceptual systems of order in addition to the physical ones of construction. A few of these which aid in eliciting positive human response to and reinforcing the perceptual and conceptual understanding of architecture are:

- spatial organization: size
                           scale
                           proportion
                           relationships
                           hierarchy

- functional organization: zoning

- circulation systems: horizontal and vertical

- physical imagery: form
                           space
                           light
                           color
                           texture
                           pattern

- context: buildings as integrated elements within the natural and man-made environment

Of primary interest to us in this book are a building's physical components which help to define, organize, and reinforce the perceptual and conceptual elements of that building. On the following page we will begin to break a building down into its physical constituent elements which will then be elaborated on in succeeding chapters.

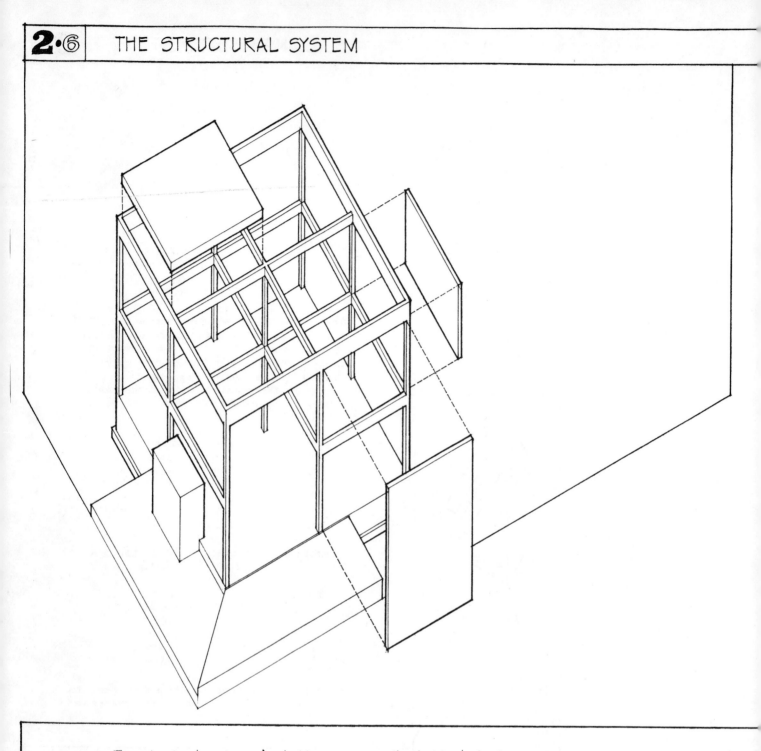

The structural system of a building supports the building's loads against the pull of gravity and enables it to resist the forces of wind pressure, shock or impact loads, vibrations, and earthquakes. In counteracting these internal and external forces which act on a building, a structural system will naturally impart a specific form to that building. In selecting a structural system one must therefore consider, in addition to building stability, function, and economy of means, the image and definition a specific structural system will tend to impart on the building's external form and internal spaces.

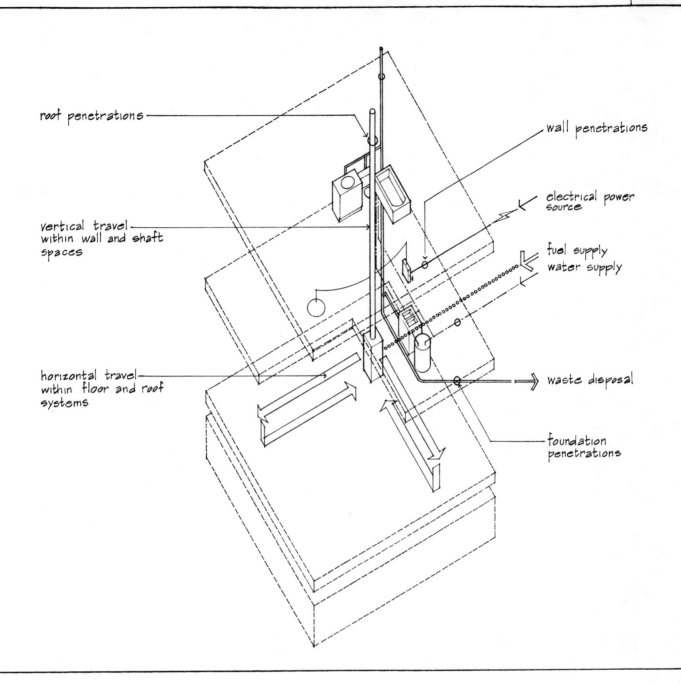

roof penetrations

wall penetrations

electrical power source

vertical travel within wall and shaft spaces

fuel supply
water supply

horizontal travel within floor and roof systems

waste disposal

foundation penetrations

Heating, ventilating, and air conditioning systems condition a building's interior environment for human health and comfort. These systems are generally concealed from view and run vertically within wall spaces and horizontally within floor and roof systems. They must therefore be carefully integrated with the building volume and mass to provide adequate accomodation for their components as well as visually coordinated outlets and points of access.

A building's water supply, waste disposal, and electrical systems should likewise be integrated with the building's form and physical elements. Oftentimes these mechanical systems will run parallel to one another in which case close coordination between them becomes important.

*see chapter II

A building can generally be broken down physically into:

① structural framework
② exterior envelope or skin
③ interior subdivisions of space

Each of these in turn can be divided into major horizontal and vertical elements:

- horizontal elements: floor planes
                           roof planes
                           beams
- vertical elements: wall planes
                           columns

These major components of a building can come together in a number of ways depending on the materials utilized, the method of resolving and transferring forces on and within the building, and the desired physical form.

What is presented here and in the following chapters is basic information on the most typical ways in which these major components are constructed, and how they may effectively interface with one another. Implications of system and material choices on building design and form are also presented where applicable.

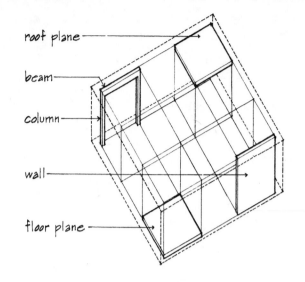

roof plane
beam
column
wall
floor plane

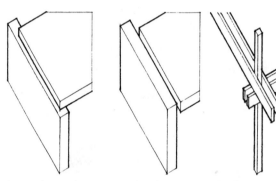

direct bearing joint   vertical butt joint   interlocking joint

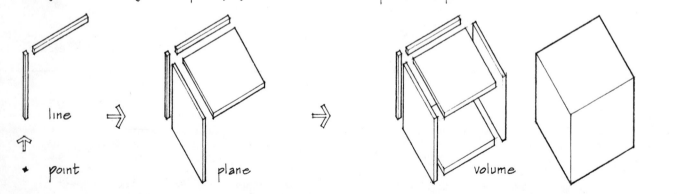

As a way of explaining the form of each major building element in a comparative manner, they are categorized according to the primary geometric elements of point, line, plane, and volume.

line

point   plane   volume

On the facing page is an expanded axonometric view of the building already illustrated on previous pages to articulate the building's major components as entities and the points at which they must be compatible with adjoining elements.

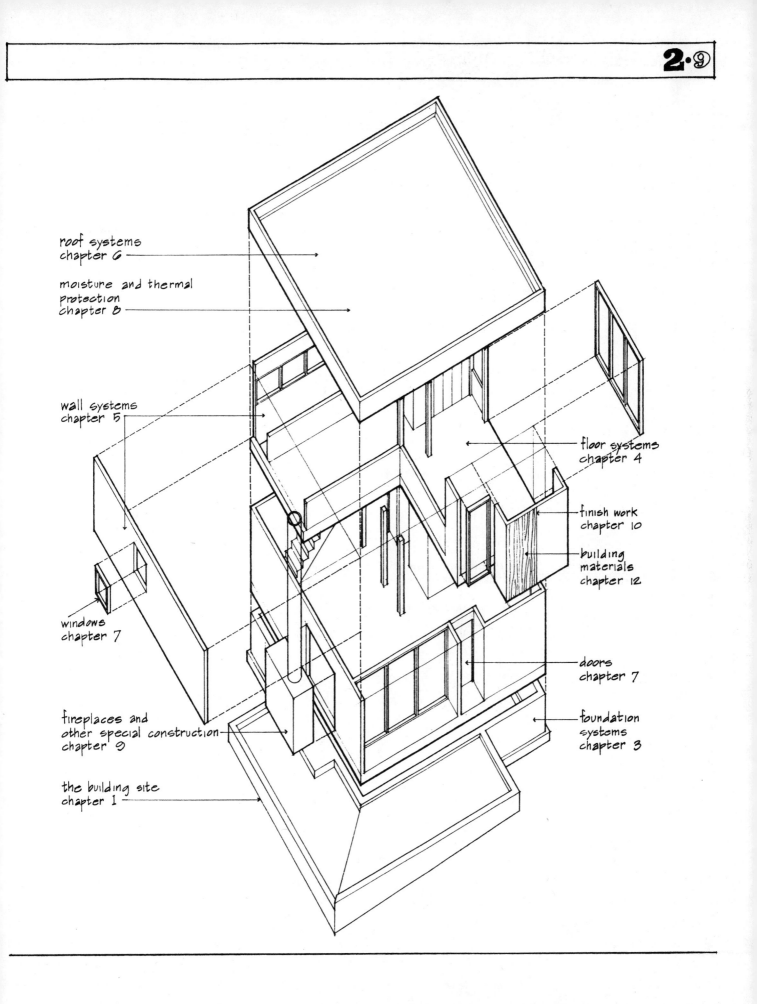

roof systems
chapter 6

moisture and thermal
protection
chapter 8

wall systems
chapter 5

floor systems
chapter 4

finish work
chapter 10

building
materials
chapter 12

windows
chapter 7

doors
chapter 7

fireplaces and
other special construction
chapter 9

foundation
systems
chapter 3

the building site
chapter 1

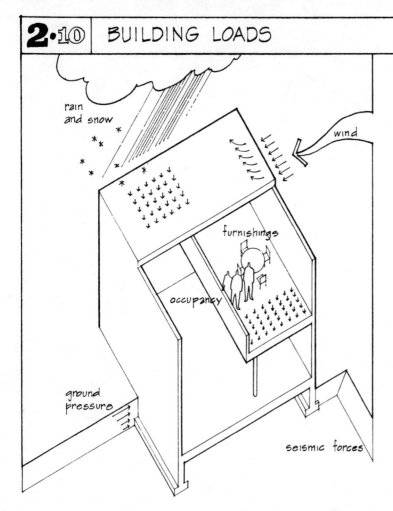

rain
and snow

wind

furnishings

occupancy

ground
pressure

seismic forces

All of the following forces must be considered
in the design of a building structure:

- **dead loads:**   static, fixed loads
  (building structure, skin,
  fixed equipment)

- **live loads:**   transient and moving loads
  (occupants, furnishings, snow, rain)

- **wind loads:**   wind pressure may result in
  lateral loading on walls and
  in downward pressure or
  uplift forces on roof planes

- **impact loads / shock waves / vibrations**

- **seismic loading:** earthquake forces

Except for a building's dead load which is fixed,
the other forces listed above can vary in
duration, magnitude, and point of application. A
building structure must nevertheless be designed
for these possibilities.

The following is a very brief outline of the factors
which must be considered in the resolution of the
above forces. For more complete information on the
structural analysis of buildings, see bibliography.

uniform loading

concentrated load

column loading

lateral loading

beam/column
connection

horizontal component

resultant

vertical component

concurrent forces

force parallelogram

non-concurrent forces

counteracting
forces

moment couple

In the structural analysis of buildings, we are interested in the magnitude, direction, and point of application of forces, and their resolution to produce a
state of equilibrium. This static balance is achieved
by counteracting these forces in an equal but
opposite direction.

Forces can be assumed to be applied either uniformly
as a live load on a floor plane or a wind load against
a wall, or as a point or concentrated load such as a
beam bearing on a column or a column bearing on a
foundation footing.

Forces can be parallel but not meet as in the case of
a point load on a beam, or they may be parallel and
concurrent as in the case of a point load on a column.
Non-concurrent forces will tend to cause a structural member to rotate which must be counteracted
by the material's internal strength.

A force can be divided into a number of components
as in the case of the force carried by a sloping
roof joist being counteracted by the vertical wall
and horizontal ceiling plane.

Understanding the type and magnitude of the forces acting on a building and how the building might deform when acted upon by these forces should give the designer and builder significant clues as to how best to resolve the forces with the building's structural system.

Here we are interested in the general characteristics of linear and planar structural elements. Both the column and beam are geometrically simple. The column (a point in plan, a line in space) transmits compressive forces vertically along its shaft. If the load is centered or evenly distributed, the column will simply compress. If, however, the load is off center or applied laterally, the column will experience curvature (similar to a beam). The thicker a column is in relation to its height, the better it will withstand eccentric or lateral loading.

The beam transmits forces laterally along its length to its supports. A beam carrying a load always experiences bending stresses. These stresses are greatest along the beam's top and bottom edges.

As a general rule of thumb the strength of a beam will increase according to the square of its increase in depth; its stiffness will generally increase according to the cube of its increase in depth. Similarly, if a beam's length is doubled, the bending stress will double and it will support only half its original maximum load. Its deflection under stress increases according to the cube of its increase in length.

When we support a beam with two columns we begin to define or qualify the space around the construction. We can envision these linear structural elements defining an invisible plane. If we make this plane solid, it too acts as a column (ie. a long, thin one) in transmitting compressive forces to the ground. This "bearing wall" however is susceptible to lateral loadings such as wind pressure or underground water and soil pressures. Stresses in a bearing wall have to flow around any openings (ie. doors and windows) within the wall plane.

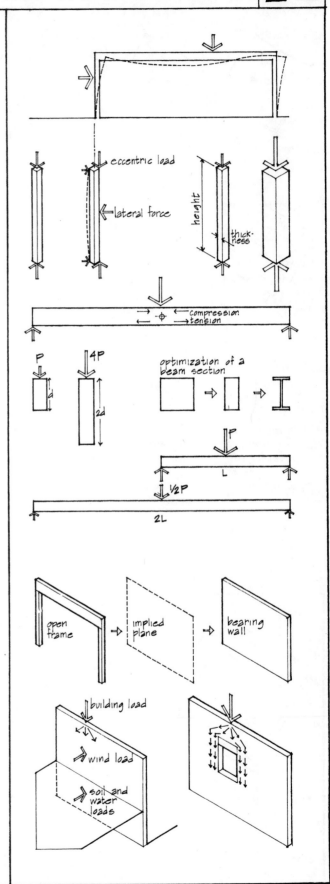

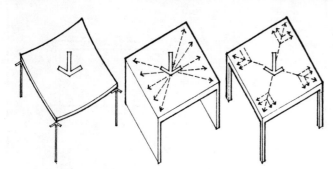

A horizontal bearing plane or slab, if supported along two parallel edges, can be seen as a wide, flat beam. A slab, however, is inherently more versatile than a narrow beam in providing paths along which stresses may travel to the slab's supports.

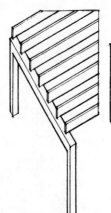
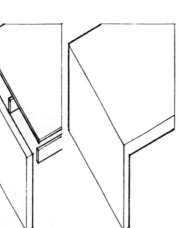

Joining these basic structural elements together (beams and horizontal slabs supported by columns and bearing walls) we compose three-dimensional form and define space. The joints between these linear and planar elements are critical in achieving structural integrity and efficiency in a building. These joints, if rigid, facilitate the transfer of stresses from one member to another and enable the overall structure to withstand heavier loads. This assumes, of course, that the individual members themselves are able to withstand these stresses internally.

• linear elements forming a horizontal plane bearing on either a linear or planar element

• a horizontal plane bearing on linear elements which in turn bear on either another linear or planar element

• a horizontal plane bearing on a vertical plane

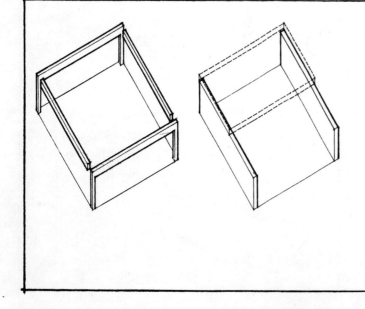

Joining linear elements (columns and beams) we form a skeletal structural system. Utilizing vertical bearing wall planes and horizontal slabs we form a planar structural system.

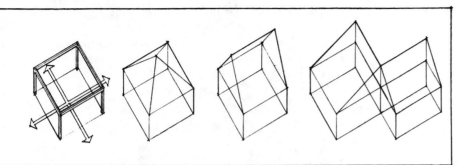

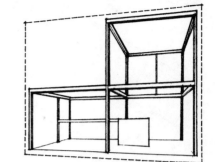

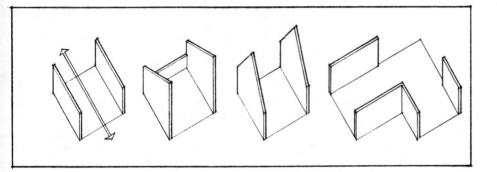

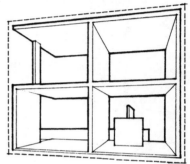

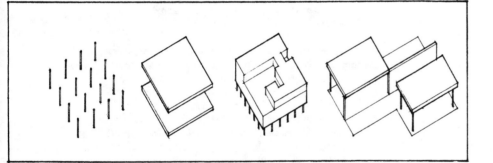

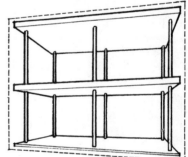

Above are a few of the many variations of form which can be achieved with both the skeletal and planar structural systems. As opposed to the skeleton frame which is characterized by its potential for openness, the bearing plane system tends to be heavier in image and more directional in form.

Combining horizontal slabs with a column grid we define horizontal layers of space which free up the use of wall elements and create the potential fusion of interior and exterior space.

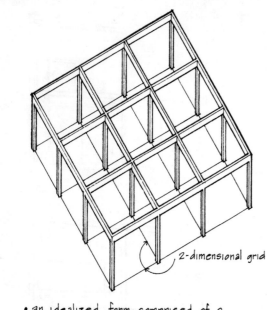

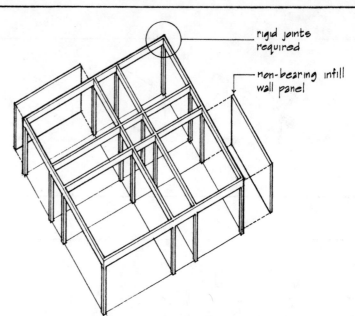

rigid joints required

non-bearing infill wall panel

2-dimensional grid

• an idealized form comprised of a regular three-dimensional grid

• in response to specific programmatic and formal requirements an irregular grid can be constructed

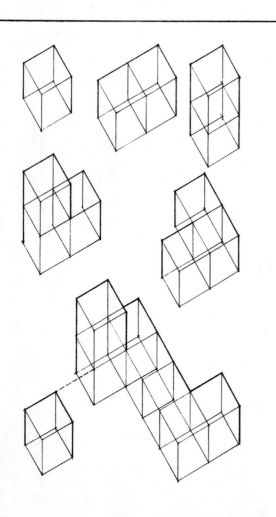

The skeletal type of structural system gives a building form through the manipulation of linear structural elements (columns and beams) which in effect form a cage.

In plan the critical points of a skeletal structural system are those at which building loads are transferred vertically along column lines. This gives rise to the use of a column grid where the grid lines represent the horizontal continuity provided by the beams and the intersections of these lines represent the location of columns. The inherent geometric order of a grid, regular or irregular, can be used in the design process to initiate and reinforce a building's functional and spatial organization.

To ensure lateral stability in a frame system rigid joints and/or shear walls and planes (both vertical and horizontal) are generally required.

To the left are diagrams which illustrate how a single module of space as defined by four columns supporting four beams can be seen as a building block that can logically be extended vertically along column lines or horizontally along beam lines.

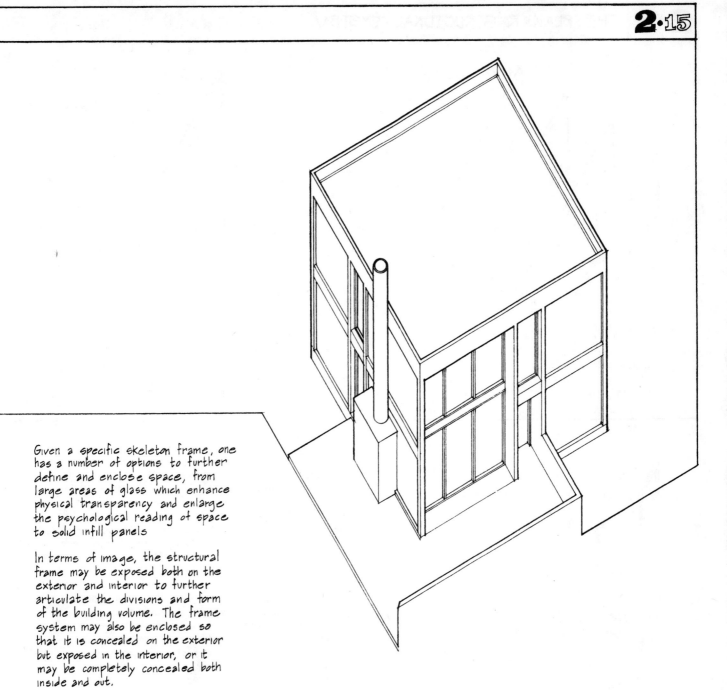

Given a specific skeleton frame, one has a number of options to further define and enclose space, from large areas of glass which enhance physical transparency and enlarge the psychological reading of space to solid infill panels

In terms of image, the structural frame may be exposed both on the exterior and interior to further articulate the divisions and form of the building volume. The frame system may also be enclosed so that it is concealed on the exterior but exposed in the interior, or it may be completely concealed both inside and out.

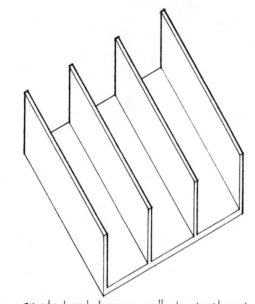

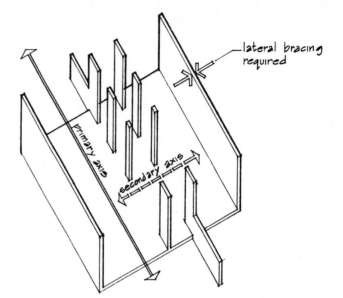

lateral bracing
required

primary axis

secondary axis

• an idealized bearing wall structural system comprised of a series of parallel planes defining equal slots of space

In response to specific programmatic and formal requirements, a series of parallel bearing walls can be manipulated in terms of height and spacing, and penetrated with openings

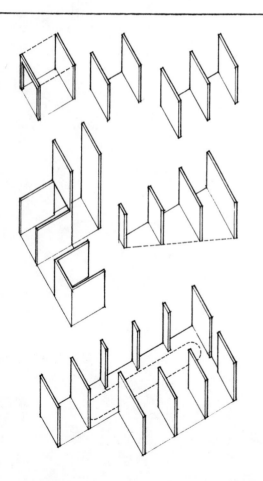

A bearing wall structural system utilizes rigid vertical planes to support building loads and transmit them down to its foundation. Using the same plan grid as that of the skeletal structural system, a planar system can be laid out. Giving preferential treatment to one direction, bearing walls can be erected parallel to one another (equally or unequally spaced) with secondary axes for penetrations through the bearing walls perpendicular to the primary axes.

Bearing walls are inherently most effective in resisting and transmitting forces along their planes, and most vulnerable to forces perpendicular to their planes. The lateral stability of bearing walls depends on their mass, rigidity, width to height ratio, and the amount of bracing effected by perpendicular walls, and horizontal roof and floor planes. Care should be taken that penetrations through bearing walls for doors and windows do not destroy the wall's integrity, strength, and rigidity.

Transferring loads horizontally requires rigid horizontal planes which may be of either homogeneous or composite construction.

To the left are diagrams illustrating the variations in form possible through the manipulation of the height, length, spacing, and direction of a series of bearing walls.

Bearing wall structures generally
project a heavier and more directional image than skeletal frame
structures due to the solidity of
the series of parallel bearing planes
employed in the structural system.
Since horizontal floor systems span
between the bearing walls, walls
perpendicular to the bearing walls
may be non-structural except to provide lateral bracing so that they
may be as opaque or transparent
as desired, and set flush with the
edges of the bearing walls or set
in from them to articulate the
structure.

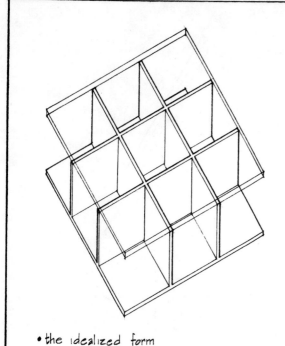

• the idealized form

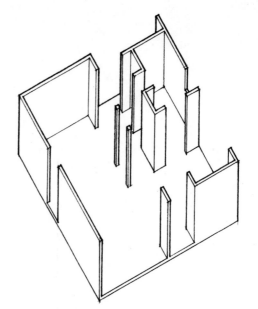

• the manipulated form in responce to specific programmatic and formal requirements

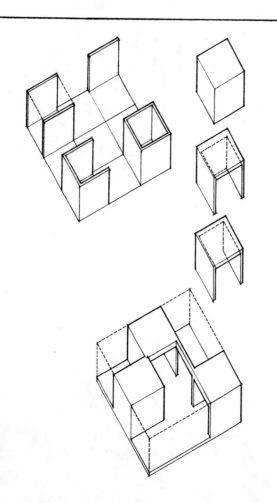

The composite structural system can be considered a combination of the two preceding structural systems, utilizing both linear columns and beams, and horizontal and vertical bearing planes to define space and provide volumetric enclosure. A plan grid is again useful in organizing and coordinating the functional, spatial, and structural systems for a building.

A building utilizing this type of structural system may appear either as a solid cubical or prismatic form with voids cut out of it or as an additive accumulation of forms.

To the left are diagrams illustrating the flexibility of form possible in the manipulation of linear and planar structural elements.

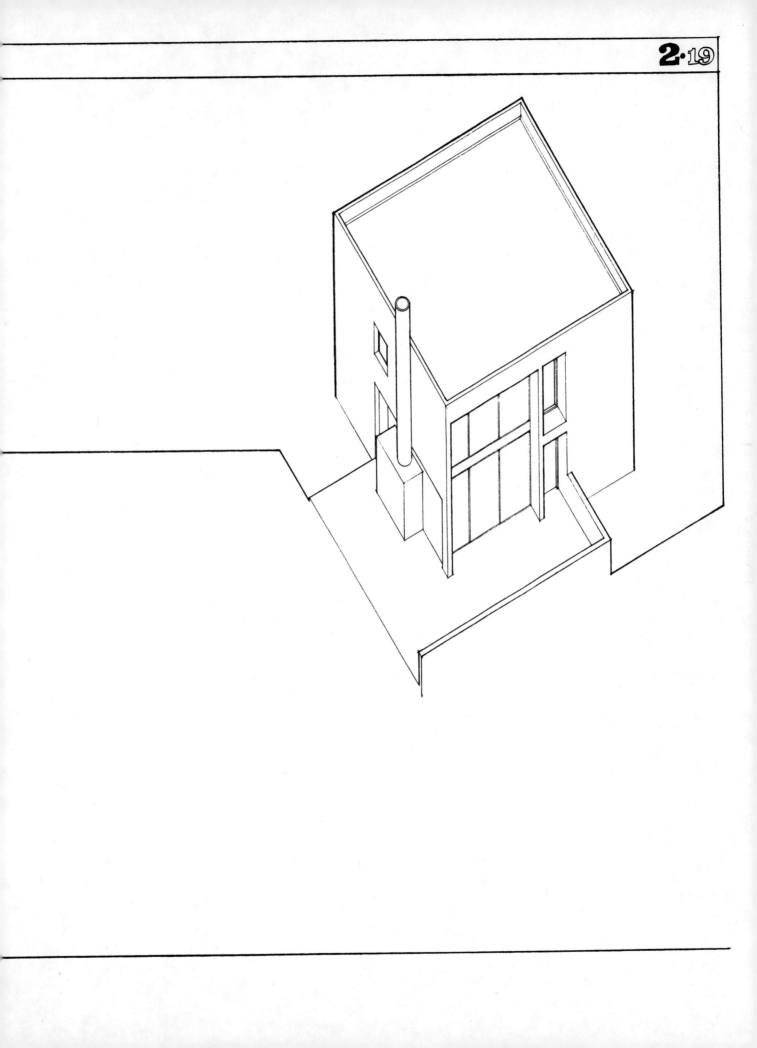

FOUNDATION SYSTEMS

The foundation system of a building, its substructure, is a critical link in the transmission of building loads down to the ground. Bearing directly on the soil, the foundation system must not only distribute vertical loads so that settlement of the building is either negligible or uniform under all parts of the building; it also has to anchor the superstructure of the building against uplift and racking forces. The most critical factor in determining the foundation system of a building is the type and bearing capacity of the soil to which the building loads are distributed.

Foundation systems are presented in three categories according to the geometric analogies of point, line, and plane. Each foundation system presented here can accept certain wall and floor systems. It must be understood that the choice of foundation system and material affects and is affected by the soil which supports the building as well as the potential form of the superstructure.

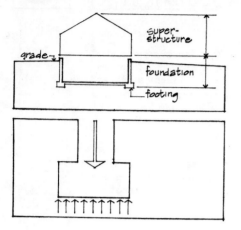

FOOTING AND FOUNDATION SYSTEMS

A building's foundation system is its substructure which supports the building loads and transmits them to the soil. Footings are those parts of the foundation which, resting directly on the soil, support specific portions of a building and distribute building loads directly to the soil. The most efficient footing and foundation system is that which transmits building loads most directly to the soil without exceeding the bearing capacity of the soil. (see 1·3)

Loads that must be carried by a foundation system would include the dead load of the building structure and the live load of its occupants and contents. Foundation systems must also resist lateral loads from both ground pressure and wind, and provide anchorage for the building superstructure against uplift and/or racking forces.

BUILDING SETTLEMENT

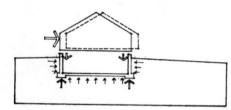

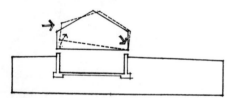

Settlement of a building must always be expected and therefore planned for. The purpose of a properly designed and constructed foundation system is to minimize this settlement, making it negligible, and insuring that whatever settlement does occur is equal under all parts of a building, minimizing any differential in settlement. Uneven settlement can cause a building to shift out of plumb and cracks to occur in the foundation, floors, walls, and ceilings. When extreme differential in settlement occurs, a structural failure may occur.

Settlement of a building is due to two factors: ① a reduction in the volume of voids in the soil and ② lateral displacement of the soil. In the first instance, settlement on dense and granular soils (ie. gravel and sand) occurs relatively quickly as loads are applied. On clayey soils, settlement is generally greater and continuous over a longer period of time. Lateral displacement of soil is not as common and usually occurs on sloped land or because of adjacent excavation.

SOIL BEARING

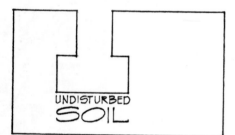

UNDISTURBED SOIL

Footings should always rest on undisturbed soil. When this is not possible the footing excavation should be filled with concrete to make up the extra depth. Footings bearing on consolidated fill or stabilized soil should be reinforced and designed by an engineer. Avoid bearing on unsettled ground, wet clays, organic soils, and ground with poor drainage.

WATER AND MOISTURE

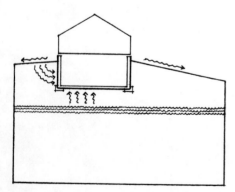

Two sources of water which may cause problems in and around a foundation system are ground water and surface water. They may cause deterioration of a soil's bearing capacity and leakage of water into a building's interior. Surface water should be drained away from a building using protective slopes: 3% minimum for grassy areas and 1% minimum for paved areas. The problem of ground water can be solved by placing the foundation sufficiently above the site's water table to prevent seasonal variations and/or capillary action from causing water to come into contact with the foundation system. Vapor barriers and a below ground drain tile system can also aid in preventing water penetration into a building and diverting it away from the foundation system.

FROST AND FOOTING LOCATION

In temperate and cool climates where frost conditions occur foundation systems are vulnerable to heaving action as frost penetrates the soil due to the freezing of soil moisture. To minimize the possibility of damage footings should be placed below the deepest frost penetration expected in the site's region. These frostlines vary from area to area and should be verified when a specific site is selected.

Never place footings on frozen ground. As the frozen soil thaws under the pressure of a building load, excess water would cause the soil to lose much of its bearing capacity, thus causing unnecessary building settlement.

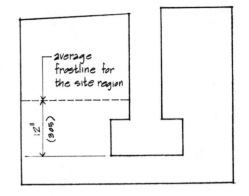

average frostline for the site region

12" (305)

FOOTING SIZE

Since footings of residential and light construction work transmit comparatively light loads, their size can usually be estimated by the following when they bear on stable soil:

$A = P/s$ where   A = horizontal bearing surface of footing
P = load in pounds
S = soil bearing capacity in pounds per square foot

and for linear foundation walls:

width of footing = 2 × thickness of foundation
depth of footing = thickness of foundation wall

In cases where the site's soil bearing capacity is low or doubtful and where heavy loads or unusual load patterns are anticipated, soil samples should be tested and an engineering analysis made to determine the type and size of footing and foundation system required.

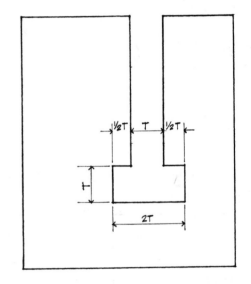

½T   T   ½T

T

2T

Additional considerations in the design of a foundation system include:

site topography   *see 1·5
desired building form and structural system   *see 2·14-10
foundation materials :   concrete
masonry
wood (treated against decay and insect attack)
requirements for: thermal insulation
waterproofing and/or moisture protection
expansion and contraction

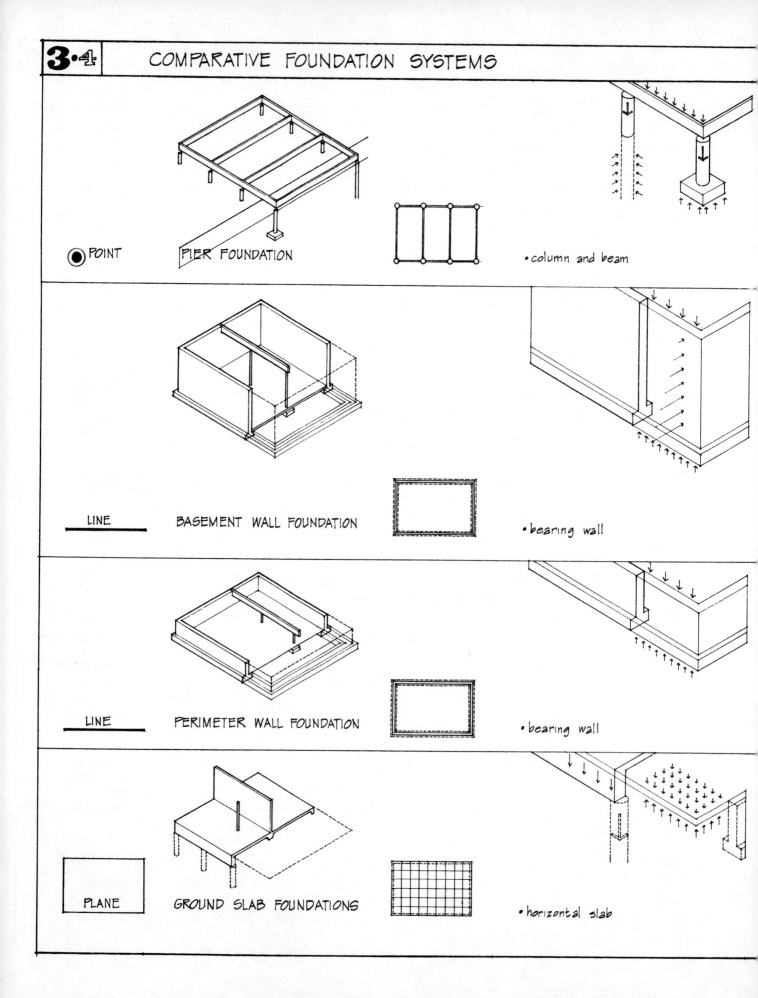

● POINT

PIER FOUNDATION

• column and beam

LINE

BASEMENT WALL FOUNDATION

• bearing wall

LINE

PERIMETER WALL FOUNDATION

• bearing wall

PLANE

GROUND SLAB FOUNDATIONS

• horizontal slab

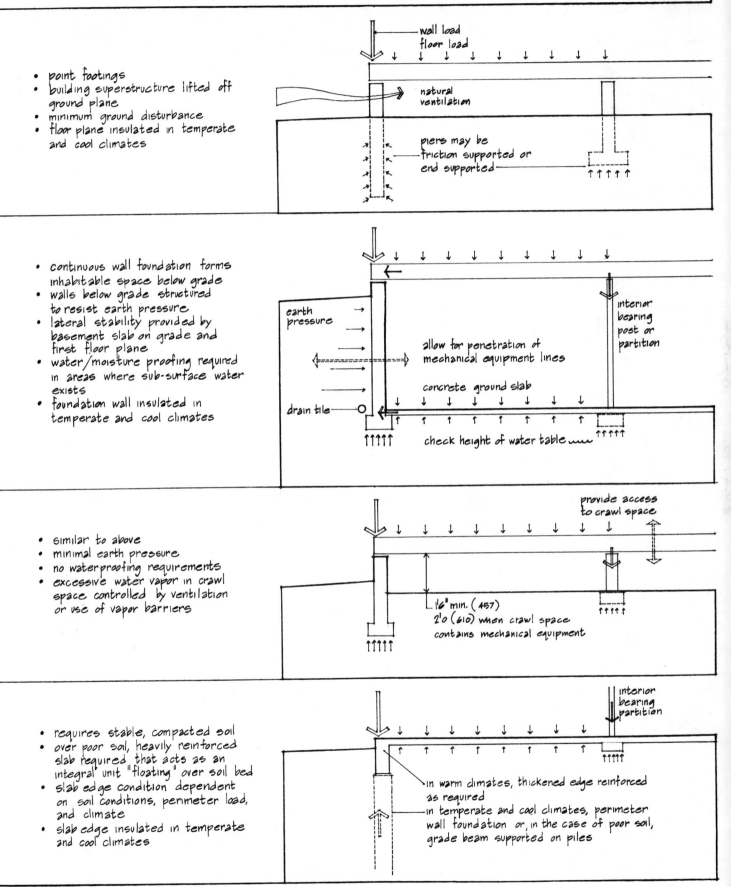

- point footings
- building superstructure lifted off ground plane
- minimum ground disturbance
- floor plane insulated in temperate and cool climates

wall load
floor load

natural ventilation

piers may be friction supported or end supported

- continuous wall foundation forms inhabitable space below grade
- walls below grade structured to resist earth pressure
- lateral stability provided by basement slab on grade and first floor plane
- water/moisture proofing required in areas where sub-surface water exists
- foundation wall insulated in temperate and cool climates

earth pressure

interior bearing post or partition

allow for penetration of mechanical equipment lines

concrete ground slab

drain tile

check height of water table

- similar to above
- minimal earth pressure
- no waterproofing requirements
- excessive water vapor in crawl space controlled by ventilation or use of vapor barriers

provide access to crawl space

16" min. (457)
2'0 (610) when crawl space contains mechanical equipment

- requires stable, compacted soil
- over poor soil, heavily reinforced slab required that acts as an integral unit "floating" over soil bed
- slab edge condition dependent on soil conditions, perimeter load, and climate
- slab edge insulated in temperate and cool climates

interior bearing partition

in warm climates, thickened edge reinforced as required
in temperate and cool climates, perimeter wall foundation or, in the case of poor soil, grade beam supported on piles

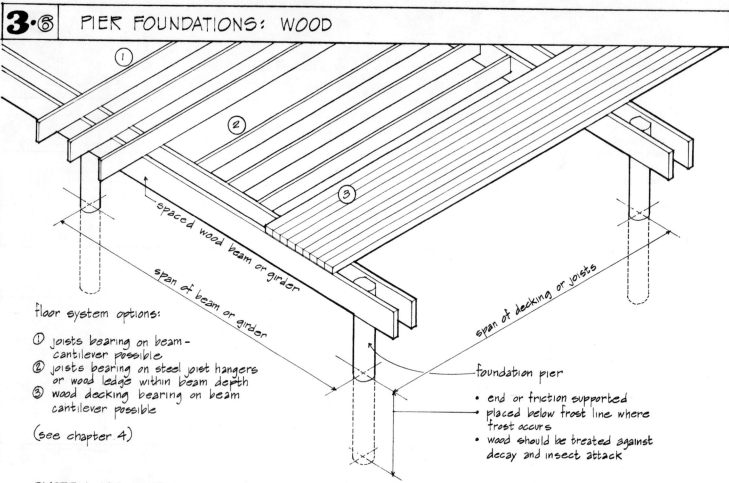

floor system options:

① joists bearing on beam — cantilever possible
② joists bearing on steel joist hangers or wood ledge within beam depth
③ wood decking bearing on beam cantilever possible

(see chapter 4)

foundation pier

- end or friction supported
- placed below frost line where frost occurs
- wood should be treated against decay and insect attack

SYSTEM ISOMETRIC

A grid system should be used to lay out the foundation piers. If irregular bays are utilized in response to programmatic and formal requirements, it is usually more efficient for the beams or girders to span the long direction with the joists or decking spanning the short direction. Likewise, it is usually better for the beams or girders to be spaced equally so that the joists or decking have equal spans and therefore constant size and depth.

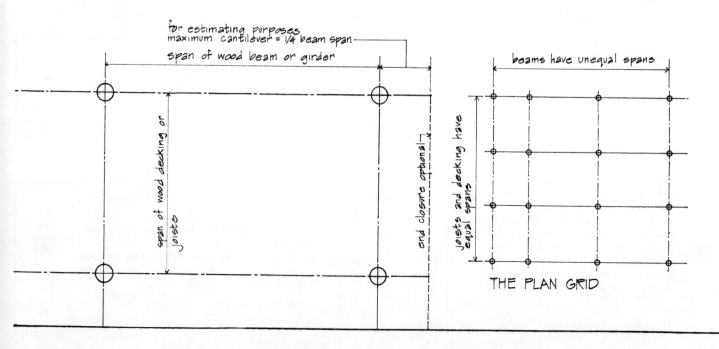

THE PLAN GRID

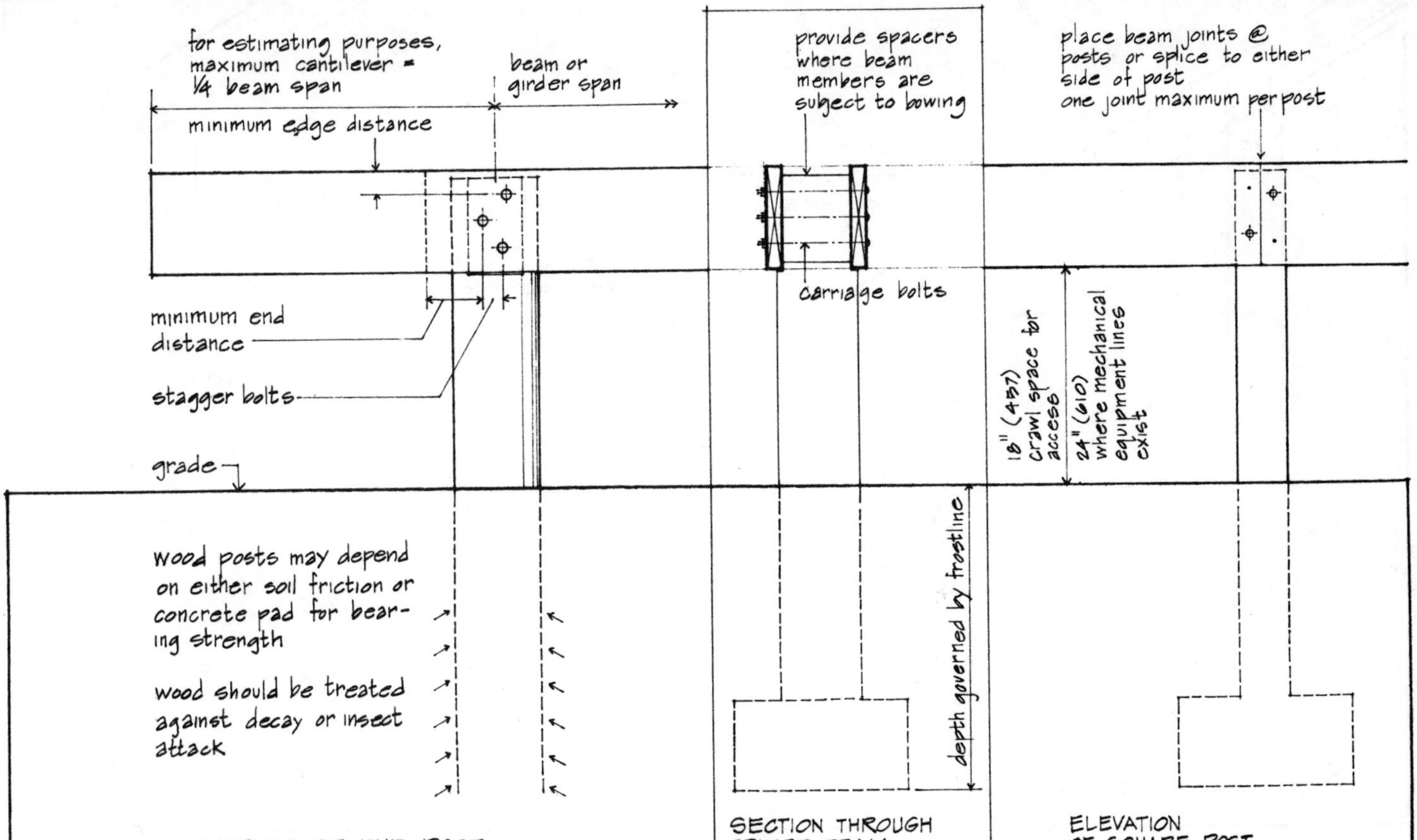

for estimating purposes,
maximum cantilever =
¼ beam span

beam or
girder span

minimum edge distance

minimum end
distance

stagger bolts

grade

wood posts may depend
on either soil friction or
concrete pad for bear-
ing strength

wood should be treated
against decay or insect
attack

ELEVATION OF END POST

provide spacers
where beam
members are
subject to bowing

carriage bolts

18" (457)
crawl space for
access

24" (610)
where mechanical
equipment lines
exist

depth governed by frostline

**SECTION THROUGH
SPACED BEAM**

place beam joints @
posts or splice to either
side of post
one joint maximum per post

**ELEVATION
OF SQUARE POST**

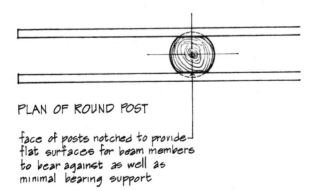

PLAN OF ROUND POST

face of posts notched to provide
flat surfaces for beam members
to bear against as well as
minimal bearing support

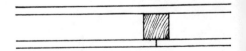

PLAN OF SQUARE POST

no bearing support -
if required, use ledger
boards

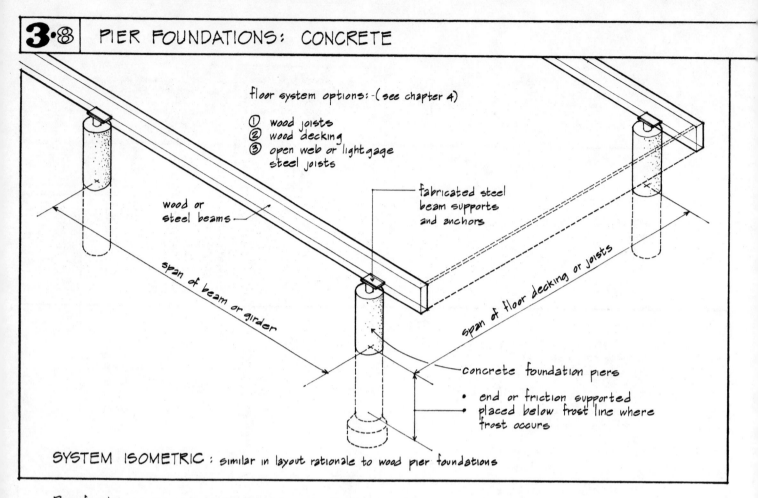

floor system options: - (see chapter 4)

① wood joists
② wood decking
③ open web or lightgage steel joists

wood or steel beams

fabricated steel beam supports and anchors

span of beam or girder

span of floor decking or joists

concrete foundation piers

• end or friction supported
• placed below frost line where frost occurs

SYSTEM ISOMETRIC: similar in layout rationale to wood pier foundations

Pier foundations are particularly suited to supporting post and beam superstructures. Refer to 4·12 through 17 and 5·12 through 17.

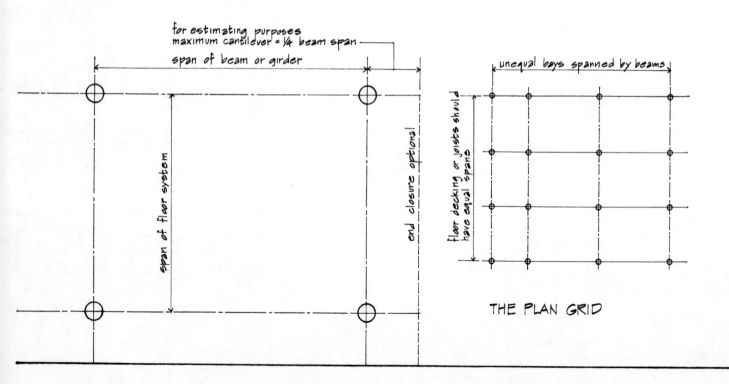

for estimating purposes
maximum cantilever = ¼ beam span

span of beam or girder

span of floor system

end closure optional

unequal bays spanned by beams

floor decking or joists should have equal spans

THE PLAN GRID

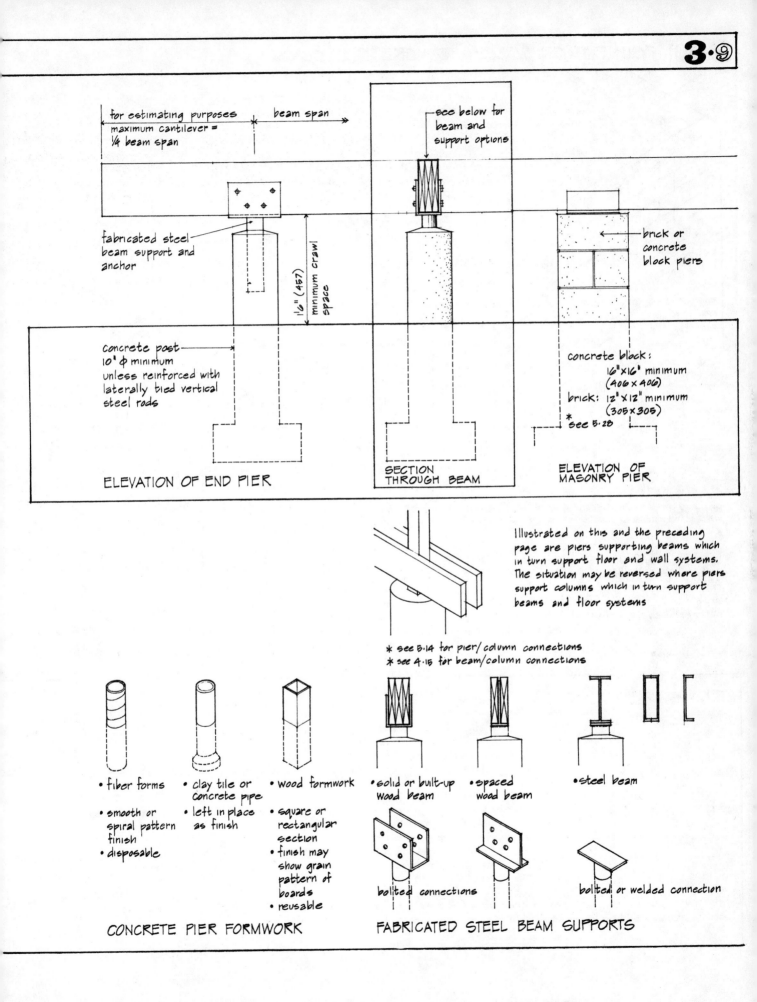

for estimating purposes
maximum cantilever = ¼ beam span

beam span

see below for beam and support options

fabricated steel beam support and anchor

1'6" (457) minimum crawl space

concrete post 10" φ minimum unless reinforced with laterally tied vertical steel rods

brick or concrete block piers

concrete block: 16"x16" minimum (406 x 406)

brick: 12"x12" minimum (305x305)

* see 5.28

ELEVATION OF END PIER

SECTION THROUGH BEAM

ELEVATION OF MASONRY PIER

Illustrated on this and the preceding page are piers supporting beams which in turn support floor and wall systems. The situation may be reversed where piers support columns which in turn support beams and floor systems

* see 5.14 for pier/column connections
* see 4.15 for beam/column connections

- fiber forms
- smooth or spiral pattern finish
- disposable

- clay tile or concrete pipe
- left in place as finish

- wood formwork
- square or rectangular section
- finish may show grain pattern of boards
- reusable

- solid or built-up wood beam

- spaced wood beam

- steel beam

bolted connections

bolted or welded connection

CONCRETE PIER FORMWORK

FABRICATED STEEL BEAM SUPPORTS

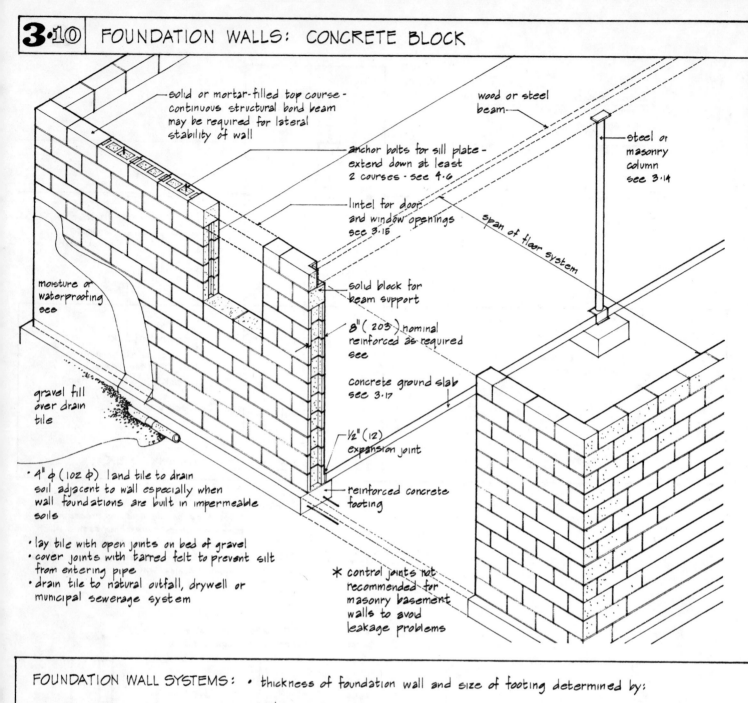

solid or mortar-filled top course -
continuous structural bond beam
may be required for lateral
stability of wall

wood or steel
beam

steel or
masonry
column
see 3·14

anchor bolts for sill plate -
extend down at least
2 courses · see 4·6

lintel for door
and window openings
see 3·15

span of floor system

solid block for
beam support

moisture or
waterproofing
see

8" (203) nominal
reinforced as required
see

concrete ground slab
see 3·17

gravel fill
over drain
tile

½" (12)
expansion joint

· 4" φ (102 φ) land tile to drain
soil adjacent to wall especially when
wall foundations are built in impermeable
soils

reinforced concrete
footing

· lay tile with open joints on bed of gravel
· cover joints with tarred felt to prevent silt
from entering pipe
· drain tile to natural outfall, drywell or
municipal sewerage system

* control joints not
recommended for
masonry basement
walls to avoid
leakage problems

FOUNDATION WALL SYSTEMS: · thickness of foundation wall and size of footing determined by:

1. building load and distribution pattern
2. soil type and bearing capacity
3. lateral loading from soil and ground water
4. lateral bracing provided by basement ground slab and first floor
   system

· presence of ground water requires waterproofing of foundation walls
and drainage of soil adjacent to walls
· allow for rough openings for windows and doors as well as pipe sleeves
for water, gas, oil and electrical lines
· wall and floor systems of superstructure above will determine top
edge condition

The form and support pattern of the foundation wall system should respond to the form of the superstructure above as well as the building site's soil and topographic conditions.

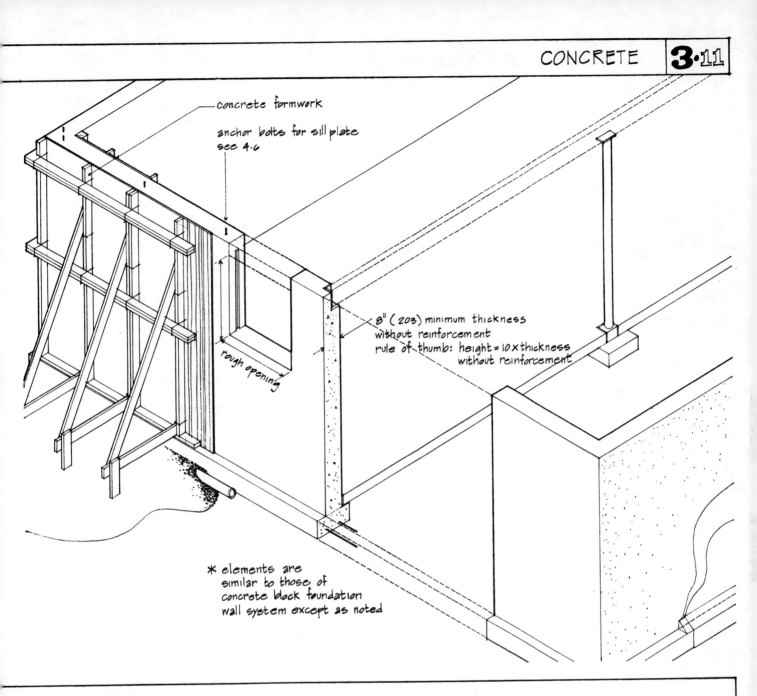

concrete formwork

anchor bolts for sill plate
see 4·6

rough opening

8" (203) minimum thickness
without reinforcement
rule of thumb: height = 10 x thickness
without reinforcement

✱ elements are
similar to those of
concrete block foundation
wall system except as noted

CONCRETE BLOCK FOUNDATION WALLS:

- no formwork required / utilizes easily handled small units / less erection time than for solid concrete walls
- since concrete block is a modular material, all major dimensions (lengths, heights, offsets, wall openings) should be modular to minimize cutting of block
- concrete block walls are susceptible to settlement and cracking and therefore susceptible to leakage
- see 5·18 through 25

SOLID CONCRETE FOUNDATION WALLS:

- formwork and access to place concrete mix required
- generally stronger and less susceptible to cracking and leakage than concrete block foundation walls
- modular dimensions not necessary unless required by superstructure above

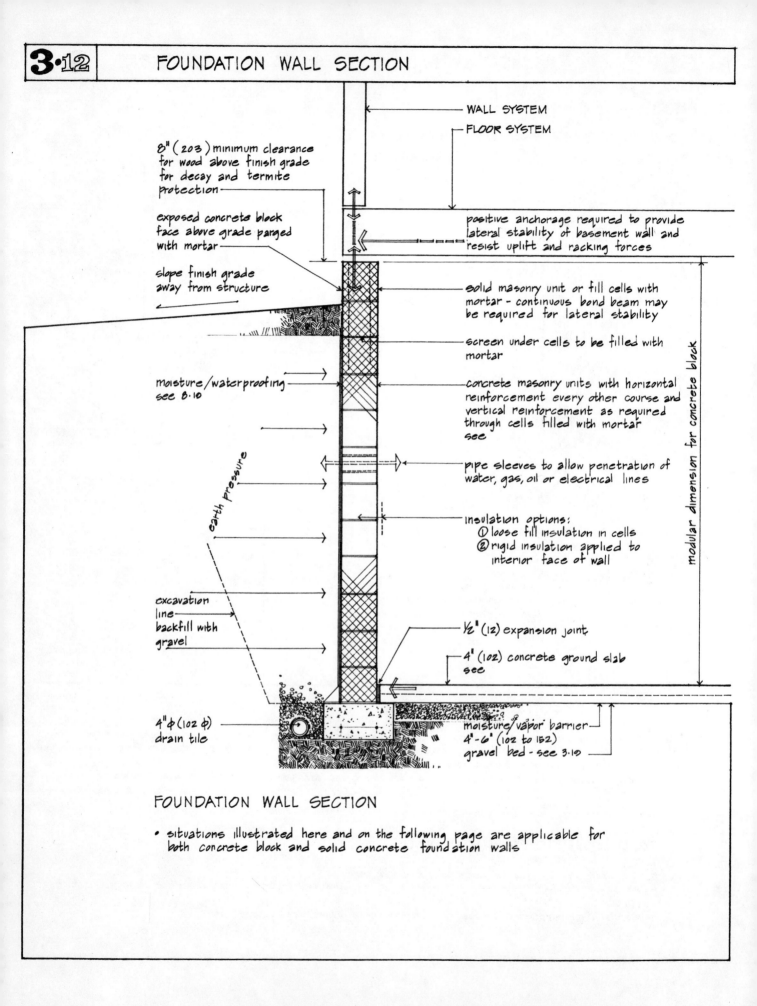

WALL SYSTEM

FLOOR SYSTEM

8" (203) minimum clearance for wood above finish grade for decay and termite protection

exposed concrete block face above grade parged with mortar

slope finish grade away from structure

positive anchorage required to provide lateral stability of basement wall and resist uplift and racking forces

solid masonry unit or fill cells with mortar - continuous bond beam may be required for lateral stability

screen under cells to be filled with mortar

moisture/waterproofing see 8·10

concrete masonry units with horizontal reinforcement every other course and vertical reinforcement as required through cells filled with mortar see

earth pressure

pipe sleeves to allow penetration of water, gas, oil or electrical lines

insulation options:
① loose fill insulation in cells
② rigid insulation applied to interior face of wall

modular dimension for concrete block

excavation line
backfill with gravel

½" (12) expansion joint

4" (102) concrete ground slab see

4"φ (102 φ) drain tile

moisture/vapor barrier
4"-6" (102 to 152) gravel bed - see 3·10

FOUNDATION WALL SECTION

• situations illustrated here and on the following page are applicable for both concrete block and solid concrete foundation walls

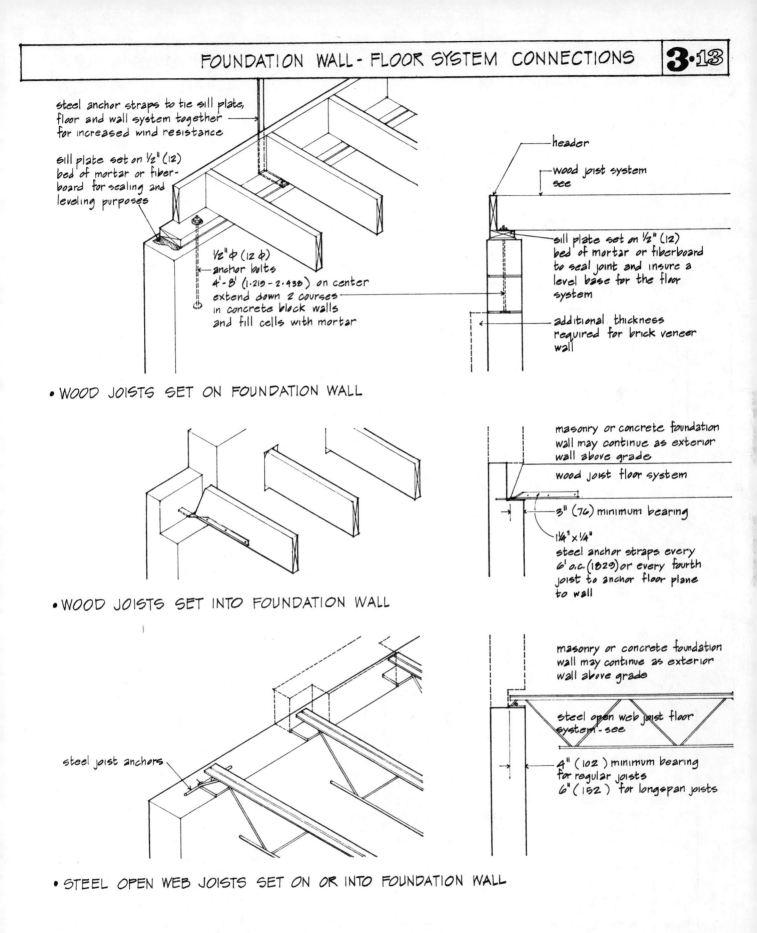

steel anchor straps to tie sill plate, floor and wall system together for increased wind resistance

sill plate set on ½" (12) bed of mortar or fiberboard for sealing and leveling purposes

½"∅ (12 ∅) anchor bolts 4'-8' (1.219 - 2.438) on center extend down 2 courses in concrete block walls and fill cells with mortar

header

wood joist system see

sill plate set on ½" (12) bed of mortar or fiberboard to seal joint and insure a level base for the floor system

additional thickness required for brick veneer wall

• WOOD JOISTS SET ON FOUNDATION WALL

masonry or concrete foundation wall may continue as exterior wall above grade

wood joist floor system

3" (76) minimum bearing

1¼" x ¼"

steel anchor straps every 6' o.c. (1829) or every fourth joist to anchor floor plane to wall

• WOOD JOISTS SET INTO FOUNDATION WALL

masonry or concrete foundation wall may continue as exterior wall above grade

steel open web joist floor system - see

4" (102) minimum bearing for regular joists 6" (152) for longspan joists

steel joist anchors

• STEEL OPEN WEB JOISTS SET ON OR INTO FOUNDATION WALL

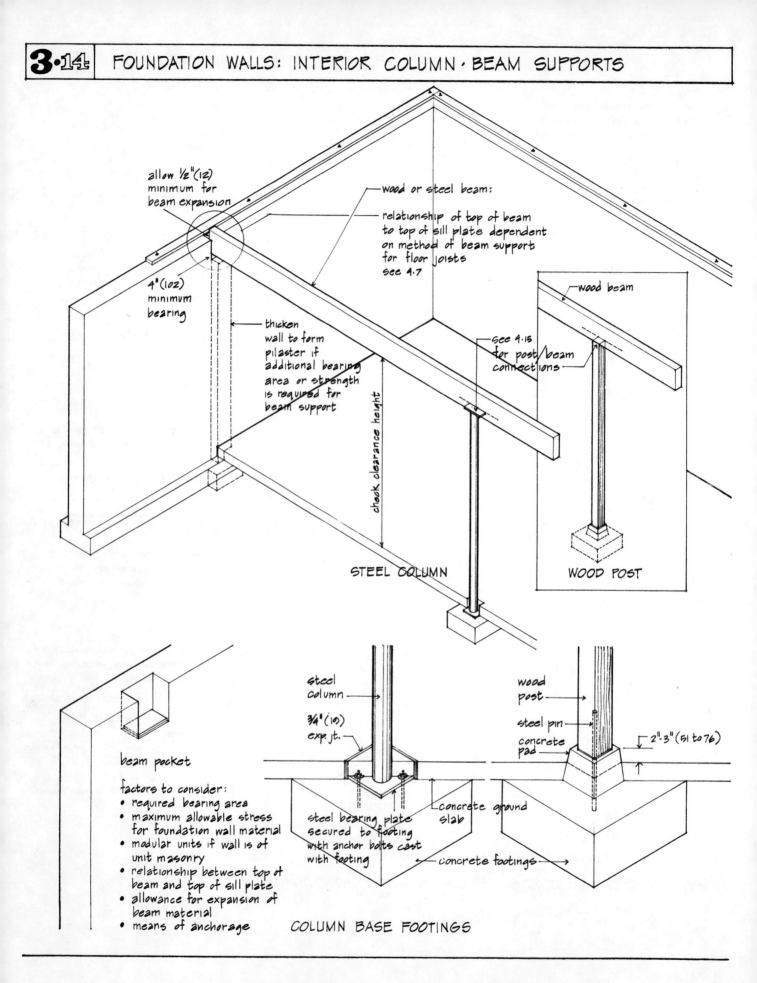

allow ½"(12) minimum for beam expansion

4"(102) minimum bearing

thicken wall to form pilaster if additional bearing area or strength is required for beam support

wood or steel beam:

relationship of top of beam to top of sill plate dependent on method of beam support for floor joists see 4·7

wood beam

see 4·15 for post/beam connections

check clearance height

STEEL COLUMN

WOOD POST

beam pocket

factors to consider:
- required bearing area
- maximum allowable stress for foundation wall material
- modular units if wall is of unit masonry
- relationship between top of beam and top of sill plate
- allowance for expansion of beam material
- means of anchorage

steel column

¾"(10) exp. jt.

steel bearing plate secured to footing with anchor bolts cast with footing

concrete slab

concrete footings

wood post

steel pin

concrete pad

2"-3" (51 to 76)

ground

COLUMN BASE FOOTINGS

minimum bearing: 8" (203)

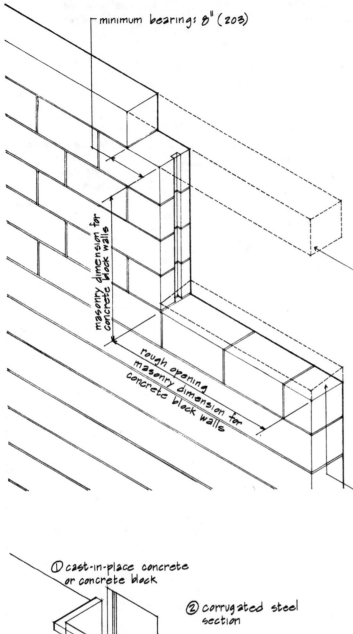

masonry dimension for concrete block walls

rough opening
masonry dimension for concrete block walls

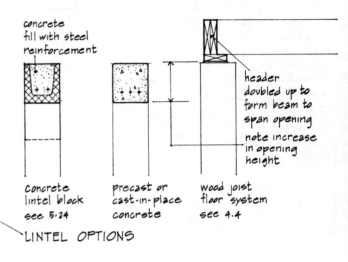

concrete fill with steel reinforcement

header doubled up to form beam to span opening

note increase in opening height

concrete lintel block see 5·24

precast or cast-in-place concrete

wood joist floor system see 4·4

LINTEL OPTIONS

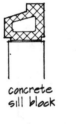

concrete sill block

precast or cast-in-place concrete

integral with window unit

SILL OPTIONS

* verify rough openings required for doors and windows with manufacturer

* see 5·24 for more information on concrete block wall openings

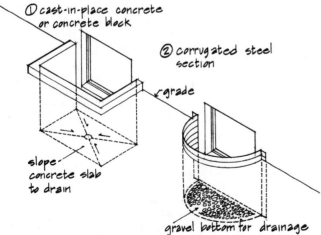

① cast-in-place concrete or concrete block

② corrugated steel section

grade

slope concrete slab to drain

gravel bottom for drainage

BASEMENT WINDOW AREAWAYS

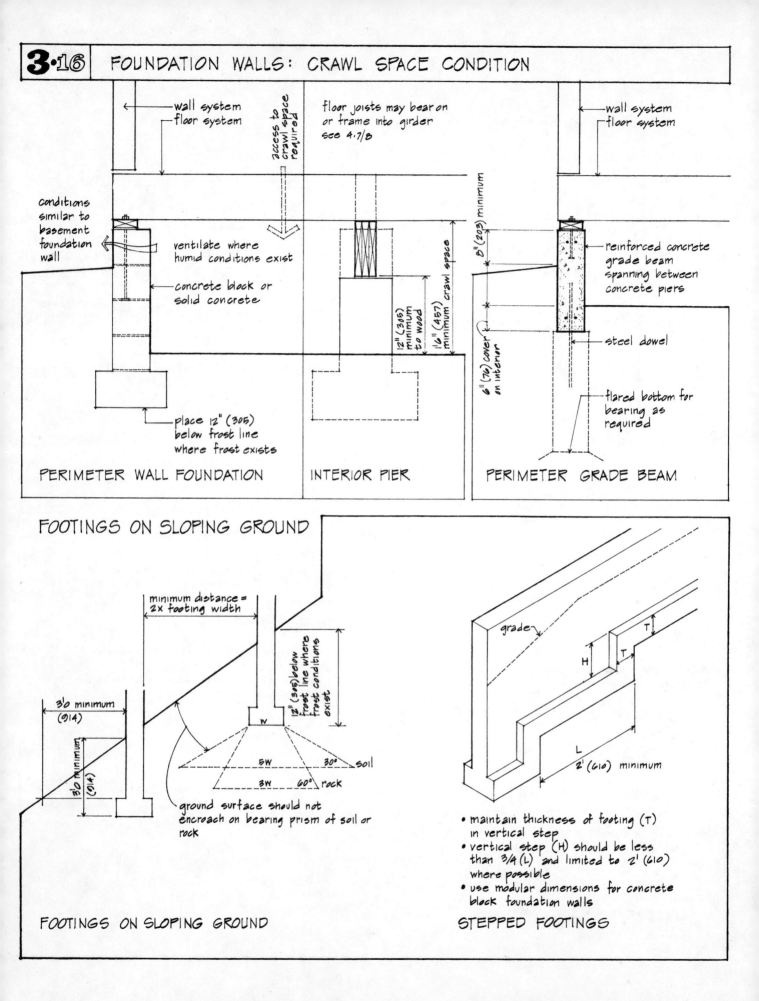

wall system
floor system

access to crawl space required

floor joists may bear on or frame into girder see 4.7/8

wall system
floor system

conditions similar to basement foundation wall

ventilate where humid conditions exist

concrete block or solid concrete

8" (203) minimum

reinforced concrete grade beam spanning between concrete piers

6" (76) cover on interior

steel dowel

flared bottom for bearing as required

12" (305) minimum to wood

18" (457) minimum crawl space

place 12" (305) below frost line where frost exists

PERIMETER WALL FOUNDATION   **INTERIOR PIER**   **PERIMETER GRADE BEAM**

FOOTINGS ON SLOPING GROUND

minimum distance = 2x footing width

12" (305) below frost line where frost conditions exist

3'0 minimum (914)

3'0 minimum (914)

5W   30° soil
3W   60° rock

ground surface should not encroach on bearing prism of soil or rock

grade

T

T

H

L

2' (610) minimum

- maintain thickness of footing (T) in vertical step
- vertical step (H) should be less than 3/4 (L) and limited to 2' (610) where possible
- use modular dimensions for concrete block foundation walls

FOOTINGS ON SLOPING GROUND   **STEPPED FOOTINGS**

- minimum slab thickness: 4" (102)
- should rest on stable, compacted soil with no organic matter
- does not carry any superstructure loads
- reinforced with steel mesh fabric which controls thermal stresses, shrinkage cracking, and any slight differential movement in the soil bed
- construction joint spacing: along perimeter = 75' (22·860) where exposed = 15'-20' (4·572 to 6·096)

GROUND SUPPORTED SLABS

- used over unstable, problem soils
- structurally reinforced slab acts as a unit
- requires engineering analysis for each specific situation

STRUCTURALLY SUPPORTED SLABS

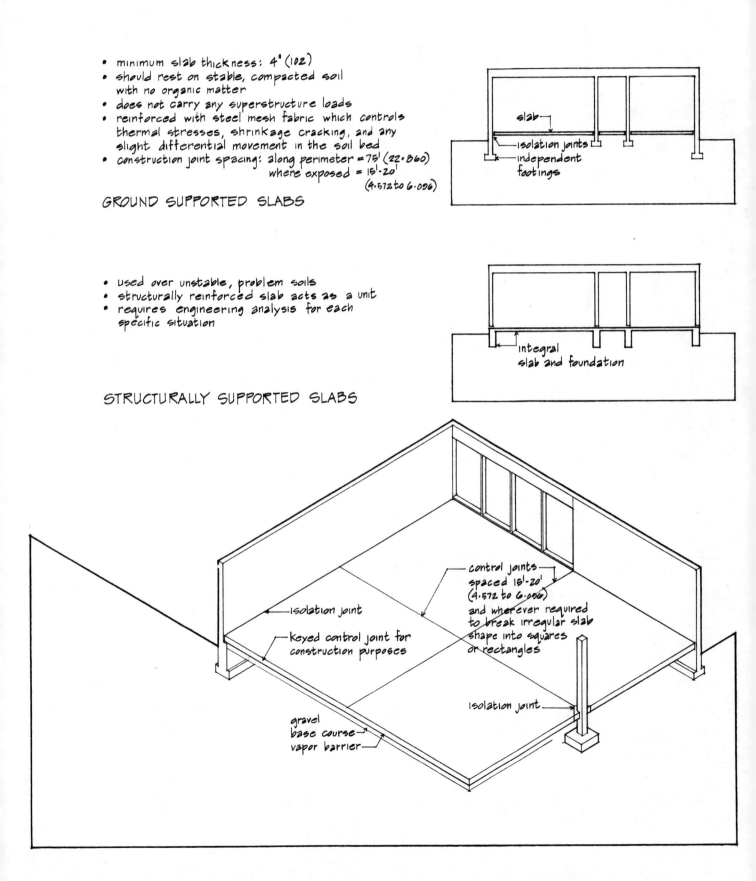

slab
isolation joints
independent footings

integral slab and foundation

control joints spaced 15'-20' (4·572 to 6·096) and wherever required to break irregular slab shape into squares or rectangles

isolation joint
keyed control joint for construction purposes

gravel base course
vapor barrier

isolation joint

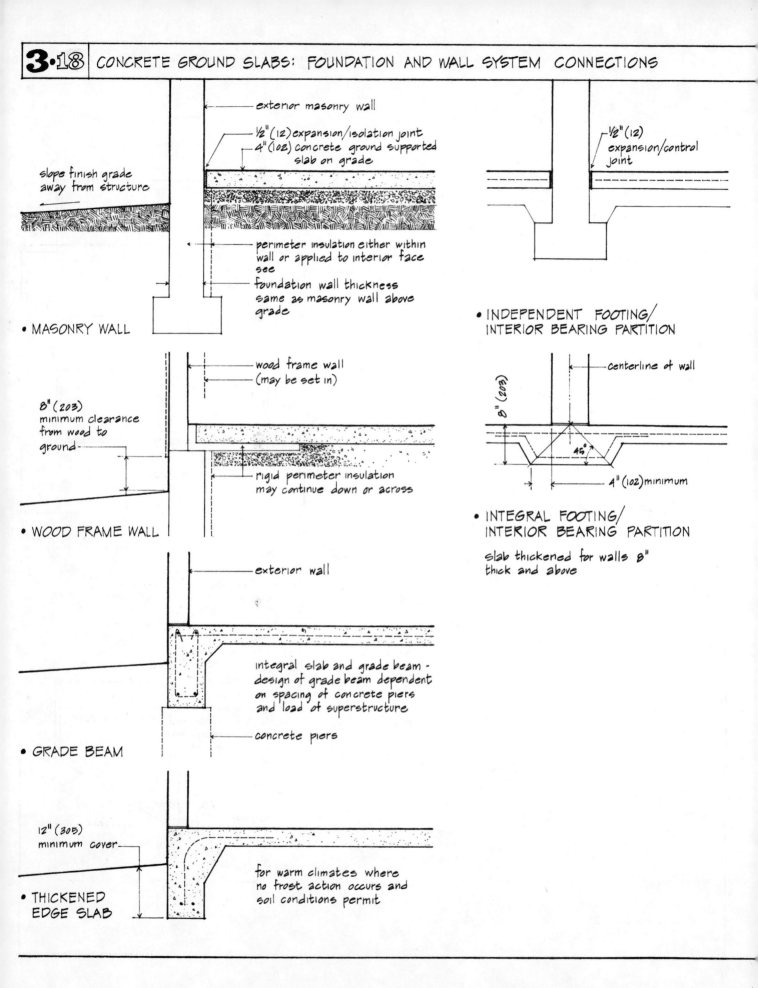

slope finish grade away from structure

exterior masonry wall

½" (12) expansion/isolation joint
4" (102) concrete ground supported slab on grade

perimeter insulation either within wall or applied to interior face see

foundation wall thickness same as masonry wall above grade

• MASONRY WALL

½" (12) expansion/control joint

• INDEPENDENT FOOTING/ INTERIOR BEARING PARTITION

wood frame wall (may be set in)

8" (203) minimum clearance from wood to ground

rigid perimeter insulation may continue down or across

• WOOD FRAME WALL

centerline of wall

8" (203)

45°

4" (102) minimum

• INTEGRAL FOOTING/ INTERIOR BEARING PARTITION

slab thickened for walls 8" thick and above

exterior wall

integral slab and grade beam - design of grade beam dependent on spacing of concrete piers and load of superstructure

concrete piers

• GRADE BEAM

12" (305) minimum cover

• THICKENED EDGE SLAB

for warm climates where no frost action occurs and soil conditions permit

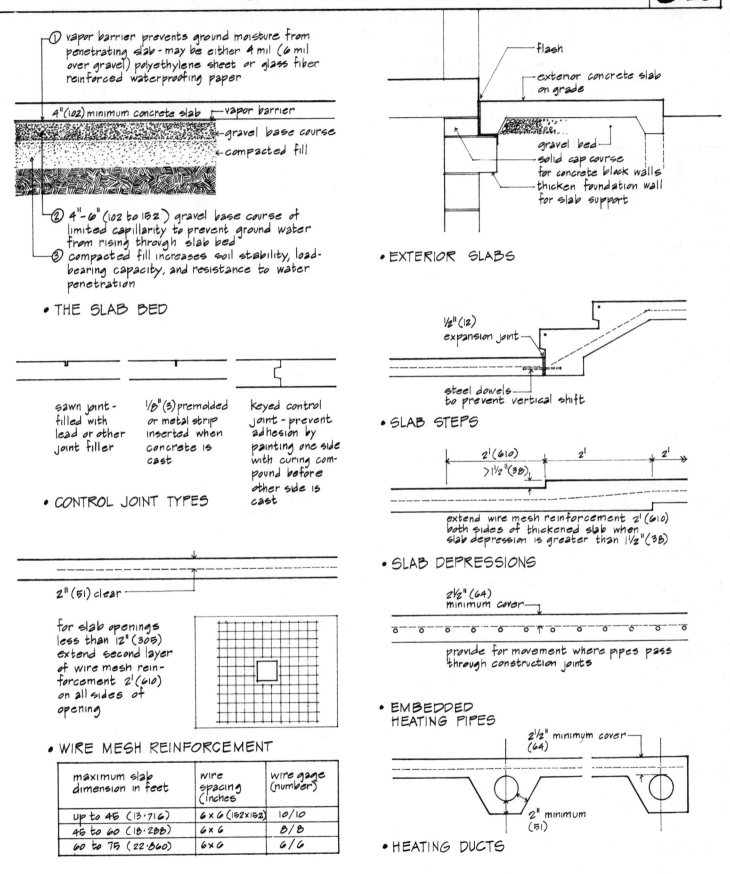

① vapor barrier prevents ground moisture from penetrating slab - may be either 4 mil (6 mil over gravel) polyethylene sheet or glass fiber reinforced waterproofing paper

4"(102) minimum concrete slab — vapor barrier
— gravel base course
— compacted fill

② 4"-6" (102 to 152) gravel base course of limited capillarity to prevent ground water from rising through slab bed

③ compacted fill increases soil stability, load-bearing capacity, and resistance to water penetration

• THE SLAB BED

sawn joint - filled with lead or other joint filler

1/8" (3) premolded or metal strip inserted when concrete is cast

keyed control joint - prevent adhesion by painting one side with curing compound before other side is cast

• CONTROL JOINT TYPES

2" (51) clear

for slab openings less than 12" (305) extend second layer of wire mesh reinforcement 2' (610) on all sides of opening

• WIRE MESH REINFORCEMENT

maximum slab dimension in feet	wire spacing (inches)	wire gage (number)
up to 45 (13·716)	6 x 6 (152x152)	10/10
45 to 60 (18·288)	6 x 6	8/8
60 to 75 (22·860)	6 x 6	6/6

— flash
— exterior concrete slab on grade
— gravel bed
— solid cap course for concrete block walls
— thicken foundation wall for slab support

• EXTERIOR SLABS

1/2" (12) expansion joint
steel dowels to prevent vertical shift

• SLAB STEPS

2' (610)   2'   2'
>1 1/2" (38)

extend wire mesh reinforcement 2' (610) both sides of thickened slab when slab depression is greater than 1 1/2" (38)

• SLAB DEPRESSIONS

2 1/2" (64) minimum cover

provide for movement where pipes pass through construction joints

• EMBEDDED HEATING PIPES

2 1/2" minimum cover (64)
2" minimum (51)

• HEATING DUCTS

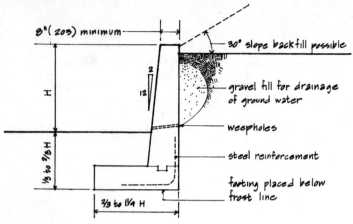

8" (203) minimum

30° slope backfill possible

2/12

gravel fill for drainage of ground water

weepholes

steel reinforcement

footing placed below frost line

H

1/3 to 2/3 H

2/3 to 1¼ H

"L" TYPE

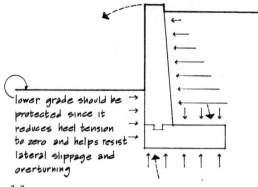

lower grade should be protected since it reduces heel tension to zero and helps resist lateral slippage and overturning

"L" TYPE

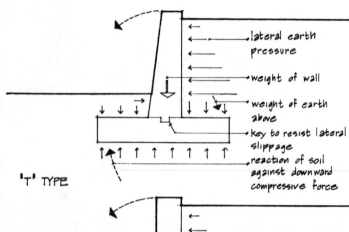

lateral earth pressure

weight of wall

weight of earth above

key to resist lateral slippage

reaction of soil against downward compressive force

"T" TYPE

Retaining walls act as cantilevered slabs. They resist the overturning moment caused by lateral ground pressure by transferring the forces onto relative wide footings. The depth of the lower grade above the footing is important to help stabilize the connection between the retaining wall and its footing.

Retaining walls may be of:

- reinforced concrete
- reinforced masonry
- stone rubble

Factors to consider:

- required expansion joints must be keyed to maintain the lateral stability of the retaining wall
- weep holes must be adequately sized and spaced to drain any ground water from behind the retaining wall and reduce the wall's surcharge

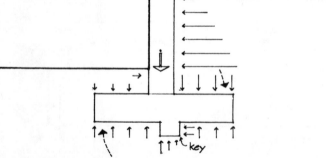

CANTILEVER TYPE   similar to "T" type

key

Below are other means of changing grade. Note that they require greater horizontal distances than do retaining walls for similar drops in grade.

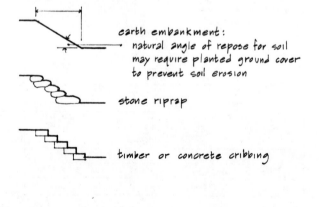

earth embankment: natural angle of repose for soil may require planted ground cover to prevent soil erosion

stone riprap

timber or concrete cribbing

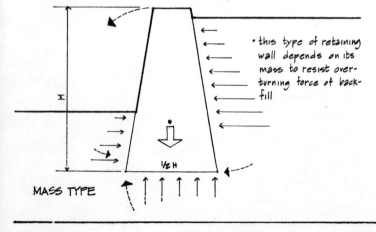

- this type of retaining wall depends on its mass to resist overturning force of backfill

H

½ H

MASS TYPE

FLOOR SYSTEMS

Floor systems are a building's primary horizontal planes which support both live loads (a building's occupants and contents) and dead loads (weight of the floor's constituent parts plus possible loading from floors and walls above). Structurally the floor system must transfer these loads laterally to either beams and columns or to bearing walls, while providing at the same time lateral support for adjacent walls.

A floor system may be composed of linear beams or joists overlaid with a plane of sheathing or it may be an almost homogeneous material. It may occur below grade, on grade, or above grade. The depth of a floor system is directly related to the size and proportion of the bay system and the strength of the materials utilized. In addition to a floor system's spans, any desired openings within the floor plane and cantilevers (their size, proportion, and placement) must be considered in the structural determination of the floor system. A floor system's edge conditions and connections to both foundation and wall systems affect the building's structural integrity and physical appearance.

Since it must safely support moving loads, the floor system must be relatively stiff while maintaining its elasticity. Deflection becomes the critical controlling factor rather than the bending stress rating of the floor structure due to desired visual appearance, human comfort, and the detrimental effects that excessive deflection and/or vibration would have on finish flooring and ceiling materials. Deflection should be reduced to visually acceptable limits: normally 1/360 th of the floor span.

For floor systems between living spaces stacked one above another, an additional factor to consider is the blockage of both air-borne and structure-borne sound by the floor system itself. The depth of a floor system and the potential cavities within it must be considered if it is necessary to accomodate heating, plumbing, or electrical lines within the floor system.

Most floor systems of a building, except for exterior decks, are not exposed to the climatic elements and their weathering effects. Since a floor system must support traffic, however, durability, resistance to wear, and easy maintenance are critical factors in the selection of a floor system and its finish. The desired flooring and ceiling finishes and their visual properties (material, color, texture and pattern) help to determine the choice of a floor system which can most easily support these finishes.

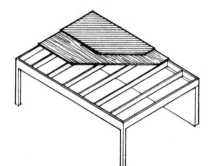

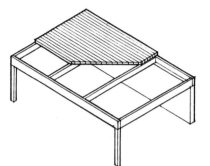

wood joist floor system

- relatively short spans for subflooring, underlayment and applied ceiling
- generally thicker construction depth than plank and beam system
- flexible in form and shape

wood joist system

- relatively small joist members closely spaced
- joists supported by either beams or walls

wood plank and beam

- larger beams spaced further apart spanned with structural planking and decking
- beams supported by girders, columns or walls

wood plank and beam system

- if underside of plank and beam system is left exposed as the finish ceiling, it is more difficult to run concealed mechanical and electrical lines and the system is less resistant to sound transmission
- concentrated loads and floor openings may require additional framing

WOOD

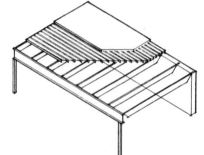

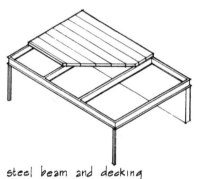

steel joist system

- relatively short spans for decking
- underside of structure left exposed or ceiling may be applied
- limited cantilever potential

steel joist system

- lightgage or open-web joists closely spaced
- joists supported by either beams or walls

steel beam and decking

- heavier steel beams spaced further apart spanned with structural decking or planks
- beams supported by girders, columns or walls

steel beam and decking

- most typical as part of a steel skeleton frame structure
- concentrated loads and floor openings may require additional framing

STEEL

- precast or cast-in-place
- essentially a planar slab system
- structural systems are classified according to the type of span and form:
  - one- and two-way slabs
  - one-way joist slab
  - two-way waffle slab
  - two-way flat slab
  - two-way flat plate
- factors in system choice include the type and magnitude of loading conditions, desired floor depth, and the desired bay size and proportions

CONCRETE

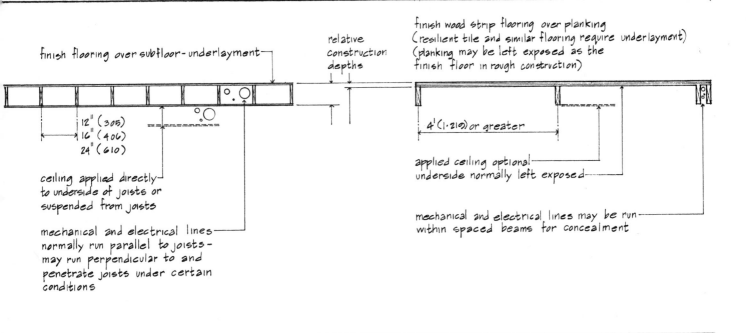

finish flooring over subfloor-underlayment

relative
construction
depths

finish wood strip flooring over planking
(resilient tile and similar flooring require underlayment)
(planking may be left exposed as the
finish floor in rough construction)

12" (305)
16" (406)
24" (610)

4' (1·210) or greater

ceiling applied directly
to underside of joists or
suspended from joists

applied ceiling optional
underside normally left exposed

mechanical and electrical lines
normally run parallel to joists-
may run perpendicular to and
penetrate joists under certain
conditions

mechanical and electrical lines may be run
within spaced beams for concealment

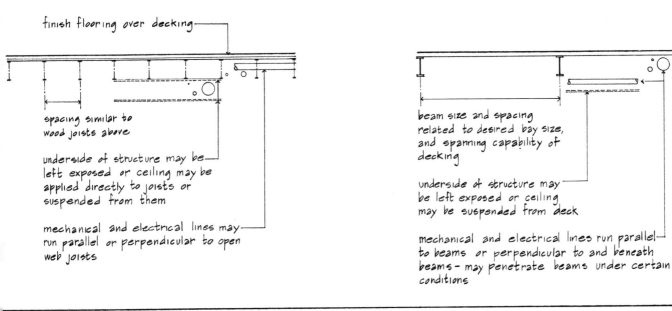

finish flooring over decking

spacing similar to
wood joists above

underside of structure may be
left exposed or ceiling may be
applied directly to joists or
suspended from them

mechanical and electrical lines may
run parallel or perpendicular to open
web joists

beam size and spacing
related to desired bay size,
and spanning capability of
decking

underside of structure may
be left exposed or ceiling
may be suspended from deck

mechanical and electrical lines run parallel
to beams or perpendicular to and beneath
beams - may penetrate beams under certain
conditions

✳ see 4·27 for reinforced concrete floor systems

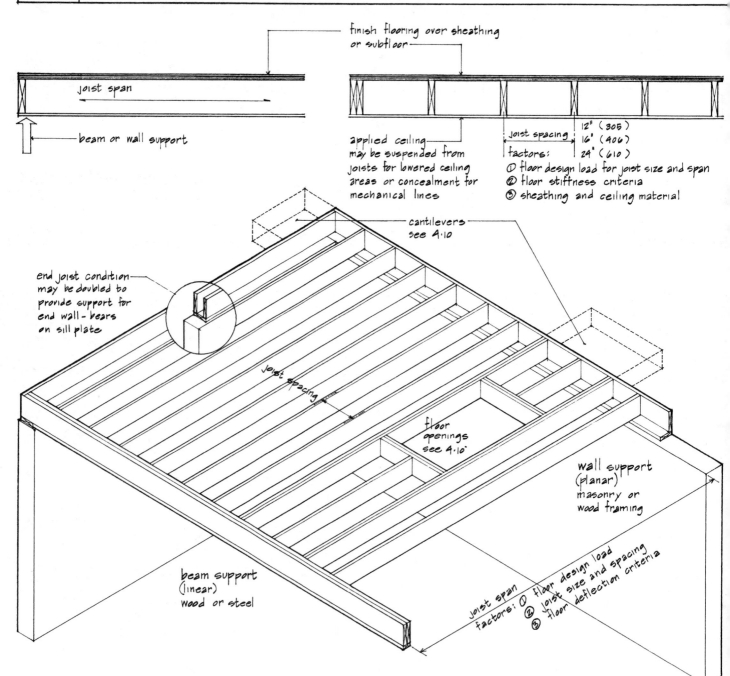

finish flooring over sheathing
or subfloor

joist span

beam or wall support

applied ceiling
may be suspended from
joists for lowered ceiling
areas or concealment for
mechanical lines

joist spacing

12" (305)
16' (406)
24" (610)

factors:
① floor design load for joist size and span
② floor stiffness criteria
③ sheathing and ceiling material

cantilevers
see A·10

end joist condition
may be doubled to
provide support for
end wall - bears
on sill plate

joist spacing

floor
openings
see A·10

wall support
(planar)
masonry or
wood framing

beam support
(linear)
wood or steel

joist span
factors: ① floor design load
② joist size and spacing
③ floor deflection criteria

WOOD JOIST FLOOR SYSTEM

- most typical wood floor system
- flexible in form and shape because of the workability
  or the material, the relatively small pieces, and the
  various means of fastening available
- fire-resistance rating depends on floor and ceiling
  finish   (* see A·11)

The joist span table below is for estimating and preliminary sizing of members only. It assumes that joists have simple spans. A rule of thumb for estimating joist spans is: (span = 24 x joist depth).

SIZE nominal	SPACING center to center	SPAN AS LIMITED BY DEFLECTION* E = 1,200,000 psi (844×10⁶ kg/m²) live load		f = live load	SPAN AS LIMITED BY BENDING			
		40 lbs/ft² (195.28 kg/m²)	60 lbs/ft² (292.02 kg/m²)		1200 psi (844×10³ kg/m²) 40 lbs/ft² (195.28 kg/m²)	60 lbs/ft² (202.02 kg/m²)	1400 psi (984×10³ kg/m²) 40 lbs/ft² (195.28 kg/m²)	60 lbs/ft² (202.02 kg/m²)
2×6 (51×152)	12" (305)	9'-8" (2.946)	8'-7" (2.616)		10'-11" (3.327)	9'-5" (2.870)	11'-9" (3.581)	10'-2" (3.099)
	16" (406)	8-10 (2.692)	7-10 (2.388)		9-6 (2.896)	8-2 (2.489)	10-3 (3.124)	8-10 (2.692)
	24" (610)	7-9 (2.362)	6-10 (2.083)		7-10 (2.388)	6-8 (2.032)	8-5 (2.565)	7-3 (2.210)
2×8 (51×203)	12	12-10 (3.912)	11-5 (3.480)		14-5 (4.394)	12-6 (3.810)	15-7 (4.750)	13-6 (4.115)
	16	11-8 (3.556)	10-5 (3.175)		12-7 (3.835)	10-10 (3.302)	13-7 (4.140)	11-9 (3.581)
	24	10-3 (3.124)	9-2 (2.794)		10-4 (3.150)	8-11 (2.718)	11-2 (3.404)	9-8 (2.946)
2×10 (51×254)	12	16-1 (4.902)	14-5 (4.394)		18-2 (5.537)	15-8 (4.775)	19-7 (5.969)	17-0 (5.182)
	16	14-9 (4.496)	13-2 (4.013)		15-10 (4.826)	13-8 (4.166)	17-2 (5.232)	14-9 (4.496)
	24	13-0 (3.962)	11-6 (3.505)		13-1 (3.988)	11-3 (3.429)	14-2 (4.318)	12-2 (3.708)
2×12 (51×305)	12	19-5 (5.918)	17-4 (5.283)		21-10 (6.655)	18-11 (5.766)	23-7 (7.188)	20-5 (6.223)
	16	17-9 (5.410)	15-10 (4.826)		19-1 (5.817)	16-6 (5.029)	20-8 (6.299)	17-10 (5.436)
	24	15-8 (4.775)	13-11 (4.242)		15-9 (4.801)	13-7 (4.140)	17-0 (5.182)	14-8 (4.470)
2×14 (51×356)	12	22-7 (6.883)	20-3 (6.172)		25-5 (7.747)	22-1 (6.731)	27-6 (8.382)	23-10 (7.260)
	16	20-9 (6.325)	18-7 (5.664)		22-4 (6.807)	19-3 (5.867)	24-1 (7.341)	20-10 (6.350)
	24	18-4 (5.588)	16-4 (4.978)		18-5 (5.613)	15-11 (4.851)	19-11 (6.071)	17-2 (5.232)
3×10 (76×254)	12	18-7 (5.664)	16-8 (5.080)		22-7 (6.883)	19-8 (5.994)	24-5 (7.442)	21-3 (6.477)
	16	17-1 (5.207)	15-3 (4.648)		19-10 (6.045)	17-2 (5.232)	21-5 (6.528)	18-7 (5.664)
	24	15-1 (4.597)	13-5 (4.089)		16-5 (5.004)	14-2 (4.318)	17-9 (5.410)	15-4 (4.674)
3×12 (76×305)	12	22-3 (6.782)	20-1 (6.121)		27-0 (8.230)	23-7 (7.188)	29-2 (8.890)	25-5 (7.747)
	16	20-6 (6.248)	18-5 (5.613)		23-10 (7.260)	20-8 (6.299)	25-9 (7.849)	22-4 (6.807)
	24	18-2 (5.537)	16-3 (4.953)		19-9 (6.020)	17-1 (5.207)	21-4 (6.502)	18-6 (5.639)

* joist deflection not to exceed 1/360th of span; stiffness of joist system under stress is more critical than its strength
• generally, if the total construction depth is acceptable, deeper joists spaced further apart are more desirable for stiffness than shallow joists spaced closer together
• E = modulus of elasticity; f = allowable unit stress in extreme fiber bending; both vary according to species and grade of wood used

BRIDGING:

Solid or criss-cross bridging should be provided for every 8' (2.438) of joist length if the joist depth is 6 or more times its thickness. Bridging prevents joists from twisting or overturning and may also improve the diaphragm action of the floor system.

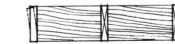

CUTS IN JOISTS:

To allow plumbing and electrical lines to penetrate floor joists, cuts may be made according to the guidelines shown.

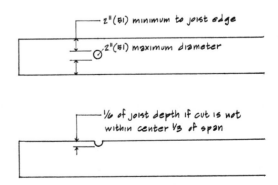

2" (51) minimum to joist edge

2" (51) maximum diameter

1/6 of joist depth if cut is not within center 1/3 of span

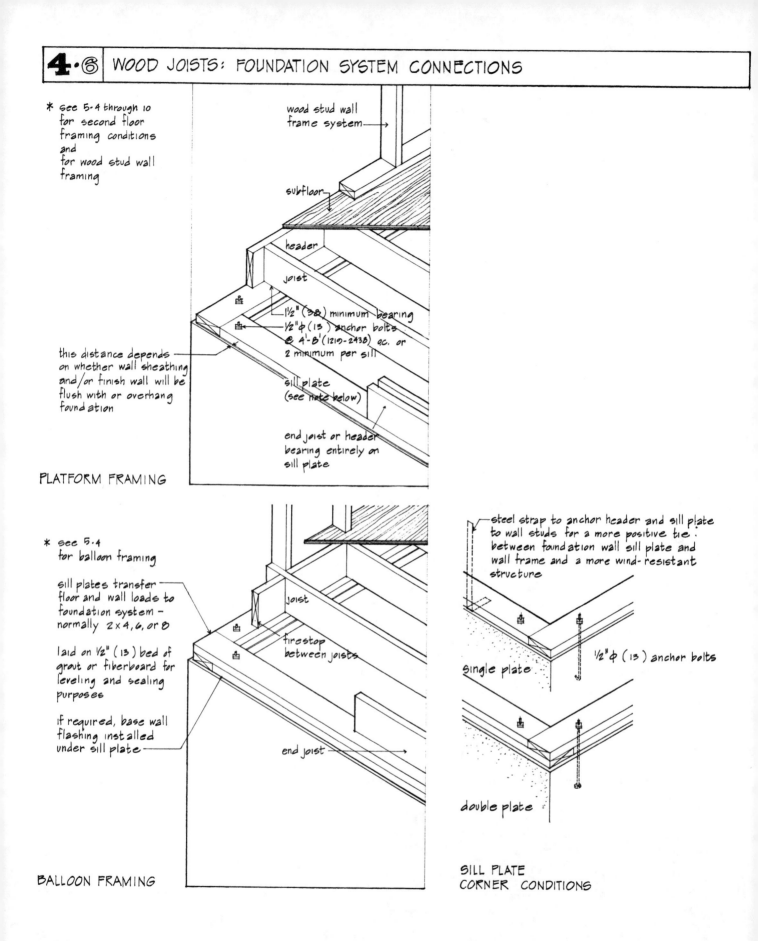

* see 5·4 through 10
for second floor
framing conditions
and
for wood stud wall
framing

wood stud wall
frame system →

subfloor

header

joist

1½" (38) minimum bearing
½"φ (13) anchor bolts
@ 4'-8' (1210-2438) oc. or
2 minimum per sill

this distance depends
on whether wall sheathing
and/or finish wall will be
flush with or overhang
foundation

sill plate
(see note below)

end joist or header
bearing entirely on
sill plate

PLATFORM FRAMING

* see 5·4
for balloon framing

sill plates transfer
floor and wall loads to
foundation system —
normally 2×4, 6, or 8

laid on ½" (13) bed of
grout or fiberboard for
leveling and sealing
purposes

if required, base wall
flashing installed
under sill plate

joist

firestop
between joists

end joist

BALLOON FRAMING

steel strap to anchor header and sill plate
to wall studs for a more positive tie
between foundation wall sill plate and
wall frame and a more wind-resistant
structure

single plate

½"φ (13) anchor bolts

double plate

SILL PLATE
CORNER CONDITIONS

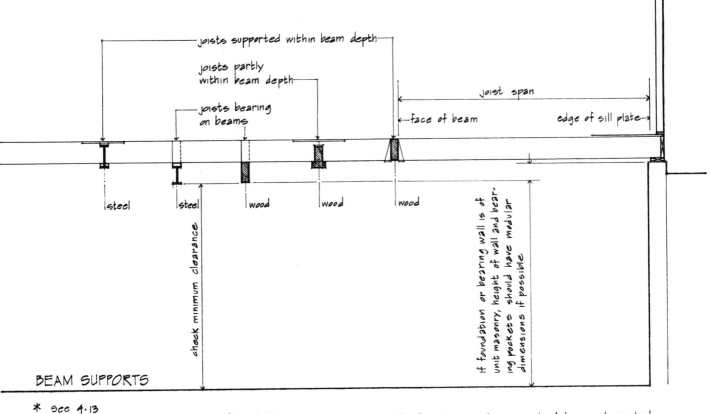

joists supported within beam depth

joists partly
within beam depth

joists bearing
on beams

joist span

face of beam

edge of sill plate

steel   steel   wood   wood   wood

check minimum clearance

If foundation or bearing wall is of unit masonry, height of wall and bearing pockets should have modular dimensions if possible

BEAM SUPPORTS

* see 4·13
for wood beam types and span/load tables

Wood joists may be supported by wood or steel beams. In either case, the height of the beam and its support should be coordinated with the type of joist support condition used and the perimeter sill plate condition to ensure a level floor plane.
(see above and following page for joist support conditions)

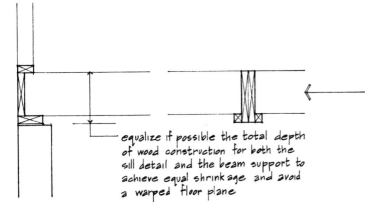

equalize if possible the total depth of wood construction for both the sill detail and the beam support to achieve equal shrinkage and avoid a warped floor plane

Wood is most susceptible to shrinkage perpendicular to its grain. For this reason, the total construction depth of a wood beam/joist connection should be minimized as much as possible.

Similarly, solid wood beams are more susceptible to shrinkage than built up or laminated wood beams.

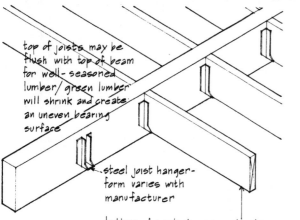

top of joists may be flush with top of beam for well-seasoned lumber/green lumber will shrink and create an uneven bearing surface

steel joist hanger- form varies with manufacturer

bottom of joist at same elevation as perimeter sill plate

• top of joists flush with top of beam

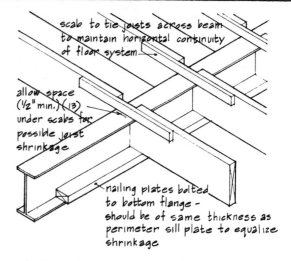

scab to tie joists across beam to maintain horizontal continuity of floor system

allow space (½" min.) (13) under scabs for possible joist shrinkage

nailing plates bolted to bottom flange - should be of same thickness as perimeter sill plate to equalize shrinkage

• ledger bearing

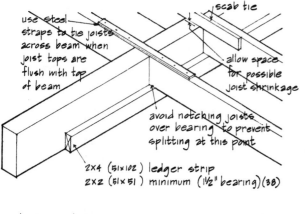

use steel straps to tie joists across beam when joist tops are flush with top of beam

scab tie

allow space for possible joist shrinkage

avoid notching joists over bearing to prevent splitting at this point

2x4 (51x102) ledger strip
2x2 (51x51) minimum (1½" bearing)(38)

• ledger bearing

WOOD BEAM BEARING

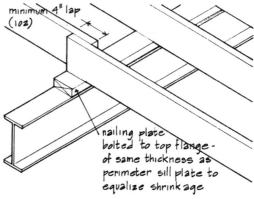

minimum 4" lap (102)

nailing plate bolted to top flange - of same thickness as perimeter sill plate to equalize shrinkage

• direct bearing

STEEL BEAM BEARING

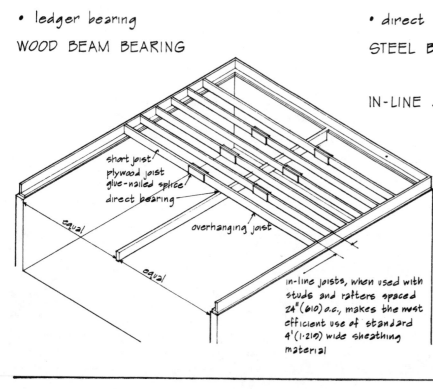

short joist
plywood joist glue-nailed splice
direct bearing

overhanging joist

equal

equal

in-line joists, when used with studs and rafters spaced 24"(610) o.c., makes the most efficient use of standard 4'(1·210) wide sheathing material

IN-LINE JOIST SYSTEM

For economy of lumber, the in-line joist system allows the use of one size smaller joists that would normally be used in conventional framing.

The system consists of uneven length joists, the longer ones overhanging the center support ⅓ to ¼ of the simple span, at a point where the bending moment approaches zero. The short joists are connected to the overhanging joists with shear-resisting metal connectors or plywood splice plates. The overhanging and short joists alternate sides and form joists continuous over two spans.

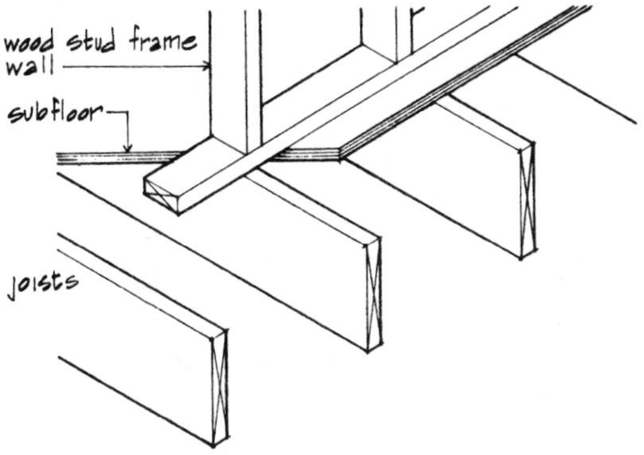

wood stud frame wall

subfloor

joists

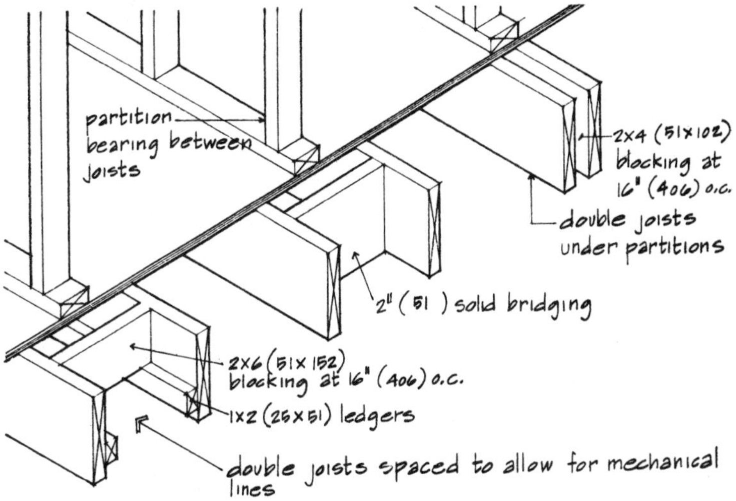

partition bearing between joists

2×4 (51×102) blocking at 16" (406) o.c.

double joists under partitions

2" (51) solid bridging

2×6 (51×152) blocking at 16" (406) o.c.

1×2 (25×51) ledgers

double joists spaced to allow for mechanical lines

NON-BEARING PARTITIONS/ NO PARTITION BELOW

NON-BEARING PARTITIONS/ NO PARTITION BELOW

wood stud frame wall

subfloor

joists

firestop and header between joists

double top plate of partition below

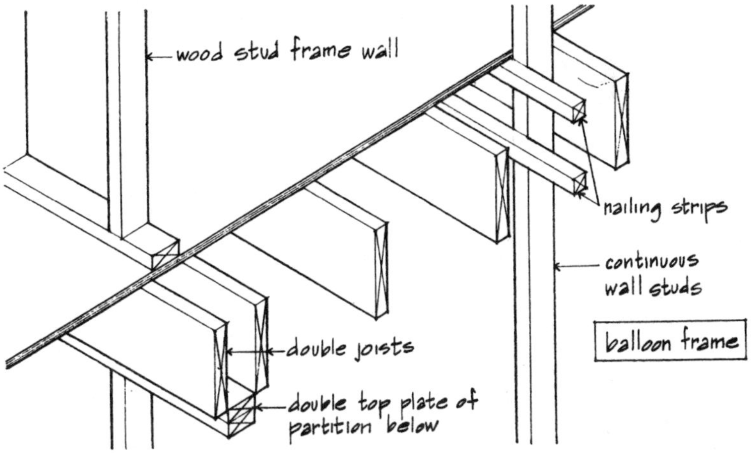

wood stud frame wall

nailing strips

continuous wall studs

double joists

double top plate of partition below

balloon frame

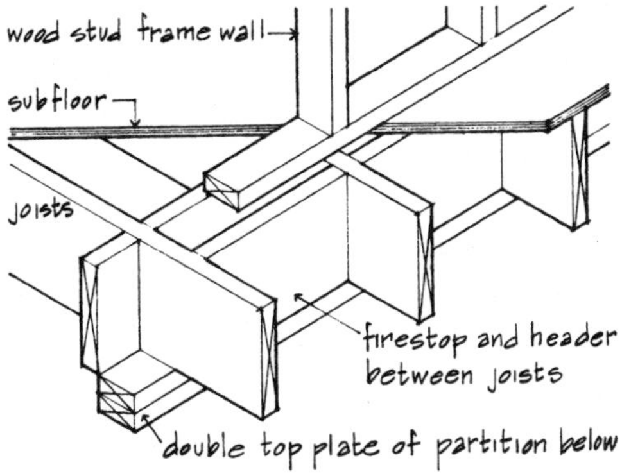

BEARING PARTITIONS

BEARING PARTITIONS

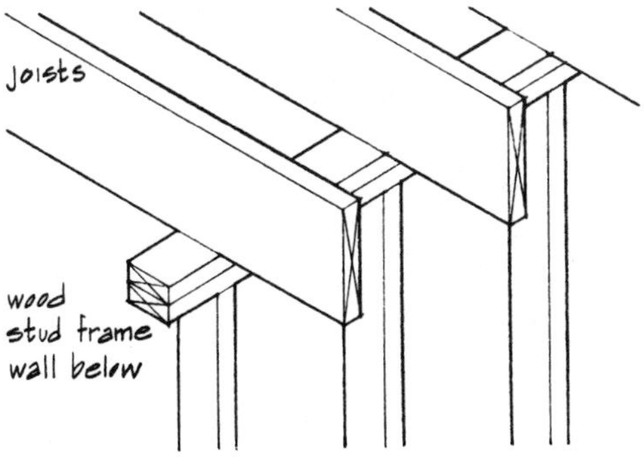

joists

wood stud wall below

2×4 (51×102) blocking at 16" (406) o.c.

1×6 (25×152) to provide nailing surface for finish ceiling

double top plate of partition below

NO PARTITION ABOVE

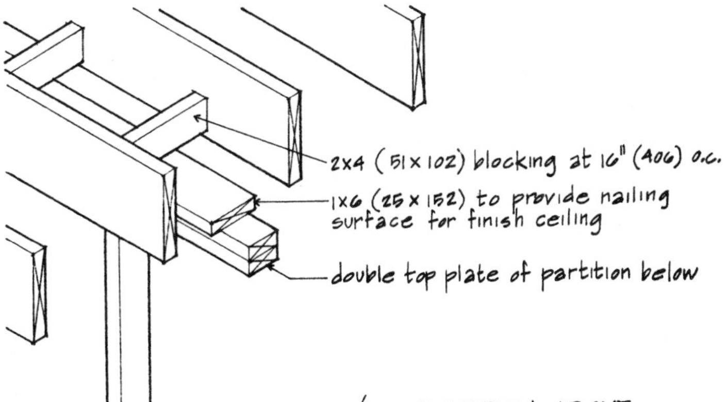

NON-BEARING PARTITION/ NO PARTITION ABOVE

INTERIOR PARTITIONS PERPENDICULAR TO JOISTS

INTERIOR PARTITIONS PARALLEL TO JOISTS

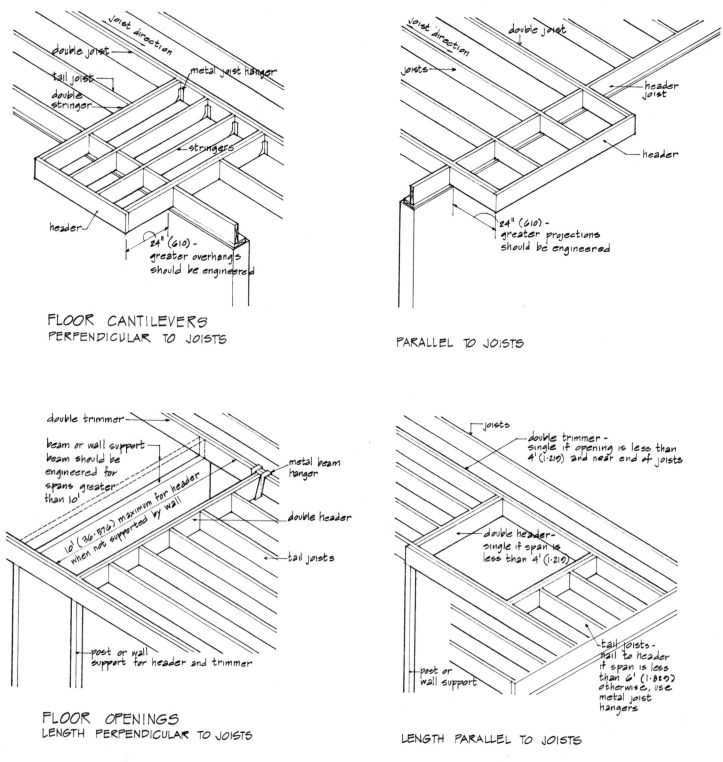

FLOOR CANTILEVERS
PERPENDICULAR TO JOISTS

joist direction
double joist
tail joist
double stringer
metal joist hanger
stringers
header
24" (610) - greater overhangs should be engineered

PARALLEL TO JOISTS

joist direction
double joist
joists
header joist
header
24" (610) - greater projections should be engineered

FLOOR OPENINGS
LENGTH PERPENDICULAR TO JOISTS

double trimmer
beam or wall support beam should be engineered for spans greater than 10'
10' (36·576) maximum for header when not supported by wall
metal beam hanger
double header
tail joists
post or wall support for header and trimmer

LENGTH PARALLEL TO JOISTS

joists
double trimmer - single if opening is less than 4' (1·210) and near end of joists
double header - single if span is less than 4' (1·210)
tail joists - nail to header if span is less than 6' (1·829) otherwise, use metal joist hangers
post or wall support

Structural subflooring and underlayment spans between joists, acts as a working platform during construction, and provides a base for the finish floor. The table below outlines the primary types of subflooring used over wood joist construction.

SUBFLOOR	THICKNESS (inches)	(mm)	PANEL INDEX	SPAN = JOIST SPACING (inches)	(mm)
• boards:					
1x4 (25 x 102)	3/4	(19)	–	16	(406)
• plywood subfloor					
DFPA struct I	5/8	(16)	32/16	16	(406)
DFPA struct II	1/2 · 5/8	(13)	36/16	16	(406)
DFPA C-C ext	5/8 · 3/4 · 7/8	(16) (19) (22)	42/20	20	(508)
DFPA standard w/ exterior glue	3/4 · 7/8	(19)	48/(24)	(24)	
• combined subfloor and underlayment					
underlayment	1/2	(13)		16	(406)
	3/4	(19)		24	(610)
underlayment w/ ext. glue	5/8	(16)		16	(406)
	7/8	(22)		24	(610)
C-C plugged	3/4	(19)		16	(406)
	1	(25.4)		24	(610)
2·4·1	1 1/8	(29)	–	48	(1·219)

plywood span can be determined visually from panel identification index

layer of underlayment required before application of resilient floor tile, carpeting or other non-structural flooring

← may be 24" (610) o.c. if 25/32" (20) wood strip flooring is laid perpendicular to joists

indicated spans assume plywood is laid continuously over 2 or more spans — concentrated floor loads might require additional construction

underlayment provides a smooth surface for the direct application of resilient floor tile, carpeting and other non-structural flooring: may be applied as a separate layer over board and plywood subfloors or be combined with the subfloor in double thickness plywood

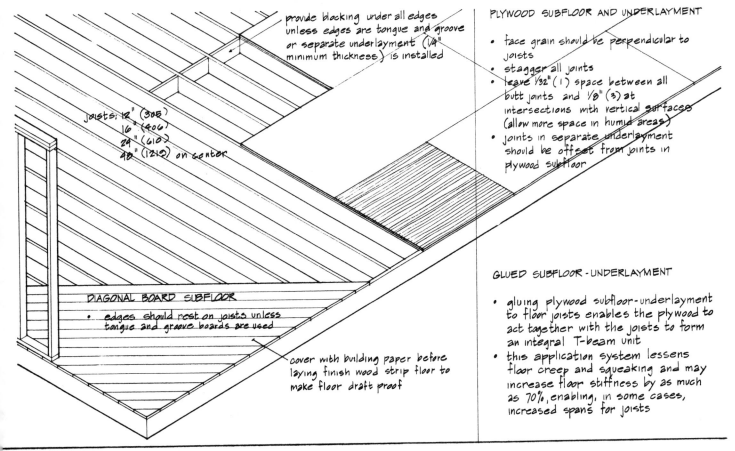

provide blocking under all edges unless edges are tongue and groove or separate underlayment (1/4" minimum thickness) is installed

joists: 12" (305)
16" (406)
24" (610)
48" (1219) on center

DIAGONAL BOARD SUBFLOOR
• edges should rest on joists unless tongue and groove boards are used

cover with building paper before laying finish wood strip floor to make floor draft proof

PLYWOOD SUBFLOOR AND UNDERLAYMENT
• face grain should be perpendicular to joists
• stagger all joints
• leave 1/32" (1) space between all butt joints and 1/8" (3) at intersections with vertical surfaces (allow more space in humid areas)
• joints in separate underlayment should be offset from joints in plywood subfloor

GLUED SUBFLOOR - UNDERLAYMENT
• gluing plywood subfloor-underlayment to floor joists enables the plywood to act together with the joists to form an integral T-beam unit
• this application system lessens floor creep and squeaking and may increase floor stiffness by as much as 70%, enabling, in some cases, increased spans for joists

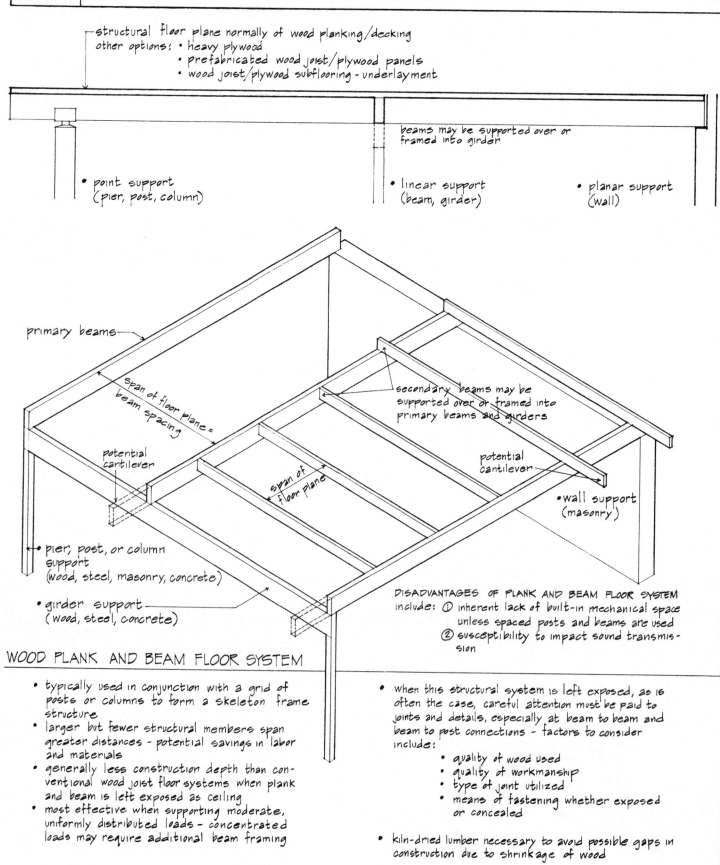

structural floor plane normally of wood planking/decking
other options: • heavy plywood
                • prefabricated wood joist/plywood panels
                • wood joist/plywood subflooring - underlayment

beams may be supported over or framed into girder

• point support
  (pier, post, column)

• linear support
  (beam, girder)

• planar support
  (wall)

primary beams

span of floor plane =
beam spacing

secondary beams may be
supported over or framed into
primary beams and girders

potential cantilever

span of floor plane

potential cantilever

• wall support
  (masonry)

• pier, post, or column
  support
  (wood, steel, masonry, concrete)

• girder support
  (wood, steel, concrete)

DISADVANTAGES OF PLANK AND BEAM FLOOR SYSTEM
include: ① inherent lack of built-in mechanical space
            unless spaced posts and beams are used
         ② susceptibility to impact sound transmission

WOOD PLANK AND BEAM FLOOR SYSTEM

- typically used in conjunction with a grid of posts or columns to form a skeleton frame structure
- larger but fewer structural members span greater distances - potential savings in labor and materials
- generally less construction depth than conventional wood joist floor systems when plank and beam is left exposed as ceiling
- most effective when supporting moderate, uniformly distributed loads - concentrated loads may require additional beam framing

- when this structural system is left exposed, as is often the case, careful attention must be paid to joints and details, especially at beam to beam and beam to post connections - factors to consider include:
  - quality of wood used
  - quality of workmanship
  - type of joint utilized
  - means of fastening whether exposed or concealed

- kiln-dried lumber necessary to avoid possible gaps in construction due to shrinkage of wood

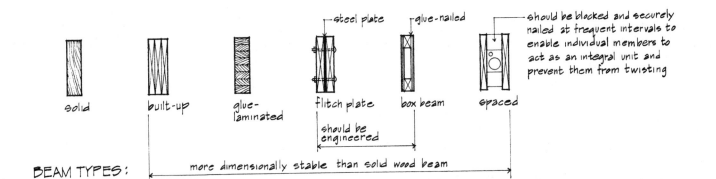

steel plate — glue-nailed — should be blocked and securely nailed at frequent intervals to enable individual members to act as an integral unit and prevent them from twisting

solid   built-up   glue-laminated   flitch plate   box beam   spaced

should be engineered

BEAM TYPES: more dimensionally stable than solid wood beam

The following load tables for the most common types of wood beams are for estimating and preliminary sizing only. The species, stress grade and allowable stresses in bending and shear, and modulus of elasticity for the lumber used, as well as the precise loading situation, joint condition, and allowable deflection should all be considered in the selection and sizing of a beam type. See bibliography for sources of detailed load tables.

SOLID AND BUILT-UP WOOD BEAMS

SPAN		SPACING		SIZE	
feet	m	feet	m	inches	mm
10	(3·048)	4	(1·219)	2 · 2 × 8	2 (51 × 203)
		6	(1·829)	2 · 2 × 10	2 (51 × 254)
		8	(2·438)	4 × 10	(102 × 254)
12	(3·658)	4		3 × 10	(76 × 254)
		6		2 · 2 × 12	2 (51 × 305)
		8		4 × 12	(102 × 305)
14	(4·267)	4		4 × 10	(102 × 254)
		6		6 × 10	(152 × 254)
		8		3 · 2 × 12	3 (51 × 305)
16	(4·877)	6		3 · 2 × 12	3 (51 × 305)
		8		4 · 2 × 12	4 (51 × 305)
18	(5·486)	6		6 × 12	(152 × 305)
		8		8 × 12	(203 × 305)
20	(6·096)	6		2 · 3 × 14	2 (76 × 356)
		8		2 · 4 × 14	2 (102 × 356)

The above assumes the following:

- total live load = 40 psf (195 kg/m²)
- fiber stress in bending = 1200 psi (844 × 10³ kg/m²)
- modulus of elasticity = 1,400,000 psi (985 × 10⁶ kg/m²)
- deflection limitation = 1/360 of beam span

(1 lb/ft² = 4.882 kg/m²)
(1 psi = 703.07 kg/m²)

GLUE-LAMINATED BEAMS

SPAN		SPACING		SIZE	
feet	m	feet	m	inches	mm
12	(3·658)	6	(1·829)	3⅛ × 9	(79 × 229)
		8	(2·438)	3⅛ × 10½	(79 × 267)
		10	(3·048)	3⅛ × 10½	(79 × 267)
		12	(3·658)	3⅛ × 12	(79 × 305)
16	(4·877)	8		3⅛ × 13½	(79 × 343)
		12		3⅛ × 15	(79 × 381)
		14		3⅛ × 15	(79 × 381)
		16		3⅛ × 15	(79 × 381)
20	(6·096)	8		3⅛ × 16½	(79 × 419)
		12		5⅛ × 15	(130 × 381)
		16		5⅛ × 18	(130 × 457)
		20		5⅛ × 18	(130 × 457)
24	(7·315)	8		5⅛ × 16½	(130 × 419)
		12		5⅛ × 18	(130 × 457)
		16		5⅛ × 21	(130 × 533)
		20		5⅛ × 22½	(130 × 572)
28	(8·534)	8		5⅛ × 19½	(130 × 495)
		12		5⅛ × 21	(130 × 533)
		16		5⅛ × 24	(130 × 610)
		20		5⅛ × 25½	(130 × 648)
32	(9·754)	8		5⅛ × 21	(130 × 533)
		12		5⅛ × 24	(130 × 610)
		16		5⅛ × 27	(130 × 686)
		20		6¾ × 27	(171 × 686)
40	(12·192)	12		6¾ × 28½	(171 × 724)
		16		6¾ × 31½	(171 × 800)
		20		6¾ × 33	(171 × 838)
		24		6¾ × 36	(171 × 914)

The above assumes the following:

- total live load = 40 psf (195 kg/m²)
- fiber stress in bending = 2400 psi (1689 × 10³ kg/m²)
- modulus of elasticity = 1,800,000 psi (1267 × 10⁶ kg/m²)
- deflection limitation = 1/360 of beam span

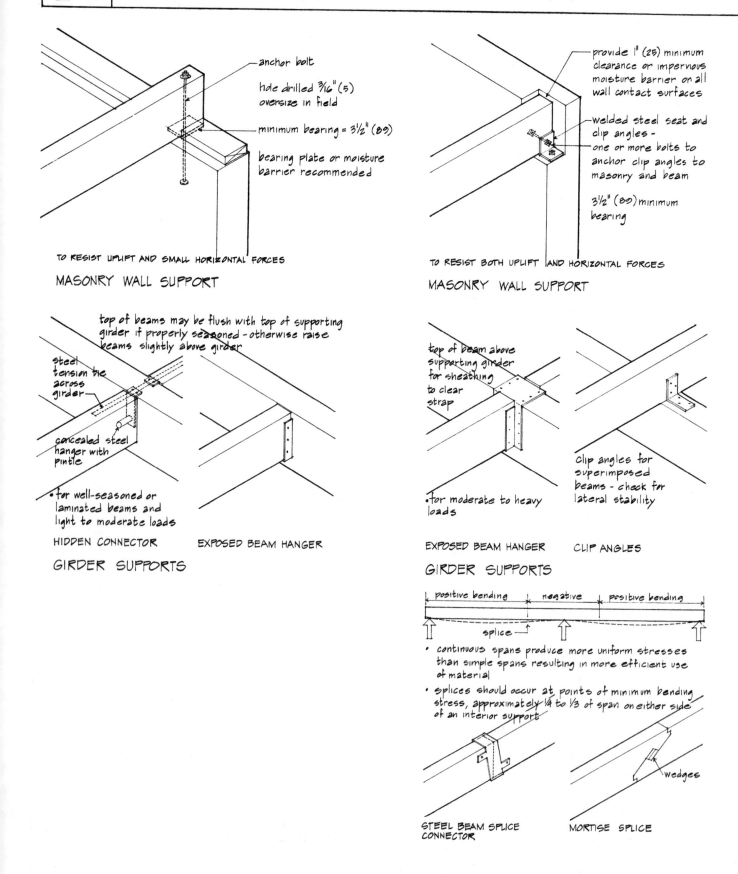

anchor bolt

hole drilled 3/16" (5) oversize in field

minimum bearing = 3½" (89)

bearing plate or moisture barrier recommended

TO RESIST UPLIFT AND SMALL HORIZONTAL FORCES

MASONRY WALL SUPPORT

provide 1" (25) minimum clearance or impervious moisture barrier on all wall contact surfaces

welded steel seat and clip angles - one or more bolts to anchor clip angles to masonry and beam

3½" (89) minimum bearing

TO RESIST BOTH UPLIFT AND HORIZONTAL FORCES

MASONRY WALL SUPPORT

top of beams may be flush with top of supporting girder if properly seasoned - otherwise raise beams slightly above girder

steel tension tie across girder

concealed steel hanger with pintle

• for well-seasoned or laminated beams and light to moderate loads

HIDDEN CONNECTOR   EXPOSED BEAM HANGER

GIRDER SUPPORTS

top of beam above supporting girder for sheathing to clear strap

• for moderate to heavy loads

clip angles for superimposed beams - check for lateral stability

EXPOSED BEAM HANGER   CLIP ANGLES

GIRDER SUPPORTS

positive bending | negative | positive bending

splice

• continuous spans produce more uniform stresses than simple spans resulting in more efficient use of material

• splices should occur at points of minimum bending stress, approximately ¼ to ⅓ of span on either side of an interior support

wedges

STEEL BEAM SPLICE CONNECTOR   MORTISE SPLICE

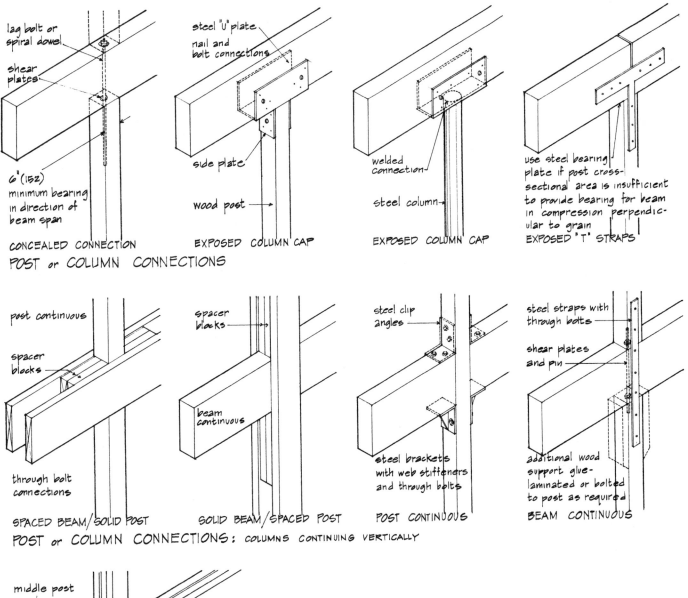

lag bolt or spiral dowel

shear plates

6" (152) minimum bearing in direction of beam span

CONCEALED CONNECTION

steel "U" plate

nail and bolt connections

side plate

wood post

EXPOSED COLUMN CAP

welded connection

steel column

EXPOSED COLUMN CAP

use steel bearing plate if post cross-sectional area is insufficient to provide bearing for beam in compression perpendicular to grain

EXPOSED "T" STRAPS

POST or COLUMN CONNECTIONS

post continuous

spacer blocks

through bolt connections

SPACED BEAM/SOLID POST

spacer blocks

beam continuous

SOLID BEAM/SPACED POST

steel clip angles

steel brackets with web stiffeners and through bolts

POST CONTINUOUS

steel straps with through bolts

shear plates and pin

additional wood support glue-laminated or bolted to post as required

BEAM CONTINUOUS

POST or COLUMN CONNECTIONS: COLUMNS CONTINUING VERTICALLY

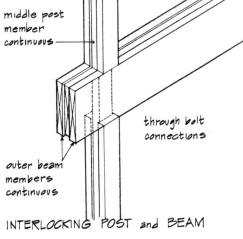

middle post member continuous

through bolt connections

outer beam members continuous

INTERLOCKING POST and BEAM

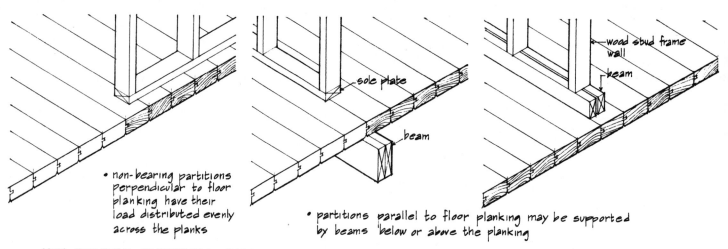

sole plate

beam

wood stud frame wall

beam

- non-bearing partitions perpendicular to floor planking have their load distributed evenly across the planks

- partitions parallel to floor planking may be supported by beams below or above the planking

NON-BEARING PARTITIONS OVER WOOD PLANK FLOOR

In the plank and beam floor system, the beam grid layout should be carefully integrated with the required placement of interior walls for both structural and visual reasons. Normally, most partitions in this system are non-structural and may be placed as shown above. If bearing partitions are required however, they should be placed over the floor beams which should be large enough to carry the additional load. When this is not possible, additional beam framing may be required.

FLOOR SYSTEMS SPANNING BETWEEN BEAMS

- Other than the conventional wood joist and plywood subfloor system, the following systems can be utilized:

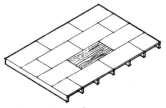

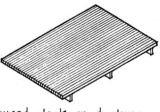

2·4·1 plywood
(combined subfloor-underlayment)

- 1⅛" (29) thick
  (may vary with wood species)
- can span up to 4'0 (1·219)
- tongue and groove edges
- laid with face plies perpendicular to beam supports with end joints staggered
- 1/16" (2) space left at all joints
- no overhang possible
* see 4·11

prefabricated panels

- plywood sheathing over nominal 2" (51) frame which acts as floor joists
- glue-nailed or bonded by adhesives under heat and pressure to form stressed skin panels
- insulation, vapor barrier, and interior finish may be installed at one time
- limited overhang possible
* see 4·11

wood plank or decking

- see facing page
- limited overhang possible
- openings require additional framing

WOOD PLANK AND DECK TYPES

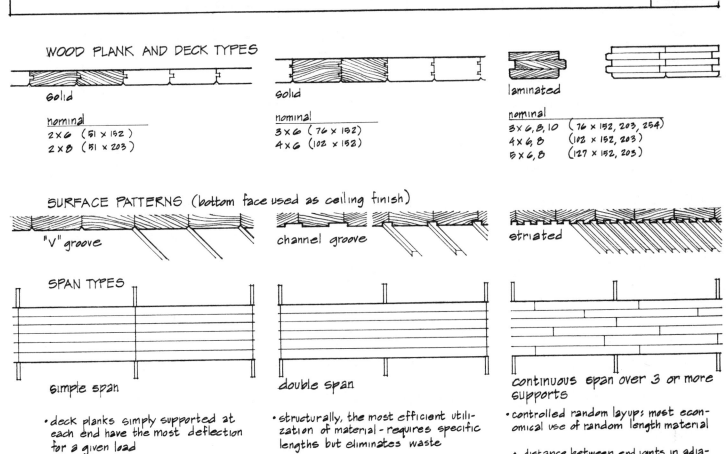

solid

nominal
2×6 (51 × 152)
2×8 (51 × 203)

solid

nominal
3×6 (76 × 152)
4×6 (102 × 152)

laminated

nominal
3×6,8,10 (76 × 152, 203, 254)
4×6,8 (102 × 152, 203)
5×6,8 (127 × 152, 203)

SURFACE PATTERNS (bottom face used as ceiling finish)

"V" groove

channel groove

striated

SPAN TYPES

simple span

double span

continuous span over 3 or more supports

• deck planks simply supported at each end have the most deflection for a given load

• structurally, the most efficient utilization of material - requires specific lengths but eliminates waste

• controlled random layups most economical use of random length material

• distance between end joints in adjacent courses must be at least 2' (610)

• joints in the same general line must rest on at least one support

• joints in rows not adjacent must be separated by 1' (305) or 2 rows of decking

• only one joint should occur in each course between supports

• a joint on a support is considered as a joint in one of the adjacent spans

• in end spans, one third of the planks should be free of joints

The following table is for estimating and preliminary sizing only

TOTAL ALLOWABLE UNIFORMLY DISTRIBUTED LOADS

NOMINAL DECK THICKNESS		SPAN		SIMPLE SPAN		CONTROLLED RANDOM LAYUP	
inches	mm	feet	m	psf	kg/m²	psf	kg/m²
2	(51)	6	(1·829)	46	(225)		
		8	(2·438)	20	(98)	25	(122)
3	(76)	8	(2·438)	62	(302)	106	(517)
		10	(3·048)	32	(156)	54	(264)
		12	(3·658)	18	(88)	31	(151)
3 (superthick)	(89)	10	(3·048)	53	(259)	90	(439)
		12	(3·658)	31	(151)	52	(254)
		14	(4·267)	19	(93)	33	(161)
4	(102)	12	(3·658)	44	(215)	74	(361)
		14	(4·267)	28	(137)	47	(229)
		16	(4·878)	19	(93)	31	(151)
5	(127)	14	(4·267)	51	(249)	86	(420)
		16	(4·878)	34	(166)	58	(283)
		18	(5·486)	24	(117)	41	(200)
		20	(6·096)	18	(88)	30	(146)

The above assumes the following: fiber stress in bending = 1500 psi (1112×10^3 kg/m²)
modulus of elasticity = 1,300,000 psi (915×10^6 kg/m²)
allowable deflection = 1/240 of deck span

structural steel framing may be spanned by:
• composite concrete/steel decking (see 4.25)
• cast-in-place or precast concrete (see 4.27/28)

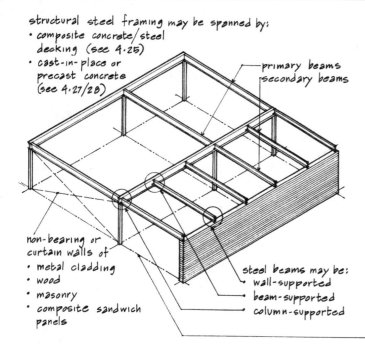

primary beams
secondary beams

non-bearing or curtain walls of
• metal cladding
• wood
• masonry
• composite sandwich panels

steel beams may be:
• wall-supported
• beam-supported
• column-supported

Structural steel is essentially a linear system that forms a skeletal frame similar in principle to the wood post-and-beam structural system. (see 4.12 and 5.12)

• steel frames are normally designed and utilized to carry relatively heavy loads over long spans, and require careful engineering analysis of moment, shear, and tensile stresses, especially at joints and connections
• slenderness and depth-to-span ratios of the steel structural members must be checked to ensure rigidity of the frame
• lateral and wind forces must be resisted by rigidly braced connections and/or shear walls

• since structural steel is difficult to work on-site, it is normally cut, shaped, and drilled by a fabricating shop according to the designer's specifications

• structural steel usually requires fire-resistant protection and, if exposed, treatment against corrosion

• a structural grid should be utilized in laying out the framing system

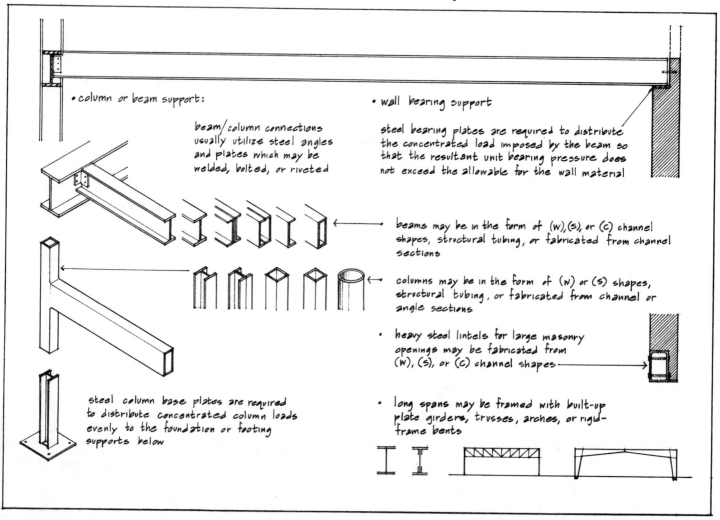

• column or beam support:

beam/column connections usually utilize steel angles and plates which may be welded, bolted, or riveted

• wall bearing support

steel bearing plates are required to distribute the concentrated load imposed by the beam so that the resultant unit bearing pressure does not exceed the allowable for the wall material

steel column base plates are required to distribute concentrated column loads evenly to the foundation or footing supports below

beams may be in the form of (w),(s), or (c) channel shapes, structural tubing, or fabricated from channel sections

columns may be in the form of (w) or (s) shapes, structural tubing, or fabricated from channel or angle sections

• heavy steel lintels for large masonry openings may be fabricated from (w), (s), or (c) channel shapes

• long spans may be framed with built-up plate girders, trusses, arches, or rigid-frame bents

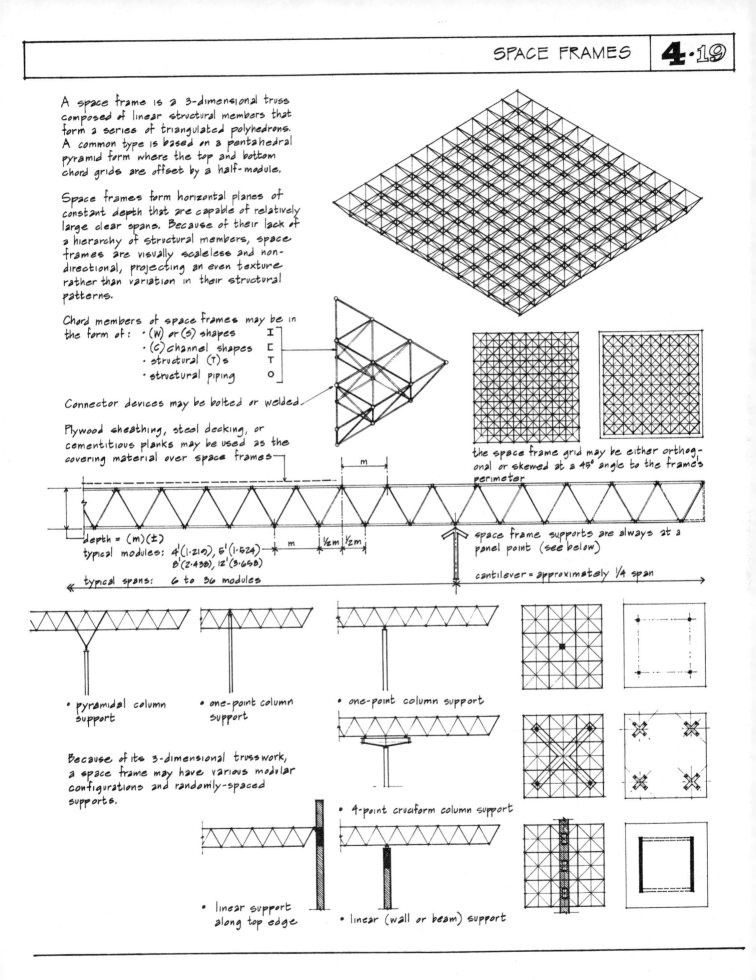

A space frame is a 3-dimensional truss composed of linear structural members that form a series of triangulated polyhedrons. A common type is based on a pentahedral pyramid form where the top and bottom chord grids are offset by a half-module.

Space frames form horizontal planes of constant depth that are capable of relatively large clear spans. Because of their lack of a hierarchy of structural members, space frames are visually scaleless and non-directional, projecting an even texture rather than variation in their structural patterns.

Chord members of space frames may be in the form of:
· (W) or (S) shapes   I
· (C) channel shapes   ⊏
· structural (T)s   T
· structural piping   O

Connector devices may be bolted or welded.

Plywood sheathing, steel decking, or cementitious planks may be used as the covering material over space frames

the space frame grid may be either orthogonal or skewed at a 45° angle to the frame's perimeter

depth = (m)(±)
typical modules: 4'(1.210), 5'(1.524), 8'(2.438), 12'(3.658)
typical spans: 6 to 36 modules

space frame supports are always at a panel point (see below)

cantilever = approximately ¼ span

· pyramidal column support

· one-point column support

· one-point column support

Because of its 3-dimensional trusswork, a space frame may have various modular configurations and randomly-spaced supports.

· 4-point cruciform column support

· linear support along top edge

· linear (wall or beam) support

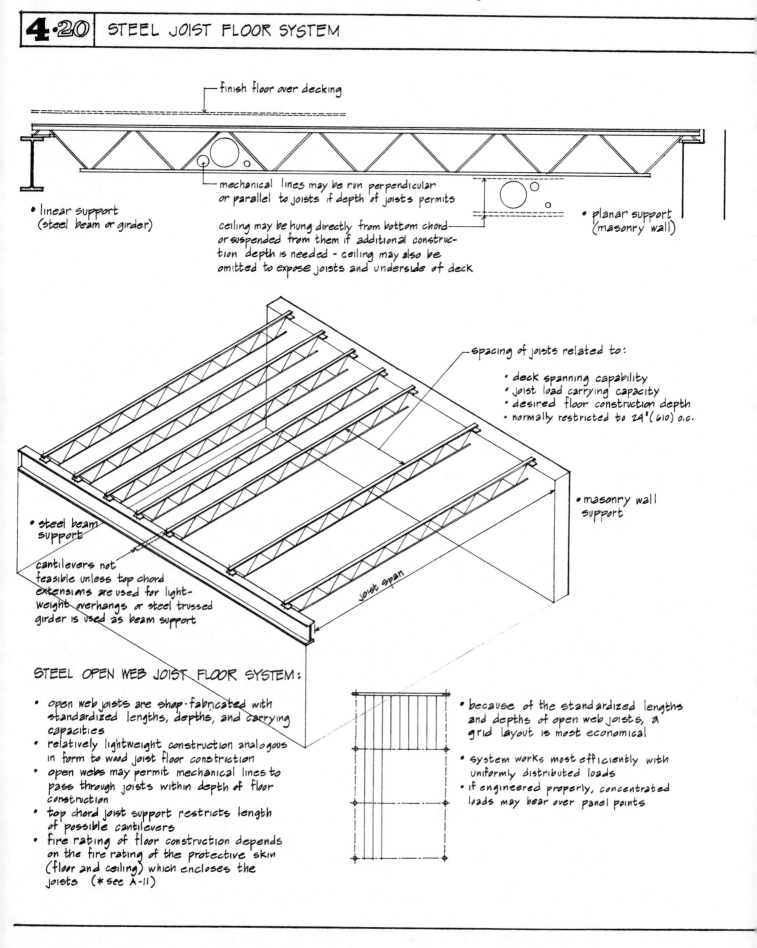

— finish floor over decking

— mechanical lines may be run perpendicular or parallel to joists if depth of joists permits

• linear support
(steel beam or girder)

• planar support
(masonry wall)

ceiling may be hung directly from bottom chord or suspended from them if additional construction depth is needed - ceiling may also be omitted to expose joists and underside of deck

spacing of joists related to:

• deck spanning capability
• joist load carrying capacity
• desired floor construction depth
• normally restricted to 24" (610) o.c.

• masonry wall
support

• steel beam
support

cantilevers not feasible unless top chord extensions are used for light-weight overhangs or steel trussed girder is used as beam support

Joist span

STEEL OPEN WEB JOIST FLOOR SYSTEM:

• open web joists are shop-fabricated with standardized lengths, depths, and carrying capacities
• relatively lightweight construction analogous in form to wood joist floor construction
• open webs may permit mechanical lines to pass through joists within depth of floor construction
• top chord joist support restricts length of possible cantilevers
• fire rating of floor construction depends on the fire rating of the protective skin (floor and ceiling) which encloses the joists (*see A-11)

• because of the standardized lengths and depths of open web joists, a grid layout is most economical
• system works most efficiently with uniformly distributed loads
• if engineered properly, concentrated loads may bear over panel points

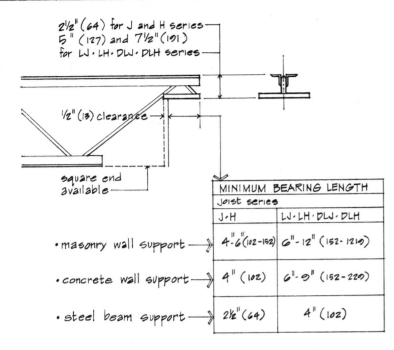

2½" (64) for J and H series —
5" (127) and 7½" (191)
for LJ · LH · DLJ · DLH series —

½" (13) clearance —

square end
available —

open web steel joist profiles vary according
to manufacturer

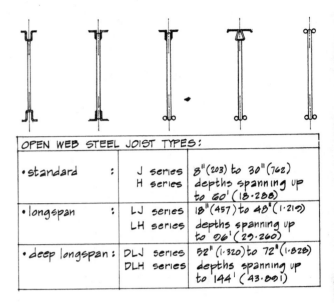

MINIMUM BEARING LENGTH	
Joist series	
J · H	LJ · LH · DLJ · DLH
• masonry wall support → 4"–6" (102–152)	6"–12" (152–1219)
• concrete wall support → 4" (102)	6"–9" (152–229)
• steel beam support → 2½" (64)	4" (102)

OPEN WEB STEEL JOIST TYPES:		
• standard :	J series H series	8" (203) to 30" (762) depths spanning up to 60' (18·288)
• longspan :	LJ series LH series	18" (457) to 48" (1·219) depths spanning up to 96' (29·260)
• deep longspan :	DLJ series DLH series	52" (1·320) to 72" (1·828) depths spanning up to 144' (43·891)

The following table is for estimating and preliminary sizing of members only. Consult the Steel Joist Institute
for specifications and more complete load tables for all joist types and sizes.

ALLOWABLE UNIFORMLY DISTRIBUTED LIVE LOADS IN LBS/FT² (1 lb/ft² = 4.882 kg/m²)														
JOIST SERIES	JOIST DESIGNATION	SPAN (feet) (m)	12 (3·658)	16 (4·878)	20 (6·096)	24 (7·314)	28 (8·534)	32 (9·754)	36 (10·972)	40 (12·192)	44 (13·411)	48 (14·630)	52 (15·850)	56 (17·069)	60 (18·288)
J	8J3		266	112											
	10J4			223	114										
	12J6				246	142									
	14J7					233	147								
	16J8					350	220								
	18J11						300	261							
	20J11							327	230						
	22J11								282						
	24J11								339	247	186	143			
	26J11									292	220	169	133		
	28J11									342	257	198	156	125	
	30J11										297	229	180	144	117

• span of open web steel joists should not exceed 24 times the joist depth

• joists are provided with positive camber so that, under loading, they will deflect and settle into a true level plane
• the following are approximate cambers for various top chord lengths:

top chord length:	camber
20' (6·096)	¼" (6)
30' (9·144)	⅜" (10)
40' (12·192)	⅝" (16)
50' (15·240)	1" (25)
60' (18·288)	1¼" (32)

• horizontal or diagonal bridging is required to prevent lateral movement of the top and bottom chords
• spacing of the bridging rows depends on the chord size and the joist span, and may vary from
10'–15' (3·048–4·782) on center

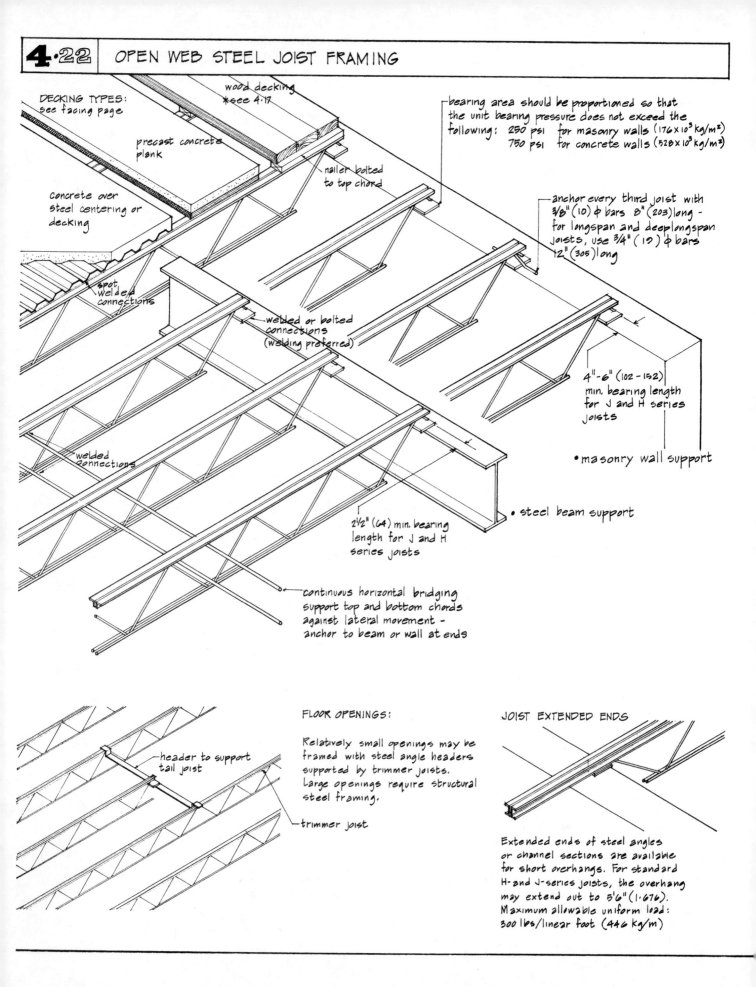

DECKING TYPES:
see facing page

wood decking
*see 4·17

precast concrete
plank

concrete over
steel centering or
decking

nailer bolted
to top chord

bearing area should be proportioned so that
the unit bearing pressure does not exceed the
following: 250 psi   for masonry walls $(176 \times 10^3 \text{kg/m}^2)$
750 psi   for concrete walls $(528 \times 10^3 \text{kg/m}^2)$

anchor every third joist with
3/8" (10) φ bars 8" (203) long -
for longspan and deeplongspan
joists, use 3/4" (19) φ bars
12" (305) long

spot
welded
connections

welded or bolted
connections
(welding preferred)

4"-6" (102 - 152)
min. bearing length
for J and H series
joists

welded
connections

• masonry wall support

• steel beam support

2½" (64) min. bearing
length for J and H
series joists

continuous horizontal bridging
support top and bottom chords
against lateral movement -
anchor to beam or wall at ends

header to support
tail joist

trimmer joist

FLOOR OPENINGS:

Relatively small openings may be
framed with steel angle headers
supported by trimmer joists.
Large openings require structural
steel framing.

JOIST EXTENDED ENDS

Extended ends of steel angles
or channel sections are available
for short overhangs. For standard
H- and J-series joists, the overhang
may extend out to 5'6" (1·676).
Maximum allowable uniform load:
300 lbs/linear foot (446 kg/m)

* see 5·23/31 for typical masonry bearing conditions

The floor deck must provide lateral support for the top chords of the open web steel joists. Deck attachments must be made at least every 36" (914) and be able to resist a lateral force of 300 lbs. (136.03 kg)

Basic types of floor decks that may be supported by steel joists are shown below:

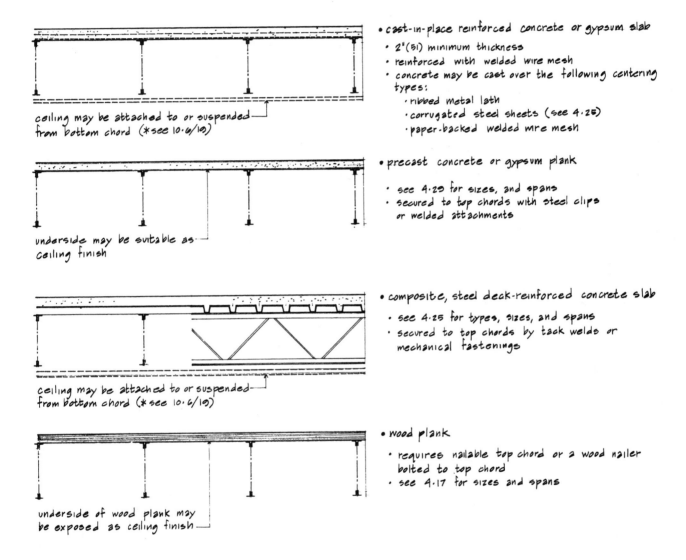

ceiling may be attached to or suspended from bottom chord (*see 10·6/10)

- cast-in-place reinforced concrete or gypsum slab
  - 2" (51) minimum thickness
  - reinforced with welded wire mesh
  - concrete may be cast over the following centering types:
    - ribbed metal lath
    - corrugated steel sheets (see 4·25)
    - paper-backed welded wire mesh

underside may be suitable as ceiling finish

- precast concrete or gypsum plank
  - see 4·29 for sizes, and spans
  - secured to top chords with steel clips or welded attachments

- composite, steel deck-reinforced concrete slab
  - see 4·25 for types, sizes, and spans
  - secured to top chords by tack welds or mechanical fastenings

ceiling may be attached to or suspended from bottom chord (*see 10·6/10)

- wood plank
  - requires nailable top chord or a wood nailer bolted to top chord
  - see 4·17 for sizes and spans

underside of wood plank may be exposed as ceiling finish

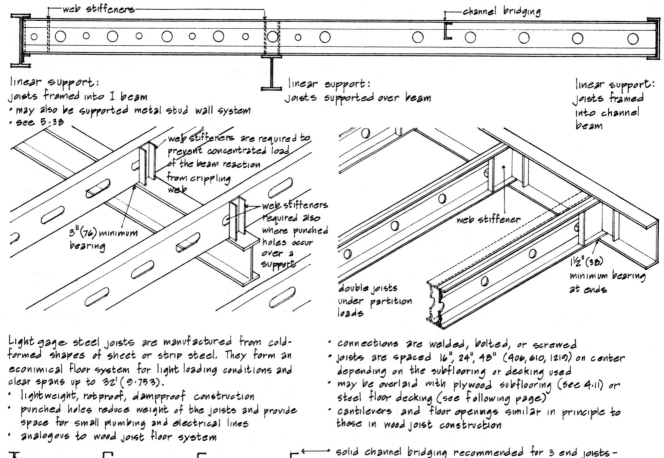

linear support:
joists framed into I beam
• may also be supported metal stud wall system
• see 5·38

linear support:
joists supported over beam

linear support:
joists framed into channel beam

web stiffeners are required to prevent concentrated load of the beam reaction from crippling web

3" (76) minimum bearing

web stiffeners required also where punched holes occur over a support

web stiffener

double joists under partition loads

1½" (38) minimum bearing at ends

Light gage steel joists are manufactured from cold-formed shapes of sheet or strip steel. They form an economical floor system for light loading conditions and clear spans up to 32' (9·753).
• lightweight, rotproof, dampproof construction
• punched holes reduce weight of the joists and provide space for small plumbing and electrical lines
• analogous to wood joist floor system

I nailable joist   [cee joist   [channel joist

• joist depths: (as listed below); flange widths: 1⅞"(48), 1¹⁵/₁₆"(40), 2³/₁₆"(56), 2¾"(70), 2⅞"(73); gages: 12 through 18

• connections are welded, bolted, or screwed
• joists are spaced 16", 24", 48" (406, 610, 1219) on center depending on the subflooring or decking used
• may be overlaid with plywood subflooring (see 4·11) or steel floor decking (see following page)
• cantilevers and floor openings similar in principle to those in wood joist construction

• solid channel bridging recommended for 3 end joists - anchored securely to end walls for lateral stability
• "v" bridging used for remaining joists
• bridging spaced 5'-8' (1·524-2·438) on center depending on span

The following table lists approximate allowable uniform loads for steel joists in lbs/ft² (for estimating purposes only)

JOIST SIZE (DEPTH)	TYPE SPAN	SPACING	SPAN IN FEET						JOIST SIZE (DEPTH)	TYPE SPAN	SPACING	SPAN IN FEET				
			10	12	14	16	18	20				14	16	18	20	22
6" (152)	S	16" (406)	114	52	33	28			10" (254)	S	16" (406)	186	125	87	64	48
		24" (610)	76	35	22	10					24" (610)	124	83	58	43	32
		48" (1219)	38	17	11	9					48" (1219)	62	42	29	21	16
	C	24	143	54	41	34				C	24	134	117	105	80	60
		48	71	27	20	17					48	67	57	52	40	30
8" (203)	S	16	233	135	85	57	53		12" (305)	S	16				163	23
		24	156	90	57	38	34				24				100	82
		48	78	45	28	19	17				48				54	41
	C	24	140	117	100	72	50			C	24				186	154
		48	70	58	50	36	25				48				93	77
9" (229)	S	16			114	76	54	39								
		24			76	51	36	26								
		48			38	26	18	13								
	C	24			92	81	67	49								
		48			46	40	33	24								

S = simple span condition
C = continuous over 3 spans
1 foot = (305)
1 lb/ft² = (4·882 kg/m²)

Steel floor decks are manufactured from copper-alloy sheet steel and may be either corrugated or cellular in form. They serve as a working platform during construction, and provide a permanent formwork and steel reinforcement for structural concrete to form a composite floor slab.

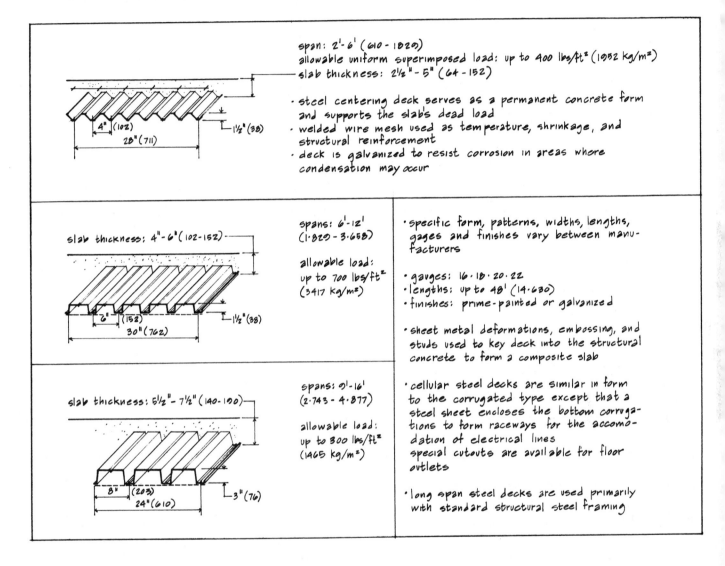

span: 2'-6' (610 - 1829)
allowable uniform superimposed load: up to 400 lbs/ft² (1952 kg/m²)
slab thickness: 2½" - 5" (64 - 152)

· steel centering deck serves as a permanent concrete form and supports the slab's dead load
· welded wire mesh used as temperature, shrinkage, and structural reinforcement
· deck is galvanized to resist corrosion in areas where condensation may occur

4" (102)
28" (711)
1½" (38)

---

slab thickness: 4" - 6" (102 - 152)

spans: 6'-12'
(1·829 - 3·658)

allowable load:
up to 700 lbs/ft²
(3417 kg/m²)

· specific form, patterns, widths, lengths, gages and finishes vary between manufacturers

· gauges: 16 · 18 · 20 · 22
· lengths: up to 48' (14·630)
· finishes: prime-painted or galvanized

· sheet metal deformations, embossing, and studs used to key deck into the structural concrete to form a composite slab

6" (152)
30" (762)
1½" (38)

---

slab thickness: 5½" - 7½" (140 - 190)

spans: 9'-16'
(2·743 - 4·877)

allowable load:
up to 300 lbs/ft²
(1465 kg/m²)

· cellular steel decks are similar in form to the corrugated type except that a steel sheet encloses the bottom corrugations to form raceways for the accomodation of electrical lines
special cutouts are available for floor outlets

· long span steel decks are used primarily with standard structural steel framing

8" (203)
24" (610)
3" (76)

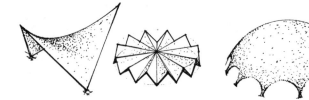

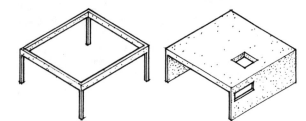

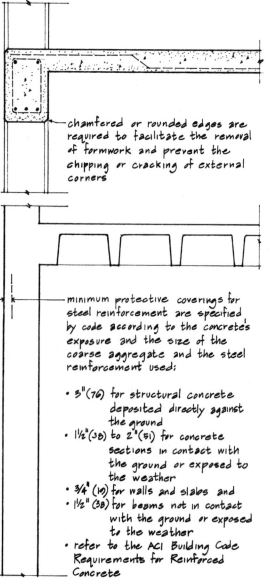

chamfered or rounded edges are required to facilitate the removal of formwork and prevent the chipping or cracking of external corners

minimum protective coverings for steel reinforcement are specified by code according to the concrete's exposure and the size of the coarse aggregate and the steel reinforcement used:

- 3" (76) for structural concrete deposited directly against the ground
- 1½" (38) to 2" (51) for concrete sections in contact with the ground or exposed to the weather
- ¾" (19) for walls and slabs and
- 1½" (38) for beams not in contact with the ground or exposed to the weather
- refer to the ACI Building Code Requirements for Reinforced Concrete

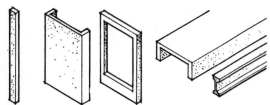

Reinforced concrete can be cast into almost any shape. Its flexibility of form is limited only by the formwork and steel reinforcement required, and the method of its placement or casting. It may be used as either a linear or planar structural element to form skeleton-frame, bearing-wall, and shell structures.

The design of reinforced concrete structures requires engineering analysis to determine the proper thickness of the concrete section and the amount and placement of the steel reinforcement required to handle tensile and shear stresses within the section. Steel reinforcement is also required to provide positive ties between vertical and horizontal structural elements, reinforce edges around openings, and control shrinkage movement.

Continuity between columns, beams, floor slabs, and bearing walls is desirable to minimize bending moments at these connections. Since such continuity is easily attainable in reinforced concrete construction, structures continuous over at least 3 spans are usually the most efficient.

Although concrete is capable of being formed into a monolithic structure with strong, continuous connections, expansion joints are required to control cracking due to shrinkage, thermal expansion, and structural settlement of the concrete. Provision should also be made for construction joints to finish off one day's pour and prepare it for the next.

The strength, durability, fire-resistance, and other properties may be altered by the type of aggregate and/or admixtures used in the concrete mix. (see 12.9)

Various surface patterns and textures may be achieved by impressions left by the formwork or treatment during or after the concrete is set. Concrete may be colored by the use of colored cement, colored aggregate, or pigments added to the concrete mix. It may also be painted or dyed after it has set.

Concrete structural elements such as columns, beams, and wall and floor panels may be precast.
- precasting allows for greater control of the quality and finish of the concrete
- precast structural elements may be prestressed or post-tensioned for greater structural efficiency and longer spans
- precast elements may be used to form a structure or be attached to other structural systems

The selection of a reinforced concrete floor system depends on the type and magnitude of the load conditions, the size and proportion of the structural bays, and the desired construction depth of the floor system.

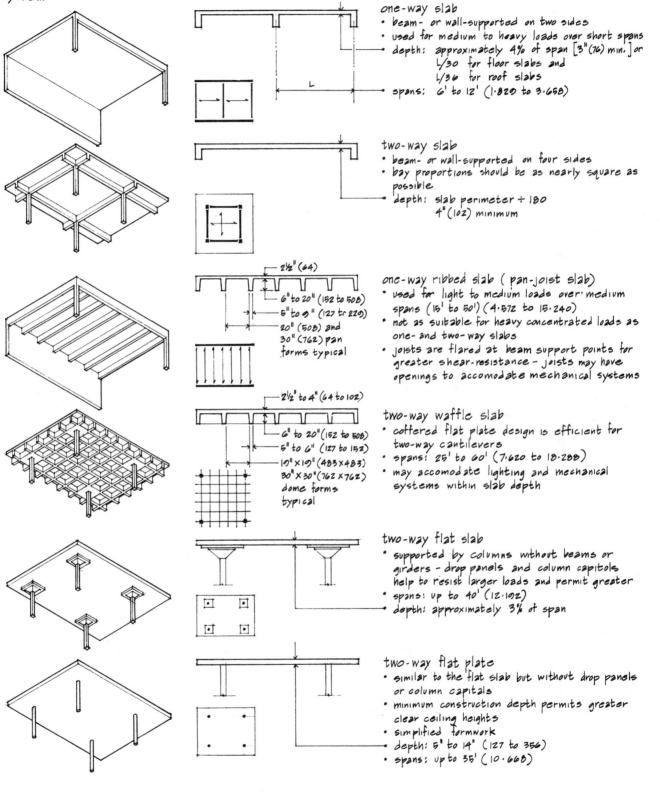

one-way slab
- beam- or wall-supported on two sides
- used for medium to heavy loads over short spans
- depth: approximately 4% of span [3"(76) min.] or
  L/30 for floor slabs and
  L/36 for roof slabs
- spans: 6' to 12' (1.829 to 3.658)

two-way slab
- beam- or wall-supported on four sides
- bay proportions should be as nearly square as possible
- depth: slab perimeter ÷ 180
  4"(102) minimum

2½" (64)
6" to 20" (152 to 508)
5" to 9" (127 to 229)
20" (508) and
30" (762) pan forms typical

one-way ribbed slab (pan-joist slab)
- used for light to medium loads over medium spans (15' to 50') (4.572 to 15.240)
- not as suitable for heavy concentrated loads as one- and two-way slabs
- joists are flared at beam support points for greater shear-resistance — joists may have openings to accomodate mechanical systems

2½" to 4" (64 to 102)
6" to 20" (152 to 508)
5" to 6" (127 to 152)
19"×19" (483×483)
30"×30" (762×762) dome forms typical

two-way waffle slab
- coffered flat plate design is efficient for two-way cantilevers
- spans: 25' to 60' (7.620 to 18.288)
- may accomodate lighting and mechanical systems within slab depth

two-way flat slab
- supported by columns without beams or girders — drop panels and column capitols help to resist larger loads and permit greater
- spans: up to 40' (12.192)
- depth: approximately 3% of span

two-way flat plate
- similar to the flat slab but without drop panels or column capitals
- minimum construction depth permits greater clear ceiling heights
- simplified formwork
- depth: 5" to 14" (127 to 356)
- spans: up to 35' (10.668)

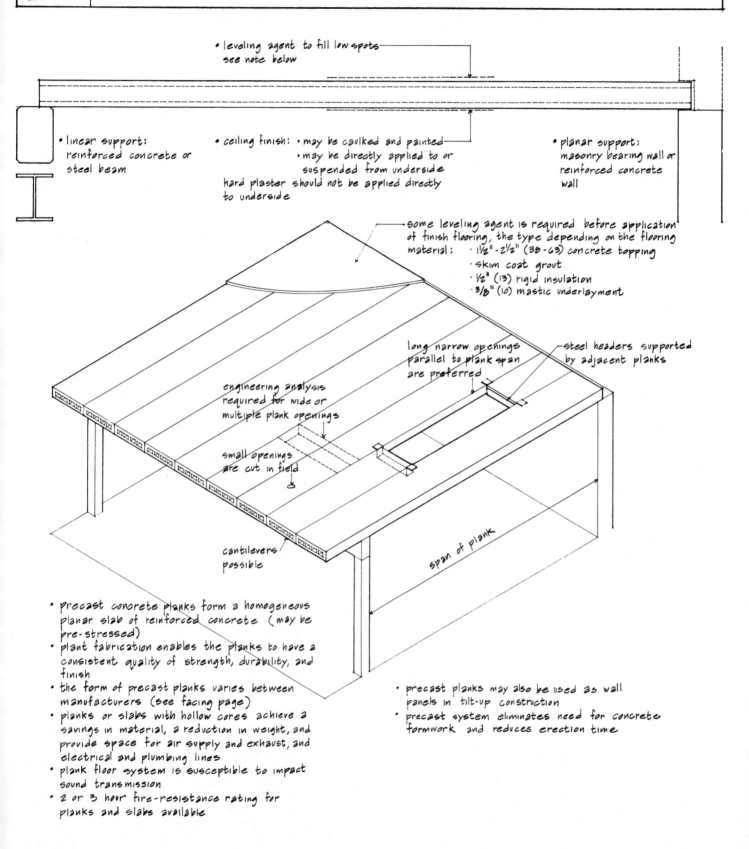

• leveling agent to fill low spots — see note below

• linear support: reinforced concrete or steel beam

• ceiling finish: • may be caulked and painted
                  • may be directly applied to or suspended from underside
hard plaster should not be applied directly to underside

• planar support: masonry bearing wall or reinforced concrete wall

• some leveling agent is required before application of finish flooring, the type depending on the flooring material: · 1½" - 2½" (38-63) concrete topping
· skim coat grout
· ½" (13) rigid insulation
· 3/8" (10) mastic underlayment

long narrow openings parallel to plank span are preferred

steel headers supported by adjacent planks

engineering analysis required for wide or multiple plank openings

small openings are cut in field

cantilevers possible

span of plank

• precast concrete planks form a homogeneous planar slab of reinforced concrete (may be pre-stressed)
• plant fabrication enables the planks to have a consistent quality of strength, durability, and finish
• the form of precast planks varies between manufacturers (see facing page)
• planks or slabs with hollow cores achieve a savings in material, a reduction in weight, and provide space for air supply and exhaust, and electrical and plumbing lines
• plank floor system is susceptible to impact sound transmission
• 2 or 3 hour fire-resistance rating for planks and slabs available

• precast planks may also be used as wall panels in tilt-up construction
• precast system eliminates need for concrete formwork and reduces erection time

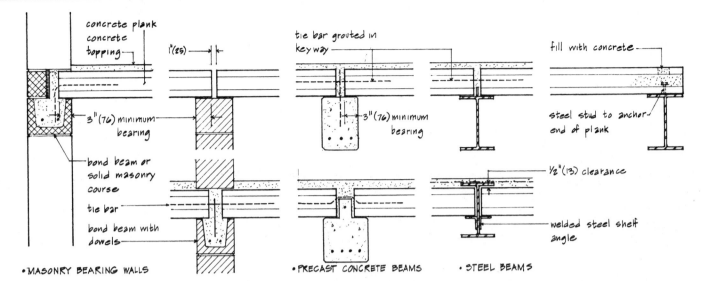

• MASONRY BEARING WALLS   **• PRECAST CONCRETE BEAMS**   **• STEEL BEAMS**

The above are typical support conditions for precast concrete planks. They may require lateral ties and/or anchorage to their support at their end joints.

Below are basic types of precast concrete floor planks and decks. Exact form varies between manufacturers

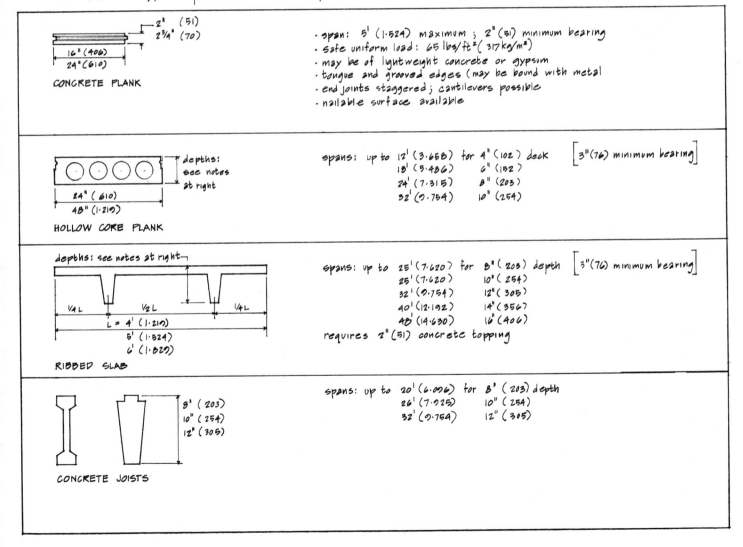

CONCRETE PLANK

- span: 5' (1·524) maximum ; 2" (51) minimum bearing
- safe uniform load: 65 lbs/ft² (317 kg/m²)
- may be of lightweight concrete or gypsum
- tongue and grooved edges (may be bound with metal
- end joints staggered; cantilevers possible
- nailable surface available

HOLLOW CORE PLANK

spans: up to 12' (3·658) for 4" (102) deck   [3" (76) minimum bearing]
18' (5·486)   6" (152)
24' (7·315)   8" (203)
32' (9·754)   10" (254)

RIBBED SLAB

spans: up to 25' (7·620) for 8" (203) depth   [3" (76) minimum bearing]
25' (7·620)   10" (254)
32' (9·754)   12" (305)
40' (12·192)   14" (356)
48' (14·630)   16" (406)
requires 2" (51) concrete topping

CONCRETE JOISTS

spans: up to 20' (6·096) for 8" (203) depth
26' (7·925)   10" (254)
32' (9·754)   12" (305)

WALL SYSTEMS

Wall systems are a building's primary vertical planar elements. They may be bearing planes of homogeneous or composite construction or they may be composed of linear bearing elements (posts and columns) with non-structural panels filling in between them. How these walls and columns support either floor or roof systems above and how they are supported in turn by wall, floor, or foundation systems below is determined by the structural compatibility of these systems, and the type of connection and materials used. Rigidity is a critical factor in the design and construction of these joints. Wall elements can also serve structurally as shear walls which provide lateral stability along the direction of their planar surfaces against horizontal and racking loads as may be caused by wind and earthquake forces.

Exterior walls serve as a protective shield against exterior conditions for a building's interior spaces. The exterior skin which may be either applied or integral with the wall structure must be durable, resistant to wear and the elements (sun, wind, rain). Depending on its orientation on the site, a wall's heat transmission properties, its reflectivity and absorptivity, and its insulation value should be important factors in the choice of a wall system. The exterior wall is also the point at which the control of air, moisture, and water vapor flow must take place.

Interior walls and partitions may be either load-bearing or non-structural, and serve as dividers and defining elements of space, visually and acoustically. Their surfaces must be durable and wear-resistant, and the desired finish, color, and texture should be compatible with the wall system used. Wall elements may also have to accomodate the vertical and horizontal travel of mechanical and electrical lines as well as their outlets.

The size and location of door and window openings in walls are determined by the type of natural light, ventilation, view and access required. In addition, these openings should comply with the restraints of the wall system construction so that, structurally, vertical loads are properly distributed around the openings and ensure that stresses around the openings are not transferred to the door and window units themselves. Visually, door and window openings are major compositional elements in a wall and can be seen either as punched openings (with the wall plane maintaining its integrity) or as separating elements (voids) between sections of wall.

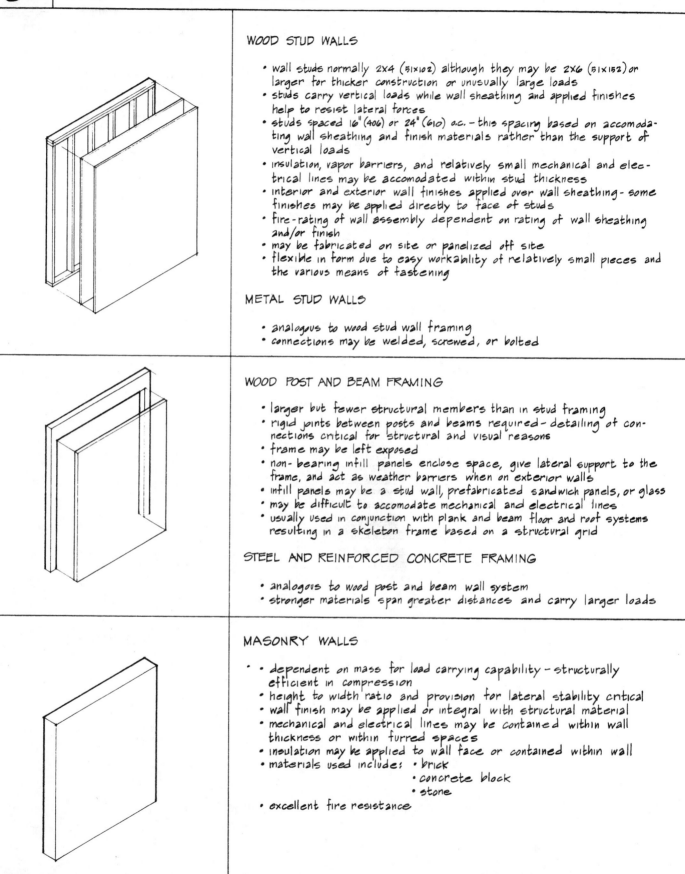

WOOD STUD WALLS

- wall studs normally 2x4 (51x102) although they may be 2x6 (51x152) or larger for thicker construction or unusually large loads
- studs carry vertical loads while wall sheathing and applied finishes help to resist lateral forces
- studs spaced 16" (406) or 24" (610) o.c. - this spacing based on accomodating wall sheathing and finish materials rather than the support of vertical loads
- insulation, vapor barriers, and relatively small mechanical and electrical lines may be accomodated within stud thickness
- interior and exterior wall finishes applied over wall sheathing - some finishes may be applied directly to face of studs
- fire-rating of wall assembly dependent on rating of wall sheathing and/or finish
- may be fabricated on site or panelized off site
- flexible in form due to easy workability of relatively small pieces and the various means of fastening

METAL STUD WALLS

- analogous to wood stud wall framing
- connections may be welded, screwed, or bolted

WOOD POST AND BEAM FRAMING

- larger but fewer structural members than in stud framing
- rigid joints between posts and beams required - detailing of connections critical for structural and visual reasons
- frame may be left exposed
- non-bearing infill panels enclose space, give lateral support to the frame, and act as weather barriers when on exterior walls
- infill panels may be a stud wall, prefabricated sandwich panels, or glass
- may be difficult to accomodate mechanical and electrical lines
- usually used in conjunction with plank and beam floor and roof systems resulting in a skeleton frame based on a structural grid

STEEL AND REINFORCED CONCRETE FRAMING

- analogous to wood post and beam wall system
- stronger materials span greater distances and carry larger loads

MASONRY WALLS

- dependent on mass for load carrying capability - structurally efficient in compression
- height to width ratio and provision for lateral stability critical
- wall finish may be applied or integral with structural material
- mechanical and electrical lines may be contained within wall thickness or within furred spaces
- insulation may be applied to wall face or contained within wall
- materials used include: • brick
                          • concrete block
                          • stone
- excellent fire resistance

FACTORS IN WALL DESIGN AND CONSTRUCTION:

- strength in:

  - supporting vertical loads from floor, wall, and roof systems above
  - resisting lateral loads from supported floor and roof systems, wind, earthquakes, etc.

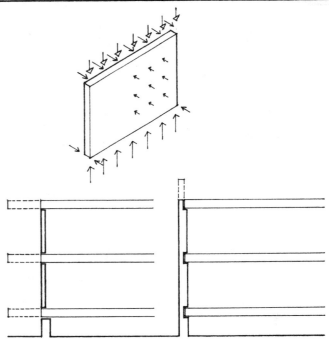

- connections with foundation, floor, and roof systems:

  - floor and roof systems may bear on the wall system so that their edges may be exposed and cantilevers and overhangs are possible, or
  - floor and roof systems may frame into the wall system which is continuous for the height of the building

- finish desired (interior and exterior):

  - compatibility between wall base and finish surface
  - appearance: color
                          texture
                          pattern

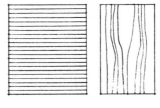

- door and window openings:

  - size, proportion, and location
  - structural and/or modular limitations

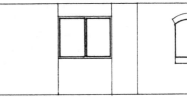

- weathertightness and control of:

  - heat flow
  - moisture and water vapor flow
  - sound transmission

- expansion and contraction

  - type and location of control and expansion joints, if required

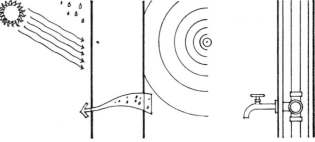

- accomodation of mechanical and electrical lines and outlets

- fire-resistance rating desired or required

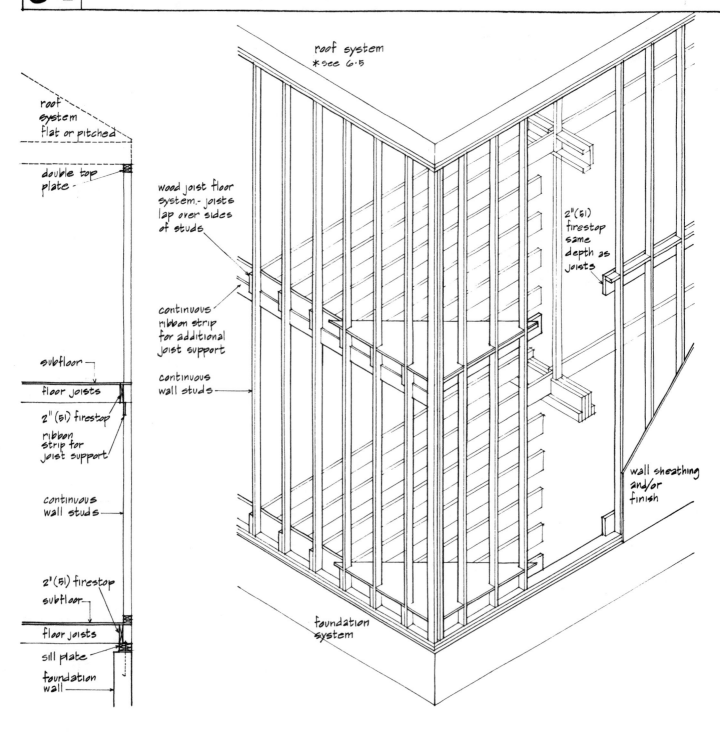

roof system
*see 6·5

double top
plate

wood joist floor
system.- joists
lap over sides
of studs

2" (51)
firestop
same
depth as
joists

continuous
ribbon strip
for additional
joist support

continuous
wall studs

roof
system
flat or pitched

subfloor

floor joists

2" (51) firestop

ribbon
strip for
joist support

continuous
wall studs

2" (51) firestop

subfloor

floor joists

sill plate

foundation
wall

wall sheathing
and/or
finish

foundation
system

- studs 16" (406) or 24" (610) o.c. are continuous for full building height
- minimum vertical movement desirable for brick veneer and stucco finishes
- first floor joists rest on sill plate
- second floor joists bear on ribbon strip let into studs
- all concealed spaces in framing require 2" (51) firestop to prevent
  drafts from one space to another

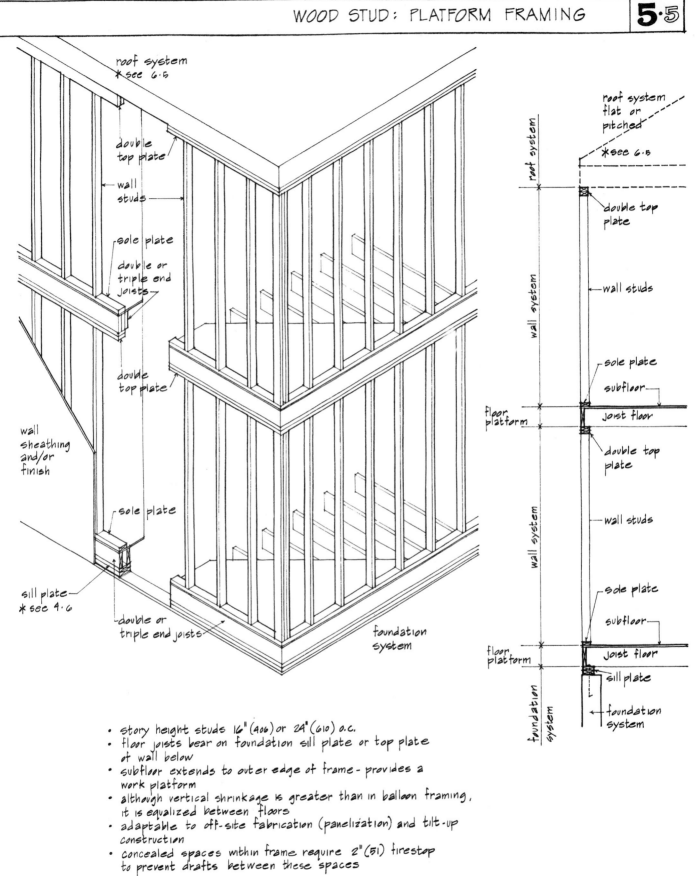

roof system
*see 6·5

double top plate

wall studs

sole plate

double or triple end joists

double top plate

wall sheathing and/or finish

sole plate

sill plate
*see 4·6

double or triple end joists

foundation system

roof system

roof system flat or pitched
*see 6·5

double top plate

wall studs

sole plate
subfloor

Joist floor

double top plate

wall studs

sole plate
subfloor

Joist floor
sill plate

foundation system

wall system

floor platform

wall system

floor platform

foundation system

- story height studs 16" (406) or 24" (610) o.c.
- floor joists bear on foundation sill plate or top plate of wall below
- subfloor extends to outer edge of frame - provides a work platform
- although vertical shrinkage is greater than in balloon framing, it is equalized between floors
- adaptable to off-site fabrication (panelization) and tilt-up construction
- concealed spaces within frame require 2" (51) firestop to prevent drafts between these spaces

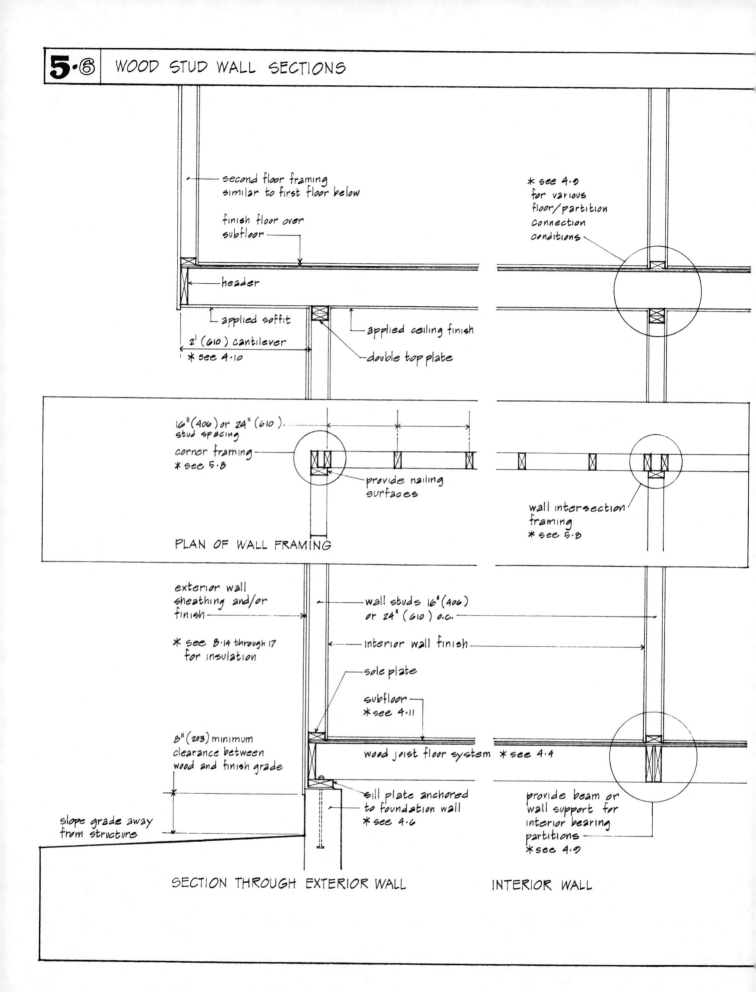

second floor framing
similar to first floor below

finish floor over
subfloor

header

applied soffit

applied ceiling finish

2' (610) cantilever
* see 4·10

double top plate

* see 4·9
for various
floor/partition
connection
conditions

16" (406) or 24" (610)
stud spacing

corner framing
* see 5·8

provide nailing
surfaces

PLAN OF WALL FRAMING

wall intersection
framing
* see 5·8

exterior wall
sheathing and/or
finish

* see 8·14 through 17
for insulation

wall studs 16" (406)
or 24" (610) o.c.

interior wall finish

sole plate

subfloor
* see 4·11

8" (203) minimum
clearance between
wood and finish grade

wood joist floor system * see 4·4

sill plate anchored
to foundation wall
* see 4·6

provide beam or
wall support for
interior bearing
partitions
* see 4·9

slope grade away
from structure

SECTION THROUGH EXTERIOR WALL   INTERIOR WALL

second floor wall
framing

sole plate

subfloor

wood joist floor system
*see 4·4

double top plate

* see 8·14 through 18
for wall insulation
and vapor barrier
installation

wood stud frame wall

blocking required
with some sheathing
and finish materials

wall sheathing flush
with face of foundation
wall so that exterior
wall finish can overlap
foundation wall

½" (13) expansion joint

4" (102) concrete
ground slab
*see 3·17/18

*see 8·14
for insulation
requirements

foundation wall

parapet wall
condition

*see 8·11
for roof flashing

roof joists
lapping studs
and bearing on
2x4 (51x102)
blocking or
ribbon strip

continuous exterior
wall finish

continuous
wall studs

finish floor

* see 3·18
for thickened
edge slabs

wood fascia or
exterior wall finish
continued up under
metal gravel stop
and edge flashing

* see 3·6/0
for pier
foundations

flashing required

grade

note: The wall sections on this and the preceding page are not intended to be complete. They exclude specific
specific wall, floor, and ceiling finishes, trim, insulation, etc. They attempt instead to indicate the ways
in which wood stud wall framing connect with various foundation, floor, and roof systems. Wood stud
walls are used typically with wood floor and roof systems.

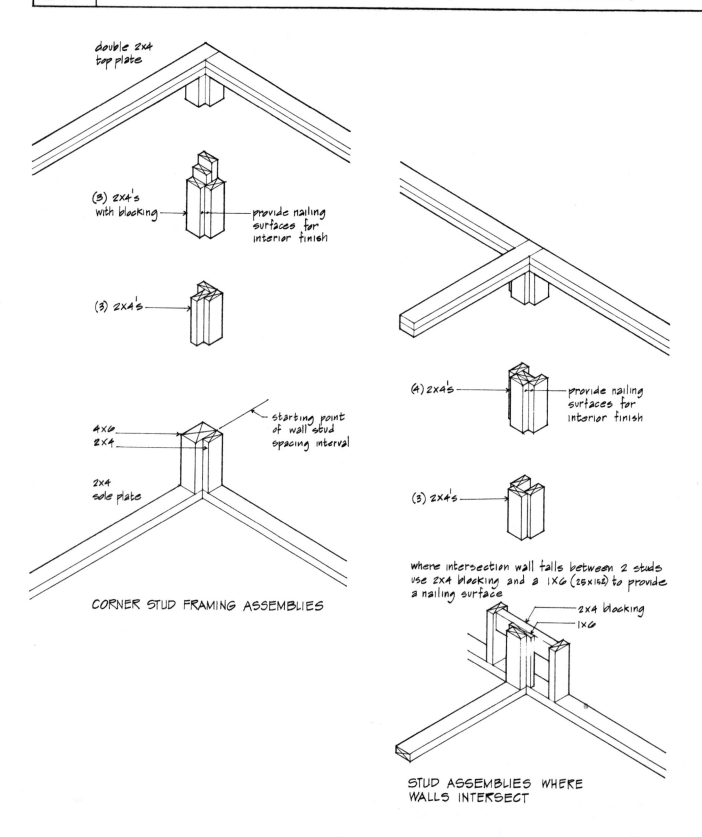

double 2x4
top plate

(3) 2x4's
with blocking — provide nailing
surfaces for
interior finish

(3) 2x4's

starting point
of wall stud
spacing interval

4x6
2x4

2x4
sole plate

CORNER STUD FRAMING ASSEMBLIES

(4) 2x4's — provide nailing
surfaces for
interior finish

(3) 2x4's

where intersection wall falls between 2 studs
use 2x4 blocking and a 1x6 (25x152) to provide
a nailing surface

2x4 blocking
1x6

STUD ASSEMBLIES WHERE
WALLS INTERSECT

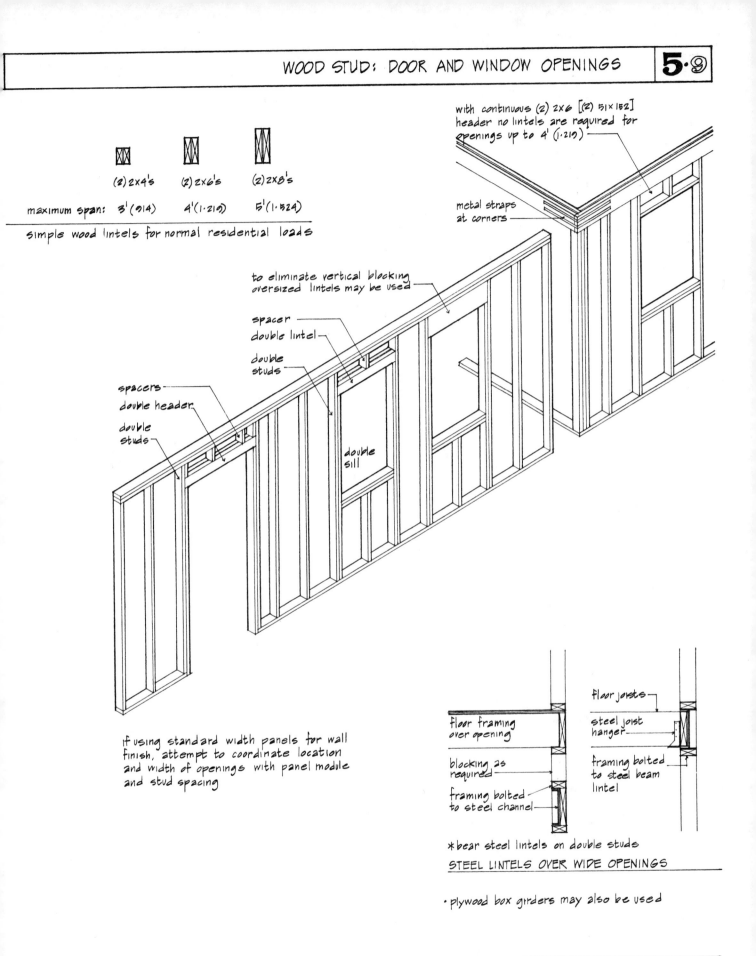

(2) 2x4's   (2) 2x6's   (2) 2x8's

maximum span: 3' (.914)   4' (1.219)   5' (1.524)

simple wood lintels for normal residential loads

with continuous (2) 2x6 [(2) 51×152] header no lintels are required for openings up to 4' (1.219)

metal straps at corners

to eliminate vertical blocking oversized lintels may be used

spacer
double lintel

double studs

spacers
double header

double studs

double sill

if using standard width panels for wall finish, attempt to coordinate location and width of openings with panel module and stud spacing

floor framing over opening

blocking as required

framing bolted to steel channel

floor joists

steel joist hanger

framing bolted to steel beam lintel

*bear steel lintels on double studs

STEEL LINTELS OVER WIDE OPENINGS

· plywood box girders may also be used

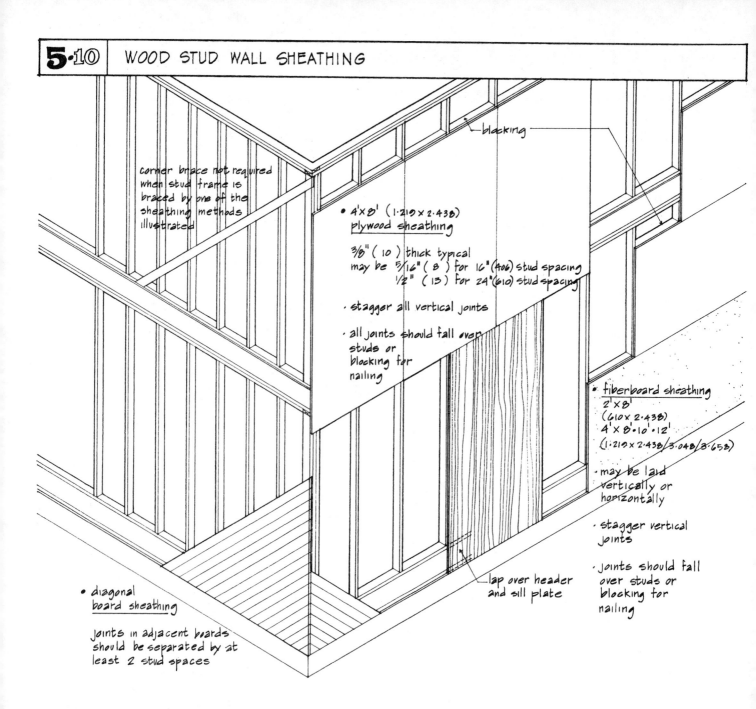

corner brace not required when stud frame is braced by one of the sheathing methods illustrated

blocking

• 4'x8' (1·219 x 2·438) plywood sheathing

3/8" (10) thick typical
may be 5/16" (8) for 16"(406) stud spacing
1/2" (13) for 24"(610) stud spacing

· stagger all vertical joints

· all joints should fall over studs or blocking for nailing

• fiberboard sheathing
2'x8'
(610 x 2·438)
4'x8'•10'•12'
(1·219 x 2·438/3·048/3·658)

· may be laid vertically or horizontally

· stagger vertical joints

· joints should fall over studs or blocking for nailing

lap over header and sill plate

• diagonal board sheathing

joints in adjacent boards should be separated by at least 2 stud spaces

EXTERIOR WALL SHEATHING

• imparts rigidity to stud frame
• forms a weather barrier
• provides a nailing base for the wall finish

• some exterior wall finishes can be applied directly to the studs

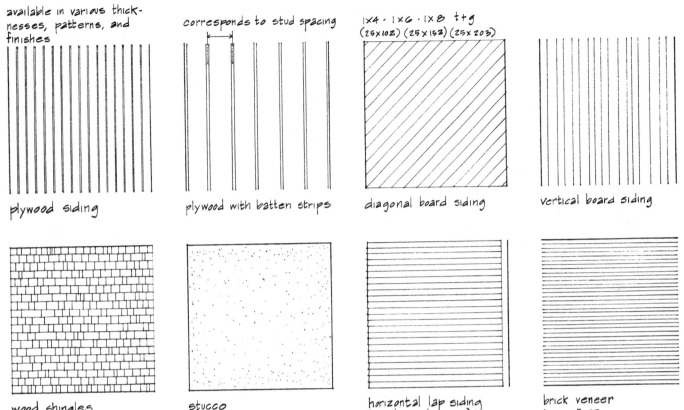

available in various thicknesses, patterns, and
finishes

plywood siding

corresponds to stud spacing

plywood with batten strips

1×4 · 1×6 · 1×8 t+g
(25×102) (25×152) (25×203)

diagonal board siding

vertical board siding

wood shingles

stucco

horizontal lap siding
(wood or aluminum)

brick veneer
*see 5·27

Above are illustrated some of the common finishes which may be applied to wood stud wall framing.
Refer to chapters 8 and 10 for more information.

Some of the factors to consider in the selection
and use of a finish for wood stud walls:

- stud spacing required
- sheathing or backing requirements
- color, pattern, and texture desired
- standard available widths and heights such as
  for plywood panels
- detailing of vertical and horizontal joints
- durability, weathering, and maintenance
  characteristics
- heat conductivity, reflectance, and porosity
  of the materials
- expansion and control joints if required
- integration of door and window openings into
  the surface pattern

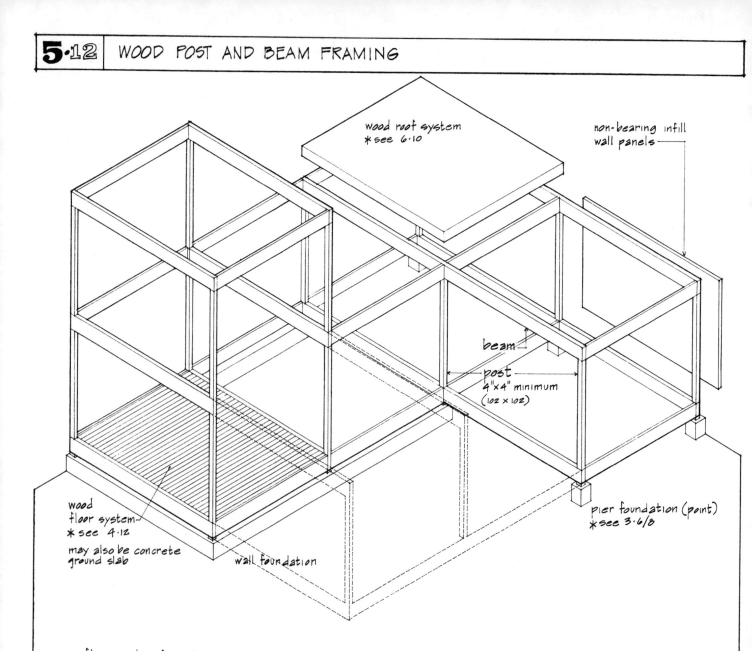

wood roof system
*see 6·10

non-bearing infill
wall panels

beam

post
4"x4" minimum
(102 x 102)

wood
floor system
*see 4·12

may also be concrete
ground slab

wall foundation

pier foundation (point)
*see 3·6/8

- floor and roof systems are supported by beams which are in turn supported by posts or columns which then transfer these loads down to the foundation system

- together with plank and beam roof and floor systems, the post and beam wall system forms a three-dimensional modular grid of spaces which may be expanded both horizontally and vertically

- this skeleton frame of posts and beams is often left exposed to form a visible framework within which wall panels, doors, and windows should be integrated

- when the post and beam frame is left exposed, the quality of wood used, the quality of workmanship, and the careful detailing of the joints between the posts and beams are important factors to consider

- non-bearing infill wall panels serve to enclose and further define space, act as weather barriers on the exterior, and impart lateral stability to the post and beam frame

- lateral stability for the post and beam frame against lateral loads such as wind is achieved through the rigidity of the joints between post, beam, and foundation, and the strength and positive tie of the infill wall panels to the structural frame

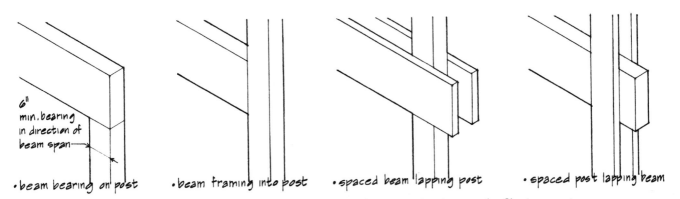

· beam bearing on post   · beam framing into post   · spaced beam lapping post   · spaced post lapping beam

6" min. bearing in direction of beam span →

Above are illustrated the primary ways in which posts and beams may be joined. Steel connections are generally used in post and beam joints to ensure rigidity and the proper transfer of forces. These steel connections may be either concealed or exposed.

solid

· should be of well-seasoned wood

built-up

· glue-laminated or mechanically fastened

spaced

· must be securely blocked internally so that individual members act in unison

The following table is for estimating and preliminary sizing of members only. Column spacing is directly related to the desired bay size and the spanning capability of the wood beams and floor system used.

LENGTH	SIZE in inches					
feet (m)	4 × 4 (102 × 102)	4 × 6 (102 × 152)	6 × 6 (152 × 152)	6 × 8 (152 × 203)	8 × 8 (203 × 203)	10 × 10 (254 × 254)
8 (2.438)	6	10	35	48	124	321
9 (2.743)	5	8	28	38	98	251
10 (3.048)	4	6	23	31	79	206
11 (3.353)	3	5	19	26	65	169
12 (3.657)		4	16	21	55	141
14 (4.267)		3	11	16	40	104
16 (4.877)			9	12	31	80
18 (5.486)			7	9	24	63
20 (6.096)			5	7	19	51
22 (6.706)			4	6	16	42
24 (7.315)			3	5	13	35

SAFE LOADS FOR WOOD POSTS AND COLUMNS in kips (1000 lbs.) · 1 kip = 453.50 kg

· the above assumes the modulus of elasticity (E) for the wood used to be 1,200,000 psi (8.44 × 10⁶ kg/m²)
· verify that the allowable unit stress in compression parallel to grain for the wood used is not exceeded

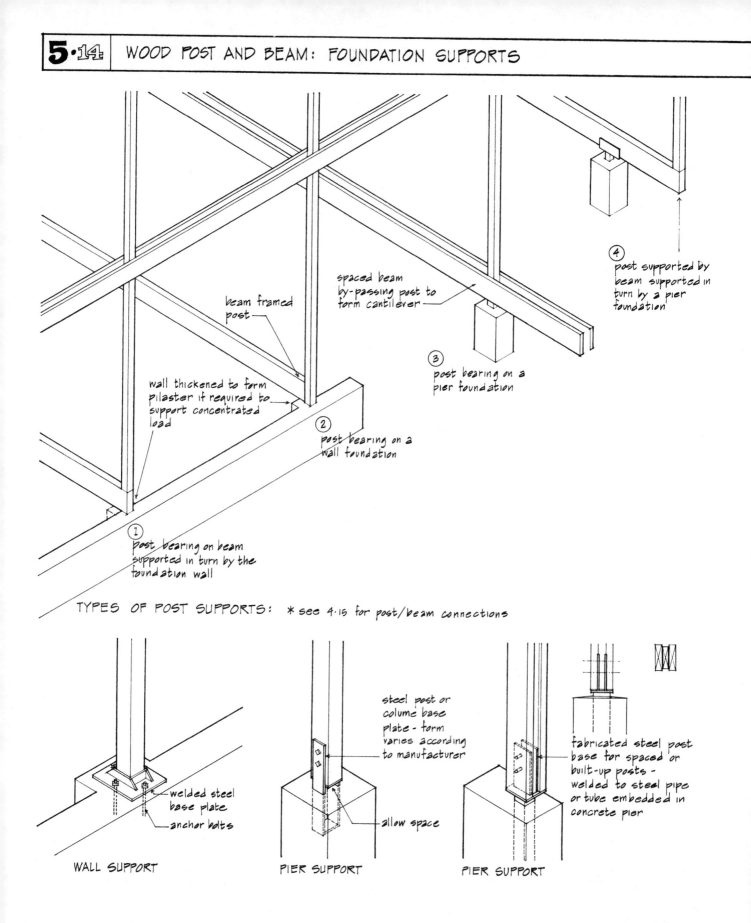

beam framed post

spaced beam by-passing post to form cantilever

④ post supported by beam supported in turn by a pier foundation

③ post bearing on a pier foundation

wall thickened to form pilaster if required to support concentrated load

② post bearing on a wall foundation

① post bearing on beam supported in turn by the foundation wall

TYPES OF POST SUPPORTS: * see 4·15 for post/beam connections

welded steel base plate

anchor bolts

WALL SUPPORT

steel post or column base plate - form varies according to manufacturer

allow space

PIER SUPPORT

fabricated steel post base for spaced or built-up posts - welded to steel pipe or tube embedded in concrete pier

PIER SUPPORT

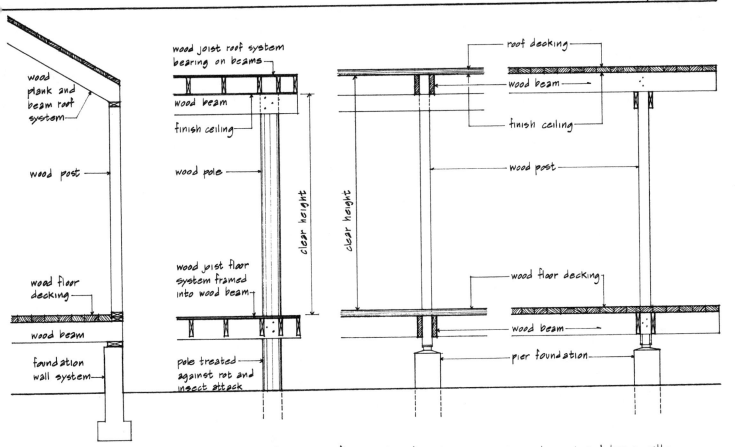

wood plank and beam roof system

wood joist roof system bearing on beams

wood beam

finish ceiling

wood pole

wood post

wood floor decking

wood beam

foundation wall system

wood joist floor system framed into wood beam

clear height

pole treated against rot and insect attack

roof decking

wood beam

finish ceiling

wood post

clear height

wood floor decking

wood beam

pier foundation

The above sections illustrate various foundation, floor, and roof system connections to post and beam walls. Note that beams are integral parts of both wall and floor or roof systems. The type of floor and roof system used and how they are supported by the wood posts affect the construction depth of the floor and roof planes, the floor to ceiling height, and the overall height of the building.

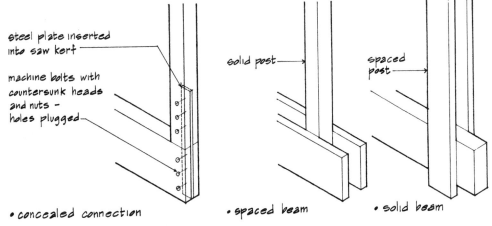

steel plate inserted into saw kerf

machine bolts with countersunk heads and nuts – holes plugged

solid post

spaced post

• concealed connection

• spaced beam

• solid beam

TYPES OF BEAM SUPPORTS

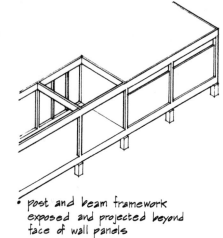

• post and beam framework exposed and projected beyond face of wall panels

• post and beam framework exposed but flush with face of wall panels

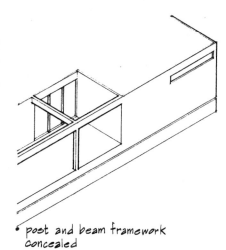

• post and beam framework concealed

Illustrated above are some of the images which may be projected utilizing the post and beam structural system. In all cases, the solid and void pattern created by the wall panels and door and window openings should be regulated by the grid set up by the post and beam framework.

Factors to consider in the design and construction of post and beam walls include:

• a positive tie between the infill wall panels and the post and beam frame to achieve lateral stability for the frame
• the maintenance of a weatherseal at the juncture between wall panel and frame through the use of offsets, flashing, and caulking
• the expansion, contraction, and shrinkage characteristics of the materials
• the detailing of the juncture between dissimilar materials
• if the wood post and beam frame is exposed on the exterior, consider also the quality, seasoning, and finish of the wood, its weathering characteristics, and the proper treatment of any exposed steel connections

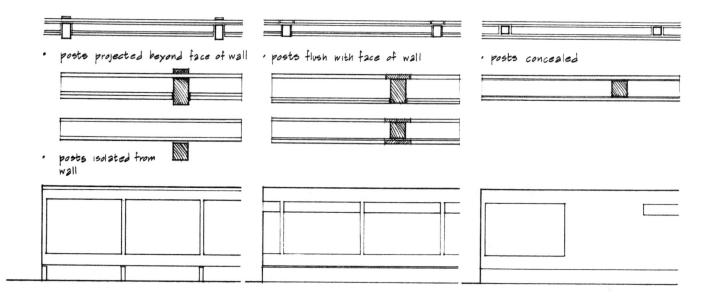

• posts projected beyond face of wall

• posts flush with face of wall

• posts concealed

• posts isolated from wall

The voids in the post and beam grid may be filled with transparent glass or solid infill panels of:

- wood stud framing with it range of finishes ✳ see 5·11
- prefabricated composite or sandwich building panels

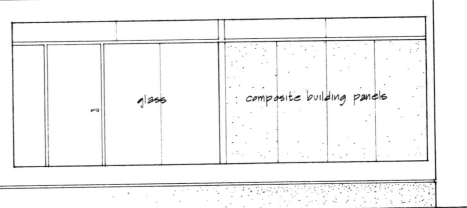

glass

composite building panels

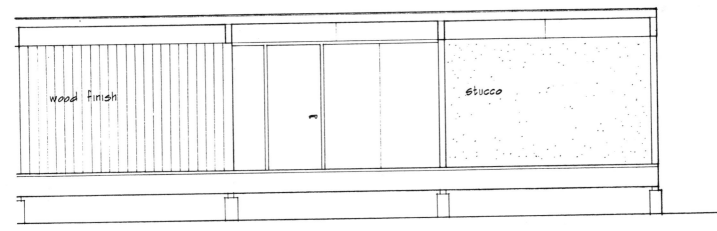

wood finish

stucco

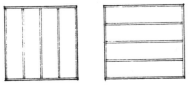

- wall stud framing may be vertical or horizontal depending on wall finish requirements

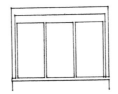

- size and proportion of frame grid should respond if possible to the standard widths and heights of pre-fabricated wall panels

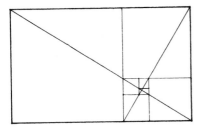

- solid and void pattern created by wall panels and door and window openings should be regulated by the size and proportion of the post and frame

MASONRY WALL THICKNESS:

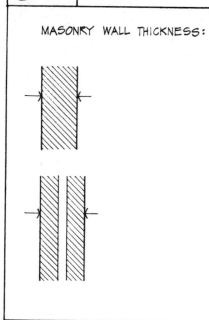

Simple bearing walls should be 12' (305) for the uppermost 35' (10·668) of the wall and increased 4" (102) in width for each additional 35' (10·668) in height.

For residences up to three stories and less than 35' (10·668) in height, this thickness may be 8" (203).

Masonry walls stiffened either by masonry crosswalls or concrete floor slabs at least 12' (3·657) o.c. may be 12" (305) in thickness up to a height of 70' (21·336)

Cavity walls (metal tied or masonry bonded) should not exceed 35' (10·668) in height. 10" (254) cavity walls should not exceed 25' (7·620) in height. Both faces should be at least 4" (102) in width with a cavity of not less than 2" (51) nor more than 3" (76).

Interior bearing walls for residences may be 6" (152) if not more than 1½ stories or 20' (6·096) in height.

Exterior non-bearing walls may be 4" (102) less in thickness than required for a bearing wall but not less than 8" (203).

LATERAL SUPPORT REQUIREMENTS:

UL = unsupported length
UH = unsupported height

wall type	maximum spacing for UL or UH
solid load bearing	20 × thickness (T)
hollow load bearing (only sum of wythes considered)	18 × T
non-load-bearing	36 × T

* for walls subject to high winds, UL or UH = 10 × T unless walls are adequately braced

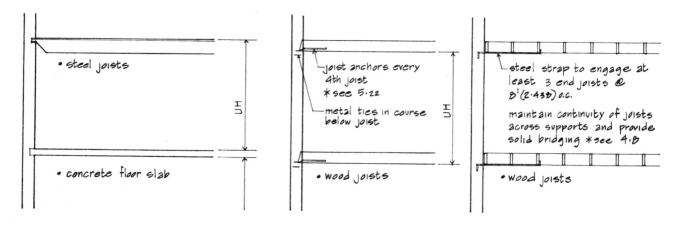

• steel joists
• concrete floor slab

joist anchors every 4th joist *see 5·22
metal ties in course below joist
• wood joists

steel strap to engage at least 3 end joists @ 8' (2·438) o.c.

maintain continuity of joists across supports and provide solid bridging *see 4·8
• wood joists

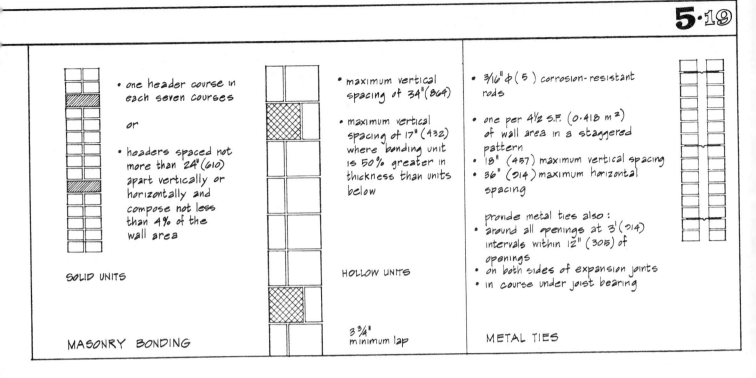

- one header course in each seven courses

or

- headers spaced not more than 24" (610) apart vertically or horizontally and compose not less than 4% of the wall area

SOLID UNITS

MASONRY BONDING

- maximum vertical spacing of 34" (864)
- maximum vertical spacing of 17" (432) where bonding unit is 50% greater in thickness than units below

HOLLOW UNITS

3¾" minimum lap

- 3/16" ⌀ (5) corrosion-resistant rods
- one per 4½ S.F. (0.418 m²) of wall area in a staggered pattern
- 18" (457) maximum vertical spacing
- 36" (914) maximum horizontal spacing

provide metal ties also:
- around all openings at 3' (914) intervals within 12" (305) of openings
- on both sides of expansion joints
- in course under joist bearing

METAL TIES

BEARING STRENGTH IN COMPRESSION

A masonry wall's bearing strength is dependent on:
- the quality of the masonry and its compressive strength
- the quality of the mortar and its compressive strength
- the quality of the workmanship

As a guide, the unit bearing pressure on masonry bearing walls should not exceed 250 psi (176×10³ kg/m²) if the masonry has a compressive strength of 3000 psi (2100×10³ kg/m²) and portland cement mortar is used.

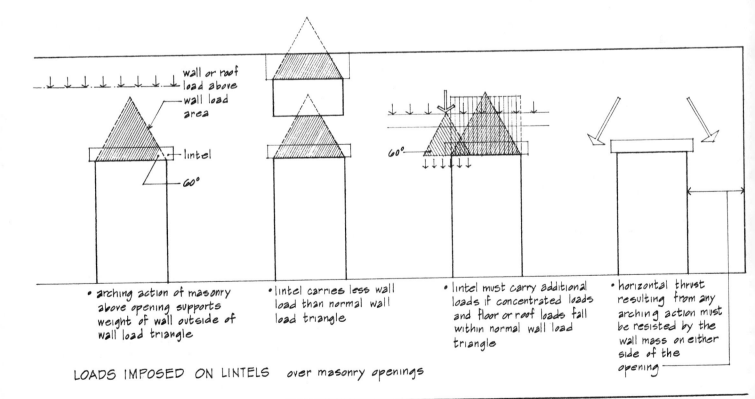

wall or roof load above
wall load area
lintel
60°

- arching action of masonry above opening supports weight of wall outside of wall load triangle

60°

- lintel carries less wall load than normal wall load triangle

60°

- lintel must carry additional loads if concentrated loads and floor or roof loads fall within normal wall load triangle

- horizontal thrust resulting from any arching action must be resisted by the wall mass on either side of the opening

LOADS IMPOSED ON LINTELS over masonry openings

direction of span for floor or roof system

all modular dimensions

masonry bearing walls

primary visual direction

masonry piers

curvilinear walls possible

- masonry walls are made up of modular building blocks bonded together with mortar to form load bearing walls which are structurally most efficient in compression

- concrete block: chemically hardened unit
- brick   : heat hardened clay unit
  (* see 12·6)

- masonry load bearing walls may be used in parallel sets or in conjunction with other wall systems to support most floor or roof systems (joists, beams, structural decking)
- proper sizing and placement of wall openings critical in maintaining the structural integrity of masonry wall planes
- masonry wall openings spanned with lintels or arches
- proper placement of expansion and control joints necessary to avoid cracking in the masonry
- masonry walls susceptible to water penetration
- masonry walls provide strong spatial definition and enclosure, weather protection, an integral and durable wall finish, and fire resistance in one material
- masonry walls generally project a heavy image
- color, pattern, and texture are important visual properties of masonry walls

- all major dimensions should conform to the modular dimensions of the masonry unit used:

  concrete block: 8" (203) vertical coursing [4" (102) coursing available]
                   8" (203) multiples for length
  brick masonry : 2⅔" (68) vertical coursing [3 courses = 8" (203)]
                  4" (102) multiples for length

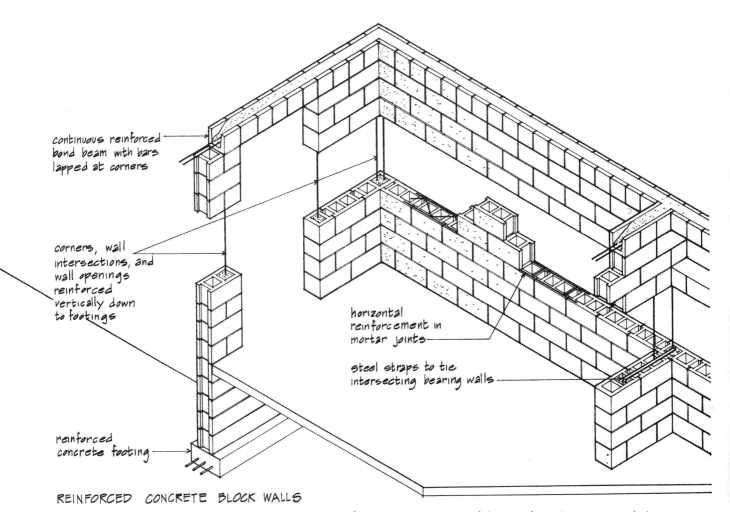

continuous reinforced
bond beam with bars
lapped at corners

corners, wall
intersections, and
wall openings
reinforced
vertically down
to footings

horizontal
reinforcement in
mortar joints

steel straps to tie
intersecting bearing walls

reinforced
concrete footing

REINFORCED CONCRETE BLOCK WALLS

When concrete block walls are subjected to lateral forces such as caused by wind, earth pressure below grade, and earthquakes, they may be reinforced as illustrated above.

CRACK CONTROL:	Differential movements within masonry walls may cause serious cracking. Masonry wall movements may be caused by the following:

- expansion and contraction of the masonry due to temperature changes or changes in moisture content of the masonry units
- structural movement caused by uneven settlement of the foundation system or the application of concentrated loads
- concentration of stresses around masonry wall openings
- localized restraint of the masonry wall at floor, roof, column, and intersecting wall junctures

CONTROL JOINTS: Movement in a concrete block wall is due primarily to drying shrinkage at the time of construction. To minimize these shrinkage cracks and cracks which may occur at points of weakness or concentrated stress, continuous vertical joints (control joints) are built into concrete block walls.

On the following page are guidelines for the location and construction of control joints in concrete masonry.

*see 5·28 for information regarding expansion joints

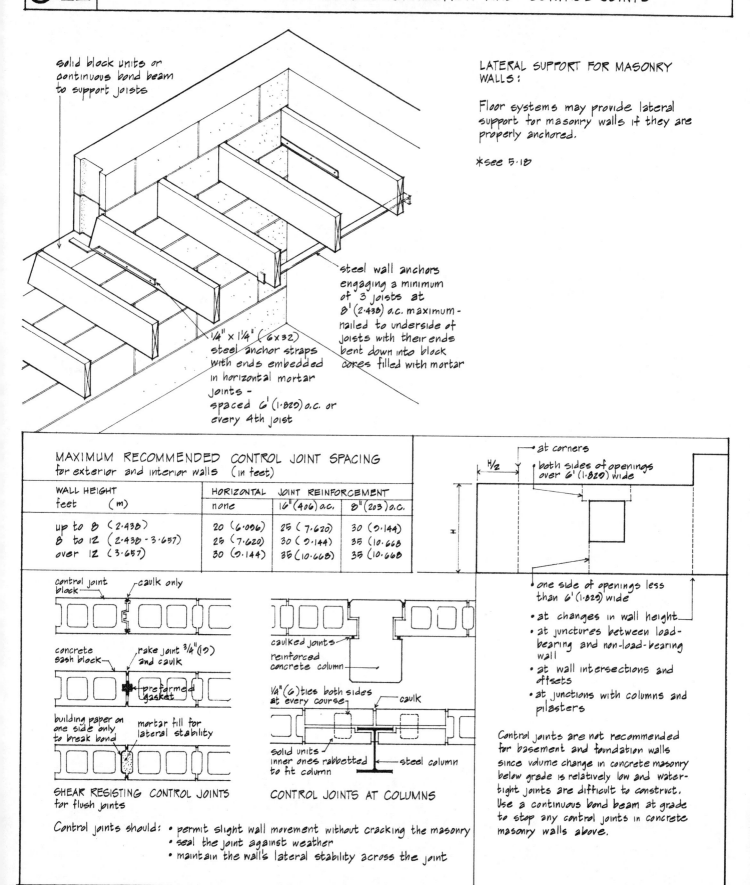

solid block units or
continuous bond beam
to support joists

¼" × 1¼" (6×32)
steel anchor straps
with ends embedded
in horizontal mortar
joints -
spaced 6' (1·829) o.c. or
every 4th joist

steel wall anchors
engaging a minimum
of 3 joists at
8' (2·438) o.c. maximum-
nailed to underside of
joists with their ends
bent down into block
cores filled with mortar

LATERAL SUPPORT FOR MASONRY
WALLS:

Floor systems may provide lateral
support for masonry walls if they are
properly anchored.

*see 5·18

MAXIMUM RECOMMENDED CONTROL JOINT SPACING
for exterior and interior walls (in feet)

WALL HEIGHT feet (m)	HORIZONTAL JOINT REINFORCEMENT		
	none	16" (406) o.c.	8" (203) o.c.
up to 8 (2·438)	20 (6·096)	25 (7·620)	30 (9·144)
8 to 12 (2·438 - 3·657)	25 (7·620)	30 (9·144)	35 (10·668)
over 12 (3·657)	30 (9·144)	35 (10·668)	35 (10·668)

at corners
H/2
both sides of openings
over 6' (1·829) wide
H

control joint
block
caulk only

concrete
sash block

rake joint ¾" (19)
and caulk

preformed
gasket

building paper on
one side only
to break bond

mortar fill for
lateral stability

SHEAR RESISTING CONTROL JOINTS
for flush joints

caulked joints
reinforced
concrete column

¼" (6) ties both sides
at every course

caulk

solid units
inner ones rabbetted
to fit column

steel column

CONTROL JOINTS AT COLUMNS

• one side of openings less
than 6' (1·829) wide
• at changes in wall height
• at junctures between load-
bearing and non-load-bearing
wall
• at wall intersections and
offsets
• at junctions with columns and
pilasters

Control joints are not recommended
for basement and foundation walls
since volume change in concrete masonry
below grade is relatively low and watertight joints are difficult to construct.
Use a continuous bond beam at grade
to stop any control joints in concrete
masonry walls above.

Control joints should: • permit slight wall movement without cracking the masonry
• seal the joint against weather
• maintain the wall's lateral stability across the joint

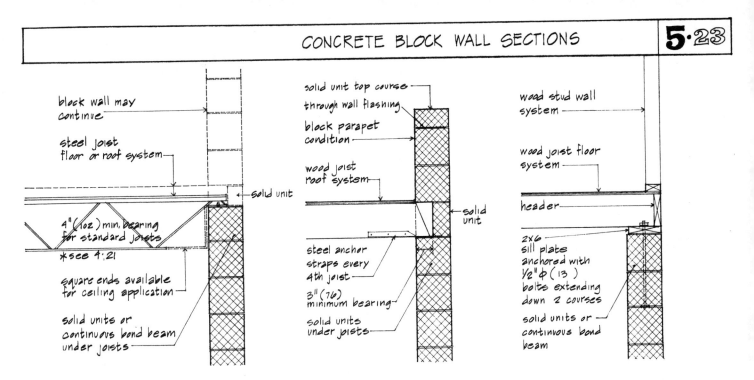

block wall may continue

steel joist floor or roof system

←— solid unit

4" (102) min. bearing for standard joists

*see 4·21

square ends available for ceiling application

solid units or continuous bond beam under joists

solid unit top course

through wall flashing

block parapet condition

wood joist roof system

←— solid unit

steel anchor straps every 4th joist

3" (76) minimum bearing

solid units under joists

wood stud wall system

wood joist floor system

header

2x6 sill plate anchored with ½"φ (13) bolts extending down 2 courses

solid units or continuous bond beam

These wall sections are not intended to be complete. They exclude floor, wall, and ceiling finishes, trim, etc. They attempt to illustrate how various floor and roof systems are supported by a concrete block bearing wall. The above-grade wall is literally an extension of the concrete block foundation wall system. Note that the edges of floor and roof planes are not visible from the exterior except at the top of the concrete block wall. All vertical dimensions should be modular, especially is the block is left exposed as the wall finish

* see 8·13 for wall flashing
* see 8·17 for wall insulation

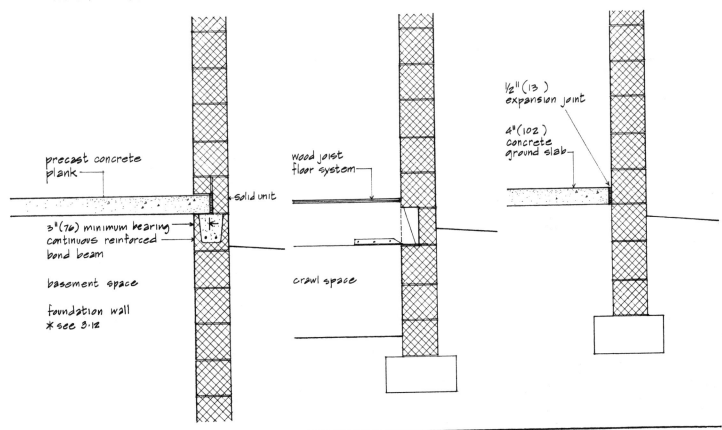

precast concrete plank

←— solid unit

3" (76) minimum bearing continuous reinforced bond beam

basement space

foundation wall
* see 3·12

wood joist floor system

crawl space

½" (13) expansion joint

4" (102) concrete ground slab

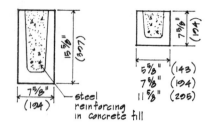

steel reinforcing in concrete fill

15 5/8" (397)
7 5/8" (194)
7 5/8" (194)

5 5/8" (143)
7 5/8" (194)
11 5/8" (295)

SPANS FOR 8" CONCRETE BLOCK WALLS

span	n° and size of reinforcement
6' (1.820)	(2) # 3
8' (2.438)	(2) # 4

CONCRETE BLOCK LINTELS

The block lintels illustrated to the left are intended to carry only concrete block wall loads and lighter construction. Other lintels which may be used to span openings in concrete masonry walls include wood, steel, and reinforced concrete.

* see 5·32

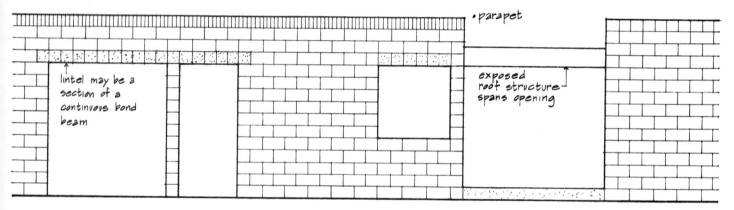

WALL OPENINGS SPANNED BY ROOF STRUCTURE · no masonry above openings

· parapet

lintel may be a section of a continuous bond beam

exposed roof structure spans opening

WALL OPENINGS SPANNED WITH LINTELS · masonry above openings

· all lengths and heights of a concrete block wall and its openings should be modular [ie. multiples of 8' (203) for standard size block]
· a change in coursing pattern may be used to articulate the tops of block walls, lintels and sills of openings, and floor and roof levels
· since control joints are visible, their effect on the appearance of a concrete block should be considered

The above drawings illustrate two different images which a concrete block wall may project, depending on how its top edge is treated, and whether the roof plane bears on the block wall or frames into it.

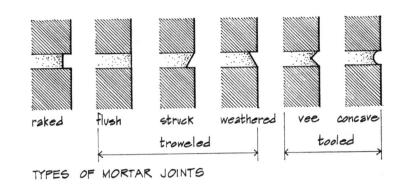

raked   flush   struck   weathered   vee   concave

troweled   tooled

TYPES OF MORTAR JOINTS

Tooled joints provide maximum protection against water penetration since tooling compresses the mortar and forces it tightly against the masonry. Tooled joints are recommended in areas of high wind, heavy rains, and where watertight walls are mandatory.

In troweled joints, the mortar is cut or struck off with a trowel. The most effective of these is the weathered joint since it sheds water

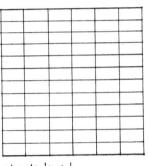

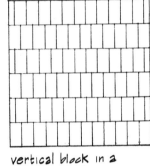

running bond

stack bond
· continuous vertical joints should be avoided - requires horizontal joint reinforcing

vertical block in a running bond

coursed ashlar: alternate rows of concrete block and brick

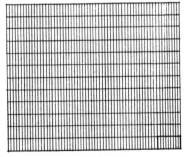

ribbed block

grooved block in a running bond

concrete brick in a running bond

stucco over block

CONCRETE BLOCK PATTERNS, BONDS AND FINISHES

· the color of the concrete block may vary according to the type of cement and aggregate used
· when using patterns with ribbed or grooved block, the color of the mortar should match the color of the block so that the joints do not stand out above the overall textural pattern
· a rough, stone-like surface texture may be achieved using split-face block
· rounded corners are possible with bullnose block
* see 12·7

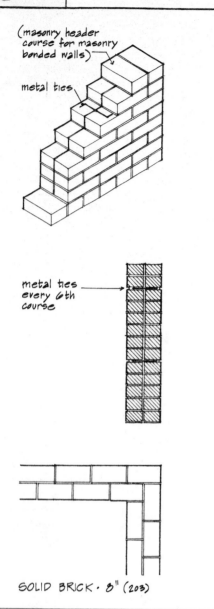

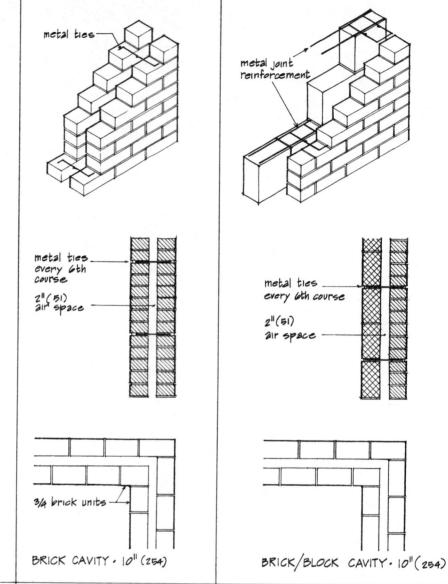

(masonry header course for masonry bonded walls)

metal ties

metal ties

metal joint reinforcement

metal ties every 6th course

metal ties every 6th course

2" (51) air space

metal ties every 6th course

2" (51) air space

3/4 brick units

SOLID BRICK · 8" (203)

BRICK CAVITY · 10" (254)

BRICK/BLOCK CAVITY · 10" (254)

Solid masonry walls act as a unit to support loads. All joints are filled with mortar.

Solid walls may be bonded with:
• masonry units (headers)
• metal ties (3/16" ⌀) (5)
• metal joint reinforcement

Metal tied walls are recommended over masonry bonded walls for better resistance to rain penetration and allowance for slight differential movement between the wythes.

Cavity walls consist of 2 wythes of masonry with an air space [not less than 2" (51) nor more than 4" (102)] between, and bonded together with metal ties or joint reinforcement. The exterior wythe is usually 4" (102) while the interior wythe may be 4" (102) · 6" (152) · 8" (203) or 10" (254). Metal wall ties enable the two wythes to act together as a unit.

Cavity walls have two advantages over solid masonry walls:

① the air space enhances the insulation value of the wall and permits installation of further insulation material
② the air space acts as a barrier against moisture penetration if the cavity is kept clear, and if proper weep holes and flashing are provided

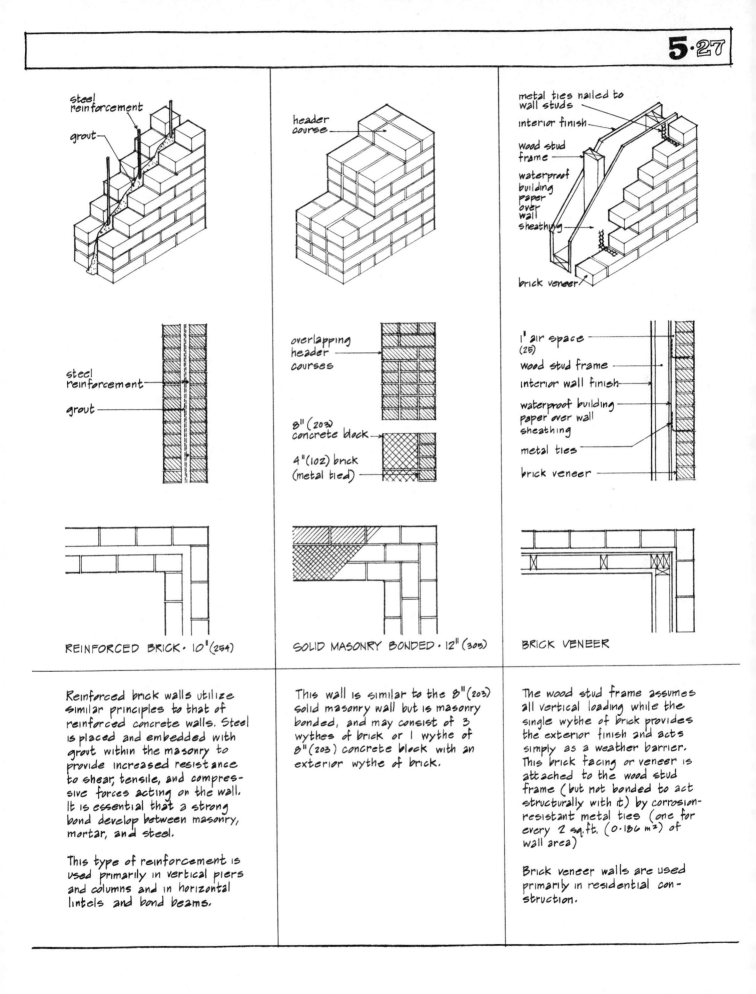

steel reinforcement

grout

steel reinforcement

grout

REINFORCED BRICK · 10" (254)

header course

overlapping header courses

8" (203) concrete block

4" (102) brick (metal tied)

SOLID MASONRY BONDED · 12" (305)

metal ties nailed to wall studs

interior finish

wood stud frame

waterproof building paper over wall sheathing

brick veneer

1' air space (25)

wood stud frame

interior wall finish

waterproof building paper over wall sheathing

metal ties

brick veneer

BRICK VENEER

Reinforced brick walls utilize similar principles to that of reinforced concrete walls. Steel is placed and embedded with grout within the masonry to provide increased resistance to shear, tensile, and compressive forces acting on the wall. It is essential that a strong bond develop between masonry, mortar, and steel.

This type of reinforcement is used primarily in vertical piers and columns and in horizontal lintels and bond beams.

This wall is similar to the 8" (203) solid masonry wall but is masonry bonded, and may consist of 3 wythes of brick or 1 wythe of 8" (203) concrete block with an exterior wythe of brick.

The wood stud frame assumes all vertical loading while the single wythe of brick provides the exterior finish and acts simply as a weather barrier. This brick facing or veneer is attached to the wood stud frame (but not bonded to act structurally with it) by corrosion-resistant metal ties (one for every 2 sq. ft. (0.186 m²) of wall area)

Brick veneer walls are used primarily in residential construction.

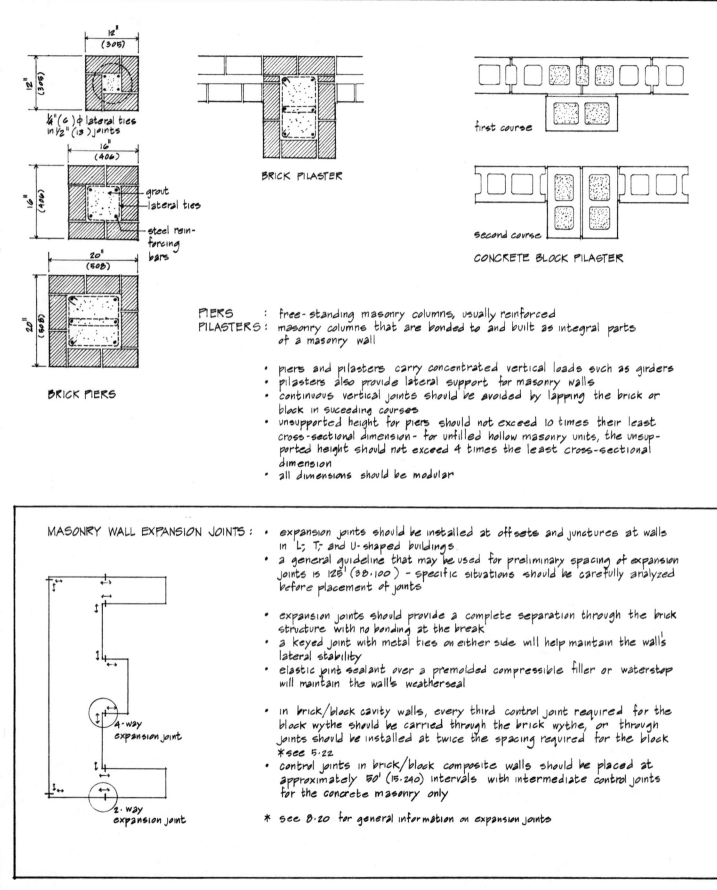

12"
(305)

12"
(305)

¼"(6) φ lateral ties
in ½"(13) joints

16"
(406)

16"
(406)

grout
lateral ties

steel rein-
forcing
bars

20"
(508)

20"
(508)

BRICK PIERS

BRICK PILASTER

first course

second course

CONCRETE BLOCK PILASTER

PIERS   : free-standing masonry columns, usually reinforced
PILASTERS: masonry columns that are bonded to and built as integral parts
             of a masonry wall

- piers and pilasters carry concentrated vertical loads such as girders
- pilasters also provide lateral support for masonry walls
- continuous vertical joints should be avoided by lapping the brick or
  block in succeeding courses
- unsupported height for piers should not exceed 10 times their least
  cross-sectional dimension - for unfilled hollow masonry units, the unsupported height should not exceed 4 times the least cross-sectional
  dimension
- all dimensions should be modular

MASONRY WALL EXPANSION JOINTS :
- expansion joints should be installed at offsets and junctures at walls
  in L-, T-, and U-shaped buildings
- a general guideline that may be used for preliminary spacing of expansion
  joints is 125' (38.100) - specific situations should be carefully analyzed
  before placement of joints

- expansion joints should provide a complete separation through the brick
  structure with no bonding at the break
- a keyed joint with metal ties on either side will help maintain the wall's
  lateral stability
- elastic joint sealant over a premolded compressible filler or waterstop
  will maintain the wall's weatherseal

- in brick/block cavity walls, every third control joint required for the
  block wythe should be carried through the brick wythe, or through
  joints should be installed at twice the spacing required for the block
  *see 5·22
- control joints in brick/block composite walls should be placed at
  approximately 50' (15.240) intervals with intermediate control joints
  for the concrete masonry only

* see 8·20 for general information on expansion joints

4-way
expansion joint

2-way
expansion joint

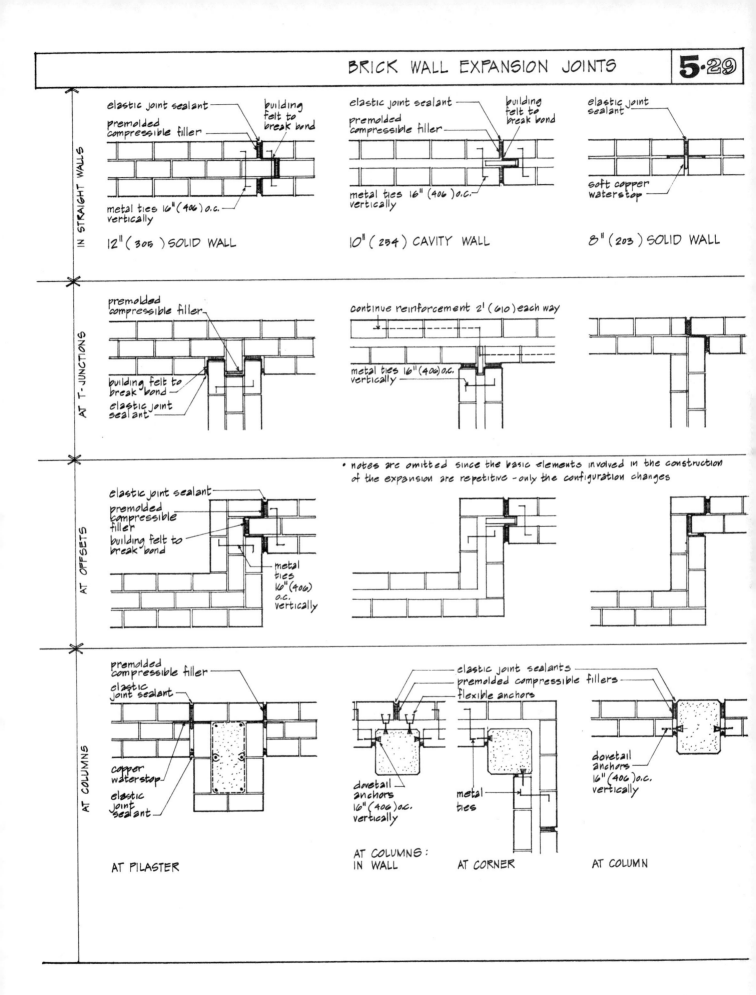

IN STRAIGHT WALLS

elastic joint sealant
premolded compressible filler
building felt to break bond
metal ties 16" (406) o.c. vertically

12" (305) SOLID WALL

elastic joint sealant
premolded compressible filler
building felt to break bond
metal ties 16" (406) o.c. vertically

10" (254) CAVITY WALL

elastic joint sealant
soft copper waterstop

8" (203) SOLID WALL

AT T-JUNCTIONS

premolded compressible filler
building felt to break bond
elastic joint sealant

continue reinforcement 2' (610) each way
metal ties 16" (406) o.c. vertically

AT OFFSETS

elastic joint sealant
premolded compressible filler
building felt to break bond
metal ties 16" (406) o.c. vertically

• notes are omitted since the basic elements involved in the construction of the expansion are repetitive - only the configuration changes

AT COLUMNS

premolded compressible filler
elastic joint sealant
copper waterstop
elastic joint sealant

AT PILASTER

elastic joint sealants
premolded compressible fillers
flexible anchors
dovetail anchors 16" (406) o.c. vertically
metal ties

AT COLUMNS: IN WALL

AT CORNER

dovetail anchors 16" (406) o.c. vertically

AT COLUMN

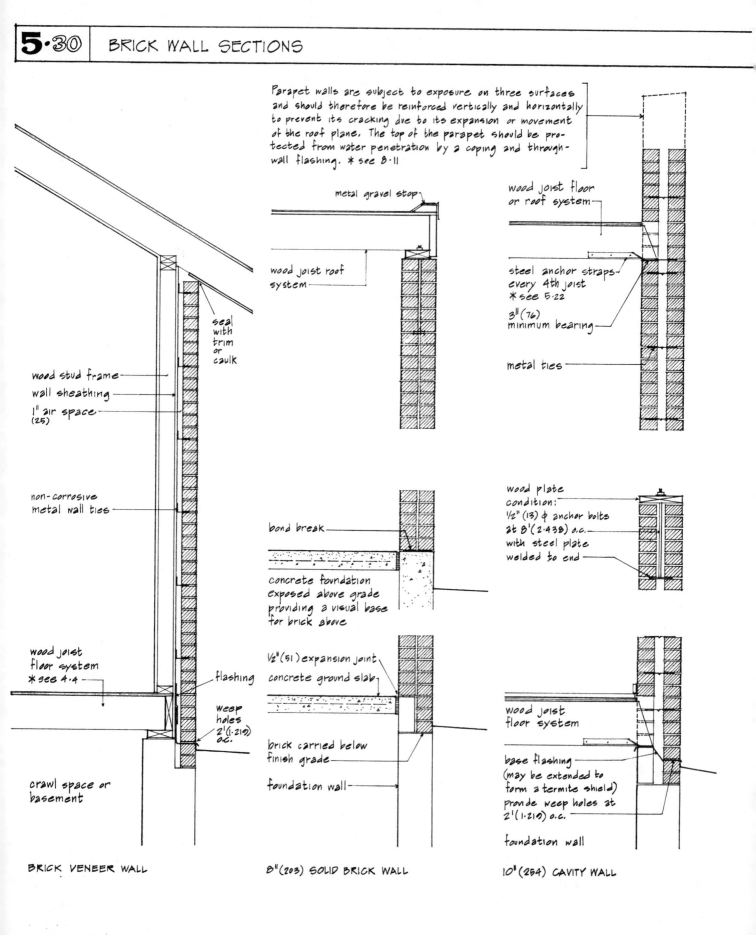

Parapet walls are subject to exposure on three surfaces and should therefore be reinforced vertically and horizontally to prevent its cracking due to its expansion or movement of the roof plane. The top of the parapet should be protected from water penetration by a coping and through-wall flashing. * see 8·11

metal gravel stop

wood joist roof system

wood joist floor or roof system

steel anchor straps every 4th joist * see 5·22

3" (76) minimum bearing

metal ties

seal with trim or caulk

wood stud frame

wall sheathing

1" air space (25)

non-corrosive metal wall ties

bond break

concrete foundation exposed above grade providing a visual base for brick above

wood plate condition: ½" (13) ⌀ anchor bolts at 8' (2.438) o.c. with steel plate welded to end

wood joist floor system * see 4·4

flashing

weep holes 2' (1.219) o.c.

½" (51) expansion joint

concrete ground slab

brick carried below finish grade

foundation wall

wood joist floor system

base flashing (may be extended to form a termite shield) provide weep holes at 2' (1.219) o.c.

foundation wall

crawl space or basement

BRICK VENEER WALL

8" (203) SOLID BRICK WALL

10" (254) CAVITY WALL

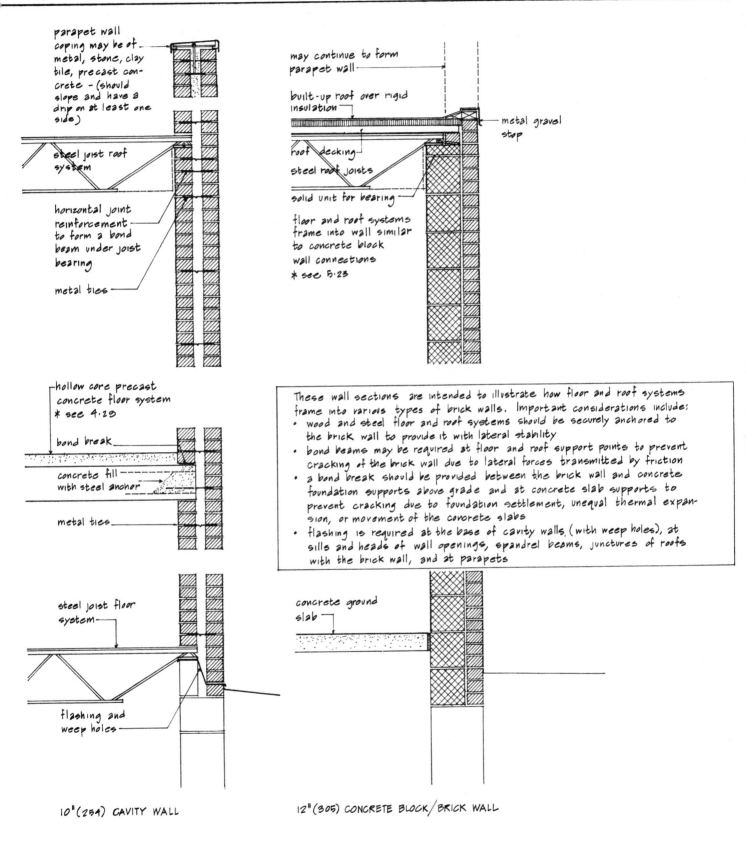

parapet wall coping may be of metal, stone, clay tile, precast concrete - (should slope and have a drip on at least one side)

steel joist roof system

horizontal joint reinforcement to form a bond beam under joist bearing

metal ties

may continue to form parapet wall

built-up roof over rigid insulation

metal gravel stop

roof decking

steel roof joists

solid unit for bearing

floor and roof systems frame into wall similar to concrete block wall connections * see 5·23

hollow core precast concrete floor system * see 4·29

bond break

concrete fill with steel anchor

metal ties

steel joist floor system

flashing and weep holes

These wall sections are intended to illustrate how floor and roof systems frame into various types of brick walls. Important considerations include:
- wood and steel floor and roof systems should be securely anchored to the brick wall to provide it with lateral stability
- bond beams may be required at floor and roof support points to prevent cracking of the brick wall due to lateral forces transmitted by friction
- a bond break should be provided between the brick wall and concrete foundation supports above grade and at concrete slab supports to prevent cracking due to foundation settlement, unequal thermal expansion, or movement of the concrete slabs
- flashing is required at the base of cavity walls (with weep holes), at sills and heads of wall openings, spandrel beams, junctures of roofs with the brick wall, and at parapets

concrete ground slab

10" (254) CAVITY WALL

12" (305) CONCRETE BLOCK/BRICK WALL

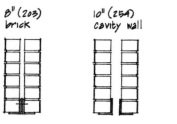 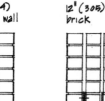 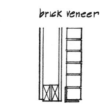

8" (203) brick   10" (254) cavity wall   12" (305) brick   brick veneer

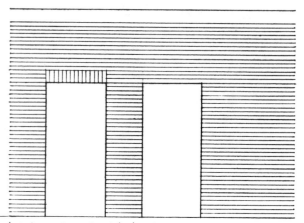

STEEL LINTELS

- size of steel angles varies according to load over opening and width of span
- minimum bearing 6" (152) - large steel angles may require 8" (203) bearing - allow for expansion of steel at ends
- other steel sections may be used, either concealed or exposed

· lintel may be articulated with a soldier course or concealed

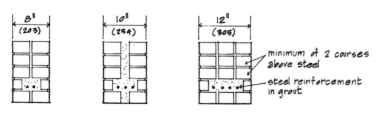

8" (203)   10" (254)   12" (305)

minimum of 2 courses above steel

steel reinforcement in grout

REINFORCED BRICK MASONRY

- width of span and the load that may be carried above opening are determined by the number and size of the steel reinforcing bars and the quality of the mortar grout

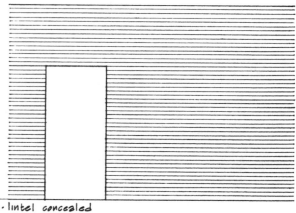

· lintel concealed

7 5/8" (194)   7 5/8" (194)   3 5/8" (92) 3 5/8" (92)   3 5/8" (92) 3 5/8" (92)

1 1/8" (29)

3 5/8" (92) 4" (102)   7 5/8" (194)   7 5/8" (194)

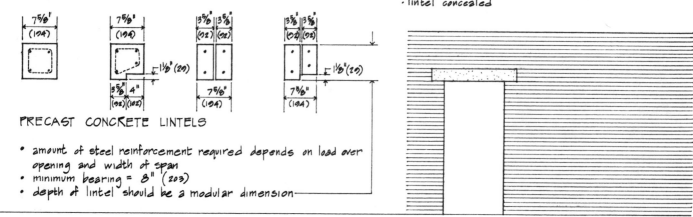

PRECAST CONCRETE LINTELS

- amount of steel reinforcement required depends on load over opening and width of span
- minimum bearing = 8" (203)
- depth of lintel should be a modular dimension

· lintel exposed

* see 5·10 for loads imposed on lintels over masonry wall openings

Instead of using steel or concrete lintels to span masonry wall openings, the compressive strength of brick or stone units may be utilized form arches.

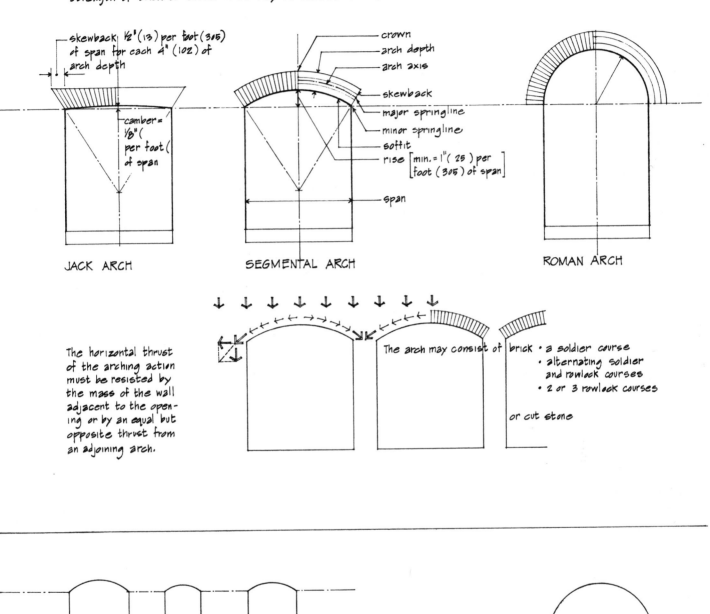

— skewback ½" (13) per foot (305) of span for each 4" (102) of arch depth

camber = ⅛" (per foot (of span

JACK ARCH

crown
arch depth
arch axis
skewback
major springline
minor springline
soffit
rise [min. = 1" (25) per foot (305) of span]
span

SEGMENTAL ARCH

ROMAN ARCH

The horizontal thrust of the arching action must be resisted by the mass of the wall adjacent to the opening or by an equal but opposite thrust from an adjoining arch.

The arch may consist of brick • a soldier course
• alternating soldier and rowlock courses
• 2 or 3 rowlock courses

or cut stone

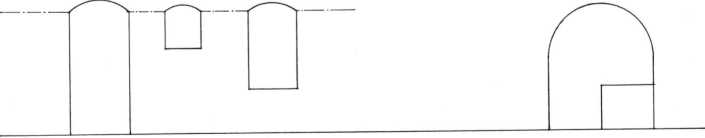

A series of arches in a wall plane will create a visual pattern and rhythm. Visual unity may be achieved by the use of: • a common springline
• a common arch type
• similar proportions

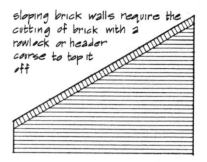

sloping brick walls require the cutting of brick with a rowlock or header course to top it off

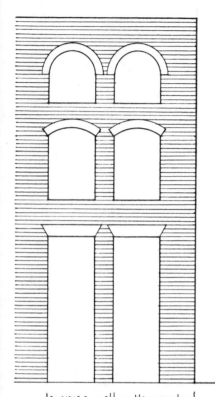

Masonry structures can project a variety of images, from a rather heavy, massive volume with door and window openings punched out, to a light, thin plane supported by a structural frame. The image projected depends on:

- the masonry wall's edge conditions (ie. whether it stands alone with corners visibly turned)
- the masonry wall's thickness (as exposed at door and window openings)
- the size, proportion, and placement of door and window openings within the wall plane

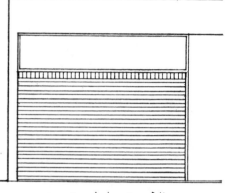

bearing wall with punched openings

non-structural brick infill panel within a steel or concrete frame

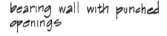
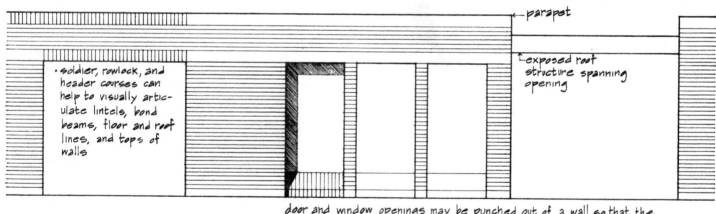

- soldier, rowlock, and header courses can help to visually articulate lintels, bond beams, floor and roof lines, and tops of walls

parapet

exposed roof structure spanning opening

door and window openings may be punched out of a wall so that the wall maintains its integrity as a plane or a section of wall can be removed with the floor or roof structure spanning the opening

- all dimensions (width, height, and length) should be modular
- because of the relatively small size of the brick unit, curvilinear walls are feasible

Illustrated here are the various positions of masonry units and mortar joints used in a brick wall

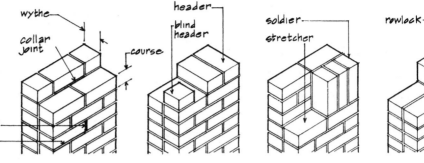

* see 5·25 for mortar joint types
* see 12·7 for brick sizes

running bond

- simplest pattern
- used in cavity and veneer walls with metal ties

common bond

3/4 brick starts header course at corners

- similar to running bond with a header course at every 5th, 6th, or 7th course

stack bond

- since vertical head joints are aligned and brick units do not overlap, this wall requires rigid metal ties to backing and steel reinforcement along the horizontal joints

flemish bond

3/4 brick used at corners

- alternating stretchers and headers in each course
- where headers are not used for masonry bonding, blind headers are used

common bond

- every 6th course composed of flemish headers (alternating stretchers and headers)

english bond

english corner: 1/4 brick

dutch corner: 3/4 brick

- alternating courses of stretchers and headers

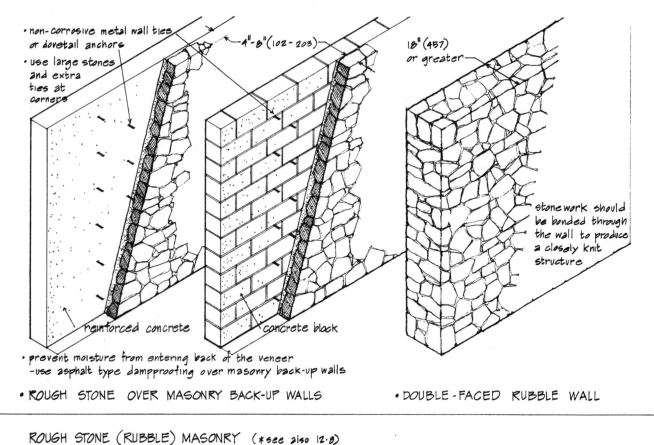

• non-corrosive metal wall ties or dovetail anchors
• use large stones and extra ties at corners

4"–8"(102–203)

18"(457) or greater

stonework should be bonded through the wall to produce a closely knit structure

reinforced concrete

concrete block

• prevent moisture from entering back of the veneer
  –use asphalt type dampproofing over masonry back-up walls

• ROUGH STONE OVER MASONRY BACK-UP WALLS

• DOUBLE-FACED RUBBLE WALL

ROUGH STONE (RUBBLE) MASONRY (*see also 12·8)

• rough stone or rubble may be bonded into a homogeneous, integral load bearing structure or used as a veneer tied to a masonry (reinforced concrete or concrete block) back-up wall
• stone is a strong (in compression), durable building material that projects a rather heavy, massive visual image
• stone must be protected against staining by:
  - using non-corrosive metal ties, fastenings, and flashing
  - using non-staining mortar with porous or light-colored stone
  - avoiding contact with bronze, copper, and unprotected steel

• stone should not be used in areas of intense heat or where fire resistance is critical since most stone is adversely affected by quick changes in temperature

• face jointing: ½"–1" (13–25) for rubble
                  ⅜"–¾" (10–19) for ashlar

• stone masonry, with its integral wall finish, may be laid out in various patterns as illustrated below - consider color, grain, and texture

RANDOM RUBBLE

• no apparent coursing
• bed joints approximately horizontal for stability and appearance
• pointing kept back of face to emphasize natural shape of stone

COURSED RUBBLE

• approximately continuous and horizontal bed joints

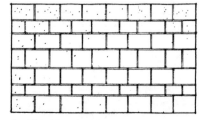

COURSED ASHLAR

• cut facing stone
• broken bond
• ranged coursing

MASONRY-BACKED
STONE WALL

DOUBLE-FACED
RUBBLE WALL

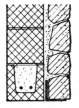
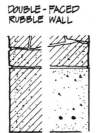

steel angle with
concrete block or
reinforced concrete
lintel

stone or
reinforced concrete
lintel

LINTEL TYPES

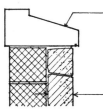

sills may be of
cut stone or
cast concrete

SILL TYPES

4" (102) minimum

Most rough stone masonry wall details:
- foundation system connections
- floor and roof system connections
- reinforcement and lateral bracing
  requirements
- flashing

are similar to those of unit masonry.
Differences lie in the non-modular
aspects of rough stone and the
varying physical properties of the
different types of stone used in
construction.

Expansion joints should be of
corrugated lead with a lead cover
or filled with non-staining, non-
hardening pointing compound.

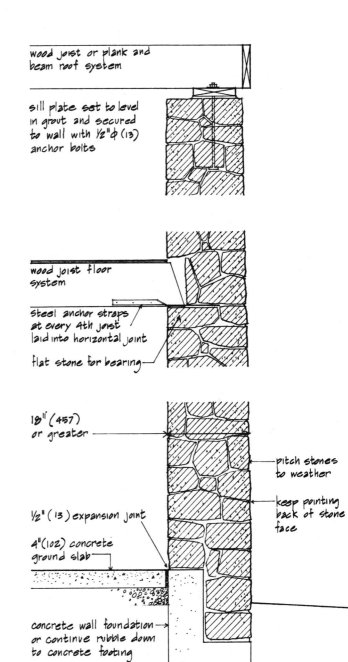

wood joist or plank and
beam roof system

sill plate set to level
in grout and secured
to wall with ½"φ (13)
anchor bolts

wood joist floor
system

steel anchor straps
at every 4th joist
laid into horizontal joint

flat stone for bearing

18" (457)
or greater

pitch stones
to weather

keep pointing
back of stone
face

½" (13) expansion joint

4" (102) concrete
ground slab

concrete wall foundation
or continue rubble down
to concrete footing

AN EXAMPLE OF A WALL SECTION THROUGH A
DOUBLE-FACED RUBBLE WALL
This type of wall is usually limited to three
stories in height

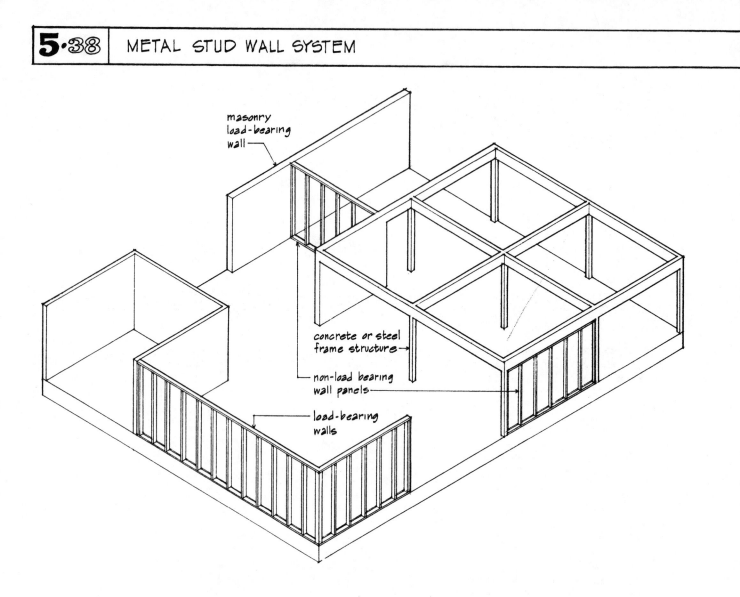

masonry
load-bearing
wall

concrete or steel
frame structure→

non-load bearing
wall panels

load-bearing
walls

- metal (steel or aluminum) stud wall systems may be used either as load bearing walls or non-load bearing infill panels within a steel or concrete structural frame

- analogous to the wood stud wall system both in overall form and configuration as well as in the type of pieces used

- metal studs spaced 12"·16"·24" (305·406·610) o.c.

- wall sheathing and finish options similar to those of the wood stud wall system

- mechanical fastening devices (nails, screws, bolts) and/or welding used

- usually used in conjunction with lightgage metal floor and roof systems

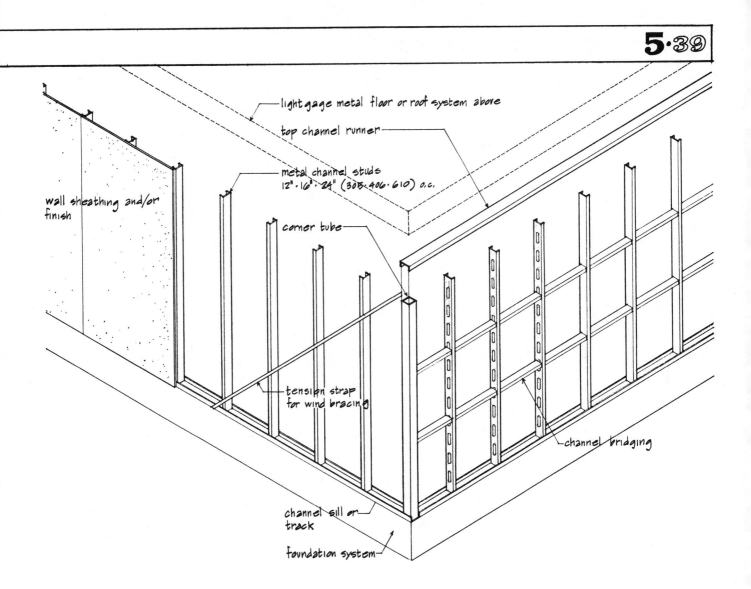

light gage metal floor or roof system above

top channel runner

metal channel studs
12"·16"·24" (305·406·610) o.c.

wall sheathing and/or finish

corner tube

tension strap
for wind bracing

channel bridging

channel sill or
track

foundation system

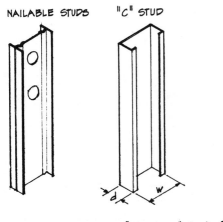

NAILABLE STUDS   "C" STUD   CHANNEL STUD

d   w

typical widths : ¾" (10) 1" (25) 1⅜" (35) 1⅝" (41) 2" (51)
typical depths: 2½" (64) 3⅝" (92) 4" (102) 6" (152) 8" (203)
typical gages : 14·15·16·18·20

• specific form, and available sizes and gages,
  vary with manufacturer

• studs may be solid or punched

• bridging and channel track (top and bottom)
  similar in form and size to channel studs

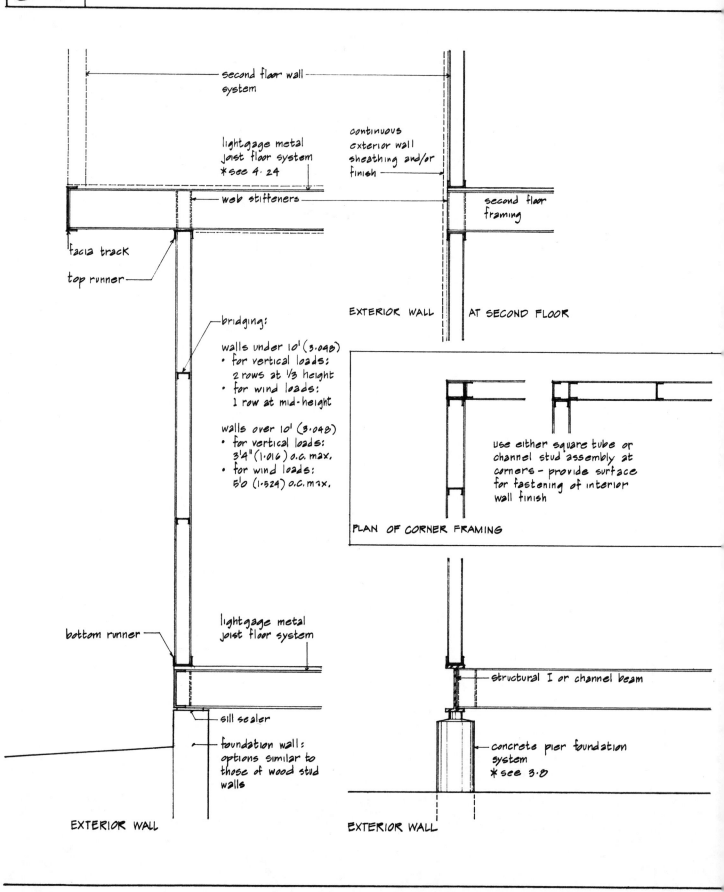

second floor wall system

lightgage metal joist floor system
* see 4·24

continuous exterior wall sheathing and/or finish

web stiffeners

facia track

top runner

second floor framing

EXTERIOR WALL   AT SECOND FLOOR

bridging:

walls under 10' (3.048)
• for vertical loads:
  2 rows at ⅓ height
• for wind loads:
  1 row at mid-height

walls over 10' (3.048)
• for vertical loads:
  3'4" (1.016) o.c. max.
• for wind loads:
  5'0 (1.524) o.c. max.

use either square tube or channel stud assembly at corners - provide surface for fastening of interior wall finish

PLAN OF CORNER FRAMING

bottom runner

lightgage metal joist floor system

sill sealer

foundation wall: options similar to those of wood stud walls

structural I or channel beam

concrete pier foundation system
* see 3·8

EXTERIOR WALL   EXTERIOR WALL

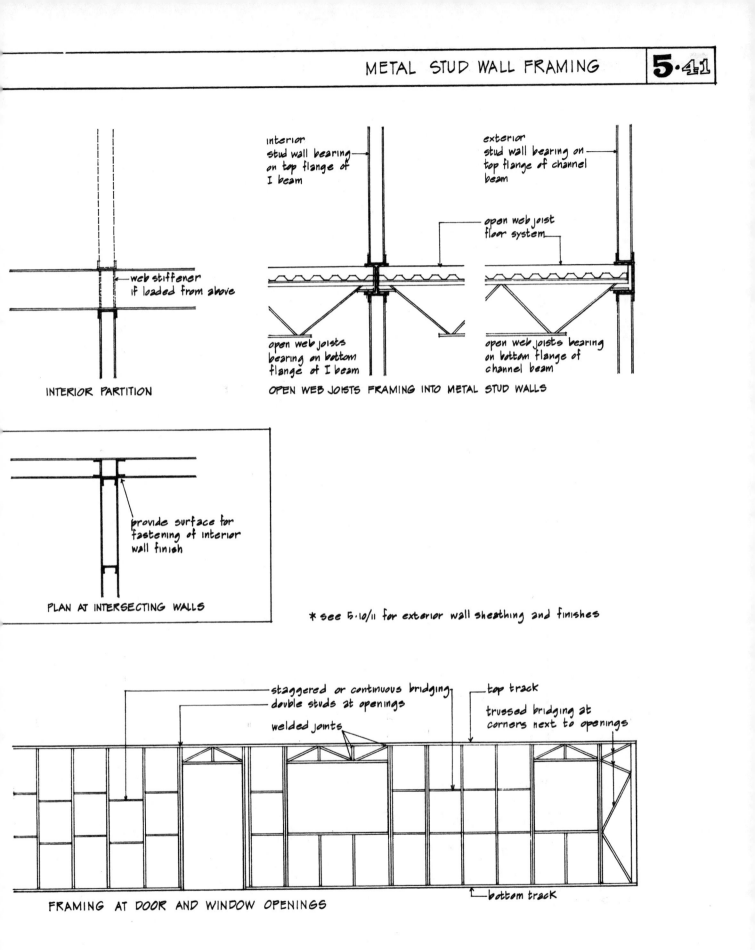

web stiffener
if loaded from above

INTERIOR PARTITION

interior
stud wall bearing
on top flange of
I beam

exterior
stud wall bearing on
top flange of channel
beam

open web joist
floor system

open web joists
bearing on bottom
flange of I beam

open web joists bearing
on bottom flange of
channel beam

OPEN WEB JOISTS FRAMING INTO METAL STUD WALLS

provide surface for
fastening of interior
wall finish

PLAN AT INTERSECTING WALLS

* see 5·10/11 for exterior wall sheathing and finishes

staggered or continuous bridging
double studs at openings
welded joints

top track

trussed bridging at
corners next to openings

bottom track

FRAMING AT DOOR AND WINDOW OPENINGS

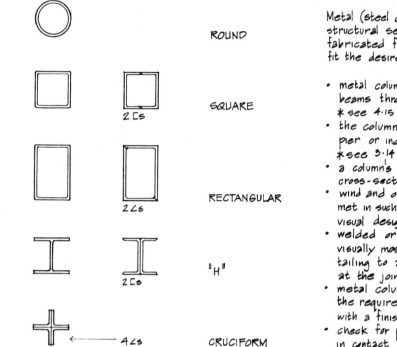

ROUND

SQUARE

2 ⊏s

RECTANGULAR

2 ⊏s

"H"

2 ⊏s

CRUCIFORM   ← 4 ∠s

Metal (steel or aluminum) columns may be of standard structural sections or tubular shapes, or they may be fabricated from a number of structural sections to fit the desired end use of the column.

- metal columns may support either wood or metal beams through the use of column caps and brackets * see 4·15
- the column connection at its base to a foundation pier or independent footing should be rigid * see 3·14
- a column's load-bearing capacity is directly related to cross-sectional area and unsupported height
- wind and other lateral bracing requirements should be met in such a way that they do not affect the desired visual design
- welded or internalized mechanical connections are visually most desirable but this requires careful detailing to achieve the necessary strength and rigidity at the joint
- metal columns may be left exposed (consistent with the required fire resistance rating) or enclosed with a finish material
- check for possible galvanic action when column comes in contact with other metals

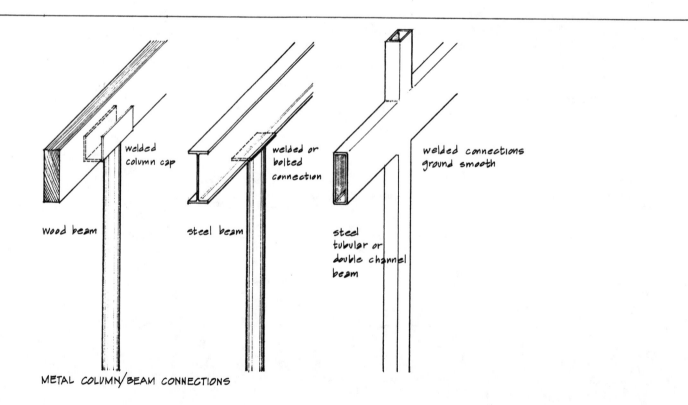

welded column cap

wood beam

welded or bolted connection

steel beam

welded connections ground smooth

steel tubular or double channel beam

METAL COLUMN/BEAM CONNECTIONS

The following tables are for estimating and preliminary sizing only.

CONCENTRATED SAFE LOADS FOR STEEL TUBULAR SHAPES in kips (kg): (1 kip = 1000 lbs = 453.50 kg)

HEAVYWEIGHT TUBULAR COLUMNS

outside diameter in inches (mm)	3 (76)	3½ (80)	4 (102)	4½ (114)	5 (127)	5½ (139)
8 (2.438)	13 (5896)	32 (14514)	43 (19504)	55 (24947)	69 (31297)	85 (38555)
10 (3.048)		27 (12246)	37 (16782)	49 (22225)	62 (28122)	77 (34926)
12 (3.657)			31 (14061)	42 (19050)	55 (24947)	70 (31571)
14 (4.267)				36 (16329)	48 (21772)	63 (28576)
16 (4.877)					41 (18597)	55 (24947)
18 (5.486)						48 (21772)

(unsupported height in feet (m))

EXTRA HEAVYWEIGHT TUBULAR COLUMNS

outside diameter in inches (mm)	4 (102)	4½ (114)	5 (127)	5½ (139)	6⅝ (168)	8⅝ (219)
8 (2.438)	54 (24493)	70 (31571)	87 (39462)	100 (49441)	161 (73027)	265 (120201)
12 (3.657)	30 (17690)	53 (24040)	69 (31297)	90 (40823)	138 (62595)	238 (107954)
16 (4.877)			51 (23133)	70 (31571)	115 (52162)	212 (96161)
20 (6.096)					93 (42183)	186 (83914)
24 (7.315)						157 (72213)
28 (8.534)						129 (51013)
32 (9.754)						

(unsupported height in feet (m))

SQUARE TUBULAR COLUMNS

face dimension in inches (mm)	3 (76)	3 (76)	3½ (80)	3½ (80)	4 (102)	4 (102)
thickness	3/16" (5)	1/4" (6)	3/16" (5)	1/4" (6)	3/16" (5)	1/4" (6)
8 (2.438)	30 (13607)	37 (16782)	43 (19504)	50 (22679)	53 (24040)	64 (29029)
10 (3.048)	25 (11339)	30 (13607)	36 (16329)	43 (19504)	48 (21772)	57 (25854)
12 (3.657)	20 (9071)	24 (10886)	30 (13607)	36 (16329)	42 (19050)	50 (22679)
14 (4.267)			25 (11339)	30 (13607)	38 (17236)	43 (19504)
16 (4.877)					31 (14061)	36 (16329)

(unsupported height in feet (m))

RECTANGULAR TUBULAR COLUMNS

width in inches (mm)	2 (51)	3 (76)	3 (76)	3 (76)	4 (102)	4 (102)
depth in inches (mm)	4 (102)	4 (102)	6 (152)	6 (152)	6 (152)	6 (152)
thickness	1/4" (6)	1/4" (6)	3/16" (5)	1/4" (6)	3/16" (5)	1/4" (6)
8 (2.438)	21 (9525)	45 (20411)	51 (23133)	61 (27668)	71 (32204)	85 (38555)
10 (3.048)		37 (16782)	42 (19050)	50 (22679)	64 (29029)	76 (34472)
12 (3.657)			33 (14968)	39 (17690)	56 (25401)	66 (29936)
14 (4.267)					49 (22225)	57 (25854)
16 (4.877)					41 (18597)	49 (22225)
18 (5.486)					33 (14968)	39 (17690)
20 (6.096)						30 (13607)

(unsupported height in feet (m))

ROOF SYSTEMS  6

The roof system of a building functions as the primary sheltering element protecting the interior spaces of the building from the natural elements. It should also control the flow of water (from rain and snow), water vapor, heat, and air. In addition, it must be structured to carry its own weight as well as live loads such as snow, ice, and wind. The roof system should be fire-resistant and may have to accomodate mechanical and electrical equipment.

Since the roof system is a primary generator of building loads, it must be compatible with the wall and/or column systems through which these loads are transferred down to the foundation system.

The roof system is potentially the most expensive system of a building because of its varied functional tasks spread over a large area. Economy of erection and maintenance, durability, and potential heat loss or gain should all be considered in the choice of a roof system and its materials.

The form of the roof system is a critical element in the visual image of a building, whether flat and hidden by a parapet wall, sloping as with a shed roof, or read as a strong horizontal cap over the building mass. The roof form, and the spacing, span and slope of its structural members, also affect the choice of the finish roofing material, the interior ceiling system, and the layout and form of the building's interior spaces. Long roof spans would open up a more flexible interior space while short spans would demand more rigidly defined spaces.

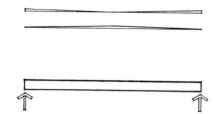

- minimum recommended slope: 4·in·12 to interior drains or perimeter gutters
- slope may result from sloping structural members, or tapering roof deck or rigid insulation
- minimum roof area for enclosed space
- requires continuous membrane roofing
- structural plane of · joists and sheathing
    · plank and beam
    · flat trusses

FLAT

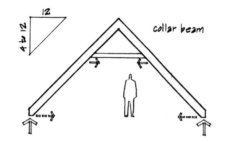

collar beam

- slope: 4·in·12 to 12·in·12
- easy runoff for rain and snow
- large roof area for enclosed space
- potential use of high interior space
- high slopes require shingle or sheet roofing
- roof structure of · sheathing over rafters
    · plank and beam
    · trusses
- possible outward thrust at eaves may require collar beam or structural tie from eave to eave

GABLE : NORMAL TO HIGH PITCH

flat ceiling plane optional

- slope: 2·in·12 to 4·in·12
- roll or continuous membrane roofing for slopes up to 3·in·12
- asphalt shingle roofing may be used
- structure similar to above

GABLE : LOW PITCH

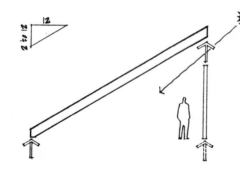

- slopes vary from 2·in·12 to 12·in·12
- roll or continuous membrane roofing for slopes up to 3·in·12
- shingle or sheet roofing for slopes 3·in·12 and higher
- structure similar to above
- potential use of high interior space with high slopes
- high wall surface on ridge side allows for additional light penetration

SHED

FACTORS IN ROOF DESIGN AND CONSTRUCTION:

- roof strength sufficient to carry:

  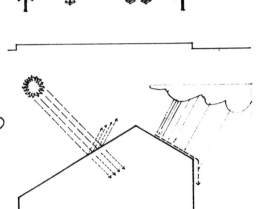

  - dead load · roof structure, roofing, insulation, ceiling,
    · suspended equipment such as light fixtures
  - live load · accumulated rain, snow, ice (and traffic, if any)
  - wind load · lateral and vertical load components, and
    vertical uplift forces, if any (*see 1·10)

- type of roofing required for slope of roof

  - shingles, tiles, sheet, or membrane types (see chapter 8)

- weatherprotection afforded

  - control of: · precipitation
    · water vapor flow
    · heat flow and solar radiation
    · ventilation

- drainage patterns and runoff outlets required

  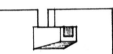

  - roof drains, scuppers, gutters, and downspouts (*see 8·9)

- flashing requirements (*see 8·11)

  - valleys
  - hips and ridges
  - edges: eaves, rakes, intersections with vertical surfaces
  - openings

- effect of roof structure support pattern on form of interior spaces

  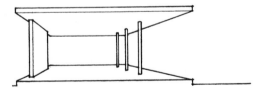

  - point or linear supports (columns or bearing walls)
  - length of spans (spacing of supports)
  - bay sizes and proportions
  - form of roof if exposed: flat or sloped
  - type of ceiling finish that may be applied or supported

- effect of roof structure on external building image

  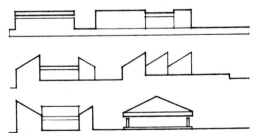

  - flat or sloped
  - single or multiple forms
  - roof edge support conditions

    - roof plane may frame into a parapet wall so that it
      is concealed
    - roof plane may bear on its beam or wall support and
      be flush with or overhang the wall plane

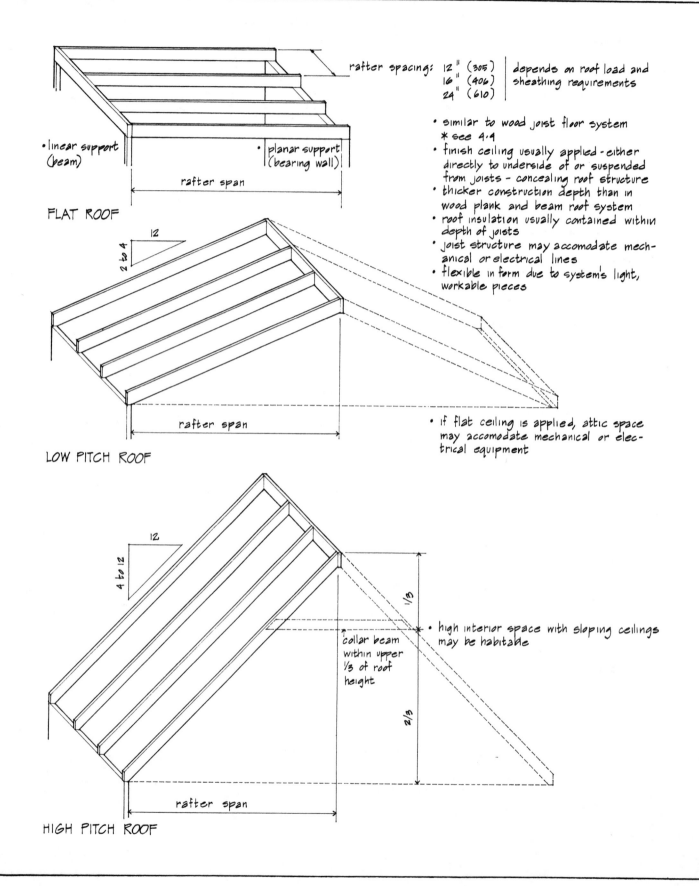

rafter spacing: 12" (305)
16" (406)
24" (610) | depends on roof load and sheathing requirements

• linear support (beam)

• planar support (bearing wall)

rafter span

FLAT ROOF

• similar to wood joist floor system
  * see 4·4
• finish ceiling usually applied - either directly to underside of or suspended from joists - concealing roof structure
• thicker construction depth than in wood plank and beam roof system
• roof insulation usually contained within depth of joists
• joist structure may accomodate mechanical or electrical lines
• flexible in form due to system's light, workable pieces

12

2 to 4

rafter span

LOW PITCH ROOF

• if flat ceiling is applied, attic space may accomodate mechanical or electrical equipment

12

4 to 12

⅓

collar beam within upper ⅓ of roof height

⅔

• high interior space with sloping ceilings may be habitable

rafter span

HIGH PITCH ROOF

The following span table is for estimating and preliminary sizing of roof joists or rafters only. It assumes that joists have simple spans.

SIZE nominal	SPACING center to center	SPAN AS LIMITED BY DEFLECTION*		f=	SPAN AS LIMITED BY BENDING			
		E = 1,200,000	1,400,000	f=	1000	1200	1400	1600
LIVE LOAD: 30 lbs/ft² (146.46 kg/m²)								
2×4 (51×102)	12" (305)	6'-0" (2.057)	7'-2" (2.184)		8'-1" (2.464)	8'-10" (2.662)	9'-6" (2.896)	10'-2" (3.099)
	16" (406)	6-2 (1.880)	6-6 (1.981)		7-0 (2.134)	7-8 (2.337)	8-3 (2.515)	8-10 (2.692)
	24" (610)	5-5 (1.651)	5-9 (1.753)		5-9 (1.753)	6-4 (1.930)	6-10 (2.083)	7-3 (2.210)
2×6 (51×152)	12	10-5 (3.175)	11-0 (3.353)		12-4 (3.759)	13-6 (4.115)	14-7 (4.445)	15-7 (4.750)
	16	9-7 (2.921)	10-1 (3.073)		10-9 (3.277)	11-10 (3.607)	12-9 (3.886)	13-8 (4.166)
	24	8-5 (2.565)	8-10 (2.692)		8-11 (2.718)	9-9 (2.972)	10-6 (3.200)	11-3 (3.429)
2×8 (51×203)	12	13-10 (4.216)	14-7 (4.445)		16-3 (4.953)	17-10 (5.436)	19-3 (5.867)	20-7 (6.274)
	16	12-8 (3.861)	13-4 (4.064)		14-3 (4.343)	15-7 (4.750)	16-10 (5.131)	18-0 (5.486)
	24	11-2 (3.404)	11-9 (3.581)		11-9 (3.581)	12-11 (3.937)	13-11 (4.242)	14-11 (4.547)
2×10 (51×254)	12	17-5 (5.309)	18-4 (5.588)		20-4 (6.198)	22-4 (6.807)	24-1 (7.341)	25-9 (7.849)
	16	15-11 (4.851)	16-9 (5.105)		17-10 (5.436)	19-7 (5.969)	21-2 (6.452)	22-7 (6.883)
	24	14-1 (4.293)	14-10 (4.521)		14-10 (4.521)	16-3 (4.953)	17-6 (5.334)	18-9 (5.715)
2×12 (51×305)	12	20-11 (6.375)	22-0 (6.706)		24-4 (7.417)	26-8 (8.128)	28-10 (8.788)	30-10 (9.398)
	16	19-2 (5.842)	20-2 (6.147)		21-5 (6.528)	23-6 (7.163)	25-5 (7.747)	27-2 (8.280)
	24	16-11 (5.156)	17-10 (5.436)		17-10 (5.436)	19-6 (5.944)	21-1 (6.426)	22-6 (6.858)
2×14 (51×356)	12	24-4 (7.417)	25-7 (7.798)		28-4 (8.636)	31-0 (9.449)		
	16	22-5 (6.833)	23-7 (7.188)		25-0 (7.620)	27-4 (8.331)	29-6 (8.992)	
	24	19-10 (6.045)	20-10 (6.350)		20-9 (6.325)	22-9 (6.934)	24-7 (7.493)	26-4 (8.026)
LIVE LOAD: 40 lbs/ft² (195.28 kg/m²)								
2×6 (51×152)	12	9-8 (2.946)	10-2 (3.099)		11-0 (3.353)	12-0 (3.658)	13-0 (3.962)	13-10 (4.216)
	16	8-10 (2.692)	9-3 (2.819)		9-7 (2.921)	10-6 (3.200)	11-4 (3.454)	12-1 (3.683)
	24	7-9 (2.362)	8-2 (2.489)		7-10 (2.388)	8-7 (2.616)	9-4 (2.845)	9-11 (3.023)
2×8 (51×203)	12	12-10 (3.912)	13-6 (4.115)		14-6 (4.420)	15-10 (4.826)	17-0 (5.182)	18-4 (5.588)
	16	11-8 (3.556)	12-4 (3.759)		12-8 (3.861)	13-10 (4.216)	15-2 (4.623)	16-0 (4.877)
	24	10-3 (3.124)	10-10 (3.302)		10-5 (3.175)	11-5 (3.480)	12-4 (3.759)	13-2 (4.013)
2×10 (51×254)	12	16-1 (4.902)	17-0 (5.182)		18-2 (5.537)	19-11 (6.071)	21-6 (6.553)	23-0 (7.010)
	16	14-9 (4.496)	15-6 (4.724)		15-11 (4.851)	17-5 (5.309)	18-10 (5.740)	20-2 (6.147)
	24	13-0 (3.962)	13-8 (4.166)		13-2 (4.013)	14-5 (4.394)	15-7 (4.750)	16-8 (5.080)
2×12 (51×305)	12	19-5 (5.918)	20-5 (6.223)		21-10 (6.655)	23-11 (7.290)	25-10 (7.874)	27-7 (8.407)
	16	17-9 (5.410)	18-9 (5.715)		19-2 (5.842)	21-0 (6.401)	22-8 (6.909)	24-3 (7.391)
	24	15-8 (4.775)	16-6 (5.029)		15-10 (4.826)	17-4 (5.283)	18-9 (5.715)	20-0 (6.096)
2×14 (51×356)	12	22-7 (6.883)	23-10 (7.264)		25-5 (7.747)	27-10 (8.484)	30-0 (9.144)	
	16	20-9 (6.325)	21-10 (6.655)		22-4 (6.807)	24-5 (7.442)	26-5 (8.052)	28-3 (8.611)
	24	18-4 (5.588)	19-4 (5.893)		18-6 (5.639)	20-3 (6.172)	21-11 (6.680)	23-5 (7.137)

* maximum allowable deflection = 1/360 of span
- E = moduslus of elasticity; 1,200,000 psi = 843.6×10⁶ kg/m²
  1,400,000 psi = 984.3×10⁶ kg/m²
- both (E) and (f) varies with the species and grade of wood used

- f= allowable unit stress in extreme fiber bending
  1000 psi = 703.07×10³ kg/m²
  1200 psi = 843.68×10³ kg/m²
  1400 psi = 984.29×10³ kg/m²
  1600 psi = 1124.91×10³ kg/m²

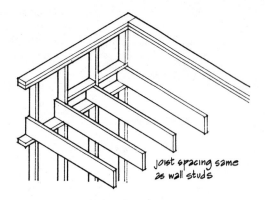

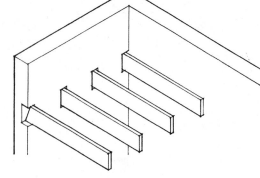

joist spacing same as wall studs

WOOD STUD WALL SUPPORT

- roof joists frame into wood stud wall similar to the way in which wood floor joists frame into a stud wall in balloon frame construction
  * see 5·4

MASONRY WALL SUPPORT

- similar to wood floor joists framing into a masonry wall
- if properly anchored, roof plane augments masonry wall's lateral stability
  * see 5·22

ROOF FRAMING INTO PARAPET WALL: exterior wall extends above roof plane concealing roof edge

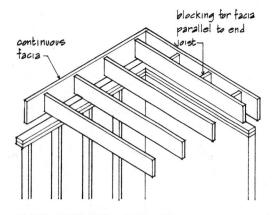

continuous facia

blocking for facia parallel to end joist

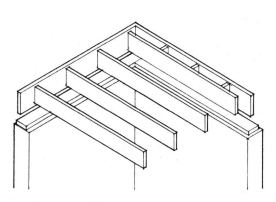

WOOD STUD WALL SUPPORT

similar to second floor wood joists bearing on wood stud wall
* see 5·6

MASONRY WALL SUPPORT

similar to wood floor joist system bearing on masonry foundation wall
* see 4·6

ROOF BEARING ON WALL: roof edge exposed - may be flush with exterior wall or cantilevered for overhang

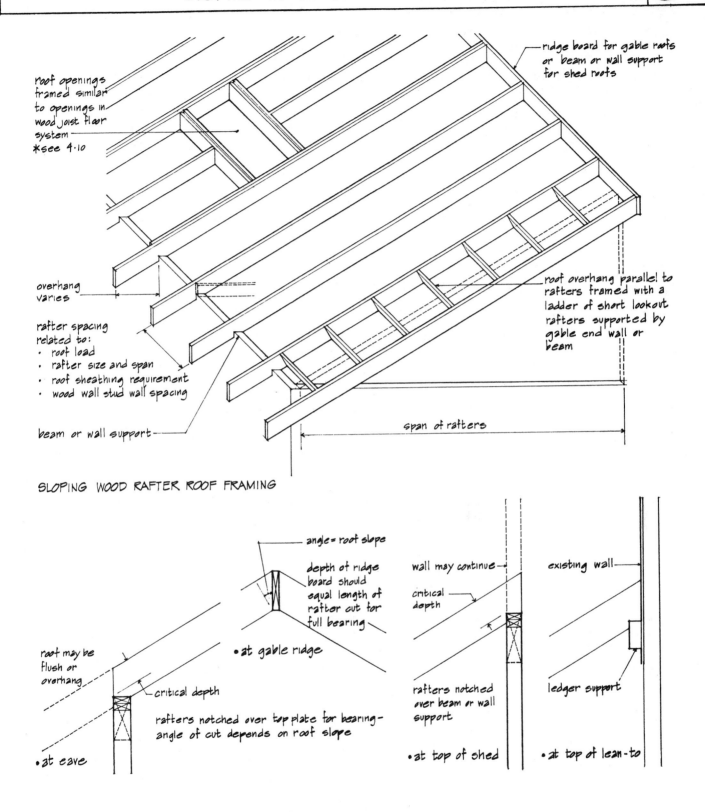

roof openings framed similar to openings in wood joist floor system *see 4·10

ridge board for gable roofs or beam or wall support for shed roofs

overhang varies

rafter spacing related to:
· roof load
· rafter size and span
· roof sheathing requirement
· wood wall stud wall spacing

beam or wall support

roof overhang parallel to rafters framed with a ladder of short lookout rafters supported by gable end wall or beam

span of rafters

SLOPING WOOD RAFTER ROOF FRAMING

angle = roof slope

depth of ridge board should equal length of rafter cut for full bearing

wall may continue

critical depth

existing wall

roof may be flush or overhang

critical depth

· at gable ridge

rafters notched over top plate for bearing- angle of cut depends on roof slope

rafters notched over beam or wall support

ledger support

· at eave

· at top of shed

· at top of lean-to

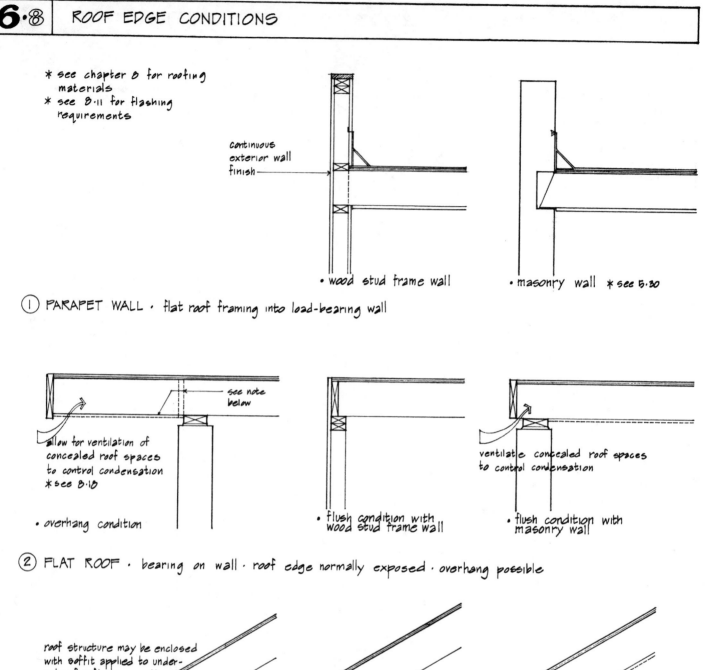

* see chapter 8 for roofing
  materials
* see 8·11 for flashing
  requirements

continuous
exterior wall
finish —

• wood stud frame wall

• masonry wall * see 5·30

① PARAPET WALL · flat roof framing into load-bearing wall

see note
below

allow for ventilation of
concealed roof spaces
to control condensation
* see 8·18

• overhang condition

• flush condition with
wood stud frame wall

ventilate concealed roof spaces
to control condensation

• flush condition with
masonry wall

② FLAT ROOF · bearing on wall · roof edge normally exposed · overhang possible

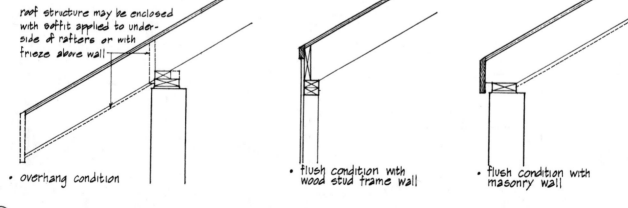

roof structure may be enclosed
with soffit applied to underside of rafters or with
frieze above wall

• overhang condition

• flush condition with
wood stud frame wall

• flush condition with
masonry wall

③ SLOPING ROOF · bearing on wall · overhang possible

Similar to subflooring over wood joists, roof sheathing over wood rafters may be of boards or plywood. Other materials, such as gypsum, fiberboard, or cementitious decking, may also be used as roof sheathing. In any case, sheathing requirements should be verified to be in accordance with the recommendations of the manufacturer of the finish roofing material.

PLYWOOD ROOF SHEATHING

ALLOWABLE GRADES	PANEL IDENT. INDEX	THICKNESS inches (mm)	MAXIMUM SPAN inches (mm)	ALLOWABLE ROOF LIVE LOAD IN LBS/S.F. ACCORDING TO SUPPORT SPACING IN INCHES						1 lb/ft² = 4.882 kg/m²
				12	16	24	32	48	72	
DFPA struct I	16/0	5/16"·3/8" (8)(10)	16 (406)	130	55					
	24/0	3/8"·1/2" (10)(13)	24 (610)		150	45				
DFPA struct II	32/16	1/2"·5/8" (13)(16)	32 (813)			90	40			
DFPA standard w/	48/24	3/4"·7/8" (19)(22)	48 (1219)				105	40		
exterior glue	2·4·1	1 1/8" (29)	72 (1829)					80	30	

maximum plywood span may be determined visually from panel identification index

above guidelines are based on uniformly distributed loads supported by plywood laid continuously over 2 or more spans

board sheathing:
- nominal 1" thickness (25)
- 6" maximum nominal thickness (152) to minimize shrinkage
- 24" (610) maximum support spacing
- tongue and groove boards recommended

- boards laid diagonally across flat roof joists with all joints staggered and falling on joists

plywood sheathing:
- laid with face grain perpendicular to supports
- all joints staggered
- provide blocking for unsupported edges unless tongue and groove edges or plyclips are used
- use exterior-grade DFPA plywood for open or exposed soffits
- protect edges of interior grade plywood from weather

board sheathing on sloping roofs laid perpendicular to supports

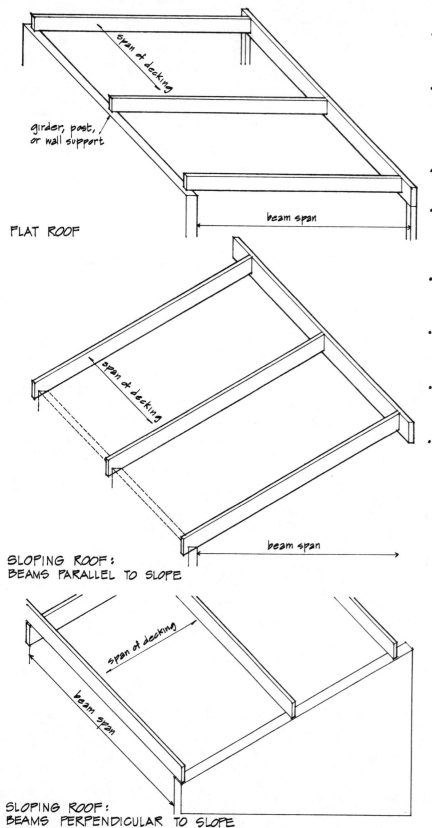

FLAT ROOF

girder, post, or wall support

span of decking

beam span

SLOPING ROOF:
BEAMS PARALLEL TO SLOPE

span of decking

beam span

SLOPING ROOF:
BEAMS PERPENDICULAR TO SLOPE

span of decking

beam span

- similar to wood plank and beam floor system
  ✳ see 4·12

- beam size and spanning capability related to: · roof design load
  · beam spacing
  · type and spanning capability of decking

- less construction depth than wood rafter roof system

- often used in conjunction with post and beam wall system and plank and beam floor system to form a skeleton frame structural grid

- structure often left exposed with the underside of the decking being the finished ceiling

- exposed structure requires careful detailing of joints, the use of quality materials, and quality workmanship

- difficult to accomodate concealed mechanical or electrical lines

- deck types: · wood plank
  · 2·4·1 plywood
  · prefabricated plywood panels
  · cementitious plank (see 6·17)

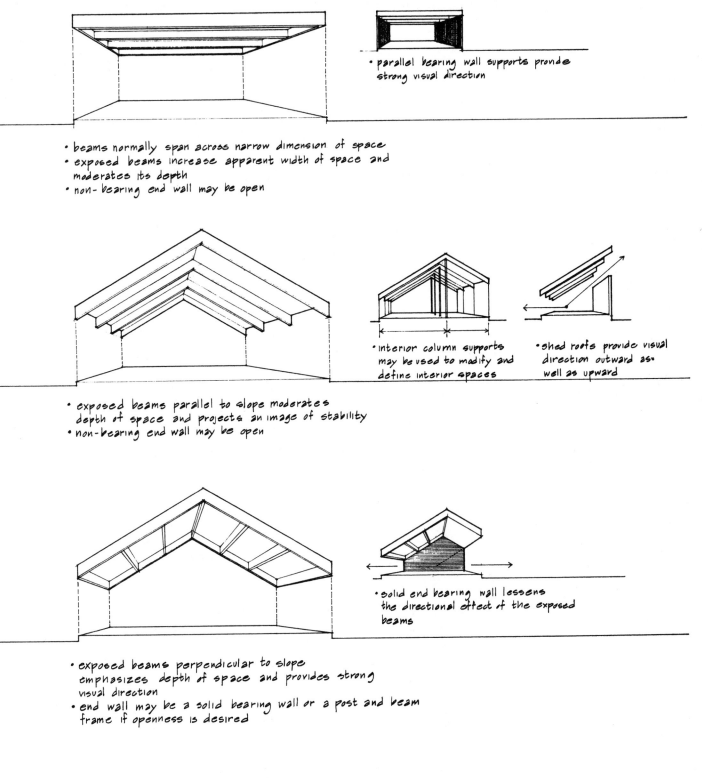

- parallel bearing wall supports provide strong visual direction

- beams normally span across narrow dimension of space
- exposed beams increase apparent width of space and moderates its depth
- non-bearing end wall may be open

- interior column supports may be used to modify and define interior spaces

- shed roofs provide visual direction outward as well as upward

- exposed beams parallel to slope moderates depth of space and projects an image of stability
- non-bearing end wall may be open

- solid end bearing wall lessens the directional effect of the exposed beams

- exposed beams perpendicular to slope emphasizes depth of space and provides strong visual direction
- end wall may be a solid bearing wall or a post and beam frame if openness is desired

*see 8·11 for flashing requirements

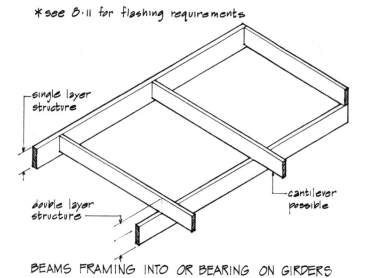

single layer structure

double layer structure

cantilever possible

BEAMS FRAMING INTO OR BEARING ON GIRDERS

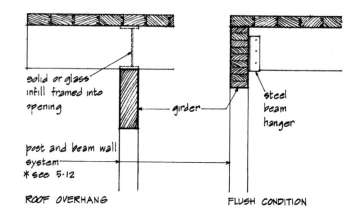

solid or glass infill framed into opening

girder

steel beam hanger

post and beam wall system *see 5·12

ROOF OVERHANG

FLUSH CONDITION

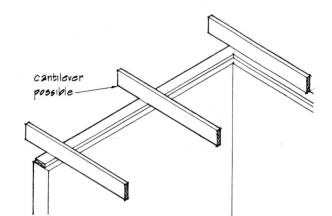

cantilever possible

BEAMS BEARING ON MASONRY WALL

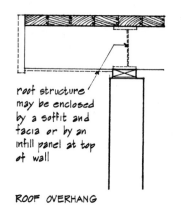
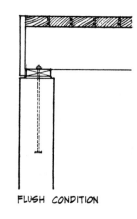

roof structure may be enclosed by a soffit and facia or by an infill panel at top of wall

ROOF OVERHANG

FLUSH CONDITION

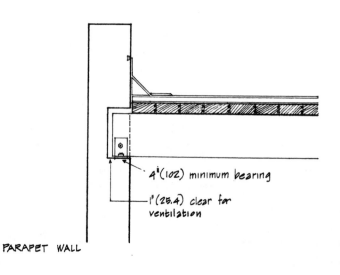

parapet condition

BEAMS FRAMING INTO MASONRY WALL

$4"$ (102) minimum bearing

$1"$ (25.4) clear for ventilation

PARAPET WALL

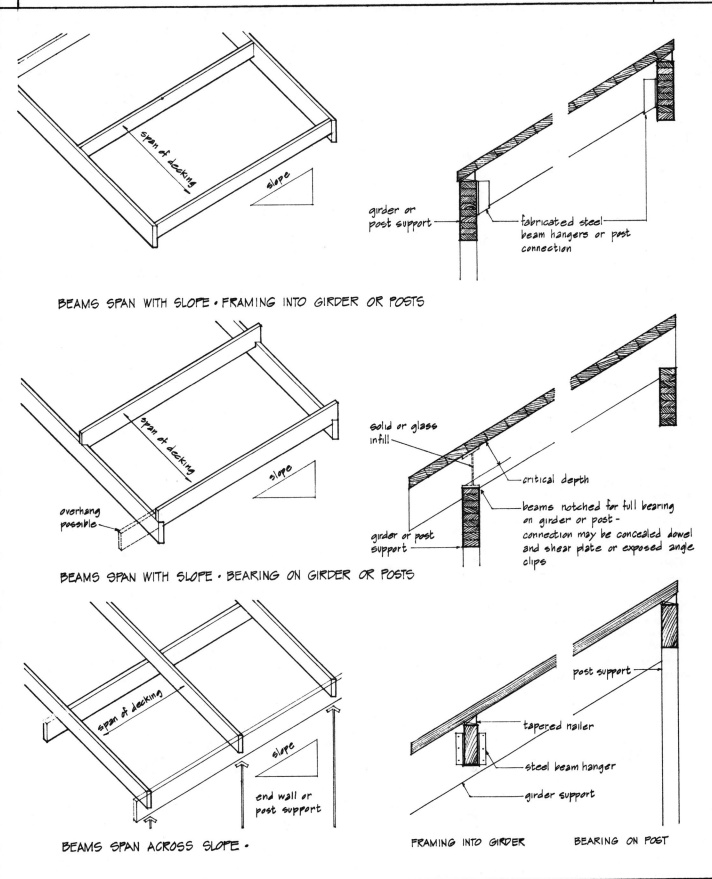

span of decking

slope

girder or post support

fabricated steel beam hangers or post connection

BEAMS SPAN WITH SLOPE · FRAMING INTO GIRDER OR POSTS

span of decking

slope

overhang possible

solid or glass infill

critical depth

girder or post support

beams notched for full bearing on girder or post - connection may be concealed dowel and shear plate or exposed angle clips

BEAMS SPAN WITH SLOPE · BEARING ON GIRDER OR POSTS

span of decking

slope

end wall or post support

post support

tapered nailer

steel beam hanger

girder support

BEAMS SPAN ACROSS SLOPE ·

FRAMING INTO GIRDER   BEARING ON POST

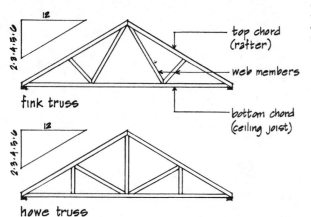

fink truss

top chord (rafter)

web members

bottom chord (ceiling joist)

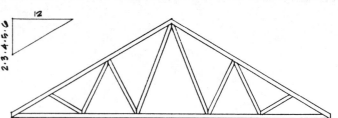

double fink truss

typical spans for 50 PSF roof load (244 kg/m²)
20'-60' (6.096 - 18.288)
spacing: 24"-48" o.c. (610 - 1219)

EXAMPLES OF PITCHED TRUSSES

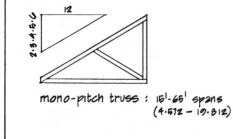

howe truss

mono-pitch truss : 15'-65' spans
(4.572 - 19.812)

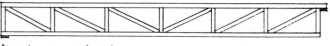

flat truss : 16'-48' spans (4.877 - 14.630)
16"-48" depths (406 - 1219)
top chord or bottom chord supported

A wood trussed rafter is a framework of wood framing members which form a light, strong, rigid structural unit capable of relatively large clear spans. Because of these clear spans, wood trussed rafters permit the use of non-load bearing interior partitions and flexibility in the design of a building's interior spaces.

Because of its triangulated structural framework, a wood trussed rafter's members resist primarily compressive and tensile forces and relatively small bending stresses unlike the normal roof rafter. Truss members, therefore, can be relatively small, normally 2x4 or 2x6.

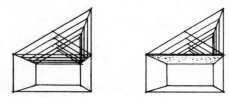

- truss members are connected by:
    - plywood gusset plates, glued and nailed
    - metal gang-nail plates
    - metal split-ring connectors (for heavy loads)

- wood trussed rafters should be engineered and are normally shop-fabricated

- trusses can accomodate insulation, and mechanical or electrical lines and equipment within their depth
- concentrated loads may require additional framing

- trusses may be girder or wall supported
- edge condition adaptable to parapet wall, flush roof edge or roof overhang

- fire-rating of truss construction depends on the applied ceiling finish and finish roofing

- a finish ceiling may be applied to the bottom chords to conceal the trusses or the trusses may be left exposed in which case the bottom chords would form an implied secondary plane

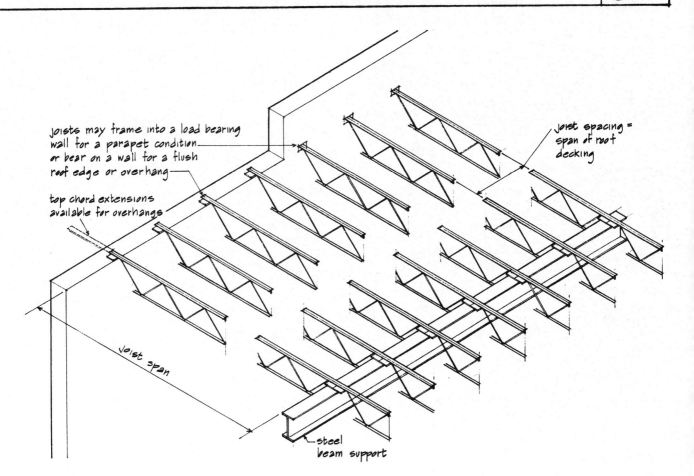

joists may frame into a load bearing wall for a parapet condition or bear on a wall for a flush roof edge or overhang

top chord extensions available for overhangs

joist span

steel beam support

joist spacing = span of roof decking

top and bottom chords parallel

top chord pitched one way

top chord pitched two ways

· standard pitch = 1/8" per foot (1%)

The open web steel joist system is similar in form and composition to the floor system utilizing the same type of steel joists.

* see 4·20/21/22
  for · steel joist sizes, spacing, and span
     · bearing and anchorage requirements
     (all roof joists must be anchored to their masonry support instead of every third joist as with floor joists - use anchor bolts instead of anchor bars if no parapet wall is present)
     · framing openings, bridging, and joist extensions for overhangs

For use as roof joists, longspan (LJ·LH) and deep longspan (DLJ·DLH) joists are available with single or double pitched chords.

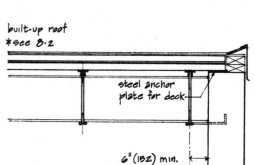

flash and counterflash over 4"(102) cant strip

8"(205)

minimum bearing: 4"(102) for J·H series joists

ceiling extension for attached ceilings only

PARAPET WALL · bearing wall

continuous bridging anchored to end wall

joists may be left exposed or ceiling may be applied to underside of joists or suspended from them

· **end wall**

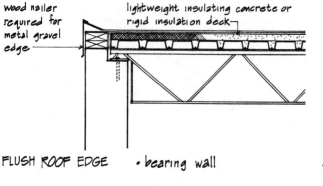

wood nailer required for metal gravel edge

lightweight insulating concrete or rigid insulation deck

FLUSH ROOF EDGE · bearing wall

built-up roof *see 8·2

steel anchor plate for deck

6"(152) min.

· **end wall**

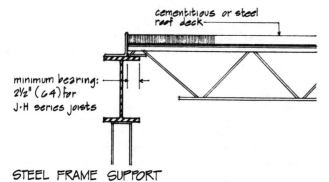

cementitious or steel roof deck

minimum bearing: 2½" (64) for J·H series joists

STEEL FRAME SUPPORT

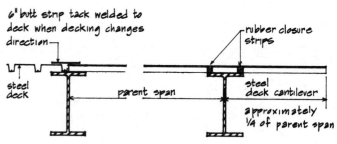

6" butt strip tack welded to deck when decking changes direction

rubber closure strips

steel deck

parent span

steel deck cantilever

approximately ¼ of parent span

· **steel roof deck bearing directly on steel frame**

Because of potential uplift forces due to wind:

- steel roof joists should be firmly anchored to their beam or wall support
  *see 4·22
- positive adhesion of roof deck to top chords of steel roof joists through tack welds or mechanical fastenings and adhesion of rigid insulation layer to the roof deck is critical
- roof edge is generally the weak spot: requires careful detailing of fascia, gravel stop, and edge flashing

- recommended minimum slope for flat, built-up roofs = ¼"/ft (2%)
- this slope may be achieved by the pitch of the top chords of the steel joists or by tapering the insulating deck

Open web steel joists may support a number of decking types: solid wood decking (*see 4·17), steel deck, and cementitious roof plank. Factors to consider in their use are: size (thickness, width, and length), span and load carrying capability, means of fastening to the support system, method of application of the finish roofing, edge conditions, allowance for expansion, roof openings, and desired fire-resistance rating.

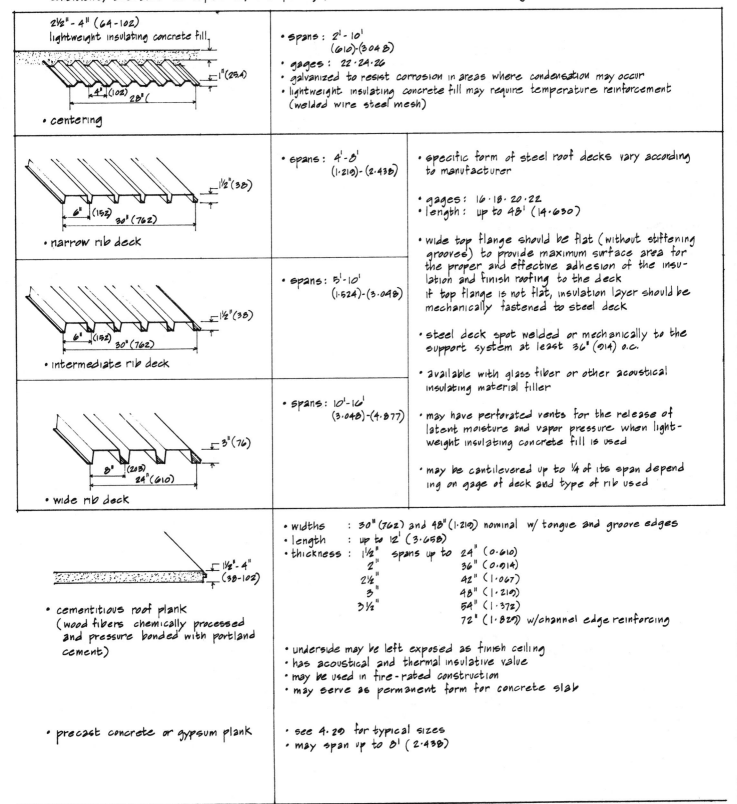

2½" - 4" (64-102)
lightweight insulating concrete fill

1" (25.4)

4" (102) 28'

• centering

• spans: 2'- 10'
     (610)-(3048)
• gages: 22·24·26
• galvanized to resist corrosion in areas where condensation may occur
• lightweight insulating concrete fill may require temperature reinforcement (welded wire steel mesh)

1½" (38)

6" (152) 30" (762)

• narrow rib deck

• spans: 4'-8'
     (1.219)-(2.438)

• specific form of steel roof decks vary according to manufacturer

• gages: 16·18·20·22
• length: up to 48' (14.630)

• wide top flange should be flat (without stiffening grooves) to provide maximum surface area for the proper and effective adhesion of the insulation and finish roofing to the deck
 if top flange is not flat, insulation layer should be mechanically fastened to steel deck

1½" (38)

6" (152) 30" (762)

• intermediate rib deck

• spans: 5'-10'
     (1.524)-(3.048)

• steel deck spot welded or mechanically to the support system at least 36" (914) o.c.

• available with glass fiber or other acoustical insulating material filler

3" (76)

8" (203) 24" (610)

• wide rib deck

• spans: 10'-16'
     (3.048)-(4.877)

• may have perforated vents for the release of latent moisture and vapor pressure when lightweight insulating concrete fill is used

• may be cantilevered up to ¼ of its span depending on gage of deck and type of rib used

1½" - 4"
(38-102)

• cementitious roof plank
 (wood fibers chemically processed and pressure bonded with portland cement)

• widths : 30" (762) and 48" (1.219) nominal w/ tongue and groove edges
• length : up to 12' (3.658)
• thickness : 1½"   spans up to 24" (0.610)
     2"   36" (0.914)
     2½"   42" (1.067)
     3"   48" (1.219)
     3½"   54" (1.372)
                       72" (1.829) w/channel edge reinforcing

• underside may be left exposed as finish ceiling
• has acoustical and thermal insulative value
• may be used in fire-rated construction
• may serve as permanent form for concrete slab

• precast concrete or gypsum plank

• see 4·29 for typical sizes
• may span up to 8' (2.438)

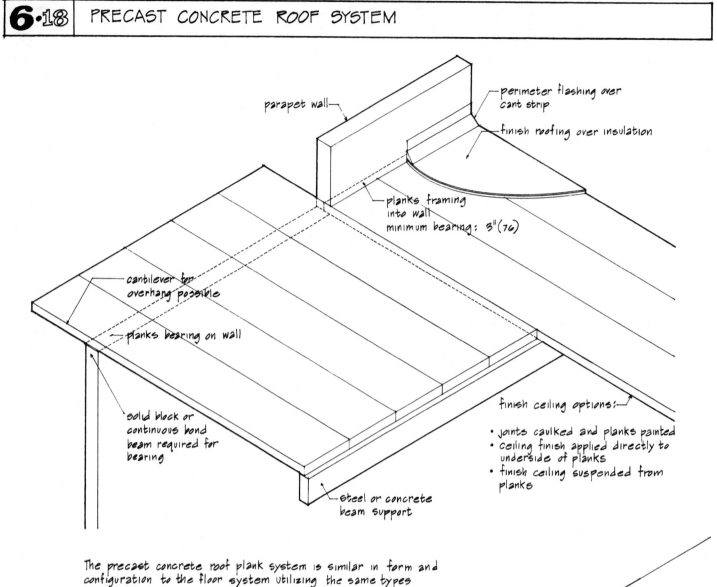

parapet wall

perimeter flashing over cant strip

finish roofing over insulation

planks framing into wall
minimum bearing: 3" (76)

cantilever for overhang possible

planks bearing on wall

solid block or continuous bond beam required for bearing

finish ceiling options:—
• joints caulked and planks painted
• ceiling finish applied directly to underside of planks
• finish ceiling suspended from planks

steel or concrete beam support

The precast concrete roof plank system is similar in form and configuration to the floor system utilizing the same types structural planking.

* see 4·28/29
   for: • types, sizes, span and load carrying capability of precast concrete planks
        • bearing and anchorage requirements
        • possibilities for and restrictions on roof openings and projections

Lightweight precast concrete or gypsum planks may be used for sloping roofs.
   • supported by light steel framing or trusses
   • steel angle stops are required to absorb downward thrust of planks and prevent them from slipping, especially for slopes above 4:12
   • decking requirements should be in accordance with the recommendations of the roofing manufacturer

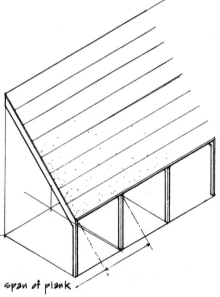

span of plank

DOORS & WINDOWS

Doors and windows provide for physical, visual, and light penetration into and through a building's interior while enclosing interior space and maintaining the continuity of the building's skin.

Doors and doorways provide means of access into a building's interior from the exterior and passage between interior spaces. Exterior doors must provide weathertight seals when closed, maintain the approximate insulative value of the building's exterior wall, and minimize the possibility of condensation forming on their interior surfaces. At the same time, they must be large enough to move through easily and accomodate the moving of interior furnishings and equipment. Ease of operation, privacy and security requirements, and the possible need for light, ventilation, and view must also be considered in a door's performance.

Interior doors provide for passage, visual privacy, and sound control between interior spaces. Doors into closet and storage spaces are primarily for visual screening although ventilation may also be a requirement.

Windows provide for light, ventilation, and view. As with exterior doors, windows should provide a weathertight seal when closed, have insulative value, and be free from condensation. There are many types and sizes of windows, the choice of which affects not only the physical appearance of a building but also the natural lighting, ventilation, view potential, and spatial quality of a building's interior.

From an exterior point of view, doors and windows are important compositional and scale-giving elements in a building's facade. The manner in which they break up a building's surface affects the massing, visual weight, scale, and articulation of the building's major planes, whether filling spaces within a skeleton structural frame, or puncturing a masonry wall.

The size, proportion, and location of doors and windows in a building must be carefully planned for so that adequate rough openings with properly-sized lintels can be built into the building's wall systems. Since door and window units are normally factory-built, manufacturers have standard sizes and rough opening requirements for the various door and window types.

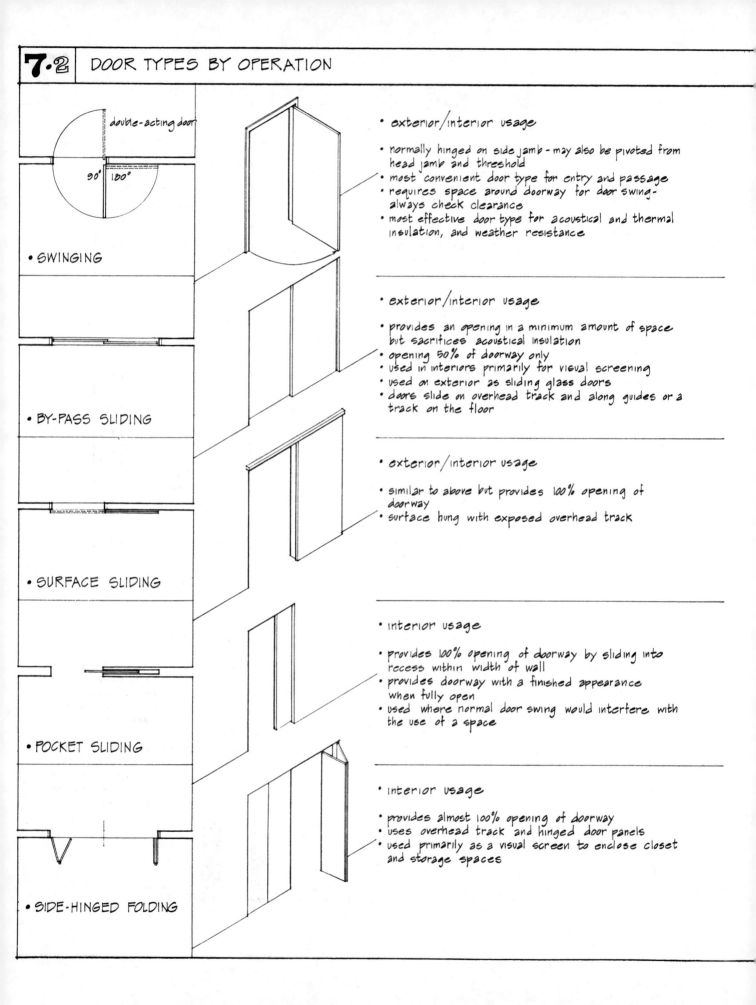

double-acting door

90° 180°

• SWINGING

- exterior/interior usage

- normally hinged on side jamb - may also be pivoted from head jamb and threshold
- most convenient door type for entry and passage
- requires space around doorway for door swing - always check clearance
- most effective door type for acoustical and thermal insulation, and weather resistance

• BY-PASS SLIDING

- exterior/interior usage

- provides an opening in a minimum amount of space but sacrifices acoustical insulation
- opening 50% of doorway only
- used in interiors primarily for visual screening
- used on exterior as sliding glass doors
- doors slide on overhead track and along guides or a track on the floor

• SURFACE SLIDING

- exterior/interior usage

- similar to above but provides 100% opening of doorway
- surface hung with exposed overhead track

• POCKET SLIDING

- interior usage

- provides 100% opening of doorway by sliding into recess within width of wall
- provides doorway with a finished appearance when fully open
- used where normal door swing would interfere with the use of a space

• SIDE-HINGED FOLDING

- interior usage

- provides almost 100% opening of doorway
- uses overhead track and hinged door panels
- used primarily as a visual screen to enclose closet and storage spaces

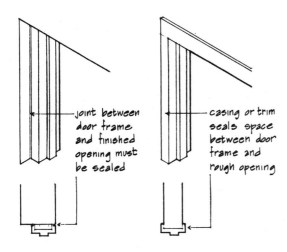

joint between door frame and finished opening must be sealed

casing or trim seals space between door frame and rough opening

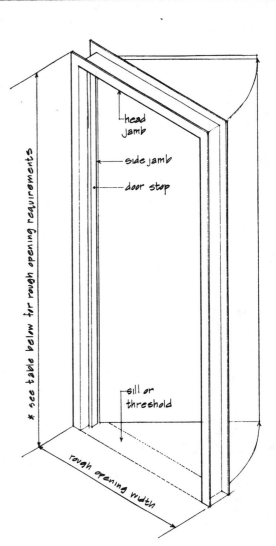

head jamb

side jamb

door stop

sill or threshold

* see table below for rough opening requirements

rough opening width

• the door frame detail determines the appearance of the opening, whether the frame is set within a finished opening or wrapped around a rough opening

• the type, size, and location of a door is related to the following :
  · physical access requirements
  · amount of usage anticipated
  · traffic pattern desired
  · weather-resistance, insulation, and durability requirements
  · light, view, and ventilation requirements
  · acoustical privacy desired
  · code (fire and exit) requirements
  · visual appearance desired

• the exact rough or masonry openings required depends on the manner in which the door frame is detailed - as a guideline, the following may be used:

  · rough openings (r.o.) in stud walls :
      width = nominal door width + 3½" (89)
      height = nominal door height + 3½" (89)
  · masonry openings (m.o.)
      width = nominal door width + 4" (102)
      height = nominal door height + 2"-4" (51)-(102)

BASIC ELEMENTS :

① door frame
  • head and side jambs with stops
  • sill or threshold
  • casing or trim if applicable

② the door itself

③ door hardware : primarily hinges and locksets - others include closers, panic hardware, weather-stripping, etc.

PHYSICAL DOOR TYPES :

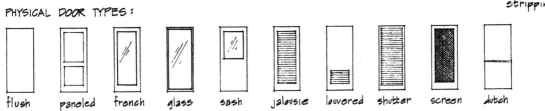

flush   paneled   french   glass   sash   jalousie   louvered   shutter   screen   dutch

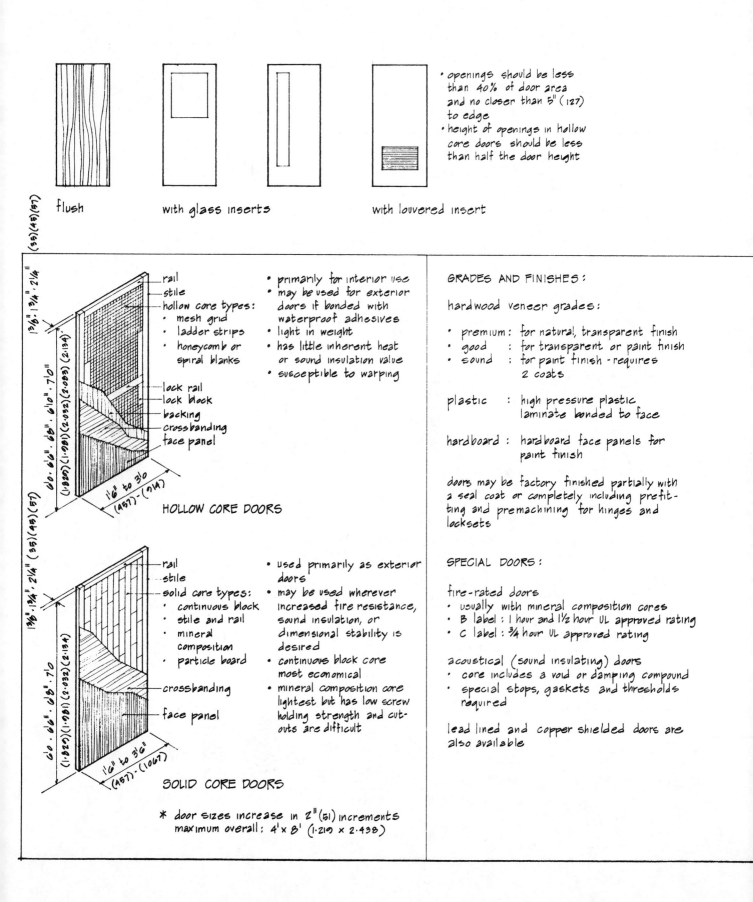

flush   with glass inserts   with louvered insert

- openings should be less than 40% of door area and no closer than 5" (127) to edge
- height of openings in hollow core doors should be less than half the door height

HOLLOW CORE DOORS

- rail
- stile
- hollow core types:
  - mesh grid
  - ladder strips
  - honeycomb or spiral blanks
- lock rail
- lock block
- backing
- crossbanding
- face panel

- primarily for interior use
- may be used for exterior doors if bonded with waterproof adhesives
- light in weight
- has little inherent heat or sound insulation value
- susceptible to warping

SOLID CORE DOORS

- rail
- stile
- solid core types:
  - continuous block
  - stile and rail
  - mineral composition
  - particle board
- crossbanding
- face panel

- used primarily as exterior doors
- may be used wherever increased fire resistance, sound insulation, or dimensional stability is desired
- continuous block core most economical
- mineral composition core lightest but has low screw holding strength and cut-outs are difficult

* door sizes increase in 2" (51) increments
maximum overall: 4' x 8' (1.219 x 2.438)

GRADES AND FINISHES:

hardwood veneer grades:

- premium: for natural, transparent finish
- good : for transparent or paint finish
- sound : for paint finish - requires 2 coats

plastic : high pressure plastic laminate bonded to face

hardboard : hardboard face panels for paint finish

doors may be factory finished partially with a seal coat or completely including prefitting and premachining for hinges and locksets

SPECIAL DOORS:

fire-rated doors
- usually with mineral composition cores
- B label : 1 hour and 1½ hour UL approved rating
- C label : ¾ hour UL approved rating

acoustical (sound insulating) doors
- core includes a void or damping compound
- special stops, gaskets and thresholds required

lead lined and copper shielded doors are also available

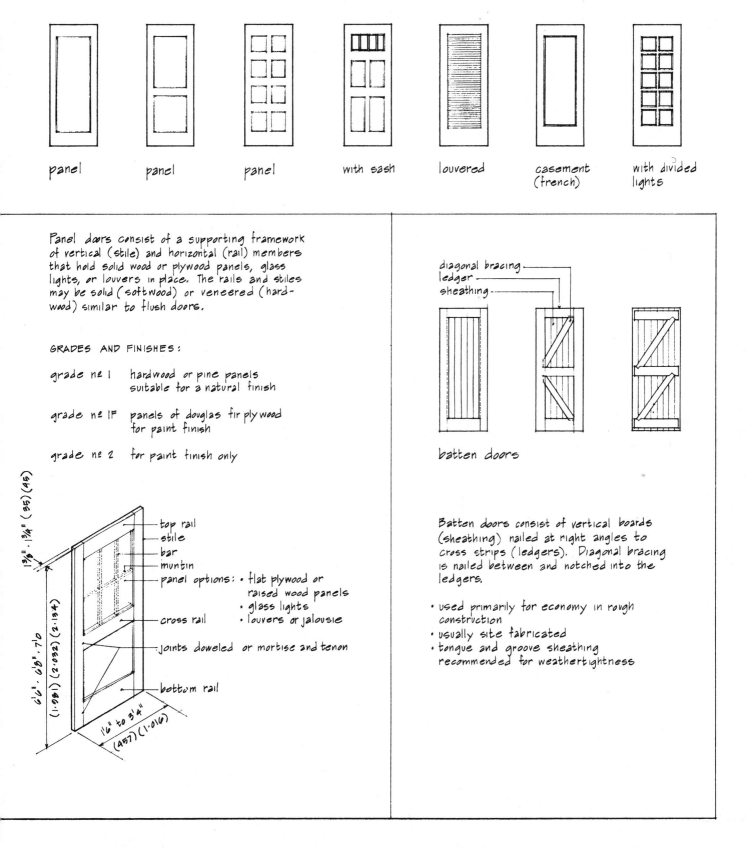

panel   panel   panel   with sash   louvered   casement (french)   with divided lights

Panel doors consist of a supporting framework of vertical (stile) and horizontal (rail) members that hold solid wood or plywood panels, glass lights, or louvers in place. The rails and stiles may be solid (softwood) or veneered (hardwood) similar to flush doors.

GRADES AND FINISHES:

grade nº 1   hardwood or pine panels suitable for a natural finish

grade nº 1F   panels of douglas fir plywood for paint finish

grade nº 2   for paint finish only

top rail
stile
bar
muntin
panel options: • flat plywood or raised wood panels
       • glass lights
       • louvers or jalousie
cross rail
joints doweled or mortise and tenon
bottom rail

1⅜" 1¾" (35)(45)
6'6" 6'8" 7'0 (1·981)(2·032)(2·134)
1'6" to 3'4" (457)(1·016)

diagonal bracing
ledger
sheathing

batten doors

Batten doors consist of vertical boards (sheathing) nailed at right angles to cross strips (ledgers). Diagonal bracing is nailed between and notched into the ledgers.

• used primarily for economy in rough construction
• usually site fabricated
• tongue and groove sheathing recommended for weathertightness

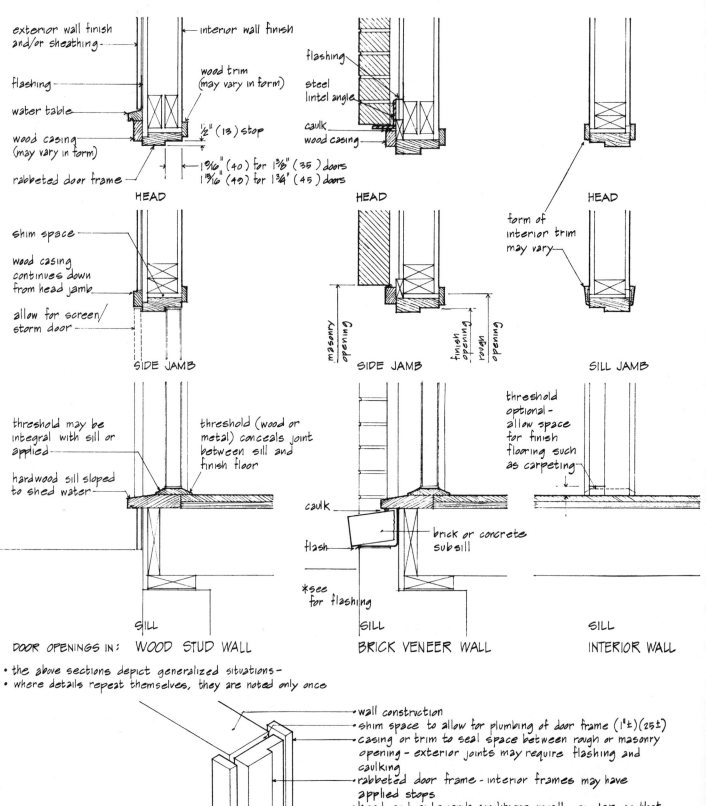

exterior wall finish and/or sheathing-

interior wall finish

wood trim (may vary in form)

flashing-

water table-

wood casing (may vary in form)

rabbeted door frame-

½" (13) stop

1⁹⁄₁₆" (40) for 1³⁄₈" (35) doors
1¹³⁄₁₆" (45) for 1³⁄₄" (45) doors

HEAD

flashing

steel lintel angle

caulk

wood casing

HEAD

form of interior trim may vary-

HEAD

shim space-

wood casing continues down from head jamb

allow for screen/ storm door-

SIDE JAMB

masonry opening

finish opening

rough opening

SIDE JAMB

SILL JAMB

threshold may be integral with sill or applied-

threshold (wood or metal) conceals joint between sill and finish floor

hardwood sill sloped to shed water-

SILL

caulk-

flash-

brick or concrete subsill

*see for flashing

SILL

threshold optional - allow space for finish flooring such as carpeting-

SILL

DOOR OPENINGS IN: **WOOD STUD WALL**   **BRICK VENEER WALL**   **INTERIOR WALL**

• the above sections depict generalized situations-
• where details repeat themselves, they are noted only once

wall construction
shim space to allow for plumbing of door frame (1"±)(25±)
casing or trim to seal space between rough or masonry opening - exterior joints may require flashing and caulking
rabbeted door frame - interior frames may have applied stops
head and side jamb conditions usually similar so that casing or trim profile is continuous around doorway

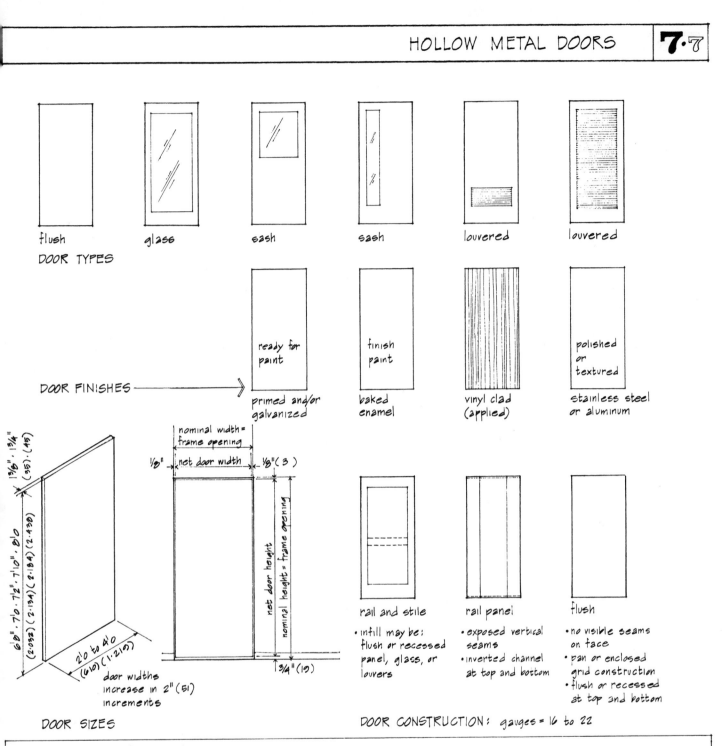

DOOR TYPES

flush   glass   sash   sash   louvered   louvered

DOOR FINISHES ⟶

ready for paint
primed and/or galvanized

finish paint
baked enamel

vinyl clad (applied)

polished or textured
stainless steel or aluminum

1⅜", 1¾" (35), (45)

6'0", 7'0", 7'2", 7'10", 8'0" (2·052) (2·134) (2·184) (2·438)

2'0 to 4'0 (610) (1·219)
door widths increase in 2" (51) increments

nominal width = frame opening
⅛" net door width ⅛" (3)
net door height   nominal height = frame opening
¾" (19)

DOOR SIZES

rail and stile
• infill may be: flush or recessed panel, glass, or louvers

rail panel
• exposed vertical seams
• inverted channel at top and bottom

flush
• no visible seams on face
• pan or enclosed grid construction
• flush or recessed at top and bottom

DOOR CONSTRUCTION: gauges = 16 to 22

FIRE DOORS: for use in fire-resistance rated construction (* see A·10)

U.L. label	rating	glazing [¼"(6) wire glass] permitted	general requirements for labelled fire doors
A	3 hr.	no glazing permitted	• maximum door size: 4'x10' (1·219 x 3·048)
B	1½ hr.	100 sq.in. (64516 mm²) per leaf	• door frame and hardware must have a rating similar to that of door
C	¾ hr.	1296 sq.in. (836170 mm²) per light 54" (1372) max. dimension	• door must be self-latching and be equipped with closers
D	1½ hr.	no glazing permitted	• louvers with fusible links permitted for B and C label doors - maximum area = 576 sq.in. (371635 mm²)
E	¾ hr.	720 sq.in. (464544 mm²) per light 54" (1372) max. dimension	• no louver and glass light combinations are allowed

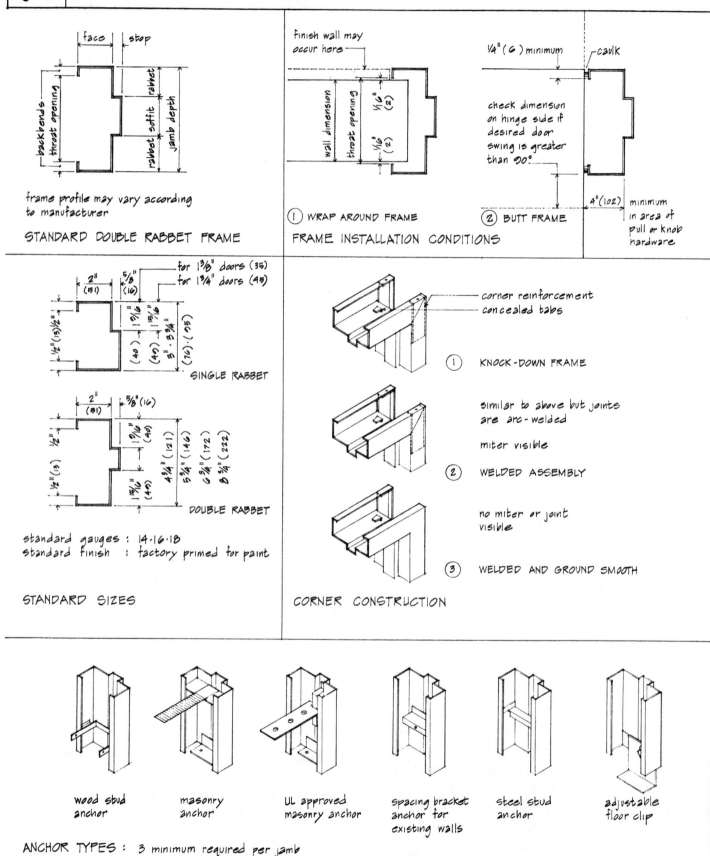

STANDARD DOUBLE RABBET FRAME

face | stop

backbends
throat opening
rabbet soffit
rabbet
jamb depth

frame profile may vary according to manufacturer

FRAME INSTALLATION CONDITIONS

finish wall may occur here

wall dimension
throat opening
1/16" (2)
1/16" (2)

① WRAP AROUND FRAME

1/4" (6) minimum — caulk

check dimension on hinge side if desired door swing is greater than 90°

② BUTT FRAME

4" (102) minimum in area of pull or knob hardware

STANDARD SIZES

2" (51) | 5/8" (16)
for 1 3/8" doors (35)
for 1 3/4" doors (45)
1/2" (13)
1 9/16" (40)
1 15/16" (49)
3" · 3 3/4" (76)

SINGLE RABBET

2" (51) | 5/8" (16)
1/2"
1/2" (13)
1 9/16" (40)
1 15/16" (49)
4 3/4" (121)
5 1/4" (146)
6 3/4" (172)
8 3/4" (222)

DOUBLE RABBET

standard gauges : 14·16·18
standard finish : factory primed for paint

CORNER CONSTRUCTION

corner reinforcement
concealed tabs

① KNOCK-DOWN FRAME

similar to above but joints are arc-welded
miter visible

② WELDED ASSEMBLY

no miter or joint visible

③ WELDED AND GROUND SMOOTH

wood stud anchor | masonry anchor | UL approved masonry anchor | spacing bracket anchor for existing walls | steel stud anchor | adjustable floor clip

ANCHOR TYPES : 3 minimum required per jamb

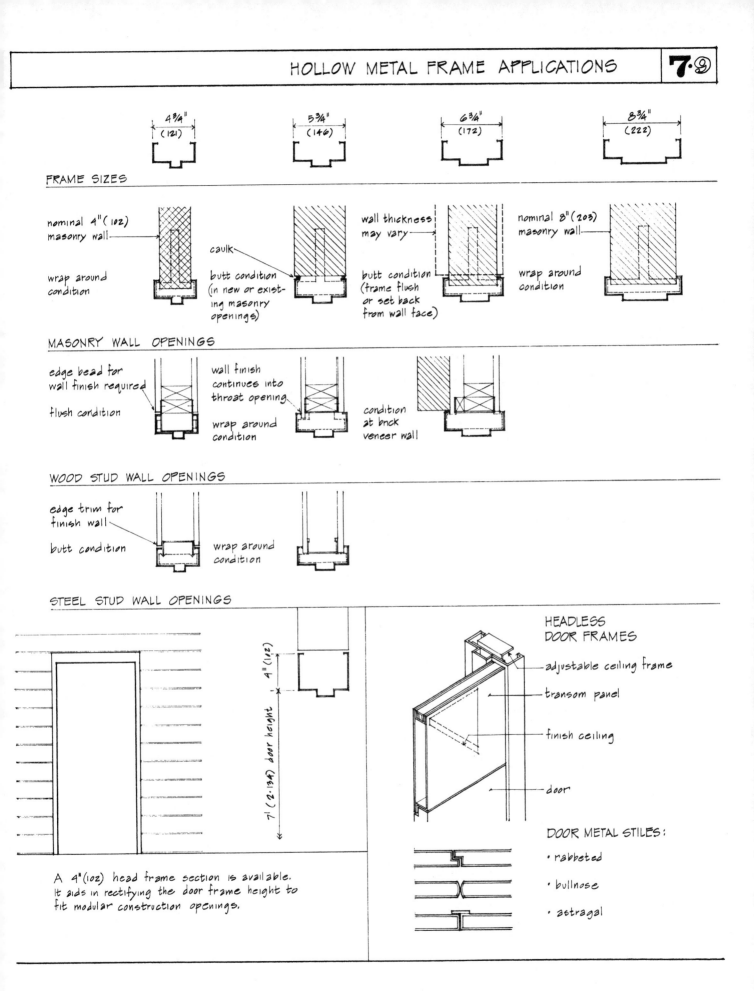

4 3/4" (121)   5 3/4" (146)   6 3/4" (172)   8 3/4" (222)

FRAME SIZES

nominal 4" (102) masonry wall

wrap around condition

caulk

butt condition (in new or existing masonry openings)

wall thickness may vary

butt condition (frame flush or set back from wall face)

nominal 8" (203) masonry wall

wrap around condition

MASONRY WALL OPENINGS

edge bead for wall finish required

flush condition

wall finish continues into throat opening

wrap around condition

condition at brick veneer wall

WOOD STUD WALL OPENINGS

edge trim for finish wall

butt condition

wrap around condition

STEEL STUD WALL OPENINGS

4" (102)

7' (2.134) door height

A 4" (102) head frame section is available. It aids in rectifying the door frame height to fit modular construction openings.

HEADLESS DOOR FRAMES

adjustable ceiling frame

transom panel

finish ceiling

door

DOOR METAL STILES:
• rabbeted
• bullnose
• astragal

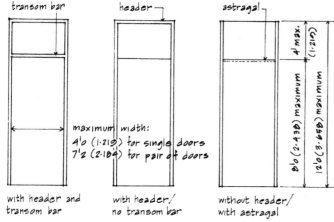

transom bar   header   astragal

4' max.

6'10 (2·436) maximum   12'0 (3·658) maximum

maximum width:
4'0 (1·219) for single doors
7'2 (2·184) for pair of doors

with header and transom bar   with header/ no transom bar   without header/ with astragal

TRANSOM PANEL CONDITIONS

Transom panels permit the continuation of the door plane up to the finish ceiling. They may have an A or B label fire-resistance rating.

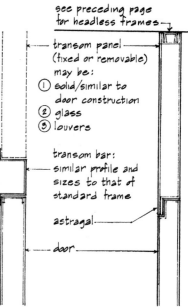

see preceding page for headless frames

transom panel (fixed or removable) may be:
① solid/similar to door construction
② glass
③ louvers

transom bar: similar profile and sizes to that of standard frame

astragal

door

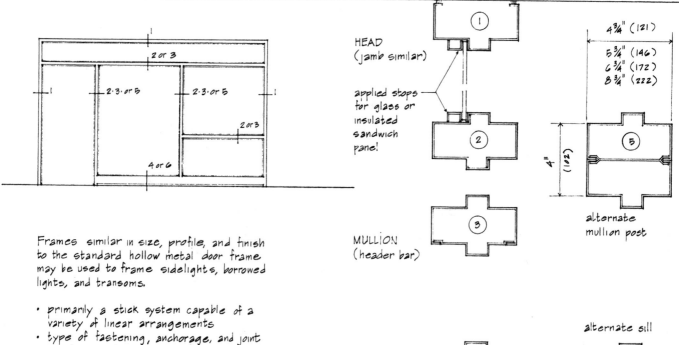

2 or 3

2·3·or 5   2·3·or 5

2 or 3

4 or 6

Frames similar in size, profile, and finish to the standard hollow metal door frame may be used to frame sidelights, borrowed lights, and transoms.

• primarily a stick system capable of a variety of linear arrangements
• type of fastening, anchorage, and joint used varies between manufacturers

HOLLOW METAL FRAMES FOR WINDOW WALLS

HEAD (jamb similar)

applied stops for glass or insulated sandwich pane!

①

②

③

MULLION (header bar)

4¾" (121)
5¾" (146)
6¾" (172)
8¾" (222)

⑤

4" (101)

alternate mullion post

alternate sill

④

⑥

2", 4", 6⅝" (51)(102)(212)

SILL

ENTRANCE DOOR TYPES:

typical widths:
2'6" (762)
3'0" (914)
3'6" (1067)

7'0 typical (2·134)

narrow stile   medium stile   wide stile

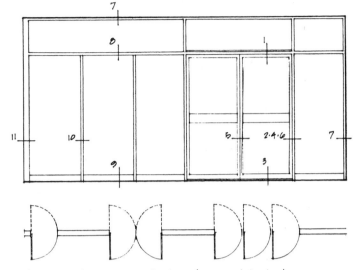

Factors to consider in determining finished appearance
include: • overall profile (face width and frame depth)
   • material and color of frame:
      aluminum, bronze, stainless steel
   • type and size of glass
   • composition of linear frame elements

• doors may be single or double acting, and banked in various ways

Consult manufacturer's data for profiles, sizes, application to metal or masonry surfaces, type of thermal break supplied,
insulation value of assembly, and provision for expansion and contraction of frame.

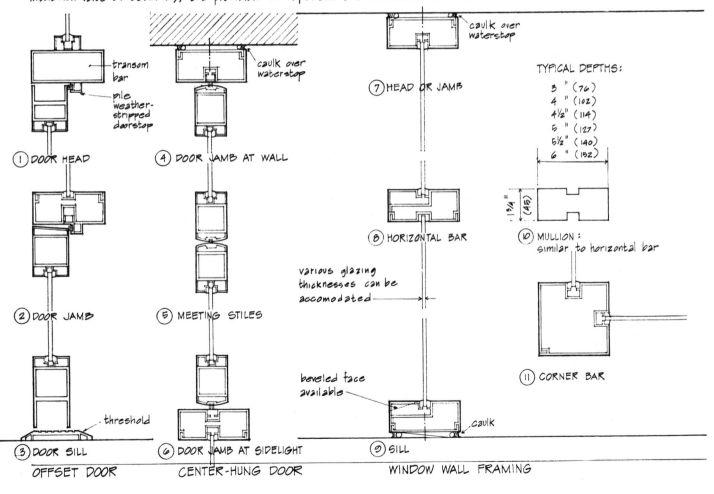

transom bar

pile weather-stripped doorstop

caulk over waterstop

caulk over waterstop

1 DOOR HEAD

4 DOOR JAMB AT WALL

7 HEAD OR JAMB

TYPICAL DEPTHS:
3 " (76)
4 " (102)
4½" (114)
5 " (127)
5½" (140)
6 " (152)

1¾" (45)

8 HORIZONTAL BAR

10 MULLION:
similar to horizontal bar

2 DOOR JAMB

5 MEETING STILES

various glazing thicknesses can be accomodated

11 CORNER BAR

beveled face available

threshold

caulk

3 DOOR SILL

6 DOOR JAMB AT SIDELIGHT

9 SILL

OFFSET DOOR   CENTER-HUNG DOOR   WINDOW WALL FRAMING

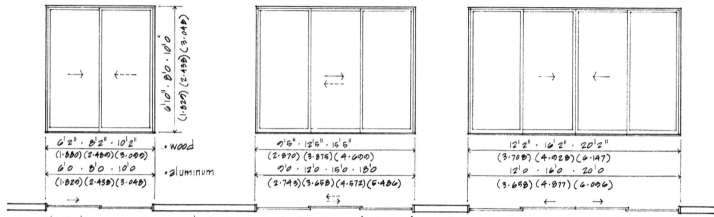

- above dimensions are nominal stock sizes · check with manufacturer for rough or masonry openings required
- as a guide: add 1" (25) to nominal width for rough openings, and 3" (76) for masonry openings

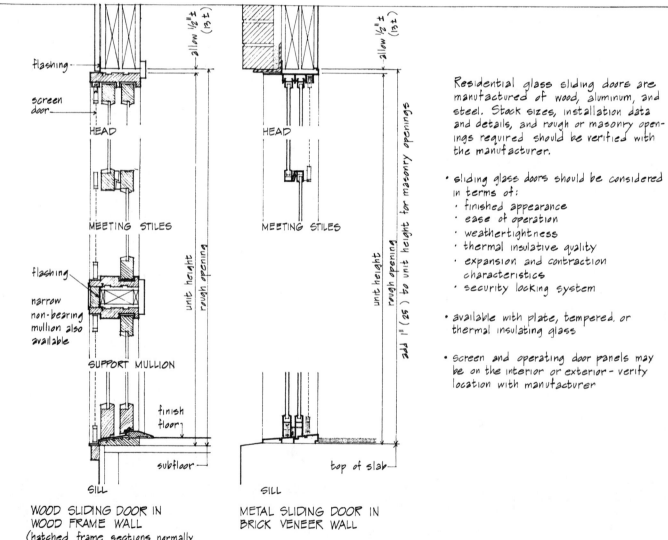

WOOD SLIDING DOOR IN
WOOD FRAME WALL
(hatched frame sections normally
supplied by manufacturer)

METAL SLIDING DOOR IN
BRICK VENEER WALL

Residential glass sliding doors are manufactured of wood, aluminum, and steel. Stock sizes, installation data and details, and rough or masonry openings required should be verified with the manufacturer.

- sliding glass doors should be considered in terms of:
  - finished appearance
  - ease of operation
  - weathertightness
  - thermal insulative quality
  - expansion and contraction characteristics
  - security locking system

- available with plate, tempered, or thermal insulating glass

- screen and operating door panels may be on the interior or exterior - verify location with manufacturer

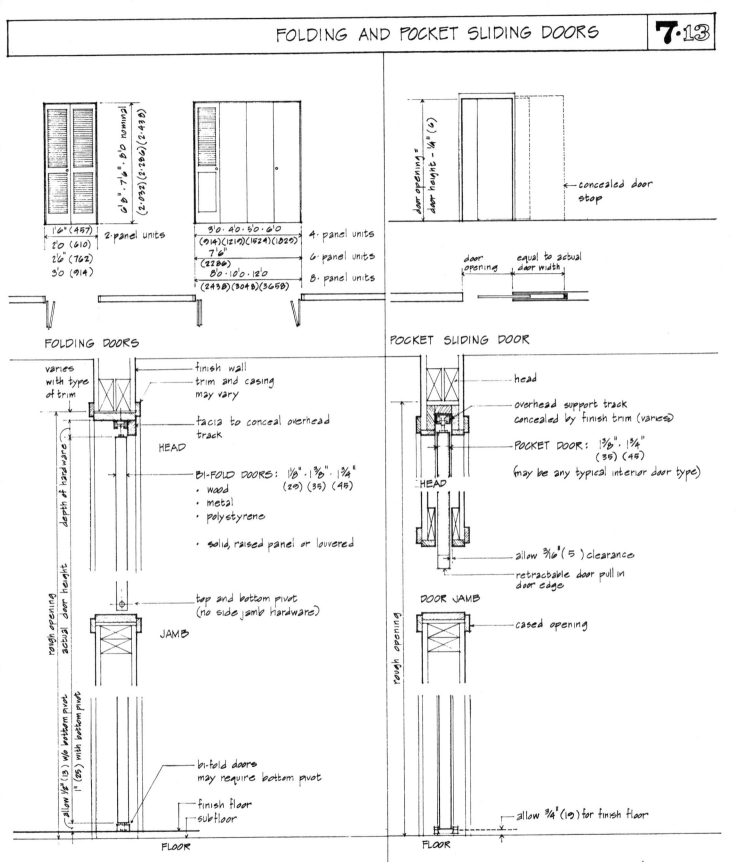

FOLDING DOORS

2 panel units
1'6" (457)
2'0 (610)
2'6" (762)
3'0 (914)

3'0 · 4'0 · 5'0 · 6'0
(914)(1219)(1524)(1829)   4 panel units
7'6"
(2286)   6 panel units
8'0 · 10'0 · 12'0
(2438)(3048)(3658)   8 panel units

6'0" · 7'6" · 8'0 nominal
(2032)(2286)(2438)

POCKET SLIDING DOOR

door opening = door height – ¼" (6)

concealed door stop

door opening   equal to actual door width

FOLDING DOORS

varies with type of trim

finish wall
trim and casing may vary

HEAD

facia to conceal overhead track

BI·FOLD DOORS: 1⅛" · 1⅜" · 1¾"
                (29) (35) (45)
· wood
· metal
· polystyrene

· solid, raised panel or louvered

depth of hardware

rough opening

actual door height

top and bottom pivot (no side jamb hardware)

JAMB

(allow ½" (13) w/o bottom pivot)
1" (25) with bottom pivot

bi-fold doors may require bottom pivot

finish floor
subfloor

FLOOR

POCKET SLIDING DOOR

head

overhead support track concealed by finish trim (varies)

POCKET DOOR: 1⅜" · 1¾"
              (35) (45)
(may be any typical interior door type)

HEAD

allow 3/16" (5) clearance

retractable door pull in door edge

DOOR JAMB

cased opening

rough opening

allow ¾" (19) for finish floor

FLOOR

Check with door manufacturer for standard sizes, hardware dimensions, and installation data. Generalized conditions for wood frame construction are illustrated. Details for hollow metal doors and frames are similar.

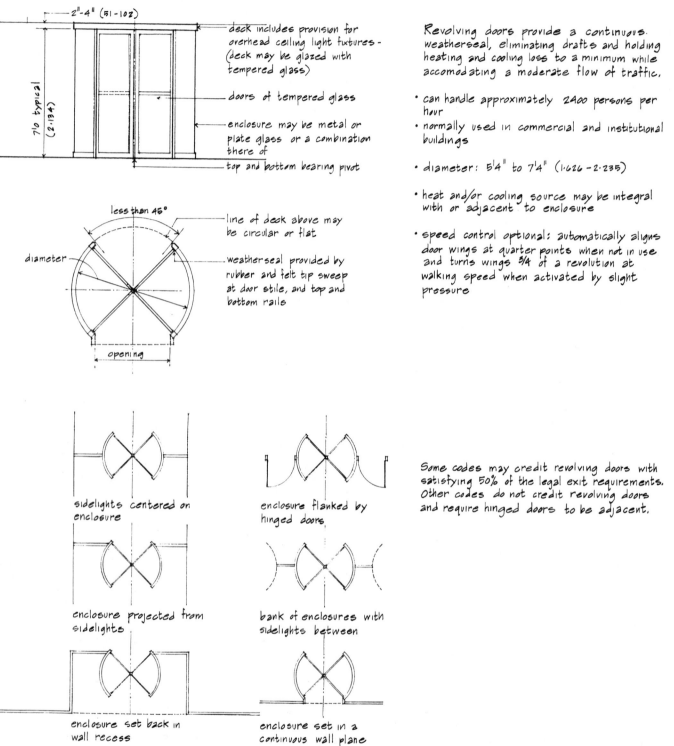

2"-4" (51-102)

deck includes provision for overhead ceiling light fixtures - (deck may be glazed with tempered glass)

doors of tempered glass

7'0 typical (2·134)

enclosure may be metal or plate glass or a combination there of

top and bottom bearing pivot

less than 45°

diameter

line of deck above may be circular or flat

weatherseal provided by rubber and felt tip sweep at door stile, and top and bottom rails

opening

sidelights centered on enclosure

enclosure projected from sidelights

enclosure set back in wall recess

enclosure flanked by hinged doors

bank of enclosures with sidelights between

enclosure set in a continuous wall plane

Revolving doors provide a continuous weatherseal, eliminating drafts and holding heating and cooling loss to a minimum while accomodating a moderate flow of traffic.

• can handle approximately 2400 persons per hour

• normally used in commercial and institutional buildings

• diameter: 5'4" to 7'4" (1·626 - 2·235)

• heat and/or cooling source may be integral with or adjacent to enclosure

• speed control optional: automatically aligns door wings at quarter points when not in use and turns wings 3/4 of a revolution at walking speed when activated by slight pressure

Some codes may credit revolving doors with satisfying 50% of the legal exit requirements. Other codes do not credit revolving doors and require hinged doors to be adjacent.

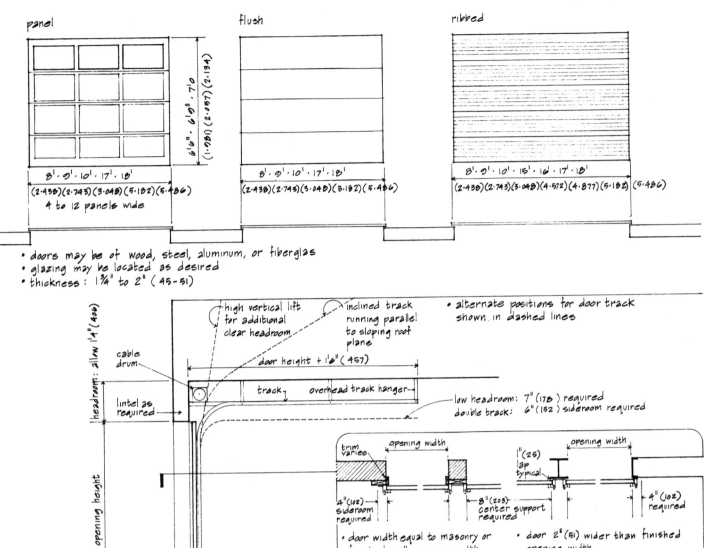

panel

8'·9'·10'·17'·18'
(2·438)(2·743)(3·048)(5·182)(5·486)
4 to 12 panels wide

6'6"·6'9"·7'0 (1·981)(2·057)(2·134)

flush

8'·9'·10'·17'·18'
(2·438)(2·743)(3·048)(5·182)(5·486)

ribbed

8'·9'·10'·15'·16'·17'·18'
(2·438)(2·743)(3·048)(4·572)(4·877)(5·182)(5·486)

- doors may be of wood, steel, aluminum, or fiberglas
- glazing may be located as desired
- thickness: 1¾" to 2" (45-51)

high vertical lift for additional clear headroom

inclined track running parallel to sloping roof plane

- alternate positions for door track shown in dashed lines

headroom: allow 1'4"(406)

cable drum

lintel as required

door height + 1'6" (457)

track | overhead track hanger

low headroom: 7" (178) required
double track: 6" (152) sideroom required

door opening height

trim varies

opening width

opening width

1"(25) lap typical

4"(102) sideroom required

8"(203) center support required

4"(102) required

- door width equal to masonry or finished wall opening width
- track anchored to 2"(51) thick wood casing

WOOD JAMBS

- door 2"(51) wider than finished opening width
- track anchod to steel angles or channels

STEEL JAMBS

- overhead door operation may be manual, by chain-hoist, or by electric motor
- chain-hoists and motor operations may require additional side, head, and back room
- side, head, and back room requirements, and installation should be verified with manufacturer

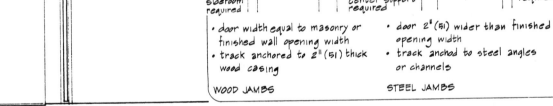

- industrial overhead doors are available up to 25' (7·620) in height and width not to exceed 340 S.F. in area (31.6 m²)
- wide doors require heavy duty lintels - may also require moveable door post supports

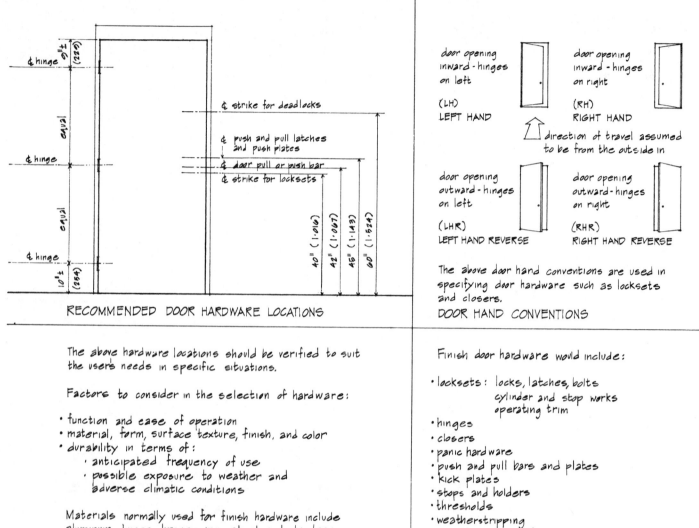

RECOMMENDED DOOR HARDWARE LOCATIONS

DOOR HAND CONVENTIONS

The above door hand conventions are used in specifying door hardware such as locksets and closers.

The above hardware locations should be verified to suit the user's needs in specific situations.

Factors to consider in the selection of hardware:

- function and ease of operation
- material, form, surface texture, finish, and color
- durability in terms of:
  - anticipated frequency of use
  - possible exposure to weather and adverse climatic conditions

Materials normally used for finish hardware include aluminum, brass, bronze, iron, steel and stainless steel.

Finish door hardware would include:

- locksets: locks, latches, bolts cylinder and stop works operating trim
- hinges
- closers
- panic hardware
- push and pull bars and plates
- kick plates
- stops and holders
- thresholds
- weatherstripping
- door tracks and hangers

HARDWARE FINISHES

BHMA CODE NO.	US NO.	FINISH
600	US P	primed for painting
605	US 3	bright brass, clear coated
606	US 4	satin brass, clear coated
612	US 10	satin bronze, clear coated
613	US 10B	oxidized satin bronze, oil rubbed
618	US 14	bright nickel plated, clear coated
619	US 15	satin nickel plated, clear coated
622	US 19	flat black coated
623	US 20	light oxidized bright bronze, clear coated
624	US 20D	dark oxidized statuary bronze, clear coated
625	US 26	bright chromium plated
626	US 26D	satin chromium plated
628	US 28	satin aluminum, clear anodized
629	US 32	bright stainless steel
630	US 32D	satin stainless steel

- Builders Hardware Manufacturers Association (BHMA) code symbols are given with the nearest US equivalent

- there are other finishes - verify available finishes with manufacturer

- consider exposure to weather, and climatic conditions in the selection of hardware material and finish - aluminum and stainless steel recommended in humid climates and where corrosive conditions exist (ie. sea air)

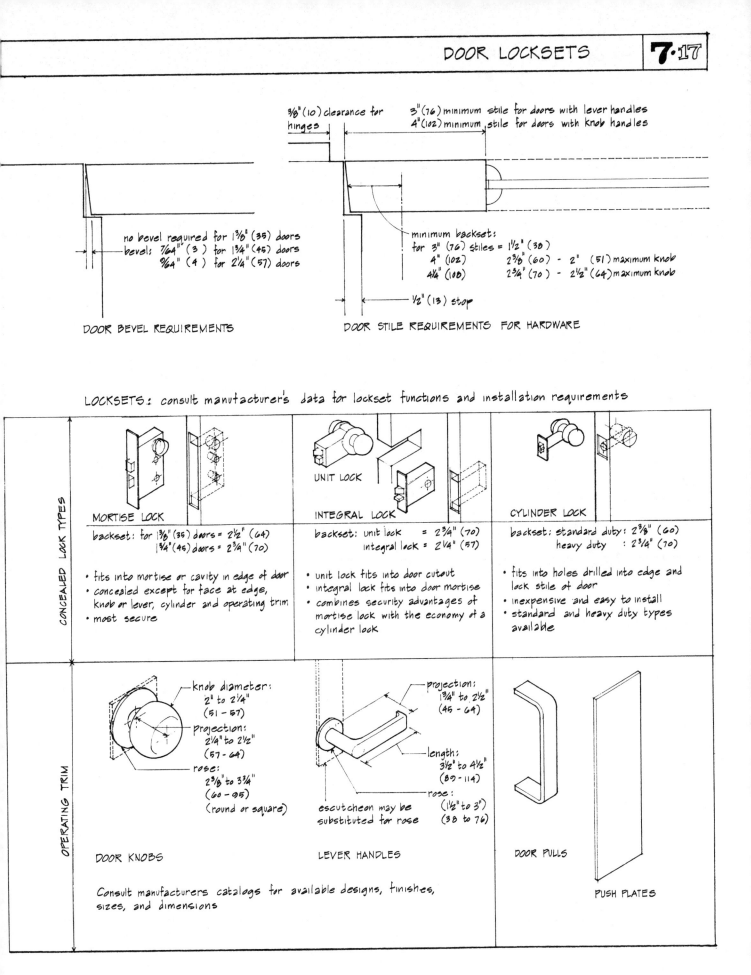

3/8" (10) clearance for hinges

3" (76) minimum stile for doors with lever handles
4" (102) minimum stile for doors with knob handles

no bevel required for 1 3/8" (35) doors
bevel: 7/64" (3) for 1 3/4" (45) doors
       9/64" (4) for 2 1/4" (57) doors

minimum backset:
for 3" (76) stiles = 1 1/2" (38)
    4" (102)   2 3/8" (60) - 2" (51) maximum knob
    4 1/4" (108)   2 3/4" (70) - 2 1/2" (64) maximum knob

1/2" (13) stop

DOOR BEVEL REQUIREMENTS   DOOR STILE REQUIREMENTS FOR HARDWARE

LOCKSETS: consult manufacturer's data for lockset functions and installation requirements

CONCEALED LOCK TYPES

MORTISE LOCK

backset: for 1 3/8" (35) doors = 2 1/2" (64)
         1 3/4" (45) doors = 2 3/4" (70)

• fits into mortise or cavity in edge of door
• concealed except for face at edge, knob or lever, cylinder and operating trim
• most secure

UNIT LOCK

INTEGRAL LOCK

backset: unit lock   = 2 3/4" (70)
         integral lock = 2 1/4" (57)

• unit lock fits into door cutout
• integral lock fits into door mortise
• combines security advantages of mortise lock with the economy of a cylinder lock

CYLINDER LOCK

backset: standard duty: 2 3/8" (60)
         heavy duty   : 2 3/4" (70)

• fits into holes drilled into edge and lock stile of door
• inexpensive and easy to install
• standard and heavy duty types available

OPERATING TRIM

DOOR KNOBS

knob diameter:
2" to 2 1/4"
(51 - 57)

projection:
2 1/4" to 2 1/2"
(57 - 64)

rose:
2 3/8" to 3 3/4"
(60 - 95)
(round or square)

Consult manufacturers catalogs for available designs, finishes, sizes, and dimensions

LEVER HANDLES

projection:
1 3/4" to 2 1/2"
(45 - 64)

length:
3 1/2" to 4 1/2"
(89 - 114)

rose:
(1 1/2" to 3")
(38 to 76)

escutcheon may be substituted for rose

DOOR PULLS

PUSH PLATES

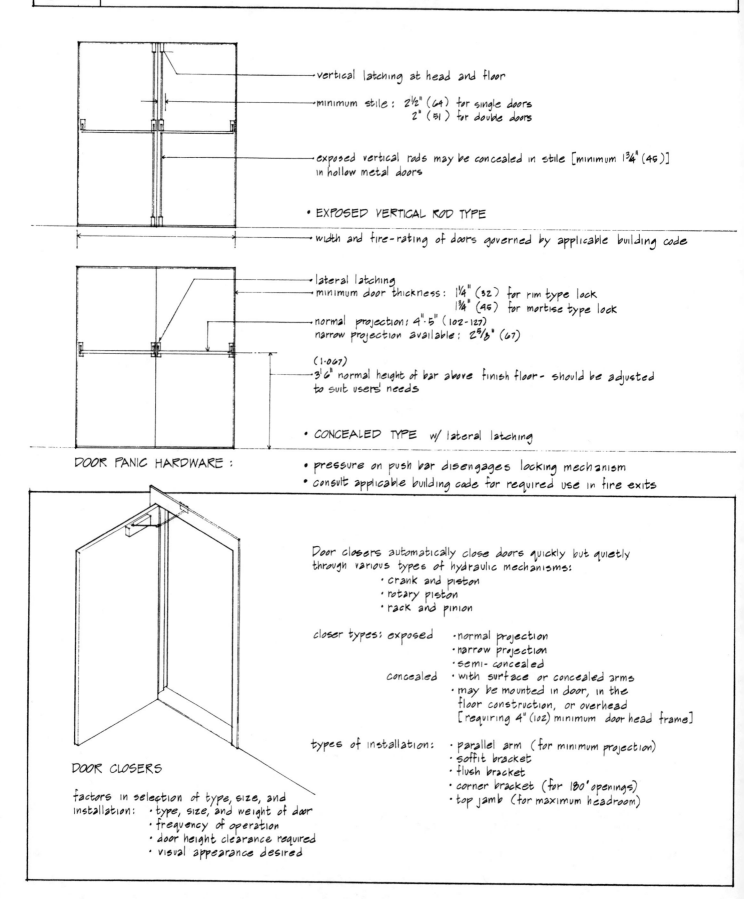

— vertical latching at head and floor

— minimum stile: 2½" (64) for single doors
2" (51) for double doors

— exposed vertical rods may be concealed in stile [minimum 1¾" (45)] in hollow metal doors

• EXPOSED VERTICAL ROD TYPE

— width and fire-rating of doors governed by applicable building code

— lateral latching
— minimum door thickness: 1¼" (32) for rim type lock
1¾" (45) for mortise type lock

— normal projection: 4"·5" (102-127)
narrow projection available: 2⅝" (67)

(1·067)
— 3'6" normal height of bar above finish floor- should be adjusted to suit users' needs

• CONCEALED TYPE w/ lateral latching

DOOR PANIC HARDWARE :

• pressure on push bar disengages locking mechanism
• consult applicable building code for required use in fire exits

Door closers automatically close doors quickly but quietly through various types of hydraulic mechanisms:
· crank and piston
· rotary piston
· rack and pinion

closer types: exposed   ·normal projection
·narrow projection
·semi-concealed
concealed   ·with surface or concealed arms
·may be mounted in door, in the floor construction, or overhead [requiring 4" (102) minimum door head frame]

types of installation: · parallel arm (for minimum projection)
· soffit bracket
· flush bracket
· corner bracket (for 180° openings)
· top jamb (for maximum headroom)

DOOR CLOSERS

factors in selection of type, size, and installation: · type, size, and weight of door
· frequency of operation
· door height clearance required
· visual appearance desired

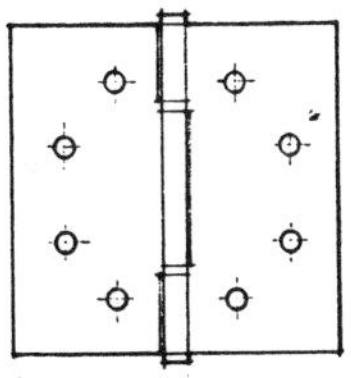

template

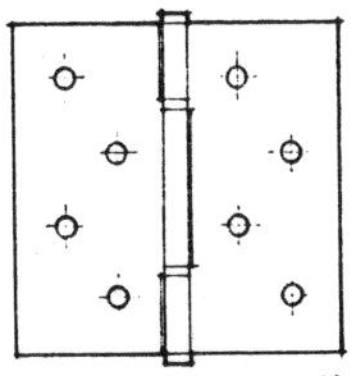

non-template (for wood doors)

Butt hinges are mortised into the door edge and jamb so that only the knuckle is visible when the door is closed.

The pin in the knuckle may be removable (loose), or fixed (non-rising). Self-locking pins which cannot be removed when the door is closed are also available for security.

Butt hinges are normally used with wood and hollow metal doors and frames.

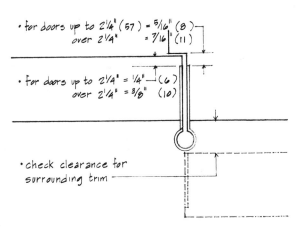

• for doors up to 2¼" (57) = 5/16" (8)
  over 2¼" = 7/16" (11)

• for doors up to 2¼" = ¼" (6)
  over 2¼" = 3/8" (10)

• check clearance for surrounding trim

TABLE FOR HINGE SIZE: width as determined by door thickness and clearance required
height as determind by door width and thickness

DOOR THICKNESS	DOOR WIDTH	CLEARANCE REQUIRED	HINGE HEIGHT	HINGE WIDTH
¾" to 1⅛" (19-29)	to 24" (610)		2½" (64)	
⅞" to 1⅛" (22-29)	to 36" (914)		3" (76)	
1⅜" (35)	to 36"	1¼" (32)	3"	3½" (89)
		1¾" (35)	3"	4" (102)
1¾" (45)	to 36"	1" (25)	4" (102)	4"
	over 36"	1½" (38)	4½" (114)	4½" (114)
		2" (51)		5" (127)
2¼" (57)	to 42" (1.067)	1" (25)	5" (127)	5"
	over 42"	2" (51)	6" (152)	6" (152)

Several types of hinges are made for special purposes. They include the following:

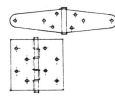

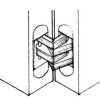

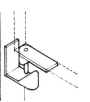

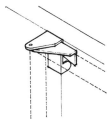

• surface hinges:

• where mortising of door or jamb is not possible (ie. channel iron jambs, kalamein doors) or where the visual appearance is desired

• invisible hinges:

• completely concealed when door is closed
• mortised into door edge and jamb

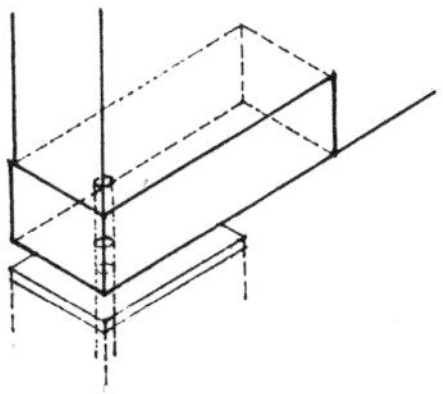

• floor hinges:

• used with mortise pivots at door heads for double-acting doors
• may be provided with door closer mechanism

• gravity type pivots:

• used with double-acting swing doors (ie. cafe or dwarf doors)

• pivot hinges:

• for use with cabinet doors
• usually supplied by manufacturer with pre-hung doors

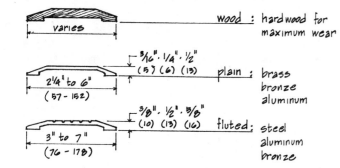

wood : hardwood for maximum wear

3/16", 1/4", 1/2"
(5) (6) (13)

2 1/4" to 6"
(57 - 152)

plain : brass
bronze
aluminum

3/8", 1/2", 5/8"
(10) (13) (16)

3" to 7"
(76 - 178)

fluted: steel
aluminum
bronze

varies

Thresholds conceal joints between flooring materials at doorways and act as a weather barrier at exterior sills

• recessed on the underside to fit snugly against flooring or sill
• when installed at exterior sills, joint sealant applied to underside for a tight seal
• metal thresholds may be cast with, covered, or filled with abrasive material to provide a non-slip surface

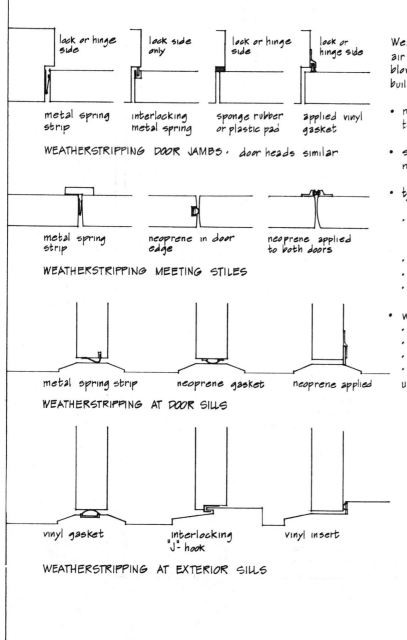

lock or hinge side

lock side only

lock or hinge side

lock or hinge side

metal spring strip

interlocking metal spring

sponge rubber or plastic pad

applied vinyl gasket

WEATHERSTRIPPING DOOR JAMBS· door heads similar

metal spring strip

neoprene in door edge

neoprene applied to both doors

WEATHERSTRIPPING MEETING STILES

metal spring strip

neoprene gasket

neoprene applied

WEATHERSTRIPPING AT DOOR SILLS

vinyl gasket

interlocking "J"-hook

vinyl insert

WEATHERSTRIPPING AT EXTERIOR SILLS

Weatherstripping of exterior doors reduces air infiltration, and prevents dust and wind-blown rain from penetrating the interior of a building.

• may be applied to door edge or face, or to the door frame and threshold

• should be durable under extended usage, non-corrosive, and easily replaceable

• types of weatherstripping include:

· metal spring tensioned strip (aluminum, bronze, stainless or galvanized steel)
· vinyl and neoprene gaskets
· sponge plastic or rubber
· woven pile

• weatherstripping for:
· sliding glass doors
· glass entrance doors
· revolving doors
· garage and overhead doors
usually supplied by door manufacturer

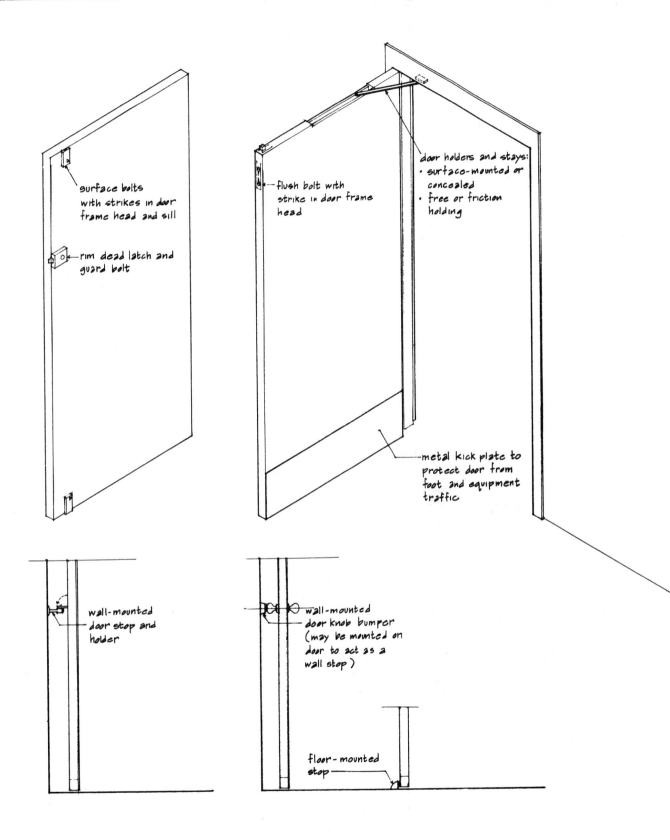

surface bolts
with strikes in door
frame head and sill

rim dead latch and
guard bolt

flush bolt with
strike in door frame
head

door holders and stays:
· surface-mounted or
  concealed
· free or friction
  holding

metal kick plate to
protect door from
foot and equipment
traffic

wall-mounted
door stop and
holder

wall-mounted
door knob bumper
(may be mounted on
door to act as a
wall stop)

floor-mounted
stop

			ventilation	
		FIXED	0%	• consists of a frame and glazed stationary sash • when used in conjunction with operable window units, thickness of fixed sash should approximate cross-sectional dimensions of the adjacent operating sash
		CASEMENT	100%	• operating sash side-hinged, usually swinging outward pair of operating sash may close on themselves or on a vertical mullion • able to direct incoming ventilation
		AWNING	100%	• similar to casement windows but hinged at top (awning type) or bottom (hopper type) • may be stacked vertically with sash closing on themselves or on meeting rails • able to direct incoming ventilation
		HOPPER	100%	
		SLIDING	50-66%	• may consist of 2 sash of which one slides horizontally (50% ventilation) or 3 sash of which the middle is fixed while the other 2 slide (66% ventilation)
		DOUBLE-HUNG	50%	• sash move vertically, held in desired position by friction fit against the window frame or by various balancing devices • single-hung windows are similar with one sash fixed
		JALOUSIE	100%	• similar to awning type windows • may be opaque or transparent • used generally in warm climates where ventilation is desired along with a flush appearance • able to direct ventilation
		PIVOTING	100%	• similar to casement window but a top and bottom pivot is used instead of side hinges • screening not possible

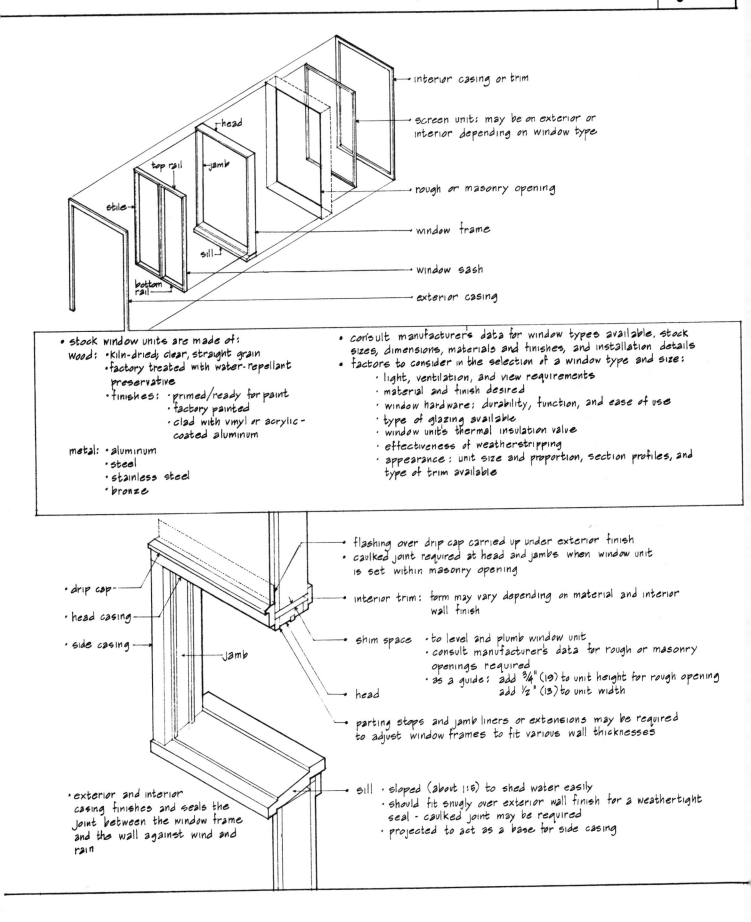

- interior casing or trim
- screen unit: may be on exterior or interior depending on window type
- rough or masonry opening
- window frame
- window sash
- exterior casing

head
top rail
jamb
stile
sill
bottom rail

- stock window units are made of:
  wood: • kiln-dried; clear, straight grain
  • factory treated with water-repellant preservative
  • finishes: • primed/ready for paint
  • factory painted
  • clad with vinyl or acrylic-coated aluminum

  metal: • aluminum
  • steel
  • stainless steel
  • bronze

- consult manufacturer's data for window types available, stock sizes, dimensions, materials and finishes, and installation details
- factors to consider in the selection of a window type and size:
  · light, ventilation, and view requirements
  · material and finish desired
  · window hardware: durability, function, and ease of use
  · type of glazing available
  · window unit's thermal insulation value
  · effectiveness of weatherstripping
  · appearance: unit size and proportion, section profiles, and type of trim available

· drip cap
· head casing
· side casing
Jamb

- flashing over drip cap carried up under exterior finish
- caulked joint required at head and jambs when window unit is set within masonry opening
- interior trim: form may vary depending on material and interior wall finish
- shim space · to level and plumb window unit
  · consult manufacturer's data for rough or masonry openings required
  · as a guide: add ¾" (19) to unit height for rough opening add ½" (13) to unit width
- head
- parting stops and jamb liners or extensions may be required to adjust window frames to fit various wall thicknesses

· exterior and interior casing finishes and seals the joint between the window frame and the wall against wind and rain

- sill · sloped (about 1:5) to shed water easily
  · should fit snugly over exterior wall finish for a weathertight seal - caulked joint may be required
  · projected to act as a base for side casing

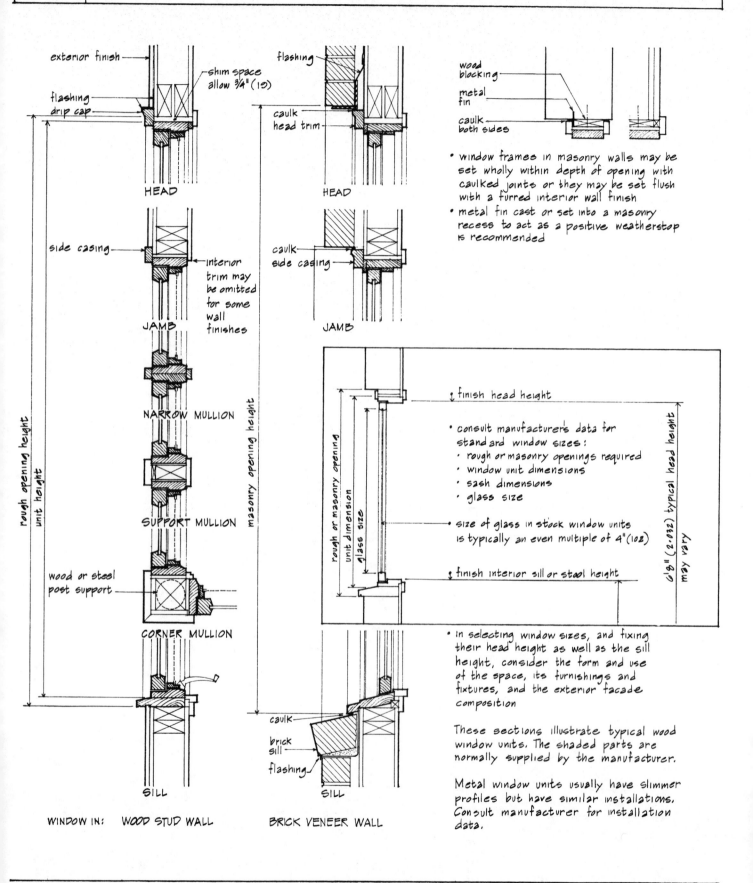

exterior finish
shim space allow ¾" (19)
flashing drip cap
HEAD

side casing
interior trim may be omitted for some wall finishes
JAMB

NARROW MULLION

SUPPORT MULLION

wood or steel post support
CORNER MULLION

rough opening height
unit height

SILL

WINDOW IN: WOOD STUD WALL

flashing
caulk
head trim
HEAD

caulk
side casing
JAMB

masonry opening height

caulk
brick sill
flashing
SILL

BRICK VENEER WALL

wood blocking
metal fin
caulk both sides

- window frames in masonry walls may be set wholly within depth of opening with caulked joints or they may be set flush with a furred interior wall finish
- metal fin cast or set into a masonry recess to act as a positive weatherstop is recommended

finish head height

- consult manufacturer's data for standard window sizes:
  - rough or masonry openings required
  - window unit dimensions
  - sash dimensions
  - glass size

- size of glass in stock window units is typically an even multiple of 4" (102)

finish interior sill or stool height

rough or masonry opening
unit dimension
glass size

6'8" (2·032) typical head height
may vary

- in selecting window sizes, and fixing their head height as well as the sill height, consider the form and use of the space, its furnishings and fixtures, and the exterior facade composition

These sections illustrate typical wood window units. The shaded parts are normally supplied by the manufacturer.

Metal window units usually have slimmer profiles but have similar installations. Consult manufacturer for installation data.

Fixed glass windows may be framed in wood or metal. They may also be set into masonry or concrete wall openings with neoprene or rubber gaskets. Attention should be paid to:

- maximum stock glass sizes available (*see 12·12)
- structure around window opening : - should be strong enough that structural movements and thermal stresses are not transferred to the glass
- wind load on the glass plane: - anticipated wind loads affect the maximum size of the glass panels permitted between supports according to the glass type and its thickness (consult glass manufacturer's data)
- concentrations of thermal stresses: - large temperature differentials within the glass may cause it to break
  - sources of thermal stresses may be hot air supply grilles or lack of ventilation around blinds or drapes which act as heat traps when in direct sunlight
- method of glazing : - glass should be set on neoprene or similar resilient blocking 4"(102) long at quarter points
  - glazing compound should provide a seal between the face of the glass and the glazing stop
  - edge of glass should be kept free from the bottom of the glazing rabbet

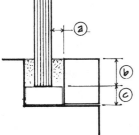

GUIDELINES FOR GLASS EDGE CLEARANCES:

glass type:	dimension	(a)	(b)	(c)
sheet glass (ss)		1/16" (2)	1/4" (6)	1/8" (3)
(ds)		1/8" (3)	1/4" (6)	1/8" (3)
(hs)		1/8" (3)	3/8" (10)	1/4" (6)
plate glass	1/4" (6)	3/16" (5)	3/8" (10)	1/4" (6)
insulating glass		3/16" (5)	1/2" (13)	1/4" (6)

- glazing stops must be removable for glass replacement
- a weatherseal must be maintained between the glass, its frame, and the wall opening

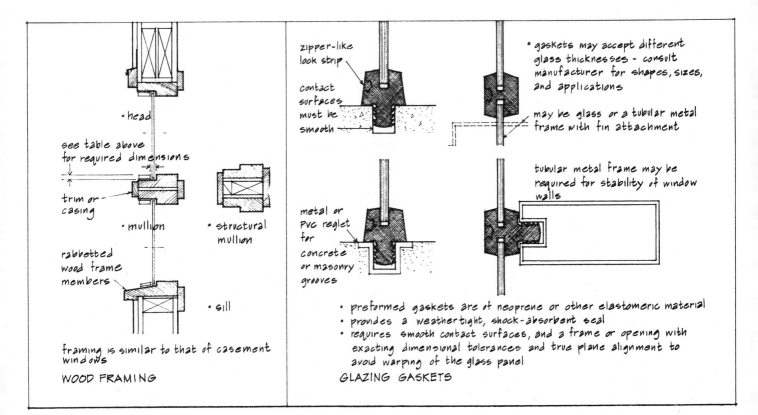

· head

see table above for required dimensions

trim or casing

· mullion

rabbetted wood frame members

· structural mullion

· sill

framing is similar to that of casement windows

WOOD FRAMING

zipper-like lock strip

contact surfaces must be smooth

metal or PVC reglet for concrete or masonry grooves

· gaskets may accept different glass thicknesses - consult manufacturer for shapes, sizes, and applications

· may be glass or a tubular metal frame with fin attachment

tubular metal frame may be required for stability of window walls

- preformed gaskets are of neoprene or other elastomeric material
- provides a weathertight, shock-absorbent seal
- requires smooth contact surfaces, and a frame or opening with exacting dimensional tolerances and true plane alignment to avoid warping of the glass panel

GLAZING GASKETS

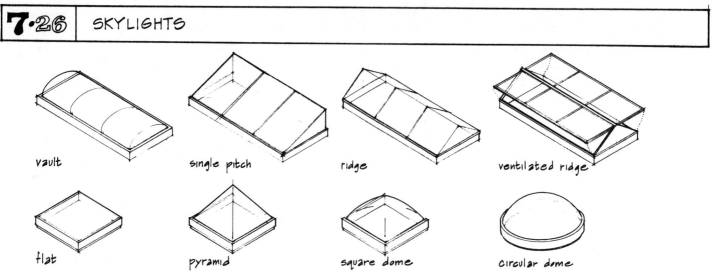

vault   single pitch   ridge   ventilated ridge

flat   pyramid   square dome   circular dome

SKYLIGHT FORMS

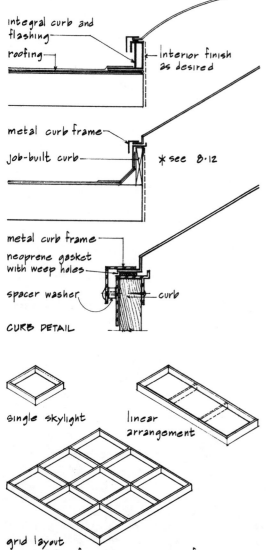

integral curb and flashing
roofing
Interior finish as desired

metal curb frame
Job-built curb   * see 8·12

metal curb frame
neoprene gasket with weep holes
spacer washer   curb

CURB DETAIL

single skylight   linear arrangement

grid layout
over modular framing or a space frame

Skylights permit interior spaces to be lit from above in place of or in addition to normal window lighting. Stock skylight units are commercially available in the configurations illustrated above. The glazing may be of

- glass : - clear, tinted, or translucent
          - plain, tempered, or wire glass
- plastic: - clear, tinted, or translucent
  (acrylic) - single sheet or sandwich panel

Skylight frames are usually of metal:
aluminum, galvanized or stainless steel, monel, copper, lead-coated steel or copper

Curbs are generally required to prevent rain or snow from penetrating into the interior. Stock skylight units may have integral curbs and flashing or only curb frames requiring job-built curbs.

Dimensions of stock skylight units range from 1' (305) to 8' (2.438). Consult manufacturer's data for actual dimensions, configurations, and curb details.

Provision should be made to allow any condensation collecting on the interior surface of a skylight to drain to the outside through weep holes in the curb frame.

Neoprene gaskets or glazing strips are normally used to act as a cushion for the glazing and allow for differential expansion and contraction of the glazing and the skylight frame.

The structural framing required to support skylight units depends on the size and layout pattern of the skylights. Gutters must be installed between adjacent skylight units to carry off condensation and precipitation.

MOISTURE & THERMAL PROTECTION

The form of the roof system and its finish roofing material are the primary means of shielding a building's interiors from the natural elements. The type of finish roofing that may be used depends on the roof structure and deck, its slope, and the appearance desired. While a sloping roof form easily sheds waters, a flat roof must depend on a continuous waterproof membrane to contain the water while it drains and/or evaporates. A flat roof (and any well-insulated sloped roof that may hold snow) should therefore be designed to support a greater live load than a moderately or highly pitched roof.

The roofing skin can range from a virtually continuous impervious membrane to a fabric of small, overlapping pieces of material. Color, pattern, texture, and form are important considerations in terms of a roofing material's visual appearance. Resistance to uplift forces caused by wind, fire-resistance and possible traffic are factors to consider in gauging a roofing material's performance, maintenance, and durability characteristics.

At roof edges, where roofs change slopes or abut vertical planes, and where roofs are penetrated by chimneys, flues, vent pipes, skylights, etc., flashing must be installed to provide weathertight and watershedding seals to prevent leakage into the roof construction and eventually the interior of a building. Exterior walls must also be flashed where leakage might occur, primarily at door and window openings and joints between materials in the wall plane.

A waterproof membrane must be applied to those floors and walls below grade where water may be present in sufficient quantity or under sufficient pressure to cause leakage into a building's interior.

Moisture is normally present in a building's interior in the form of water vapor. When this water vapor reaches a surface cooled by heat loss to the cold outside air, condensation may occur. This condensation may become visible, such as on an uninsulated window during the winter, or it may collect in concealed wall, floor, or roof spaces. Means of combatting condensation include the correct placement of vapor barriers and insulation, and the proper ventilation of concealed spaces such as attics and crawl spaces.

The expansion and contraction of building materials due to heat and cold within the natural temperature range, as well as exposure to solar radiation and wind, must be allowed for in the design and construction of a building to minimize the cracking or deterioration of its materials. In allowing for movement and relieving the stresses caused by a material's expansion and contraction, expansion joints must be flexible, weathertight, durable, and correctly placed to be effective.

Potential heat loss or gain through a building's exterior structure is an important factor in the consideration of human comfort and the amount of mechanical equipment and energy required to maintain conditions of comfort within a building's interior. The proper selection of building material, and the correct construction and insulation of a building's exterior structure are basic means of controlling heat loss or gain.

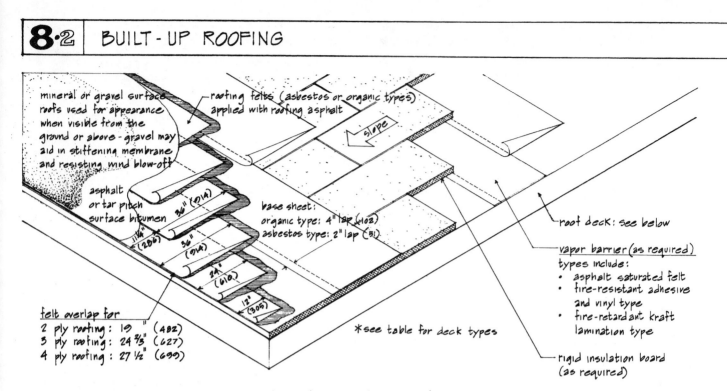

mineral or gravel surface roofs used for appearance when visible from the ground or above — gravel may aid in stiffening membrane and resisting wind blow-off

roofing felts (asbestos or organic types) applied with roofing asphalt

slope

asphalt or tar pitch surface bitumen

36" (914)
1¼" (206)
36" (914)
24" (610)
12" (305)

base sheet: organic type: 4" lap (102) asbestos type: 2" lap (51)

roof deck: see below

vapor barrier (as required) types include:
• asphalt saturated felt
• fire-resistant adhesive and vinyl type
• fire-retardant kraft lamination type

rigid insulation board (as required)

felt overlap for
2 ply roofing: 19" (482)
3 ply roofing: 24 ⅔" (627)
4 ply roofing: 27 ½" (699)

*see table for deck types

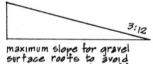

¼:12

recommended minimum slope (except for water-cooled roofs)

3:12

maximum slope for gravel surface roofs to avoid gravel runoff

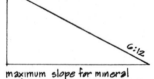

6:12

maximum slope for mineral surface or smooth surface roofs

For slopes in excess of 1:12, treated wood nailers should be provided for non-nailable decks parallel to the eave at 36" (914) o.c.

Correctly applied built-up roofing over a structurally sound roof structure and deck acts as a continuous impervious membrane for flat and low slope roofs. Alway consult manufacturer's specifications for material and asphalt types and recommended application procedures over various roof decks. Proper adhesion of the roofing to its base, correct flashing at roof edges, terminations, and penetrations, and control of water vapor in the roofing substrata are essential to the performance of the built-up roof.

Vapor barriers are required where condensation might occur under the built-up roof within the insulation chamber. As a guideline, vapor barriers are normally required where the average outdoor January temperature is lower than 40°F (4.4 °C) or where high relative humidity (over 50%) conditions within the building are anticipated. Vapor barriers should provide a continuous seal across the roof plane, including all roof penetrations and terminations, against the source of the water vapor.

When a vapor barrier is present and the heat flow cycle is primarily upward or when the built-up roofing is applied over a moisture-prone deck, the roofing may have to be vented to allow any moisture-laden air to escape to the outside and not collect under the roofing membrane and cause it to blister and deteriorate. Consult manufacturer's specifications for details.

ROOF DECK OR SUBSTRATE TYPES	
steel deck	• 22 gage minimum / layer of rigid insulation required before appication of roof
wood board (nailable)	• ¾" (19) minimum tongue and groove boards / dry, well-seasoned wood only / loose knots and large cracks should be covered with sheet metal
plywood (nailable)	• ½" (13) minimum thickness / face ply laid at right angle to supports spaced not more than 24" (610) o.c. / tongue and groove joints or blocking under all joints
structural wood fiber deck (nailable)	• roofing must be fastened mechanically
poured concrete (require wood nailers)	• should be smooth, dry, unfrozen, and properly graded to drain
precast concrete or gypsum plank (may be nailable)	• should be well-cured / joints should be grouted / unevenness between units must be compensated for with a vented leveling fill
lightweight aggregate poured concrete (may be nailable)	• beause of relatively high moisture content, 5 days minimum drying time required / should be placed over a base which permits venting from beneath / if insulation deck is laid over slab, vapor barrier should be placed between

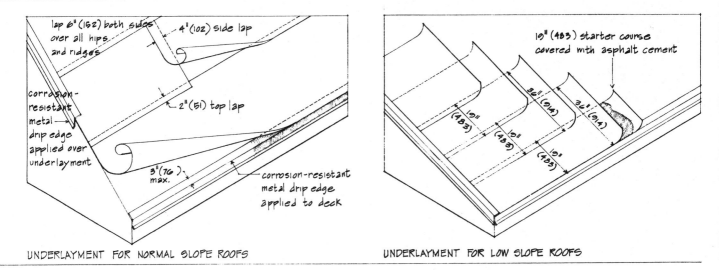

UNDERLAYMENT FOR NORMAL SLOPE ROOFS   UNDERLAYMENT FOR LOW SLOPE ROOFS

Underlayment for shingle roofs
- protects the roof sheathing from moisture absorption until the shingles are applied;
- provides additional protection against wind-driven rain from penetrating onto the roof sheathing and into the structure;
- protects asphalt shingles from resinous wood sheathing

Underlayment should have low water vapor resistance to prevent moisture and water vapor from accumulating between the underlayment and the roof sheathing. Underlayment is mechanically fastened to the roof sheathing only to hold it in place until the roofing shingles are applied.

Metal drip edges protect the deck edge and allow water to drip free of the roof edge. They should be of corrosion-resistant metal, and may be omitted on wood shingle roofs when the shingles themselves form drips by projecting beyond the roof edge.

Eave flashing is recommended in cold climates where ice might form along the eaves and cause water to back up under the roofing shingles. For normal slope roofs, eave flashing is formed by an additional course of underlayment extending to a point 12"(305) inside of interior wall line.

For low slope roofs, eave flashing consists of an additional course of underlayment cemented over the roof underlayment and extending to a point 24"(610) inside of interior wall line.

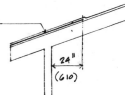

UNDERLAYMENT RECOMMENDATIONS FOR SHINGLE ROOFS

TYPE ROOFING	SHEATHING	TYPE UNDERLAYMENT	NORMAL SLOPE		LOW SLOPE	
asbestos-cement shingles	solid	no 15 asphalt saturated asbestos felt or no 30 asphalt saturated felt	5:12 and up	single layer	3:12 to 5:12	double layer - may be single layer for 4:12 slope in warm climates
asphalt shingles	solid	no 15 asphalt saturated felt	4:12 and up	single layer	2:12 to 4:12	double layer
wood shakes	spaced	no 30 asphalt saturated felt	4:12 and up	underlayment starter course; interlayment over entire roof		not recommended
	solid	no 30 asphalt saturated felt	4:12 and up	underlayment starter course; interlayment over entire roof	3:12 to 4:12	single layer underlayment
wood shingles	spaced	none required	5:12 and up	none required	3:12 to 5:12	none required
for added insulation and to minimize air infiltration →	solid	no 15 asphalt saturated felt	5:12 and up	none required	3:12 to 5:12	none - may be desirable to protect sheathing

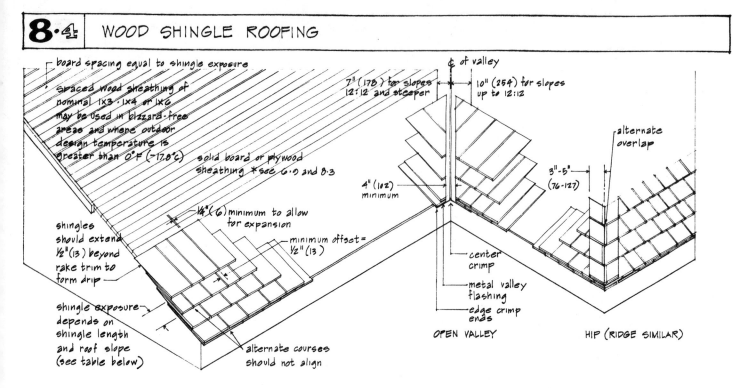

board spacing equal to shingle exposure

spaced wood sheathing of nominal 1x3 · 1x4 or 1x6 may be used in blizzard-free areas and where outdoor design temperature is greater than 0°F (-17.8°C)

solid board or plywood sheathing *see 6·0 and 8·3

shingles should extend ½"(13) beyond rake trim to form drip

¼"(6) minimum to allow for expansion

minimum offset = ½"(13)

shingle exposure depends on shingle length and roof slope (see table below)

alternate courses should not align

7" (178) for slopes 12:12 and steeper

¢ of valley

10" (254) for slopes up to 12:12

alternate overlap

3"-5" (76-127)

4" (102) minimum

center crimp

metal valley flashing

edge crimp ends

OPEN VALLEY

HIP (RIDGE SIMILAR)

Wood shingles are usually red or white cedar although redwood shingles are available. Red cedar, a common shingle type, is characterized by extremely fine, even grain, low ratio of expansion and contraction with changes in moisture content, and high impermeability to liquids.

Wood shingles are available in 16"·18"·24" (406/457/610)lengths and the following grades:

- nº1 premium grade: 100% heartwood /100% clear
- nº2 good grade: 10" (254) clear on 16" (406) shingles
  11" (279) clear on 18" (457) shingles
  16" (406) clear on 24" (610) shingles
- nº3 utility grade: 6" (152) clear on 16" shingles
  10" (254) clear on 24" shingles

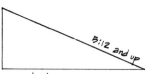

minimum slope 3:12

normal slope 5:12 and up

- should be applied with corrosion-resistant nails
- contact between copper and cedar should be avoided to avoid deterioration of the copper
- wood shingles may be left natural to weather or they may be stained

SHINGLE EXPOSURE SCHEDULE

SHINGLE LENGTH	ROOF SLOPE		
	5:12 and up	4:12	3:12
24" (610)	7½" (191)	6¾" (172)	5¾" (146)
18" (457)	5½" (140)	5" (127)	4¼" (108)
16" (406)	5" (127)	4½" (114)	3¾" (95)

wood shingles may also be applied to vertical surfaces as a wall finish

SHINGLE LENGTH	EXPOSURE	
	SINGLE COURSE	DOUBLE COURSE
24" (610)	8"-11½" (203-292)	12"-16" (305-406)
18" (457)	6"-8½" (152-216)	9"-14" (229-356)
16" (406)	6"-7½" (152-191)	8"-12" (203-305)

While wood shingles are sawn, wood shakes are split, resulting in at least one highly textured side.

- standard lengths and exposures for the recommended minimum slope of 4:12 and steeper are:
- 7½" (191) exposure for 18" (457) lengths
- 10" (254) exposure for 24" (610) lengths
- 13" (330) exposure for 32" (813) lengths

- due to their rough texture, wood shakes require 18" (457) wide interlayment of nº 30 asphalt saturated felt over the top portion of each course

SHINGLE ROOFING TERMINOLOGY
L = shingle length
E = shingle exposure
TL = top lap
HL = head lap

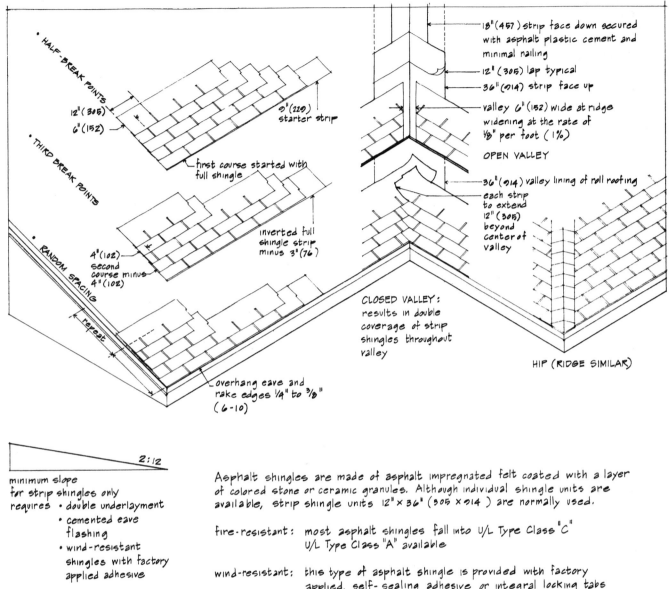

HALF-BREAK POINTS

12" (305)

6" (152)

THIRD BREAK POINTS

9" (229) starter strip

first course started with full shingle

RANDOM SPACING

4" (102) second course minus 4" (102)

inverted full shingle strip minus 3" (76)

repeat

overhang eave and rake edges ¼" to ⅜" (6-10)

18" (457) strip face down secured with asphalt plastic cement and minimal nailing

12" (305) lap typical

36" (914) strip face up

valley 6" (152) wide at ridge widening at the rate of ⅛" per foot (1%)

OPEN VALLEY

36" (914) valley lining of roll roofing each strip to extend 12" (305) beyond center of valley

CLOSED VALLEY: results in double coverage of strip shingles throughout valley

HIP (RIDGE SIMILAR)

2:12

minimum slope
for strip shingles only
requires • double underlayment
• cemented eave flashing
• wind-resistant shingles with factory applied adhesive

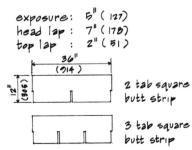

4:12 and up

normal slope

exposure: 5" (127)
head lap: 7" (178)
top lap: 2" (51)

36" (914)

12" (305)

2 tab square butt strip

3 tab square butt strip

Asphalt shingles are made of asphalt impregnated felt coated with a layer of colored stone or ceramic granules. Although individual shingle units are available, strip shingle units 12" x 36" (305 x 914) are normally used.

fire-resistant: most asphalt shingles fall into U/L Type Class "C" U/L Type Class "A" available

wind-resistant: this type of asphalt shingle is provided with factory applied, self-sealing adhesive or integral locking tabs

weight: 235 to 300 lbs. per square (100 SF) [11.5 to 14.6 kg/m²]

appearance • asphalt shingles are relatively thin producing slim shadowlines
• thickened butt edges, cutout and embossed patterns, and color range aid in giving the roof plane textural interest
• consult manufacturer for specifications

Asbestos cement (mineral fiber) and fiber glass roofing shingles are similar in appearance and application to asphalt shingles. Consult manufacturer for size, pattern, color, and application specifications.

• U/L Type Class "A" fire resistance rating
• inorganic, rot-resistant
• durable, weather-resistant

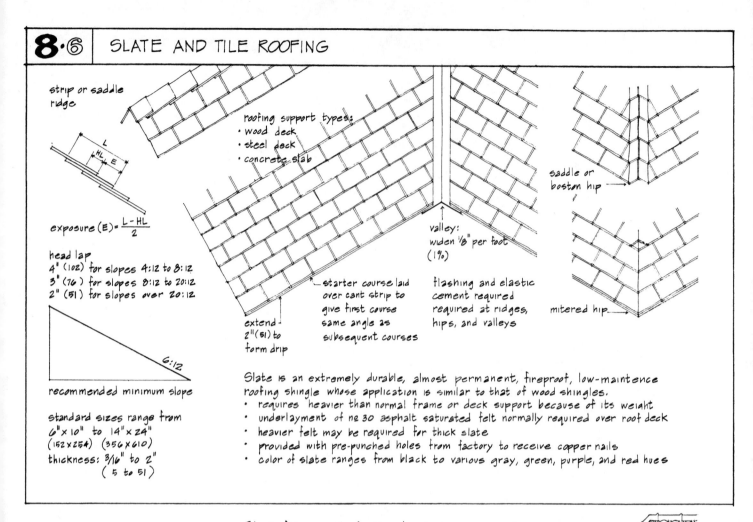

strip or saddle ridge

exposure (E) = $\frac{L - HL}{2}$

head lap
4" (102) for slopes 4:12 to 8:12
3" (76) for slopes 8:12 to 20:12
2" (51) for slopes over 20:12

6:12

recommended minimum slope

standard sizes range from
6"x10" to 14"x24"
(152x254) (356x610)
thickness: 3/16" to 2"
(5 to 51)

roofing support types:
· wood deck
· steel deck
· concrete slab

starter course laid over cant strip to give first course same angle as subsequent courses

extend 2"(51) to form drip

valley:
widen 1/8" per foot (1%)

flashing and elastic cement required required at ridges, hips, and valleys

saddle or boston hip

mitered hip

Slate is an extremely durable, almost permanent, fireproof, low-maintence roofing shingle whose application is similar to that of wood shingles.
· requires heavier than normal frame or deck support because of its weight
· underlayment of no 30 asphalt saturated felt normally required over roof deck
· heavier felt may be required for thick slate
· provided with pre-punched holes from factory to receive copper nails
· color of slate ranges from black to various gray, green, purple, and red hues

Tile roofing consists of either burnt clay or concrete units. Like slate, these roofing tiles are durable, fireproof, and require little maintenance.

· requires heavy framing because of weight of tile
· roofing tile applied with copper or other non-corrosive nails to solid sheathing covered with no 30 roofing felt
· underlayment should be doubled under ridges, hips, valleys, and other roof breaks
· strong textural pattern created - depends on shape of tile used, some of which are illustrated below
· color of unglazed clay tile ranges from yellow-orange to dark red - polychrome and bright, solid colors available with glazed tile - concrete tile more subdued in color

see table below

TILE TYPE		MINIMUM SLOPE	WIDTH	LENGTH	EXPOSURE	MINIMUM LAP	WEIGHT PER 100 SF IN LBS.
	spanish	4½:12	9¾" (248)	13¼" (337)	10¼" (260)	3" (76)	900 (44)kg/m²
	barrel mission	4½:12	8" (203)	18" (457)	15" (381)	3" (76)	1250 (61)kg/m²
	shingle	6:12	9" (229)	15" (381)	12½" (318)	2" (51)	1100 (54)kg/m²
		4½:12	12" (305)	12¾" (324)	10" (254)	3" (76)	1250 (61)kg/m²
roman	greek						

· special shapes are manufactured for ridges, hips, and rake and eave closures - consult manufacturer for shapes and application details

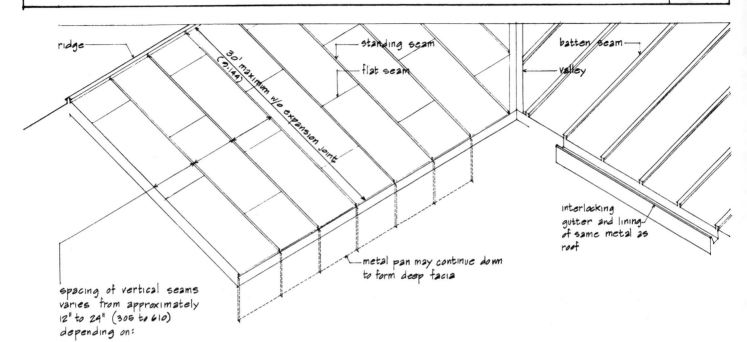

ridge

standing seam

flat seam

30' maximum w/o expansion joint (9.144)

batten seam

valley

metal pan may continue down to form deep facia

interlocking gutter and lining of same metal as roof

spacing of vertical seams varies from approximately 12" to 24" (305 to 610) depending on:

- starting width of metal sheet
- size of batten or standing seam
- even spacing of seams across the roof plane

spacing of seams on prefabricated batten roofs varies from 24" to 36" (610 to 914)

Sheet metal roofing may be of aluminum, copper, monel, galvanized and stainless steels, and terne metal. Other alloys may also be used. Factors to consider in their use include:
- corrosion-resistance
- low rate of expansion and contraction desirable
- finish, color, and weathering properties
- compatibility with other building materials when in direct contact
- maintenance characterics
- also: weight, workability, and cost

A sheet metal roof is characterized by a pattern of strong vertical lines and articulated ridges and edges created by interlocking seams and cleats.

- major vertical seams above the recommended minimum slope may be either of the standing or batten type
- horizontal and valley seams are flat and usually soldered
- maximum run = 30' (9.144) without expansion joints
- nailable deck required for fastening of cleats; if a non-nailable deck is used, nailing strips must be provided

3:12

minimum slope:

slope may be less if soldered, locked flat seams are used

Consult manufacturer for material specifications, application details, and underlayment recommendations. Metal batten roofs are available prefabricated.

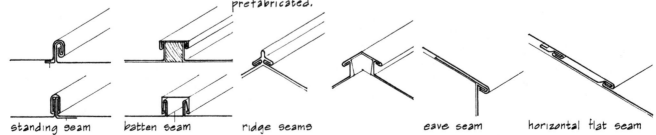

standing seam   batten seam   ridge seams   eave seam   horizontal flat seam

EXAMPLES OF SEAM TYPES

special sections are available for ridges, hips, valley flashing, and rake closures

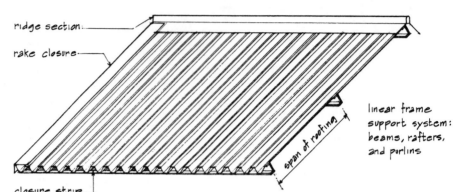

ridge section

rake closure

linear frame support system: beams, rafters, and purlins

span of roofing

closure strip
to seal open ends of corrugation at roof terminations

3:12

minimum recommended slope

- typical end lap: 6" (152)
- typical side lap: 1½ corrugations
- verify with manufacturer

Corrugated sheet material may be used as structural, self-supporting roofing spanning between linear support members.

- corrugated sheet may be of the following materials:

  aluminum
  cement asbestos   · consult manufacturer for material specifications,
  fiber glass   sizes, finishes, colors, spanning capability and
  galvanized steel   application details
  plastic
  wire glass,

- support system may consist of beams, rafters, and purlins in wood, steel, or aluminum
- corrugated sheet roofing is normally mechanically fastened to the support frame · fastening always made through upper portion of corrugation
  · washers and gaskets required
  · mastic or other sealant may also be required at side and end laps
- if insulation is required, it must be supported by and integrated with the roof structure
- expansion joint requirements depend on the material used
- appearance and color depend on the material used, and the profile and depth of the corrugations

THIN MEMBRANE ROOFING

- recently developed materials capable of forming a virtually continuous, single ply, flexible membrane roof
- requires a smooth, dry substrate support: plywood, wood or concrete decking, or any of several rigid insulation boards
- since any surface irregularity would show through the thin surface roofing, any joints or depressions in the substrate must be filled and leveled, and projections leveled
- may be applied to almost any slope from horizontal to vertical
- may be in sheet form or applied as a liquid
- sheet form   · elastomeric polymeric materials such as butyl rubber or chlorinated polyethylene: 1/32" to 3/32" thick (1 to 2)
                    · available in black or white
                    · may have a thin foam backing for resilience and slight insulation value
- liquid-applied   · synthetic elastomeric rubber such as neoprene-hypalon or roofing   · silicon rubbers
                    · ceramic granules embedded in final coat for texture
                    · light colors available

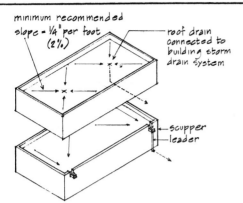

minimum recommended slope = ¼" per foot (2%)

roof drain connected to building storm drain system

scupper

leader

location of roof drains should respond to the building form and its structural and plumbing systems

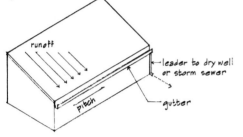

runoff

leader to dry well or storm sewer

pitch

gutter

The frequency and intensity of precipitation for the building site's region should be checked to determine the amount of water or snow the roof and drain systems will have to handle.

Flat roofs (except for water-cooled roofs) should be properly pitched to drain either into roof drains built into the roof plane or through scuppers along the building perimeter.

Rain water shed by sloped roofs should be caught by gutters along the eave line to prevent ground erosion around a building and protect entry ways. Gutters empty into vertical downspouts or leaders which in turn may discharge into a dry well or storm sewer system. Masonry or gravel strips at ground level to break the fall of water shed by a roof may be substituted for gutters and downspouts in the case of small roof areas or in regions with minimal precipitation.

Factors to consider in the use of gutters and downspouts:

size	• depends on roof area to be drained, intensity of rainfall for the region, and the slope of the roof which affects the speed of the runoff
profile	• should allow for the expansion of water if it freezes in cold climates without deforming
pitch	• should be uniform and sufficient to drain water quickly without leaving standing pockets of water
	• 1/16" per foot minimum (0.6%)
support	• should be supported often enough to prevent sagging when gutter is full of water
location	• should be sufficiently clear of eave line and below roofing edge to prevent water, ice, or snow from backing up under the roofing
expansion	• joints should be provided for metal gutters
appearance	• long gutter lengths between leaders may be undesirable if pitch becomes visually evident

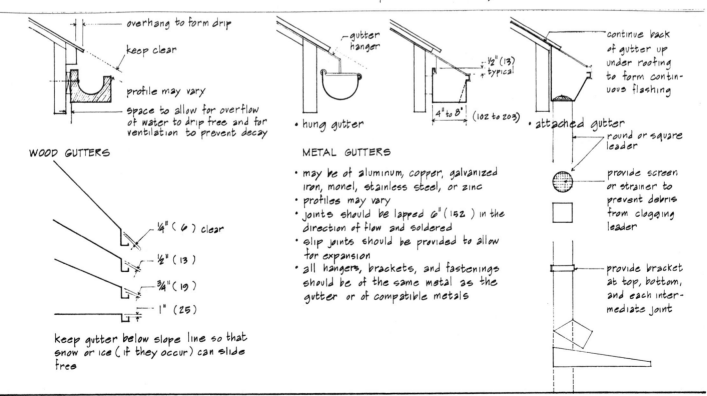

overhang to form drip

keep clear

profile may vary

space to allow for overflow of water to drip free and for ventilation to prevent decay

WOOD GUTTERS

¼" (6) clear

½" (13)

¾" (19)

1" (25)

keep gutter below slope line so that snow or ice (if they occur) can slide free

gutter hanger

• hung gutter

½" (13) typical

4" to 8" (102 to 203)

METAL GUTTERS

• may be of aluminum, copper, galvanized iron, monel, stainless steel, or zinc
• profiles may vary
• joints should be lapped 6" (152) in the direction of flow and soldered
• slip joints should be provided to allow for expansion
• all hangers, brackets, and fastenings should be of the same metal as the gutter or of compatible metals

continue back of gutter up under roofing to form continuous flashing

• attached gutter

round or square leader

provide screen or strainer to prevent debris from clogging leader

provide bracket at top, bottom, and each intermediate joint

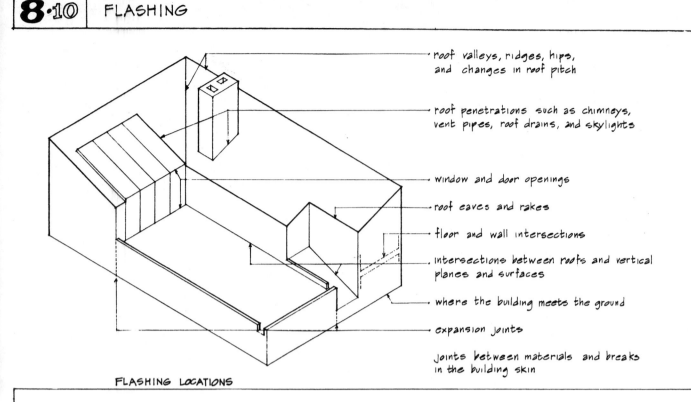

• roof valleys, ridges, hips, and changes in roof pitch

• roof penetrations such as chimneys, vent pipes, roof drains, and skylights

• window and door openings

• roof eaves and rakes

• floor and wall intersections

• intersections between roofs and vertical planes and surfaces

• where the building meets the ground

• expansion joints

• joints between materials and breaks in the building skin

FLASHING LOCATIONS

Flashing refers to pieces of sheet metal or impervious, flexible membrane material used to seal and protect joints in a building for the prevention of leakage or penetration of wind-driven rain water. Flashing generally operates on the principle that, for water to penetrate a joint, it must work itself upward against the force of gravity or, in the case of wind-driven rain, it would have to follow a tortuous path during which the force of the wind is dissipated.

Flashing may be either concealed or exposed. Flashing concealed within the construction of a building may be of either sheet metal or a waterproof membrane material. Exposed flashing is usually metal, and of the following types:

aluminum
copper
galvanized steel (painted)
stainless steel
lead
monel
terne
zinc alloy

exposed metal flashing:
• affects the appearance of a building; its color, texture, and pattern should be considered
• should be durable, weather-resistant, and maintenance-free
• must not stain or be stained by adjacent materials or react chemically with them
• should be provided with expansion joints to prevent their deformation

The flashing details on the following pages are generalized and may be applied to various building materials and constructions.

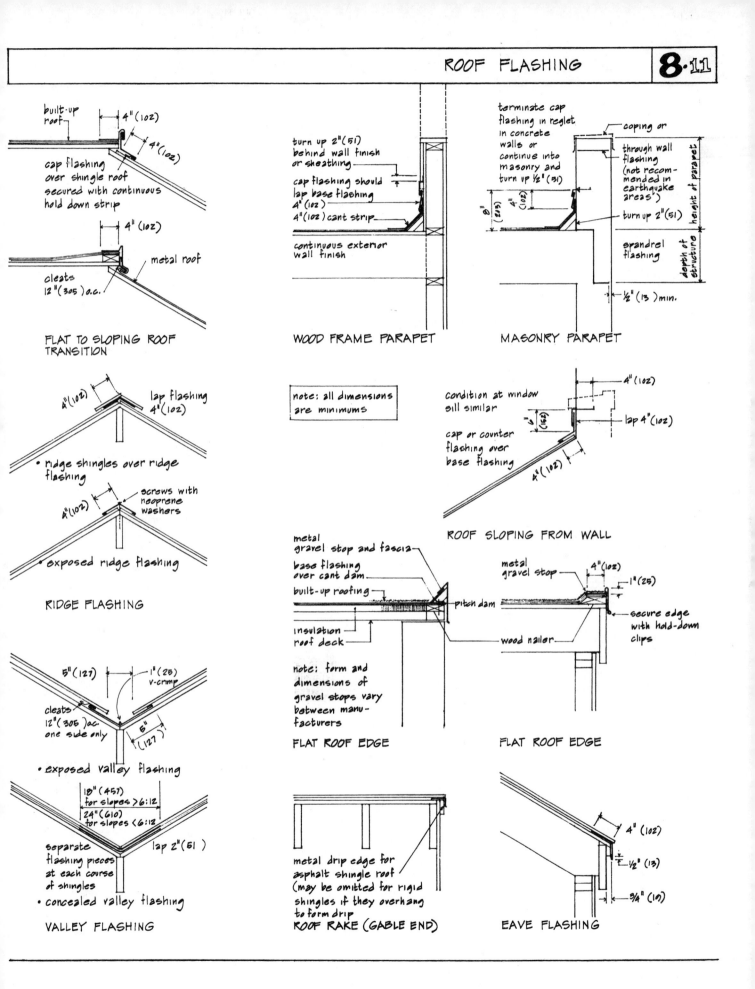

built-up roof

4" (102)

4" (102)

cap flashing over shingle roof secured with continuous hold down strip

4" (102)

metal roof

cleats 12" (305) o.c.

FLAT TO SLOPING ROOF TRANSITION

turn up 2" (51) behind wall finish or sheathing

cap flashing should lap base flashing 4" (102)

4" (102) cant strip

continuous exterior wall finish

WOOD FRAME PARAPET

terminate cap flashing in reglet in concrete walls or continue into masonry and turn up ½" (51)

coping or

through wall flashing (not recommended in earthquake areas)

turn up 2" (51)

spandrel flashing

height of parapet

depth of structure

8" (203)

4" (102)

½" (13) min.

MASONRY PARAPET

lap flashing 4" (102)

4" (102)

• ridge shingles over ridge flashing

screws with neoprene washers

4" (102)

• exposed ridge flashing

RIDGE FLASHING

note: all dimensions are minimums

condition at window sill similar

cap or counter flashing over base flashing

4" (102)

lap 4" (102)

4" (102)

ROOF SLOPING FROM WALL

5" (127)

1" (25) v-crimp

cleats 12" (305) o.c. one side only

5" (127)

• exposed valley flashing

18" (457) for slopes >6:12
24" (610) for slopes <6:12

separate flashing pieces at each course of shingles

lap 2" (51)

• concealed valley flashing

VALLEY FLASHING

metal gravel stop and fascia

base flashing over cant dam

built-up roofing

pitch dam

insulation roof deck

note: form and dimensions of gravel stops vary between manufacturers

FLAT ROOF EDGE

metal gravel stop

4" (102)

1" (25)

secure edge with hold-down clips

wood nailer

FLAT ROOF EDGE

metal drip edge for asphalt shingle roof (may be omitted for rigid shingles if they overhang to form drip

ROOF RAKE (GABLE END)

4" (102)

½" (13)

¾" (19)

EAVE FLASHING

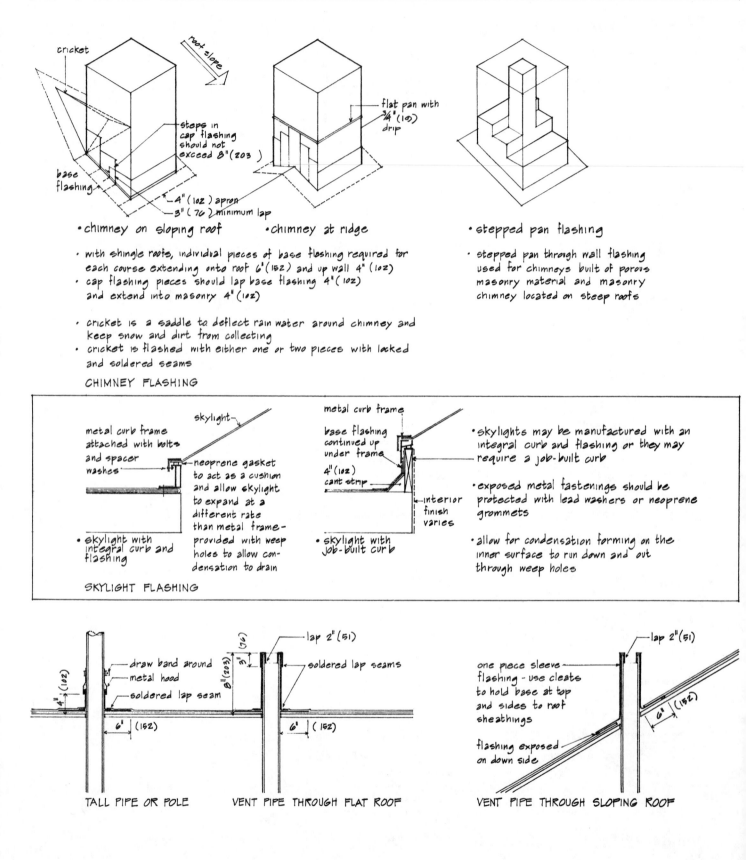

cricket

root slope

steps in
cap flashing
should not
exceed 8" (203)

base
flashing

flat pan with
¾" (19)
drip

—4" (102) apron
—3" (76) minimum lap

• chimney on sloping roof   • chimney at ridge

• stepped pan flashing

• with shingle roofs, individual pieces of base flashing required for
  each course extending onto roof 6" (152) and up wall 4" (102)
• cap flashing pieces should lap base flashing 4" (102)
  and extend into masonry 4" (102)

• cricket is a saddle to deflect rain water around chimney and
  keep snow and dirt from collecting
• cricket is flashed with either one or two pieces with locked
  and soldered seams

CHIMNEY FLASHING

• stepped pan through wall flashing
  used for chimneys built of porous
  masonry material and masonry
  chimney located on steep roofs

skylight

metal curb frame
attached with bolts
and spacer
washes

neoprene gasket
to act as a cushion
and allow skylight
to expand at a
different rate
than metal frame-
provided with weep
holes to allow con-
densation to drain

• skylight with
  integral curb and
  flashing

metal curb frame

base flashing
continued up
under frame

4" (102)
cant strip

interior
finish
varies

• skylight with
  job-built curb

• skylights may be manufactured with an
  integral curb and flashing or they may
  require a job-built curb

• exposed metal fastenings should be
  protected with lead washers or neoprene
  grommets

• allow for condensation forming on the
  inner surface to run down and out
  through weep holes

SKYLIGHT FLASHING

draw band around
metal hood
soldered lap seam

4" (102)

4" (102)

lap 2" (51)

soldered lap seams

3" (76)

8" (203)

6" (152)

6" (152)

TALL PIPE OR POLE   VENT PIPE THROUGH FLAT ROOF

lap 2" (51)

one piece sleeve
flashing - use cleats
to hold base at top
and sides to roof
sheathings

flashing exposed
on down side

6" (152)

VENT PIPE THROUGH SLOPING ROOF

Wall flashing is installed to collect moisture that may penetrate a wall and divert it to the wall's exterior through weep holes.

Locations where wall flashing is usually required include:

- where roof planes abut walls
- where floor planes abut walls
- at door and window heads
- at door and window sills
- at the base of walls where they
- meet the ground

Masonry walls are especially susceptible to water penetration. Wall flashing in masonry walls require weep holes to drain properly. Weep holes should be:
- formed in the head joints directly above the flashing
- spaced 24" (610) o.c.
- filled with glass fiber rope or similar inorganic material to block access to insects and prevent staining of the wall when placed over lintels - when filled, weep holes should be spaced 16" (406) o.c.

SOURCES OF MOISTURE:

① rain ——→ remedies: ·painting
·parging
·caulking
·tooling masonry joints

·sloping surfaces

② condensation of water vapor } requires proper placement of vapor barriers *see 8·18

③ capillary action where wall is in contact with the ground } requires dampproofing *see 8·19

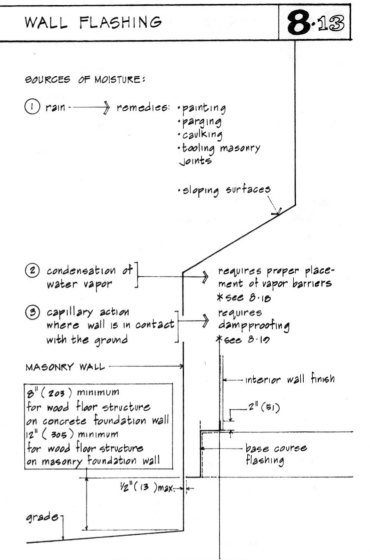

MASONRY WALL

8" (203) minimum for wood floor structure on concrete foundation wall
12" (305) minimum for wood floor structure on masonry foundation wall

interior wall finish

2" (51)

base course flashing

½" (13) max.

grade

DAMP COURSE AT FLOOR CONSTRUCTION

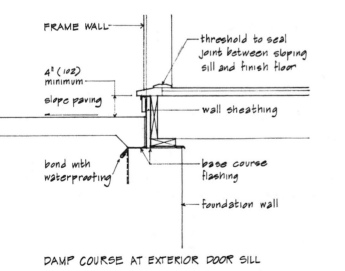

FRAME WALL

4" (102) minimum
slope paving

bond with waterproofing

threshold to seal joint between sloping sill and finish floor

wall sheathing

base course flashing

foundation wall

DAMP COURSE AT EXTERIOR DOOR SILL

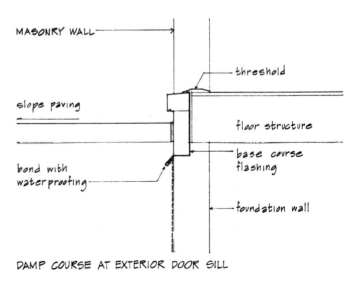

MASONRY WALL

slope paving

bond with waterproofing

threshold

floor structure

base course flashing

foundation wall

DAMP COURSE AT EXTERIOR DOOR SILL

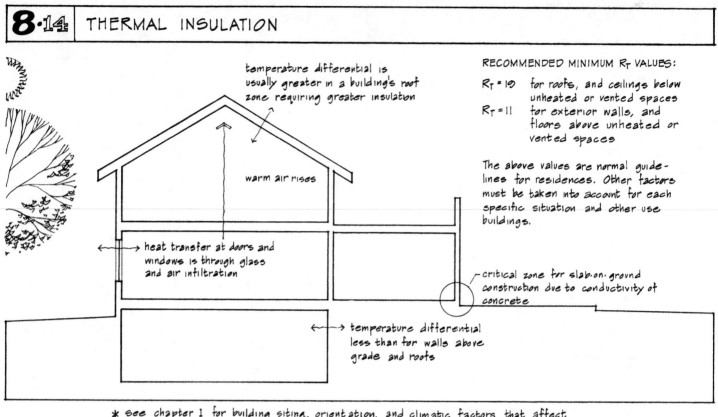

temperature differential is usually greater in a building's roof zone requiring greater insulation

warm air rises

heat transfer at doors and windows is through glass and air infiltration

temperature differential less than for walls above grade and roofs

RECOMMENDED MINIMUM R_T VALUES:

$R_T = 19$ for roofs, and ceilings below unheated or vented spaces

$R_T = 11$ for exterior walls, and floors above unheated or vented spaces

The above values are normal guidelines for residences. Other factors must be taken into account for each specific situation and other use buildings.

critical zone for slab·on·ground construction due to conductivity of concrete

* see chapter 1 for building siting, orientation, and climatic factors that affect a building's heat loss or gain

The primary purpose of a building's thermal insulation is to control heat transfer and thereby protect a building from excessive heat loss during cold seasons and heat gain during hot seasons. This control can effectively reduce the amount of energy required by a building's heating and cooling equipment to maintain conditions for human comfort. [For further discussion of the factors affecting human comfort: air temperature, radiant temperature differentials, relative humidity, and air velocity, see chapter 11]

Heat may be transferred by:
1. convection: air currents from warm to cold air zones
2. conduction: transmission through the mass of a material
3. radiation :   emission of radiant heat energy from warm surfaces through air to cooler surfaces

Effective thermal insulation combats any or all of the above sources of heat loss or gain:

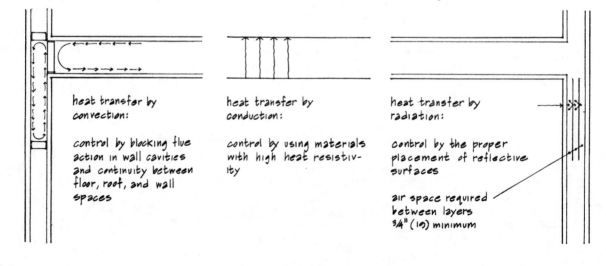

heat transfer by convection:

control by blocking flue action in wall cavities and continuity between floor, roof, and wall spaces

heat transfer by conduction:

control by using materials with high heat resistivity

heat transfer by radiation:

control by the proper placement of reflective surfaces

air space required between layers 3/4" (19) minimum

The following table lists the thermal resistivity (r) for some common building materials and may be used to compare their relative value for thermal insulation and estimate the total thermal resistance (R$_T$) of various wall, floor, and roof constructions. (Resistivities may be added to find R$_T$.) (r) is given per inch (25.4 mm) of thickness unless material thickness is specified. Consult material manufacturer for more detailed information and specifications.

MATERIAL		(r) VALUE	MATERIAL		(r) VALUE
WOOD	plywood	1.25	ROOFING	asphalt shingle	.44
	hardwood	.91		wood shingle	.87
	softwood	1.25		slate	.05
	1¾" (45) solid core door (45) 1¾"	1.96		built-up roof	.33
MASONRY	common brick	.20	GLASS	single thickness	.88
	concrete block (203) 8"	1.11	INSULATING MATERIALS	batt : mineral wool	3.12
	block w/ lt.wt. aggregate (203) 8"	2.00		loose fill: mineral wool	3.70
CONCRETE	cement mortar	.20	• value increases with decrease in temperature	perlite	2.78
	w/ lt.wt. aggregate	.59		boards : expanded polystyrene	4.00
	stucco	.20		mineral fiber board	2.94
	sand, gravel, stone aggregate	.11		glass fiber	4.17
METAL	aluminum	.0007	AIR SPACE	between non-reflective surfaces	1.34
	steel	.0032	• value does not increase significantly for thicknesses above 3/4" (19)	between a reflective and non-reflective surface	4.64
	copper	.0004			
PLASTER		.20			
GYPSUM	gypsum or plaster board (16) 5/8"	.30			
	(13) ½"	.32			
FINISH FLOORING	carpet	2.08			
	cork (3) 1/8"	.28			
	vinyl tile	.05			

(r) = rate of heat flow through a homogeneous material one inch thick measured by the temperature difference in degrees (F) between the two exposed faces required to cause one british thermal unit (BTU) to flow through one square foot per hour. [1 ft² h degF/BTU in = 6.933 m°C/W (meter degree Celsius per watt)]

The steady state method of calculating heat loss or gain takes into account primarily the thermal resistance (R$_T$) of the construction assembly and the air temperature differential. Other critical factors which should also be taken into consideration include:

- the mass of the wall which affects the time lag or delay caused by heat storage and its subsequent release by the structure; time lag generally increases as the mass of the structure increases
- the surface color, reflectivity, and specific heat of the materials used
- the position of the insulation
- the orientation of the building which affects solar heat gain as well as wind exposure and the attendant air movement and potential air infiltration
- latent heat sources and heat gain from building occupants, lighting, and equipment

Building materials, and therefore wall, floor, and roof construction assemblies, have their inherent thermal insulation value that can be enhanced by the addition of an insulating material, either applied to or contained within the construction. Insulating materials may be categorized as follows:

• batt or blanket	• wood fibers; glass or mineral wool; enclosed by paper, aluminum; available with vapor barrier	• fill air spaces, particular in frame walls, floors, and roofs
• board or sheet	• wood, glass, mineral fibers; foamed plastics; cork; available with vapor barrier	• wall sheathing or cavity fill; rigid roof insulation; perimeter slab insulation
• loose fill	• vermiculite; perlite; glass or mineral wool; shredded wood	• fill wall cavities and flat areas above ceilings
• reflective	• aluminum foil; combined in layers with air spaces	• roofs, walls, and floors above vented or unheated spaces
• foamed in place	• concrete; plastics	• roof decks; irregular spaces

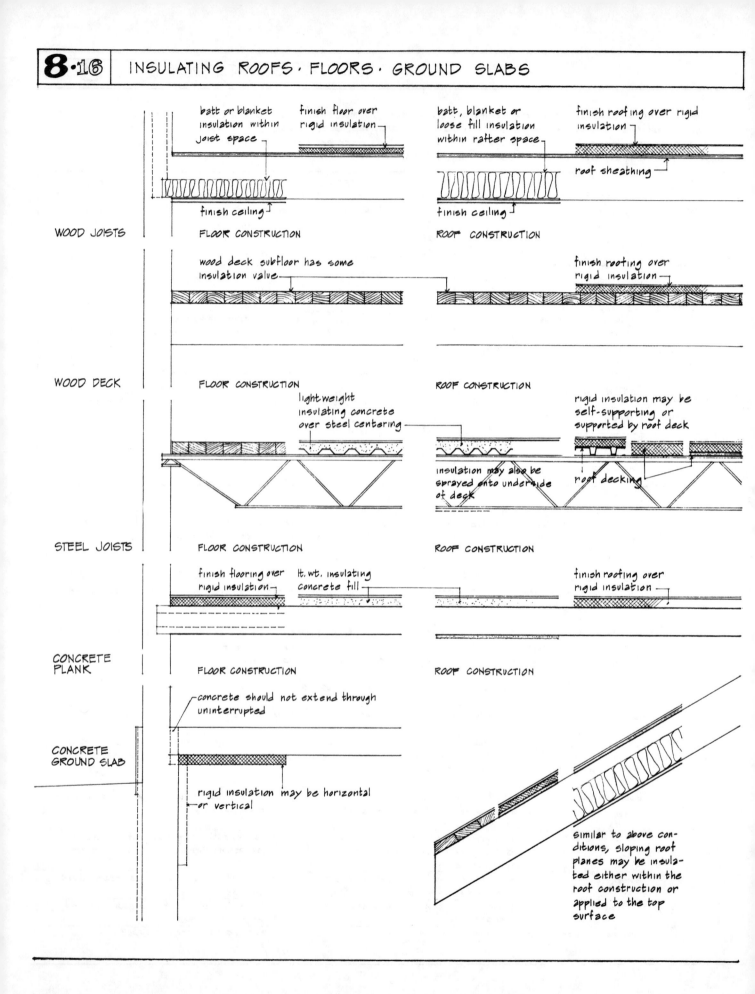

WOOD JOISTS

batt or blanket insulation within joist space

finish floor over rigid insulation

finish ceiling

FLOOR CONSTRUCTION

batt, blanket or loose fill insulation within rafter space

finish roofing over rigid insulation

roof sheathing

finish ceiling

ROOF CONSTRUCTION

WOOD DECK

wood deck subfloor has some insulation value

FLOOR CONSTRUCTION

finish roofing over rigid insulation

ROOF CONSTRUCTION

STEEL JOISTS

lightweight insulating concrete over steel centering

FLOOR CONSTRUCTION

rigid insulation may be self-supporting or supported by roof deck

insulation may also be sprayed onto underside of deck

roof decking

ROOF CONSTRUCTION

CONCRETE PLANK

finish flooring over rigid insulation

lt. wt. insulating concrete fill

FLOOR CONSTRUCTION

finish roofing over rigid insulation

ROOF CONSTRUCTION

CONCRETE GROUND SLAB

concrete should not extend through uninterrupted

rigid insulation may be horizontal or vertical

similar to above conditions, sloping roof planes may be insulated either within the roof construction or applied to the top surface

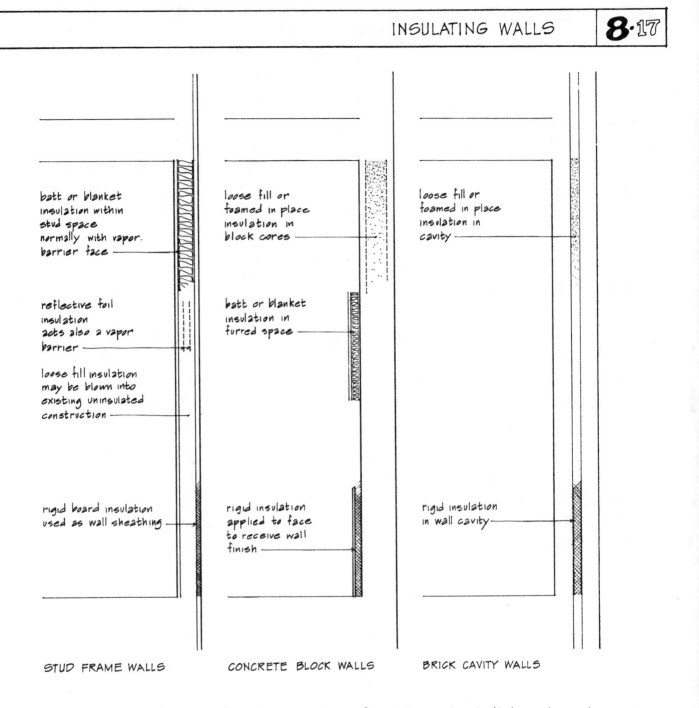

batt or blanket
insulation within
stud space
normally with vapor
barrier face

reflective foil
insulation
acts also a vapor
barrier

loose fill insulation
may be blown into
existing uninsulated
construction

rigid board insulation
used as wall sheathing

loose fill or
foamed in place
insulation in
block cores

batt or blanket
insulation in
furred space

rigid insulation
applied to face
to receive wall
finish

loose fill or
foamed in place
insulation in
cavity

rigid insulation
in wall cavity

STUD FRAME WALLS   CONCRETE BLOCK WALLS   BRICK CAVITY WALLS

This and the preceding page illustrate various types of insulating materials that may be used
in different construction assemblies and locations of a building. Continuity must be maintained
at foundation, floor, wall, and roof junctures to form an unbroken envelope of protection
against heat transmission through a building's exterior surfaces.

Moisture is normally present in the air as water vapor. Evaporation from a building's occupants and equipment may tend to raise the air's humidity level. This moisture vapor will transform itself into a liquid state (condense) when the air in which it exists, at any temperature, becomes completely saturated with all the vapor it can hold and reaches its dew-point temperature. It should be noted that warm air is capable of holding more moisture vapor and has a higher dew-point temperature than cooler air.

Since it is a gas, moisture vapor always moves from high to lower pressure areas. This normally means it tends to diffuse from the higher humidity levels of a building's interior towards the lower humidity levels outside. (This flow is reversed when hot, humid conditions exist outdoors and a building's interior spaces are cool.) A building's exterior wall and roof construction materials often offer little resistance to the vapor's passage. When this moisture vapor comes into contact with a cold surface whose temperature coincides with the air's dew-point, it will condense.

Since condensation may be absorbed by building materials, lessen the efficiency of insulating materials, freeze in cold weather, and deteriorate finishes, moisture vapor must either be prevented from penetrating into concealed spaces in a building's construction (by the use of vapor barriers), or be allowed to escape without transforming itself into a liquid state (through ventilation).

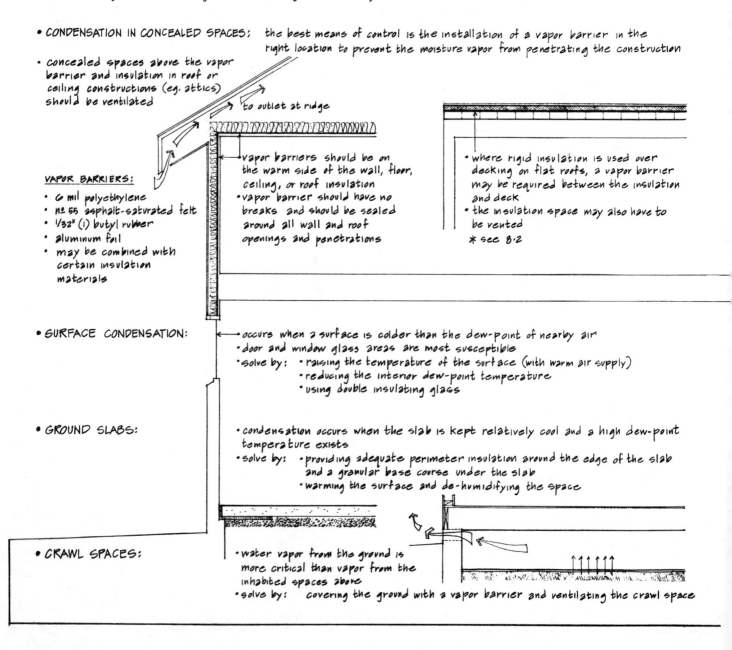

- CONDENSATION IN CONCEALED SPACES: the best means of control is the installation of a vapor barrier in the right location to prevent the moisture vapor from penetrating the construction

- concealed spaces above the vapor barrier and insulation in roof or ceiling constructions (eg. attics) should be ventilated

to outlet at ridge

- vapor barriers should be on the warm side of the wall, floor, ceiling, or roof insulation
- vapor barrier should have no breaks and should be sealed around all wall and roof openings and penetrations

- where rigid insulation is used over decking on flat roofs, a vapor barrier may be required between the insulation and deck
- the insulation space may also have to be vented
  * see 8·2

VAPOR BARRIERS:
- 6 mil polyethylene
- nº 55 asphalt-saturated felt
- 1/32" (1) butyl rubber
- aluminum foil
- may be combined with certain insulation materials

- SURFACE CONDENSATION:
  - occurs when a surface is colder than the dew-point of nearby air
  - door and window glass areas are most susceptible
  - solve by:
    - raising the temperature of the surface (with warm air supply)
    - reducing the interior dew-point temperature
    - using double insulating glass

- GROUND SLABS:
  - condensation occurs when the slab is kept relatively cool and a high dew-point temperature exists
  - solve by:
    - providing adequate perimeter insulation around the edge of the slab and a granular base course under the slab
    - warming the surface and de-humidifying the space

- CRAWL SPACES:
  - water vapor from the ground is more critical than vapor from the inhabited spaces above
  - solve by: covering the ground with a vapor barrier and ventilating the crawl space

Waterproofing: the prevention of the flow of free water and moisture, usually under hydrostatic pressure, into a building by sealing off those parts which come into direct contact with the earth (exterior or foundation walls below grade, basement slabs, ground slabs at grade).

methods:
- membrane - layers of asphalt or tar bitumens alternating with plies of bituminous saturated felt or woven cotton and glass fabric
- hydrolithic - coatings of asphatic bitumens and plastics
- admixtures - liquid, paste, or powder admixtures to concrete to render it impermeable

Dampproofing: the means of stopping dampness (from the earth or from surface water caused by rain) from penetrating a building.

methods:
- below grade
  - 2 coats asphalt base coating or paint
  - dense cement plaster
  - silicones and plastics

- above grade concrete block walls   · paint; stucco; or portland cement and sand grout
- above grade concrete walls   · properly constructed and caulked joints; · where required, a surface coat of grout or mortar
- above grade brick walls   · wetting of brick to reduce the rate of moisture absorption (as required) · tooled joints

• BASEMENT SPACES:
- normally remain relatively cool
- condensation occurs when the dew point temperature rises above the temperature of the basement surfaces and pipes
- solve by: · reducing the fresh air intake
  · warming the surfaces
  · de-humidifying the space

bond with damp course or end in reglet at grade

waterproofing (protect when backfilling)

waterproofing may occur within masonry when more than one wythe thick

metal sheet (lead or copper) waterproofing

4" (102) granular base or a second slab

Allowance should be made for the expansion and contraction of building materials which occur in responce to normal temperature changes in the form of expansion joints to prevent distortion, cracks, and breaks in the building materials. These expansion joints must provide a complete separation of material and allow free movement while maintaining at the same time the weathertightness and watertightness of the structure.

EXPANSION JOINTS :

- joint width varies from ½" to 1" (13 to 26)
- should be calculated for each specific situation
- depends on: · temperature range
  · materials involved
  · appearance of joint and whether it is caulked or not

- for surfaces with severe solar exposure, joints should be provided at more frequent intervals

- provide joints through parapet walls near corners to prevent their displacement

- provide additional joints in exterior wythe of masonry cavity walls and secure to back-up masonry with flexible anchors

- provide horizontal expansion joints for steel shelf angles in masonry walls

- separate partitions at their top and bottom with expansion joints in structures of exposed concrete bearing or shear walls - also where deflection might crush the partition

- provide expansion joints in long, linear building elements such as handrails, fascias, gravel stops, plate glass window walls, pavements

LOCATION GUIDELINES:

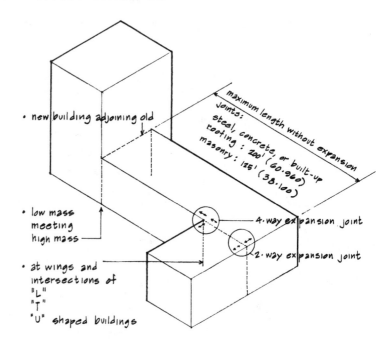

- new building adjoining old
- low mass meeting high mass
- at wings and intersections of "L" "T" "U" shaped buildings

maximum length without expansion joints:
steel, concrete, or built-up roofing : 200' (60.960)
masonry: 125' (38.100)

4-way expansion joint
2-way expansion joint

* see 5·28 masonry wall guidelines

- coefficient of surface expansion is approximately twice the linear coefficient
- coefficient of volume expansion is approximately three times the linear coefficient

COEFFICIENT OF LINEAR EXPANSION PER UNIT LENGTH PER CHANGE OF ONE DEGREE IN TEMPERATURE :									
	C° $\times 10^{-7}$	F° $\times 10^{-7}$		C° $\times 10^{-7}$	F° $\times 10^{-7}$		C° $\times 10^{-7}$	F° $\times 10^{-7}$	
aluminum	231	128	(parallel to fiber)			brick masonry	61	34	
brass	188	104	fir	37	21	portland cement	126	70	
bronze	181	101	maple	64	36	concrete	99	55	
copper	168	93	oak	49	27	granite	80	44	
iron, cast	106	59	pine	54	30	limestone	76	42	
iron, wrought	120	67	(perpendicular to fiber)			marble	81	45	
lead	286	159	fir	580	320	plaster	166	92	
nickel	126	70	maple	480	270	rubble masonry	63	35	
steel, mild	117	65	oak	540	300	slate	80	44	
steel, stainless	178	99	pine	340	190	glass	83	47	

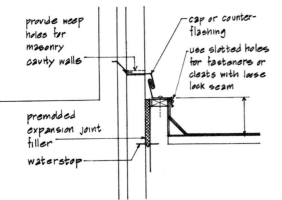

provide weep holes for masonry cavity walls

cap or counter-flashing

use slotted holes for fasteners or cleats with loose lock seam

premolded expansion joint filler

waterstop

EXPANSION JOINT AT WALL AND ROOF

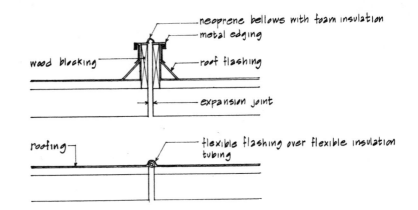

neoprene bellows with foam insulation
metal edging
wood blocking
roof flashing
expansion joint

roofing

flexible flashing over flexible insulation tubing

ROOF EXPANSION JOINT COVERS

✳ see 5·21/22/28/29 for masonry control and expansion joints

These expansion joint details, although general in nature, have the following elements in common:

- joint
  (½" to 1")
  (13 to 25)

- a complete break through the structure - usually filled with a premolded expansion joint filler

- weatherstop: may be in the form of:
  - caulking or elastic joint sealant at the exterior face of the joint in walls
  - a flexible waterstop embedded within a wall
  - a flexible membrane or metal flashing over joints in roofs

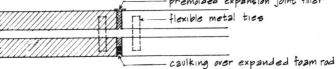

premolded expansion joint filler
waterstop
waterproofing

CONCRETE FOUNDATION WALL

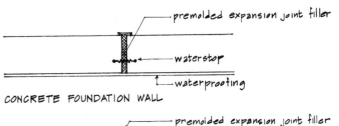

premolded expansion joint filler
flexible metal ties
caulking over expanded foam rod

MASONRY CAVITY WALL

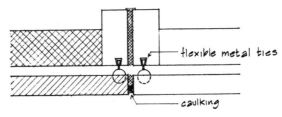

flexible metal ties
caulking

CAVITY WALL AT COLUMNS

Expansion joint covers are used to conceal joints in floor planes and interior wall and ceiling surfaces. They consist of a rigid plate fixed to one side of the joint with a slip joint on the other.

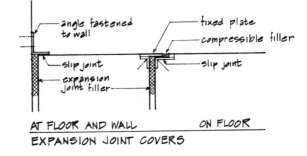

angle fastened to wall
fixed plate
compressible filler
slip joint
slip joint
expansion joint filler

AT FLOOR AND WALL   ON FLOOR
EXPANSION JOINT COVERS

SPECIAL CONSTRUCTION

This chapter discusses those areas of a building which possess unique characteristics that need to be covered as separate entities. While not always influencing the exterior form of a building, they influence the internal organization of spaces, their relationship to the building's structural system, and in some cases, the organization of heating, plumbing, and electrical systems.

Stairs provide a means of vertical circulation between stories of a building, and as such is an important link in the overall circulation scheme of a building, whether punctuating a two story volume of space or rising through a narrow shaft of space. A stair should be logically integrated into the building's structural system at its landing points to avoid overly complicated structural framing conditions. Safety and ease of travel are, in the end, probably the most important considerations in the design and placement of stairs.

A fireplace is a source of heat as well as a focal point for visual attraction. The placement and size of a fireplace in a room or space should be related to the proportion and scale of the space, whether the fireplace is attached to or contained within a wall, or is a free-standing element within the space. Fireplaces can become sources of serious problems if they are not constructed to draft properly. The size (width, height, and depth) of the fireplace opening, the corresponding damper and flue sizes, and precautions against fire hazards are important areas of considerations in fireplace construction.

Kitchens and bathrooms are unique areas of a building that demand careful integration of plumbing, electrical, and ventilating systems with the functional and spatial requirements of the spaces. These areas also require special fixtures, equipment, and furnishings, as well as durable, easy to maintain, and sanitary surfaces and finishes.

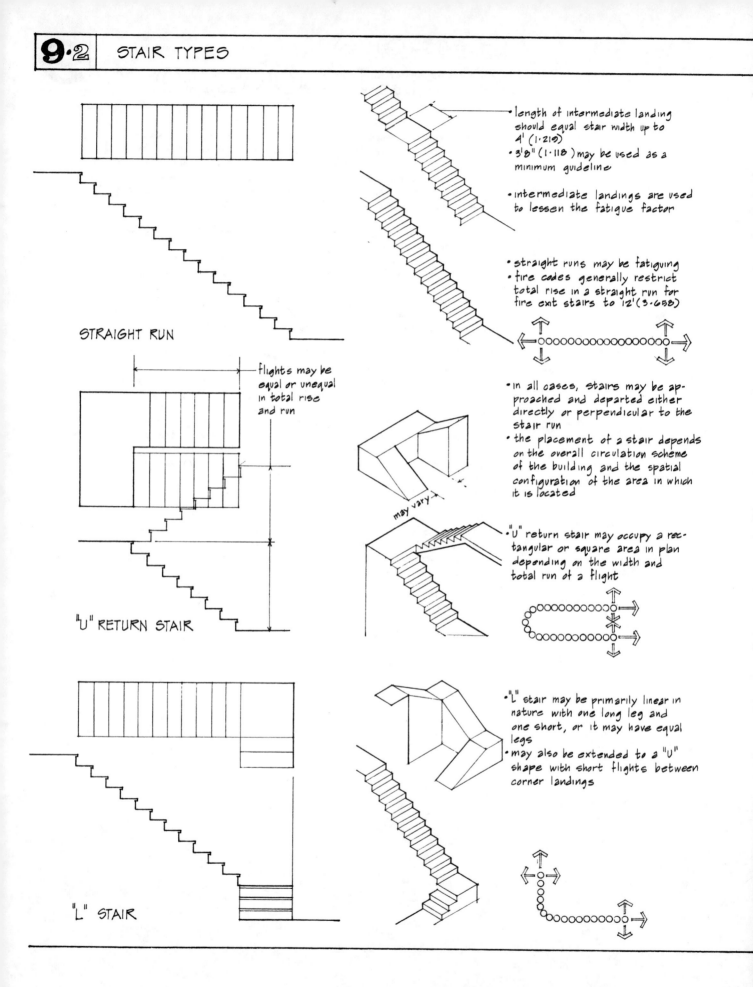

STRAIGHT RUN

"U" RETURN STAIR

"L" STAIR

flights may be equal or unequal in total rise and run

may vary

- length of intermediate landing should equal stair width up to 4' (1·219)
- 3'8" (1·118) may be used as a minimum guideline

- intermediate landings are used to lessen the fatigue factor

- straight runs may be fatiguing
- fire codes generally restrict total rise in a straight run for fire exit stairs to 12' (3·658)

- in all cases, stairs may be approached and departed either directly or perpendicular to the stair run
- the placement of a stair depends on the overall circulation scheme of the building and the spatial configuration of the area in which it is located

- "U" return stair may occupy a rectangular or square area in plan depending on the width and total run of a flight

- "L" stair may be primarily linear in nature with one long leg and one short, or it may have equal legs
- may also be extended to a "U" shape with short flights between corner landings

- used where there is insufficient space for a normal "L" stair
- landing is omitted and the corner treads angled to meet at a point at the turn of the stair
- should be avoided since it may be hazardous due to the minimal foothold at the turn of the stair
- if used, the point of convergence of the angled treads should be offset

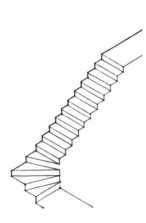

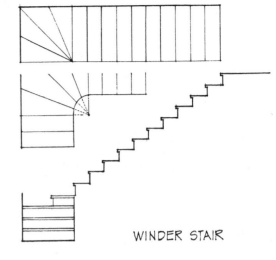

WINDER STAIR

landing: 90°

- occupies a minimum amount of space in plan
- used in residences and in low traffic areas
- not acceptable as a fire exit stair except possibly for residences
- provides strong vertical emphasis (line in space, point in plan)

landing platforms always occur in a 90° quadrant section

SPIRAL STAIR

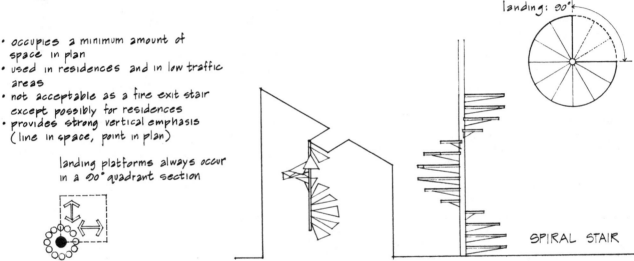

RAMPS

Ramps allow smooth, easy transitions to be made between changes in level. Utilizing comfortably low slopes, they require relatively long horizontal runs. They may be used to provide:

- access for the handicapped
- access for equipment traffic
- smooth vertical travel through, around, or along a high space

Short, straight ramps act as beams and may be constructed as linear wood, steel, or concrete floor systems. Long, curvilinear ramps must be of reinforced concrete or steel construction. Ramps should have non-slip surfaces, especially when exposed to the weather.

The ramp configuration depends on the size and form of the space, and the required length of run for the vertical change in level.

- maximum slope 1:8
- consult local codes

- for the handicapped 1:12

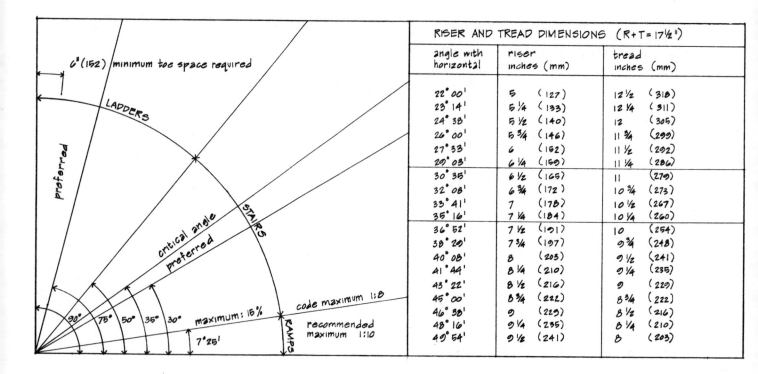

angle with horizontal	riser inches (mm)	tread inches (mm)
22° 00'	5 (127)	12 ½ (318)
23° 14'	5 ¼ (133)	12 ¼ (311)
24° 38'	5 ½ (140)	12 (305)
26° 00'	5 ¾ (146)	11 ¾ (299)
27° 33'	6 (152)	11 ½ (292)
29° 03'	6 ¼ (159)	11 ¼ (286)
30° 35'	6 ½ (165)	11 (279)
32° 08'	6 ¾ (172)	10 ¾ (273)
33° 41'	7 (178)	10 ½ (267)
35° 16'	7 ¼ (184)	10 ¼ (260)
36° 52'	7 ½ (191)	10 (254)
38° 29'	7 ¾ (197)	9 ¾ (248)
40° 08'	8 (203)	9 ½ (241)
41° 44'	8 ¼ (210)	9 ¼ (235)
43° 22'	8 ½ (216)	9 (229)
45° 00'	8 ¾ (222)	8 ¾ (222)
46° 38'	9 (229)	8 ½ (216)
48° 16'	9 ¼ (235)	8 ¼ (210)
49° 54'	9 ½ (241)	8 (203)

RISER AND TREAD DIMENSIONS (R+T= 17½")

Stairs can be physically tiring as well as psychologically forbidding. They should be neither too steep nor too shallow. For most situations, a riser slightly over 7"(178) is recommended. This dimension however should be adjusted to satisfy specific user requirements.

For comfort as well as safety, certain proportions between riser and tread should be maintained. The table and rules of thumb to the right give guidelines for the determination of these proportions for interior stairs. Exterior stairs are generally less steep than interior stairs, especially where dangerous conditions such as snow and ice exist.

All risers must be identical in height, again for comfort and safety. The total rise should be divided by a whole number which would give a riser height closest to what is desired.

Since in any flight of stairs there is always one less tread than riser, the total run may easily be determined once the height and number of risers are known and the riser: tread ratio fixed.

• 3 rules of thumb for the determination of the riser to tread ratio:

  • riser x run = 72 to 75   (dimensions in inches)
  • riser + run = 17 to 17½
  • 2(riser)+ run = 24 to 25

• for exterior stairs:

  • 2(riser) + run = 26   (dimensions in inches)

• always check local or applicable codes for minimum and maximum dimensions for stairs

• some guidelines are:

  • maximum riser = 7½" (191)
  • minimum tread = 10 " (254)

• for residences:

  • maximum riser = 8" (203)
  • minimum tread = 9 " (229)

Stairs should be designed and constructed to comfortably accommodate the passage of the human body. What is presented here are general guidelines for dimensional clearances. Specific user requirements may take precedence and should therefore be considered.

Local fire and building codes should be checked for fire exit stair requirements: location, access, size, enclosure and construction.

Stair width guidelines:
minimum for residences   : 2'8" (813)
        light occupancy : 3'0 (914)
        normal occupancy: 3'6" (1067)

Psychological sense of clearance may be more critical than physical clearance. If so, the overhead clearance should be such that a person cannot extend and touch the stair ceiling.

Some codes require wall curvature at corners in fire exit stairs in public buildings to prevent congestion in case of panic.

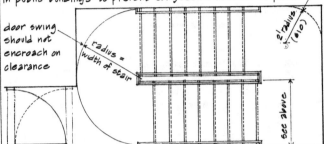

door swing should not encroach on clearance

radius = width of stair

2'radius (610)

see above

door should swing in direction of exit travel

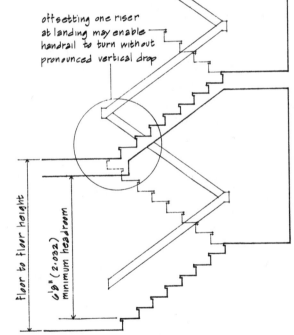

offsetting one riser at landing may enable handrail to turn without pronounced vertical drop

floor to floor height

6'8" (2.032) minimum headroom

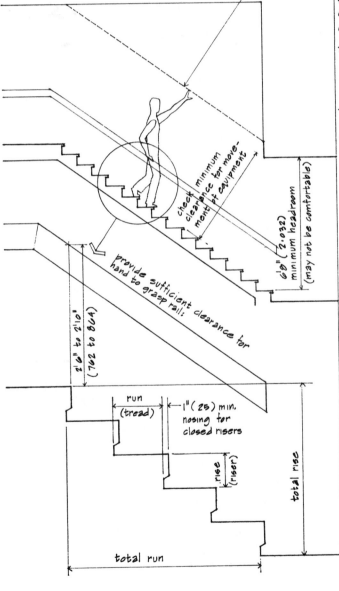

check minimum clearance for movement of equipment

6'8" (2.032) minimum headroom (may not be comfortable)

provide sufficient clearance for hand to grasp rail:

2'6" to 2'10" (762 to 864)

run (tread)

1" (25) min. nosing for closed risers

rise (riser)

total rise

total run

STAIR ELEMENTS:

• stair carriage spans between post and beam or wall supports –
• 3 carriages generally required when stair is wider than 3' (914) depending on size and spanning capability of tread material

• carriage may be entirely supported by wall framing when stair is enclosed in a walled shaft

• treads act as small beams and span between carriage supports
• size may vary but should be at least 1¼" (32) thick

• stair may have open (no riser) or closed risers

• stair stringers are usually housed or cut to the profile of the risers and treads

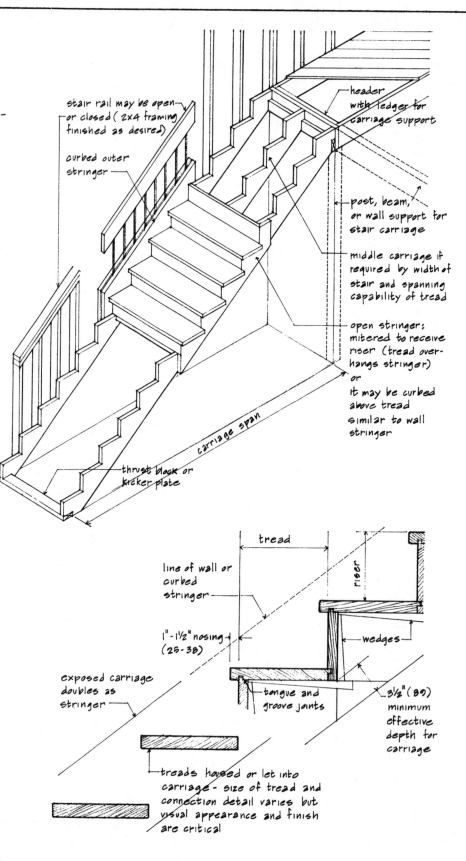

stair rail may be open or closed (2x4 framing finished as desired)

curbed outer stringer

header with ledger for carriage support

post, beam, or wall support for stair carriage

middle carriage if required by width of stair and spanning capability of tread

open stringer; mitered to receive riser (tread over-hangs stringer) or

it may be curbed above tread similar to wall stringer

carriage span

thrust block or kicker plate

tread

line of wall or curbed stringer

riser

1"-1½" nosing (25-38)

wedges

exposed carriage doubles as stringer

tongue and groove joints

3½" (89) minimum effective depth for carriage

treads housed or let into carriage - size of tread and connection detail varies but visual appearance and finish are critical

- analogous to wood stairs in form

- steel channel sections act as both carriage and stringer in supporting treads

- steel channel stringers may be post and beam, or wall supported

- steel treads span between the steel channel stringers

- steel treads are usually in the form of pans filled with lightweight concrete

- they may also be left exposed as flat plates (with textured surfaces) or open gratings for use in utility stairs

- pre-engineered and prefabricated steel stairs are available

- may also be pre-erected at the factory

railing may be supported by an adjacent wall or by posts or balustrades secured to the channel stringer

post, beam or wall support for steel channel stringers

steel treads (see below)

metal deck or pan construction for landing platform

steel channel or I-beam landing supports framed into wall or post and beam supported

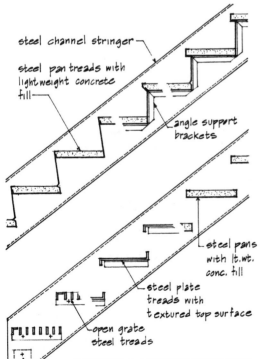

steel channel stringer

steel pan treads with lightweight concrete fill

angle support brackets

steel pans with lt.wt. conc. fill

steel plate treads with textured top surface

open grate steel treads

clip angle to anchor steel channel

CLOSED RISERS

- form of steel pan varies as shown - consult manufacturer

OPEN RISERS

- connections may be bolted or welded depending on finish appearance desired

- wood treads also possible

Reinforced concrete stairs are designed as slabs and require structural analysis of load, support, and span conditions.

- form of stair as well as the individual risers and treads may vary as desired
- cantilevered designs possible

- extensive formwork and weight of construction is an important consideration
- precast stair elements available

- used where fireproof construction is required

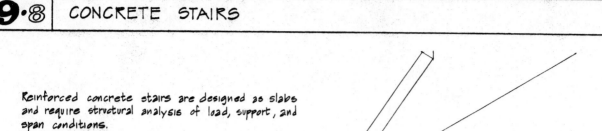

beam or wall support for stair slab

stair form may vary as desired

span of stair slab

various metal nosings are available to protect edge

resilient flooring filler

serrated surface

abrasive fillers

- treads for concrete stairs may be of metal (aluminum, bronze, or cast iron), rubber, or vinyl
- nosing form varies
- other finishes possible: slate, marble, terrazzo, carpeting

form of toe space may vary

nosing bar to strengthen edge

beam or wall support

stair slab thickness (preliminary guideline = span/26)

steel reinforcement as required

3/4" (10) radius typical

span of stair slab

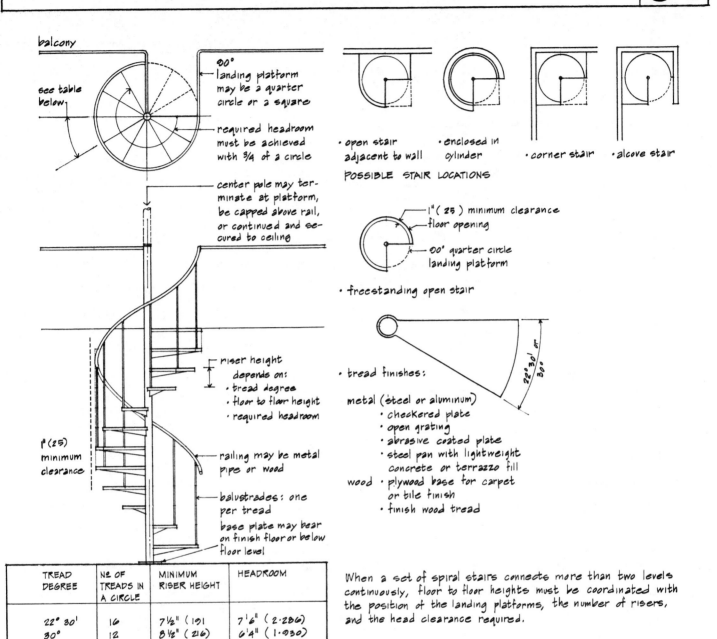

balcony

see table below

90° landing platform may be a quarter circle or a square

required headroom must be achieved with ¾ of a circle

center pole may terminate at platform, be capped above rail, or continued and secured to ceiling

riser height depends on:
· tread degree
· floor to floor height
· required headroom

railing may be metal pipe or wood

balustrades: one per tread

base plate may bear on finish floor or below floor level

1" (25) minimum clearance

· open stair adjacent to wall
· enclosed in cylinder
· corner stair
· alcove stair

POSSIBLE STAIR LOCATIONS

1" (25) minimum clearance
floor opening
90° quarter circle landing platform

· freestanding open stair

22° 30' or 30°

· tread finishes:

metal (steel or aluminum)
· checkered plate
· open grating
· abrasive coated plate
· steel pan with lightweight concrete or terrazzo fill

wood · plywood base for carpet or tile finish
· finish wood tread

TREAD DEGREE	Nº OF TREADS IN A CIRCLE	MINIMUM RISER HEIGHT	HEADROOM
22° 30'	16	7½" (191)	7'6" (2·286)
30°	12	8½" (216)	6'4" (1·930)

When a set of spiral stairs connects more than two levels continuously, floor to floor heights must be coordinated with the position of the landing platforms, the number of risers, and the head clearance required.

STAIR DIAMETER	FINISHED WELL OPENING	WIDTH FROM CENTER OF POST TO RAIL	PLATFORM SIZE: SQUARE OR ¼ CIRCLE	BASE PLATE: OUTSIDE DIAMETER	CENTER POLE OUTSIDE DIAMETER
3' 6" (1·067)	3' 8" (1·118)	17" (432)	22" (550)	10" (254)	3½" (89)
4' 0" (1·219)	4' 2" (1·270)	20" (508)	25" (635)	10" (254)	3½" (89)
4' 6" (1·372)	4' 8" (1·422)	23" (584)	28" (711)	10" (254)	3½" (89)
5' 0" (1·524)	5' 2" (1·575)	26" (660)	31" (787)	12" (305)	4½" (114)
5' 6" (1·676)	5' 8" (1·727)	29" (737)	34" (864)	12" (305)	4½" (114)
6' 0" (1·829)	6' 2" (1·880)	31½" (800)	37" (940)	12" (305)	4½" (114)
6' 6" (1·981)	6' 8" (2·032)	34½" (876)	40" (1016)	12" (305)	4½" (114)
7' 0" (2·134)	7' 2" (2·184)	37½" (953)	43" (1092)	12" (305)	6" (152)
7' 6" (2·286)	7' 8" (2·337)	40½" (1029)	46" (1168)	12" (305)	6" (152)
8' 0" (2·438)	8' 2" (2·489)	43½" (1105)	49" (1245)	12" (305)	6" (152)

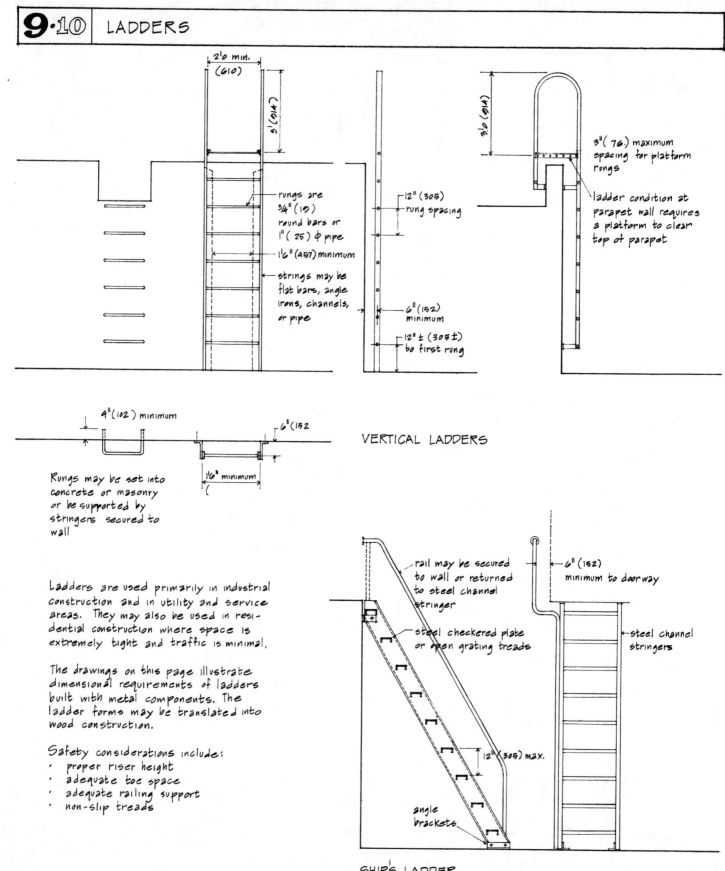

2'0 min. (610)

3' (914)

rungs are 3/4" (19) round bars or 1" (25) ∅ pipe

1'6" (457) minimum

strings may be flat bars, angle irons, channels, or pipe

12" (305) rung spacing

6" (152) minimum

12" ± (305±) to first rung

3'0 (914)

3" (76) maximum spacing for platform rungs

ladder condition at parapet wall requires a platform to clear top of parapet

4" (102) minimum

6" (152)

1'6" minimum

Rungs may be set into concrete or masonry or be supported by stringers secured to wall

VERTICAL LADDERS

Ladders are used primarily in industrial construction and in utility and service areas. They may also be used in residential construction where space is extremely tight and traffic is minimal.

The drawings on this page illustrate dimensional requirements of ladders built with metal components. The ladder forms may be translated into wood construction.

Safety considerations include:
· proper riser height
· adequate toe space
· adequate railing support
· non-slip treads

rail may be secured to wall or returned to steel channel stringer

steel checkered plate or open grating treads

6" (152) minimum to doorway

steel channel stringers

12" (305) max.

angle brackets

SHIP'S LADDER

Elevators provide means of direct, vertical traffic for a building's occupants, equipment, and supplies. The type, size, and number of elevators required is determined by:
- the type and tempo of traffic carried
- the total vertical distance traveled: (the number of floors served and the building's floor-to-floor height)
- the average round-trip time and elevator speed desired

Factors to consider in planning for elevators in a building include:
- size, material, and structural requirements for the elevator shaft
- structural support requirements for the elevator and its hoisting equipment
- space and enclosure requirements for the elevator's hoisting and control equipment
- electric power and control equipment required
- lobby space requirements for banks of elevators

The following are guidelines for preliminary planning only. Consult local codes and the elevator manufacturer for specific size, structural, and enclosure requirements.

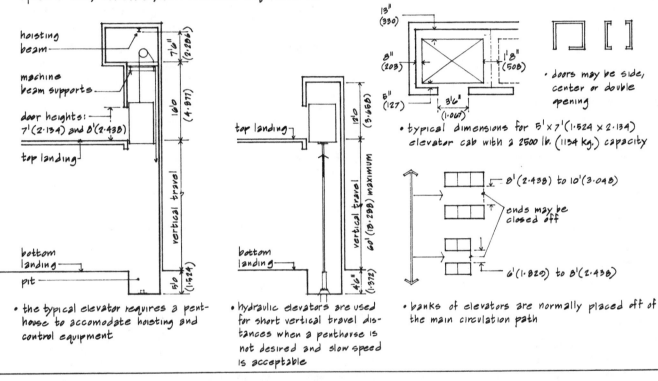

- the typical elevator requires a penthouse to accommodate hoisting and control equipment

- hydraulic elevators are used for short vertical travel distances when a penthouse is not desired and slow speed is acceptable

- doors may be side, center or double opening

- typical dimensions for 5'x7' (1·524 x 2·134) elevator cab with a 2500 lb. (1134 kg.) capacity

- ends may be closed off

- banks of elevators are normally placed off of the main circulation path

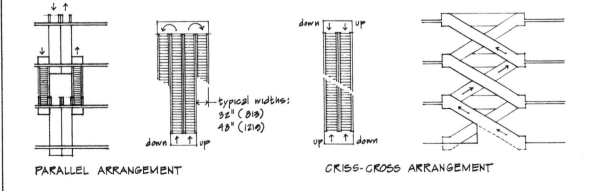

Escalators provide rapid, comfortable vertical travel without long waiting periods. They are normally installed at a 30° angle with the horizontal and may be arranged in a parallel or criss-cross (scissors) arrangement. They should be located in the line of traffic with adequate queuing space at loading and discharge points.

typical widths:
32" (813)
48" (1219)

PARALLEL ARRANGEMENT

CRISS-CROSS ARRANGEMENT

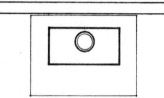

FREESTANDING

- seen as a freestanding object within room
- prefabricated, self-contained units are available in various designs
- should be set on an incombustible base
- exposed flue (metal-lined and insulated) either rises through ceiling or runs through wall to the exterior
- consult manufacturer for designs, sizes, and clearance requirements

OPEN FRONT

OPENING HEIGHT	HEARTH SIZE (width x depth)	FLUE SIZE (modular type)
29" (737)	30"x16" (762 x 406)	12"x12" (305 x 305)
29" (737)	36"x16" (914 x 406)	12"x12" (305 x 305)
29" (737)	40"x16" (1016 x 406)	12"x16" (305 x 406)
32" (813)	48"x18" (1219 x 457)	16"x16" (406 x 416)

- most common fireplace type
- of masonry or prefabricated metal
- directional (frontal) in form

OPEN FRONT AND SIDE

OPENING HEIGHT	HEARTH SIZE (width x depth)	FLUE SIZE (modular type)
26" (660)	32"x16" (813 x 406)	12"x16" (305 x 406)
29" (737)	40"x16" (1016 x 406)	16"x16" (406 x 406)
29" (737)	48"x20" (1219 x 508)	16"x16" (406 x 406)

- open corner may be cantilevered or post-supported
- bi-directional: primary visual direction along the diagonal with a secondary one perpendicular to the long face

OPEN FRONT AND BACK

OPENING HEIGHT	HEARTH SIZE (width x depth)	FLUE SIZE (modular type)
29" (737)	32"x28" (813 x 711)	16"x16" (406 x 406)
29" (737)	36"x28" (914 x 711)	16"x20" (406 x 508)
29" (737)	40"x28" (1016 x 711)	16"x20" (406 x 508)

- located within a space-dividing element
- directional (frontal) toward 2 spaces

OPEN 3 SIDES   4 SIDES

OPENING HEIGHT	HEARTH SIZE (width x depth)	FLUE SIZE (modular type)
27" (686)	36"x32" (914 x 813)	20"x20" (508 x 508)
27" (686)	36"x36" (914 x 914)	20"x20" (508 x 508)
27" (686)	44"x40" (1118 x 1016)	20"x20" (508 x 508)

- open corners may be cantilevered or post-supported
- metal fireplace hoods and flues may be suspended from above
- may be visually multi-directional or omnidirectional depending on its form and proportions

• EFFECTIVE FIREPLACE DESIGN ENSURES
- proper combustion of the fuel material
- proper exhaustion of smoke and other combustion by-products
- the radiation of maximum heat comfortably into the room
- fire safety in construction

• FACTORS TO CONSIDER IN THE DESIGN AND CONSTRUCTION OF FIREPLACES
- form, proportion, and dimensions of the combustion chamber
- size and location of the throat, damper, and smoke chamber
- free flue area in proportion to combustion chamber
- position of the flue sufficiently above roof plane for proper draft
- size and location of fireplace in relation to size and form of room

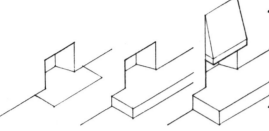

- appearance of a fireplace depends on:
  - materials and finish used in the combustion chamber
  - materials and position of the front hearth, whether flush with the finish floor or raised above it
  - material and finish of the surrounding wall plane as well as the proportion and placement of the fireplace opening within the wall plane
- the information on the following pages pertains only to those technical aspects necessary for the proper functioning of an open front fireplace and does not imply a specific visual design

- multi-faced fireplaces, even though they may be correctly designed and constructed may still have serious smoking problems due to certain draft conditions which may exist in the room
- placement and orientation of these types of fireplaces therefore is of critical importance and each specific situation should be carefully considered with regard to potential draft problems

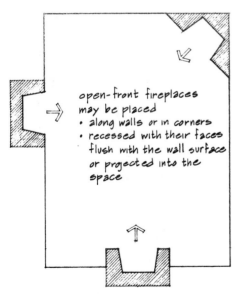

open-front fireplaces may be placed
- along walls or in corners
- recessed with their faces flush with the wall surface or projected into the space

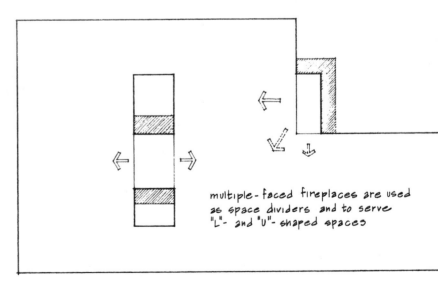

multiple-faced fireplaces are used as space dividers and to serve "L"- and "U"-shaped spaces

• FIREPLACE LOCATIONS

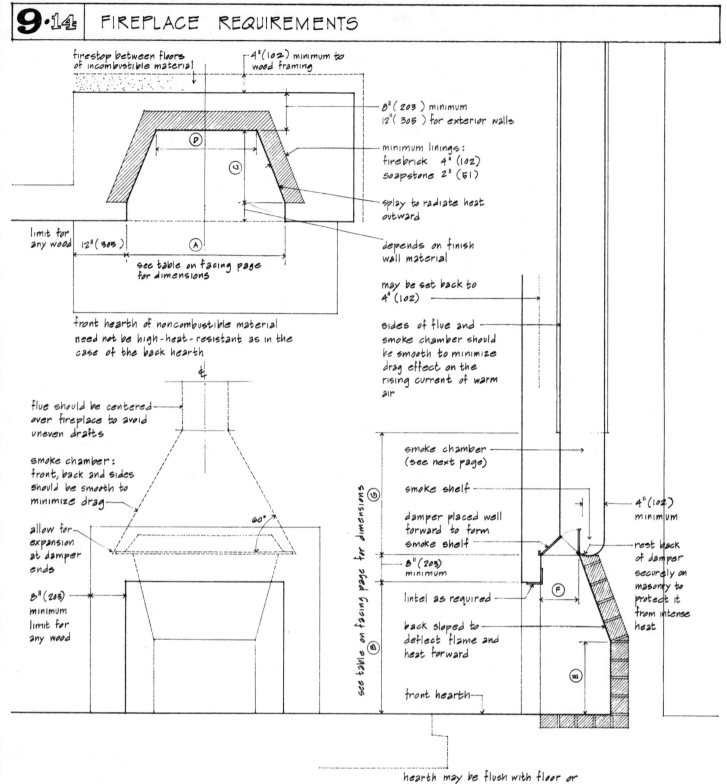

firestop between floors
of incombustible material

4" (102) minimum to
wood framing

8" (203) minimum
12" (305) for exterior walls

minimum linings:
firebrick 4" (102)
soapstone 2" (51)

splay to radiate heat
outward

depends on finish
wall material

limit for
any wood

12" (305)

see table on facing page
for dimensions

may be set back to
4" (102)

sides of flue and
smoke chamber should
be smooth to minimize
drag effect on the
rising current of warm
air

front hearth of noncombustible material
need not be high-heat-resistant as in the
case of the back hearth

flue should be centered
over fireplace to avoid
uneven drafts

smoke chamber:
front, back and sides
should be smooth to
minimize drag

allow for
expansion
at damper
ends

8" (203)
minimum
limit for
any wood

60°

see table on facing page for dimensions

smoke chamber
(see next page)

smoke shelf

damper placed well
forward to form
smoke shelf

8" (203)
minimum

lintel as required

back sloped to
deflect flame and
heat forward

front hearth

4" (102)
minimum

rest back
of damper
securely on
masonry to
protect it
from intense
heat

hearth may be flush with floor or
raised as desired

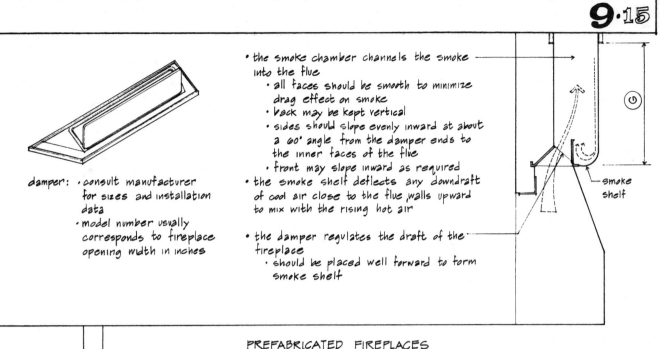

damper: · consult manufacturer for sizes and installation data
· model number usually corresponds to fireplace opening width in inches

- the smoke chamber channels the smoke into the flue
  - all faces should be smooth to minimize drag effect on smoke
  - back may be kept vertical
  - sides should slope evenly inward at about a 60° angle from the damper ends to the inner faces of the flue
  - front may slope inward as required
- the smoke shelf deflects any downdraft of cool air close to the flue walls upward to mix with the rising hot air

- the damper regulates the draft of the fireplace
  - should be placed well forward to form smoke shelf

smoke shelf

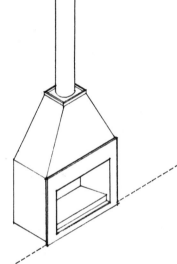

PREFABRICATED FIREPLACES

- most prefabricated fireplaces have metal exteriors with heat-resistant insulating liners
- may be used in most standard building construction systems
- may have zero clearance requirement between unit and adjacent surfaces
- standard components available include: built-in damper, chimney starter sections, prefabricated flue sections, and chimney housing tops
- may be self-trimming or finish wall may surround opening

- consult manufacturer for sizes, details, and installation data

- standard widths include: 28" (711)   typical height = 30" (762)
                           36" (914)
                           42" (1067)
                           44" (1118)
                           48" (1219)

The following table gives recommended finished dimensions for open front fireplaces (in inches and metric equivalents). Refer to drawings on the preceding page for locations of dimensions.

WIDTH (A)	HEIGHT (B)	DEPTH (C)	BACK (D)	VERTICAL BACK (E)	THROAT (F)	SMOKE CHAMBER (G)	FLUE SIZE: ROUND (H)	MODULAR (I)
30 (762)	29 (737)	16 (406)	17 (432)	14 (356)	8¾ (222)	24 (610)	10 (254)	12×12 (305×305)
32 (813)	29 (737)	16 (406)	19 (483)	14 (356)	8¾ (222)	24 (610)	10 (254)	12×12 (305×305)
36 (914)	29 (737)	16 (406)	23 (584)	14 (356)	8¾ (222)	27 (686)	12 (305)	12×12 (305×305)
40 (1016)	29 (737)	16 (406)	27 (686)	14 (356)	8¾ (222)	29 (737)	12 (305)	12×12 (305×305)
42 (1067)	32 (813)	16 (406)	29 (737)	14 (356)	8¾ (222)	32 (813)	12 (305)	16×16 (406×406)
48 (1219)	32 (813)	18 (457)	33 (838)	14 (356)	8¾ (222)	37 (940)	15 (381)	16×16 (406×406)
54 (1372)	37 (940)	20 (508)	37 (940)	16 (406)	13 (330)	45 (1143)	15 (381)	16×20 (406×508)
60 (1524)	37 (940)	22 (559)	42 (1067)	16 (406)	13 (330)	45 (1143)	15 (381)	16×20 (406×508)
60 (1524)	40 (1016)	22 (559)	42 (1067)	16 (406)	13 (330)	45 (1143)	18 (457)	16×20 (406×508)
72 (1829)	40 (1016)	22 (559)	54 (1372)	16 (406)	13 (330)	56 (1422)	18 (457)	20×20 (508×508)
84 (2134)	40 (1016)	24 (610)	64 (1626)	20 (508)	13 (330)	67 (1702)	20 (508)	20×20 (508×508)
96 (2438)	40 (1016)	24 (610)	76 (1930)	20 (508)	13 (330)	75 (1905)	22 (559)	20×20 (508×508)

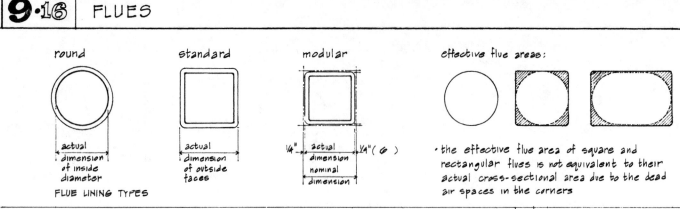

round
standard
modular

actual
dimension
of inside
diameter

actual
dimension
of outside
faces

1/4" actual
dimension
nominal
dimension 1/4" (6)

FLUE LINING TYPES

effective flue areas:

- the effective flue area of square and rectangular flues is not equivalent to their actual cross-sectional area due to the dead air spaces in the corners

Flues are open vertical shafts which carry smoke and other combustion by-products to the outside air. They are required not only for fireplaces but also for any fuel burning heating equipment and incinerators

- the size of the flue required depends on the size and draft requirements of the unit it serves
- for fireplaces, a general rule of thumb is: free or effective flue area should be 1/10 of the fireplace opening

- for maximum draft, a flue should not serve more than one heating unit

- sloped flue sections should be avoided
- if offsets are required, the angle should less than 45° (60° is preferred), and the effective area should be maintained throughout

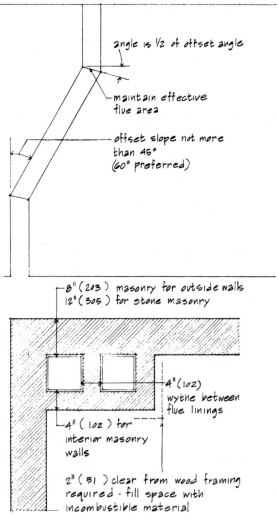

angle is 1/2 of offset angle

maintain effective flue area

offset slope not more than 45° (60° preferred)

- the interior faces of the flue should be smooth and free of rough spots to minimize drag effect on smoke and eliminate areas for soot to deposit

- masonry chimneys usually have terra cotta or expanded shale linings - consult manufacturers for available types and sizes
- required masonry protection for these flue linings are given in the drawing to the right
- all masonry around the flue should have full mortar joints, tightly packed to prevent leaks

- prefabricated chimney sections are also available
- consists of an inner lining of high heat resistant material surrounded by insulation and an outer covering of rust-resistant metal

8" (203) masonry for outside walls
12" (305) for stone masonry

4" (102) wythe between flue linings

4" (102) for interior masonry walls

2" (51) clear from wood framing required - fill space with incombustible material

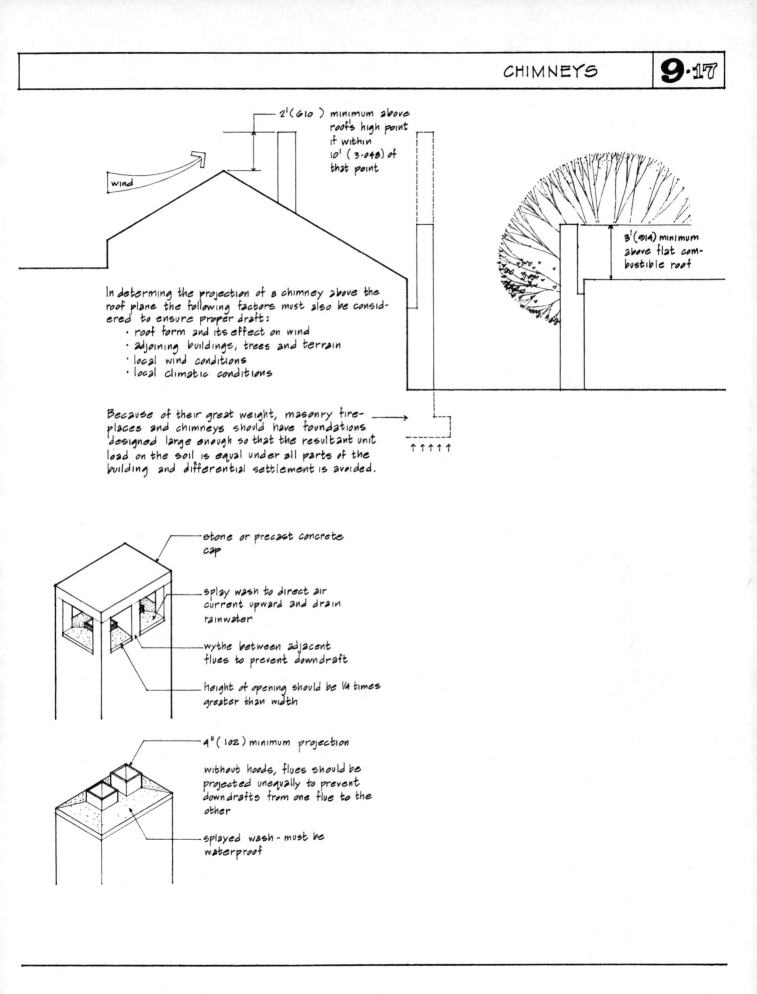

2' (610) minimum above roof's high point if within 10' (3·048) of that point

wind

3' (914) minimum above flat combustible roof

In determing the projection of a chimney above the roof plane the following factors must also be considered to ensure proper draft:
· roof form and its effect on wind
· adjoining buildings, trees and terrain
· local wind conditions
· local climatic conditions

Because of their great weight, masonry fireplaces and chimneys should have foundations designed large enough so that the resultant unit load on the soil is equal under all parts of the building and differential settlement is avoided.

stone or precast concrete cap

splay wash to direct air current upward and drain rainwater

wythe between adjacent flues to prevent downdraft

height of opening should be ¼ times greater than width

4" (102) minimum projection

without hoods, flues should be projected unequally to prevent downdrafts from one flue to the other

splayed wash - must be waterproof

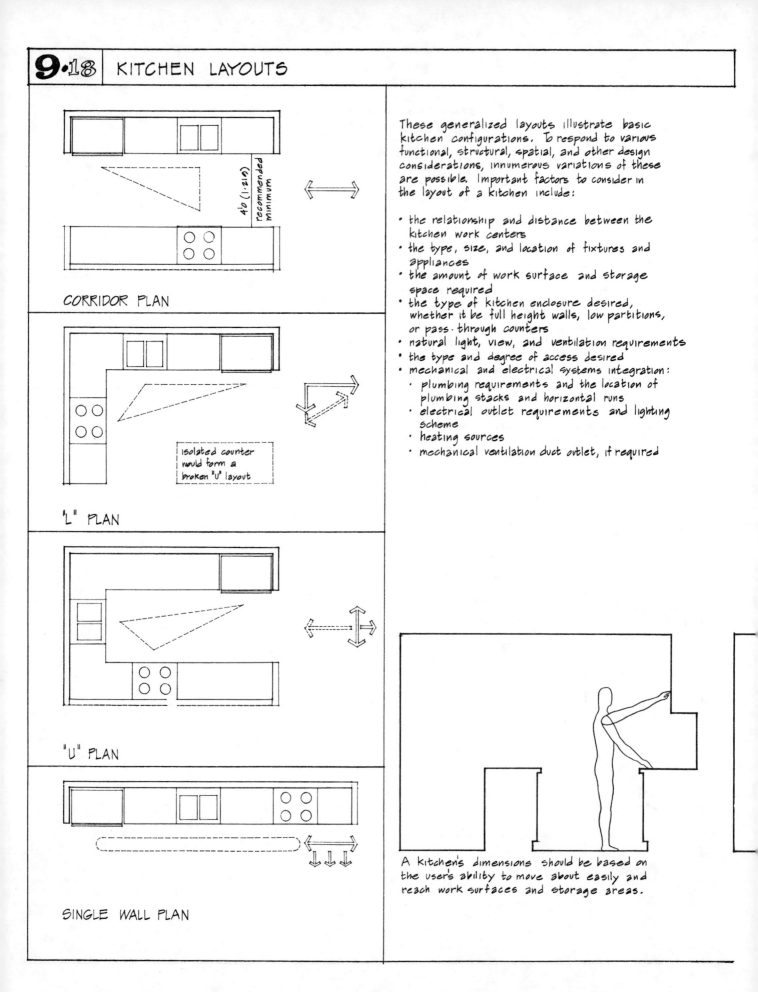

CORRIDOR PLAN

4'0 (1.210) recommended minimum

"L" PLAN

isolated counter would form a broken "U" layout

"U" PLAN

SINGLE WALL PLAN

These generalized layouts illustrate basic kitchen configurations. To respond to various functional, structural, spatial, and other design considerations, innumerous variations of these are possible. Important factors to consider in the layout of a kitchen include:

- the relationship and distance between the kitchen work centers
- the type, size, and location of fixtures and appliances
- the amount of work surface and storage space required
- the type of kitchen enclosure desired, whether it be full height walls, low partitions, or pass-through counters
- natural light, view, and ventilation requirements
- the type and degree of access desired
- mechanical and electrical systems integration:
  - plumbing requirements and the location of plumbing stacks and horizontal runs
  - electrical outlet requirements and lighting scheme
  - heating sources
  - mechanical ventilation duct outlet, if required

A kitchen's dimensions should be based on the user's ability to move about easily and reach work surfaces and storage areas.

top of cabinets may be closed off
with a furred space or fascia, or
it may be used as extra storage
for rarely used items

cabinets should
project flush with
refrigerator

pass through to
adjacent space

24"
(610)

range

1"(25) lip
typical

24" (610)
typical

36" (914)
typical

36"
(914)

sink

provide toe space

15"
(381)

18"
(457)

minimum recommended clearances

to corner

refrigerator

note:• all length dimensions should be
based upon and coordinated with
standard kitchen cabinet sizes
*see following page

• assume the following widths for appliances for
preliminary planning: range   30" (762)
refrigerator 36" (914)
sink   30" (762) * see 9·23

• verify with manufacturer

may be furred space or extra storage
for rarely used items

18" - 30" (457 - 762)

wall cabinet:
back requires
finish

12"-18"
(305)-(457)

edge condition of
counter varies
according to proximity
of appliances, outlets,
and chair height

30" (762) for chairs
36" (914) for stools

18" (457)

30" (762)

18" (457)
for range hoods

36" (914)

24" (610)

24" (610)

18" (457)
minimum

36" (914)

72" (1·829) highest shelf advisable

84" (2·134) overall

• pass through counter

• above sinks and ranges

• typical

WORK HEIGHTS AND CABINET CLEARANCES

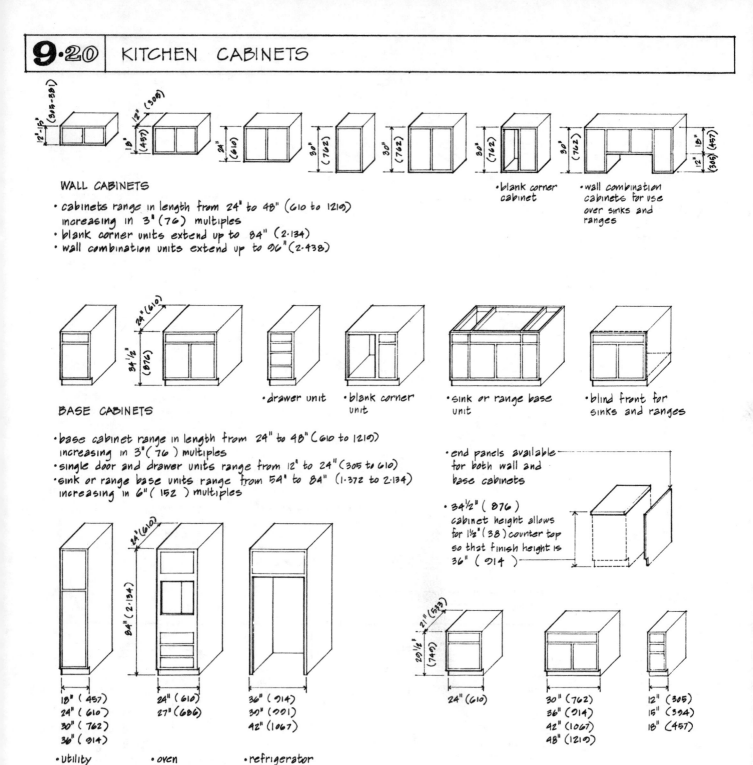

WALL CABINETS

- cabinets range in length from 24" to 48" (610 to 1219) increasing in 3" (76) multiples
- blank corner units extend up to 84" (2.134)
- wall combination units extend up to 96" (2.438)

• blank corner cabinet

• wall combination cabinets for use over sinks and ranges

BASE CABINETS

• drawer unit

• blank corner unit

• sink or range base unit

• blind front for sinks and ranges

- base cabinet range in length from 24" to 48" (610 to 1219) increasing in 3" (76) multiples
- single door and drawer units range from 12" to 24" (305 to 610)
- sink or range base units range from 54" to 84" (1.372 to 2.134) increasing in 6" (152) multiples

• end panels available for both wall and base cabinets

• 34½" (876) cabinet height allows for 1½" (38) counter top so that finish height is 36" (914)

18" (457)
24" (610)
30" (762)
36" (914)
• utility

24" (610)
27" (686)
• oven

36" (914)
30" (991)
42" (1067)
• refrigerator

MISCELLANEOUS CABINETS

24" (610)

30" (762)
36" (914)
42" (1067)
48" (1219)

12" (305)
15" (394)
18" (457)

VANITY CABINETS

- finishes available: metal   • painted
                       wood   • hardwood veneer for natural finish
                               • plastic laminate skin
                               • painted

- countertops may be: metal • stainless steel
                      wood   • laminated wood
                             • plastic laminate on wood

- consult manufacturer for type, sizes, finishes, accessories, and installation data

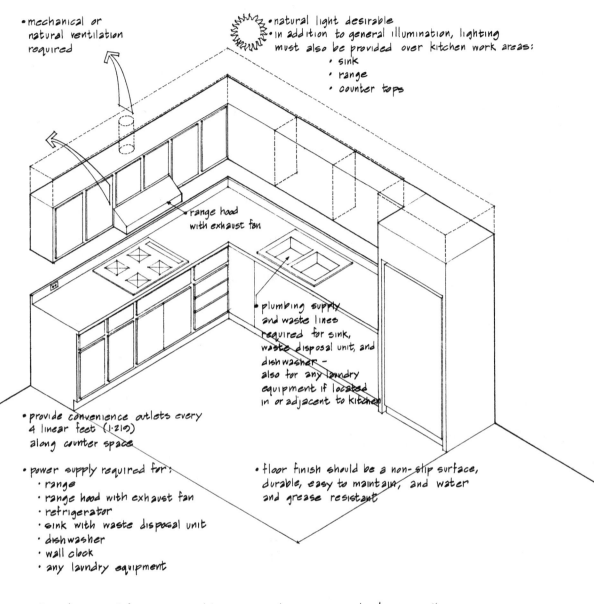

• mechanical or natural ventilation required

• natural light desirable
• in addition to general illumination, lighting must also be provided over kitchen work areas:
  • sink
  • range
  • counter tops

• range hood with exhaust fan

• plumbing supply and waste lines required for sink, waste disposal unit, and dishwasher — also for any laundry equipment if located in or adjacent to kitchen

• provide convenience outlets every 4 linear feet (1·210) along counter space

• power supply required for:
  • range
  • range hood with exhaust fan
  • refrigerator
  • sink with waste disposal unit
  • dishwasher
  • wall clock
  • any laundry equipment

• floor finish should be a non-slip surface, durable, easy to maintain, and water and grease resistant

• all surfaces and finishes should be water and grease-resistant, especially along counter tops and work areas

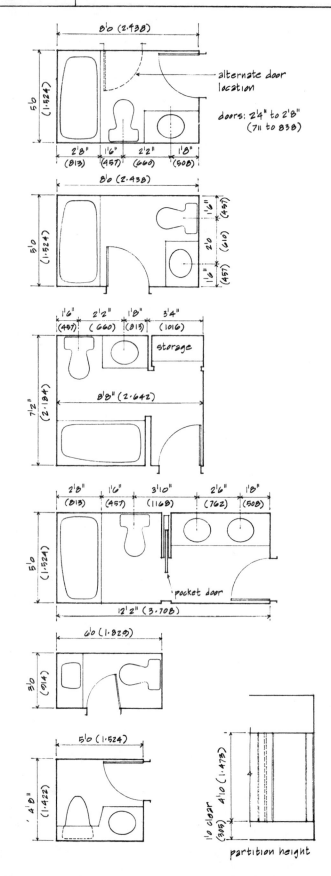

As with the kitchen layouts on page 9·18 these bathroom layouts illustrate only basic configurations and relationships and may be adjusted to suit specific situations.

Clearances between fixtures as well as between fixtures and wall surfaces are important for comfortable and safe movement within the space. Recommended clearances can be perceived through the study of these plans and the drawings on the facing page.

Because of the presence of high humidity levels within the space, materials used should be moisture-resistant. They should also be durable, sanitary, and easy to clean.

Natural or mechanical ventilation of the space is required not only to lower the humidity level but also for health and comfort reasons.

Another consideration in the layout of bathrooms and other restroom facilities is the number of plumbing walls required and the location of stacks, vents, and horizontal runs.

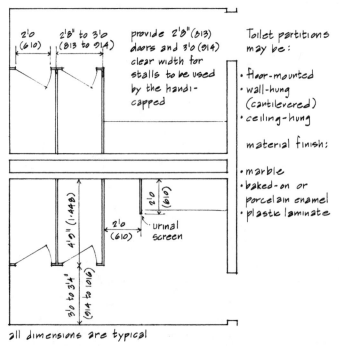

provide 2'8" (813) doors and 3'0 (914) clear width for stalls to be used by the handi-capped

Toilet partitions may be:

- floor-mounted
- wall-hung (cantilevered)
- ceiling-hung

material finish:

- marble
- baked-on or porcelain enamel
- plastic laminate

partition height

all dimensions are typical

The dimensions for the fixtures shown below are averages for preliminary planning. Consult manufacturer for the actual dimensions of the model to be used.

 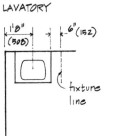 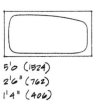 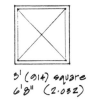

width : 1'10" (559)
depth : 2'4" (711)
height : 1'3" (381) to seat

WATER CLOSET

2'6" (762)
1'9" (533)
2'7" (787)

LAVATORY

2'0 (610)
1'8" (508)
2'7" (787)

LAVATORY

5'0 (1524)
2'6" (762)
1'4" (406)

BATHTUB

3' (914) square
6'8" (2·032)

SHOWER

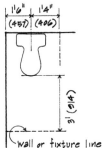 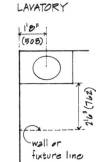 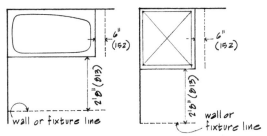

1'6" (457)   1'4" (406)

3' (914)

wall or fixture line

1'8" (508)

2'6" (762)

wall or fixture line

1'8" (508)   6" (152)

fixture line

6" (152)

2'6" (613)

wall or fixture line

6" (152)

2'6" (613)

wall or fixture line

RECOMMENDED FIXTURE CLEARANCES

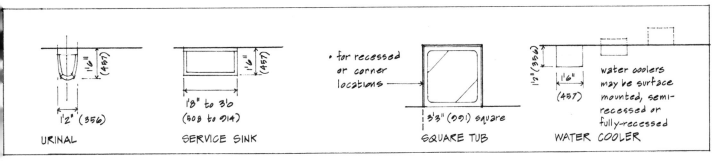

1'6" (457)

1'2" (356)

URINAL

1'6" (457)

1'8" to 3'0 (508 to 914)

SERVICE SINK

• for recessed or corner locations →

3'3" (991) square

SQUARE TUB

1'2" (356)

1'6" (457)

water coolers may be surface mounted, semi-recessed or fully-recessed

WATER COOLER

FIXTURE MATERIALS

• water closets and urinals — vitreous china

• lavatories, service sinks, and bath tubs
  — vitreous china
  — enameled cast iron
  — enameled steel

• shower receptors
  — terrazzo
  — enameled steel

• shower stalls
  — enameled or
  — stainless steel

• bathtub and shower enclosures may also be of ceramic tile or one-piece Fiberglas units

• kitchen sinks
  — enameled cast iron
  — porcelain enameled steel
  — stainless steel

1'8" (508)

2'6" (762)

1'8" (508)

2'8" (813)

 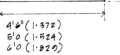

2'0 (610)

4'6" (1·372)
5'0 (1·524)
6'0 (1·829)

KITCHEN SINKS

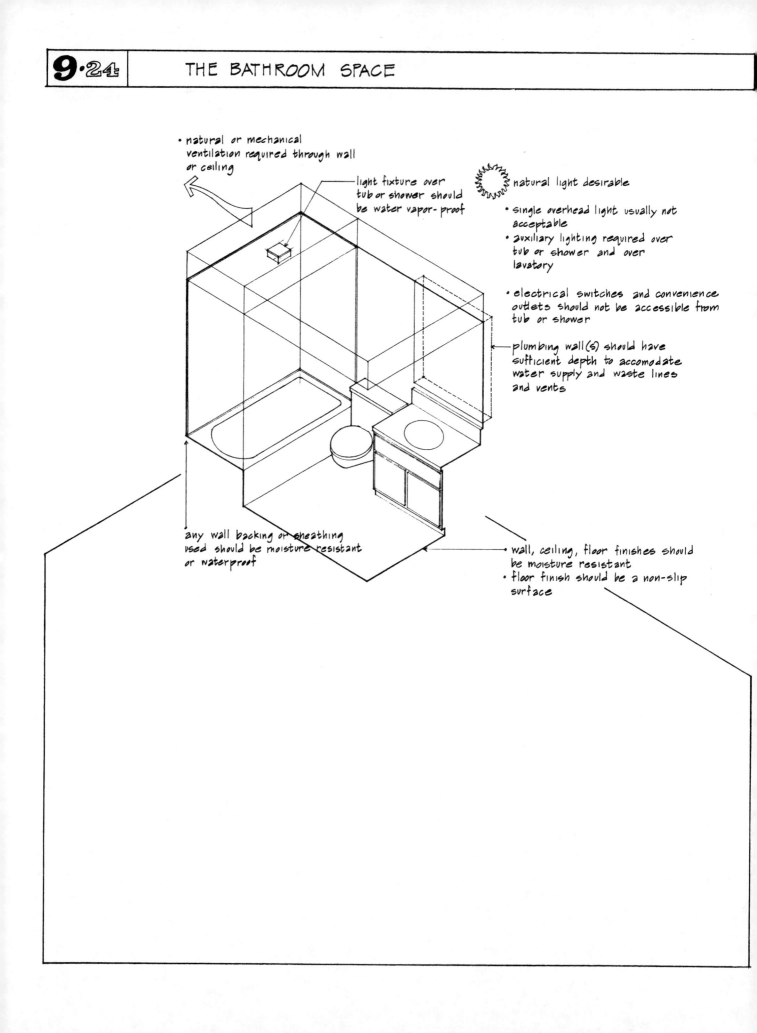

• natural or mechanical ventilation required through wall or ceiling

light fixture over tub or shower should be water vapor-proof

natural light desirable

• single overhead light usually not acceptable
• auxiliary lighting required over tub or shower and over lavatory

• electrical switches and convenience outlets should not be accessible from tub or shower

plumbing wall(s) should have sufficient depth to accomodate water supply and waste lines and vents

any wall backing or sheathing used should be moisture resistant or waterproof

• wall, ceiling, floor finishes should be moisture resistant
• floor finish should be a non-slip surface

FINISH WORK

This chapter illustrates major methods and materials used to provide the finish skin to exterior and interior surfaces, both vertical and horizontal.

Exterior wall surfaces must be weather resistant, durable, and relatively maintenance free. Interior walls should be wear resistant and cleanable; floors should be safe (non-slip) and durable against traffic wear; ceilings should be maintenance free.

The strength of a finish material depends on its stiffness and/or brittleness and the rigidity of its backing, whether a planar material or a network of thin framing members.

The modular characteristics of a finish material may dictate the dimensions of a wall, floor, or ceiling surface. A finish material's acoustical, thermal, and fire resistance values may also be important considerations in their use.

For visual appearance, all finish materials should be considered in terms of their color, texture, pattern, scale, modular characteristics, and their jointing and edge conditions.

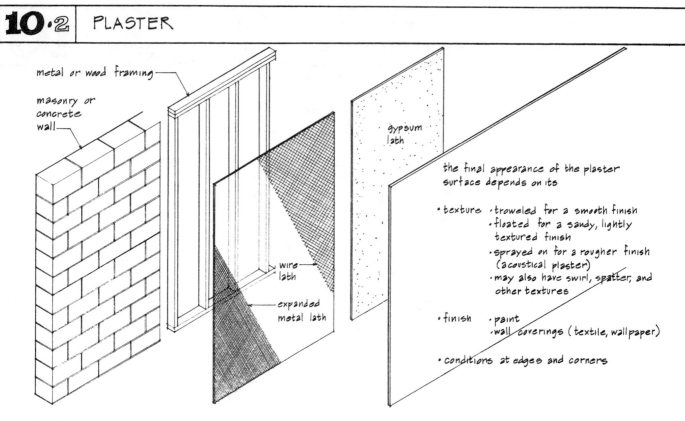

metal or wood framing

masonry or concrete wall

gypsum lath

wire lath

expanded metal lath

the final appearance of the plaster surface depends on its

- texture · troweled for a smooth finish
  - · floated for a sandy, lightly textured finish
  - · sprayed on for a rougher finish (acoustical plaster)
  - · may also have swirl, spatter, and other textures
- finish · paint
  - · wall coverings (textile, wallpaper)
- conditions at edges and corners

BASE

masonry walls:

- plaster may be applied directly to masonry surfaces
- these surfaces should be sufficiently rough and porous to allow for absorption and a good bond, and free of oil and other parting materials
- glazed tile or brick and dense, smooth concrete surfaces should not be used for direct application of plaster
- where there is a possibility of moisture or condensation getting into the wall, plaster should applied over furring

wood and metal framing:

- must be sturdy, rigid, plane and level
- deflection should be limited to 1/360 th of the framing's span
- requires support of metal or gypsum lath

LATH

metal lath:

- may be of expanded metal or of wire fabric
- usually of copper-bearing steel, galvanized or coated with rust-inhibitive paint
- weight and strength of lath used depends on the spacing of its supports

gypsum lath:

- similar to gypsum wallboard
- used as a basecoat for gypsum plaster
- adhesion provided by porous or fibrous paper covering
- perforated gypsum lath provides for better mechanical keying
- insulating and fire-resistant lath available

PLASTER

Plaster is a cementitious material that is suitable for both interior and exterior surfaces. Gypsum plaster may be used for any interior wall or ceiling surface not subject to severe moisture conditions and protected exterior surfaces not directly exposed to water. Exterior plaster or stucco (usually of portland cement) may be used for both exterior and interior walls and ceiling surfaces.

Gypsum plaster is usually composed of any or all of the following: gypsum or Keene's cement, lime, water hair, fibers, and sand. Mineral aggregates may also be added to alter the plaster's properties. Consult the manufacturer or the Gypsum Association for the types of plaster and the recommended proportions and mix of the above ingredients.

Plaster is applied in layers, the number of which depends on the type and strength of the base.

3 coat plaster:
1. scratch coat · must be strong to adhere firmly to lath, and raked to provide a keyed foundation for the following coats
2. brown coat · leveling coat (brought out to the grounds or screeds) that acts as a base for the finish coat
3. finish coat · the visible plaster surface

2 coat plaster is similar to the above except that the brown coat is doubled back before the scratch coat is set.

WOOD LATH

rarely used currently

METAL LATHS
wire fabric   expanded metal

· widths: 24". 27". 48" (610) (686) (1210)
· lengths: 8'· 10'· 12' (2·438) (3·048) (3·658)

GYPSUM LATH

· 3/8" (10) or 1/2" (13) thick
· 16" (406) wide
· 48" (1·210) long
· lengths up to 12' (3·658) are available
· covered with porous paper for adhesion of plaster
· edges tapered or rounded for better bond with plaster

LATH TYPE	LATH WEIGHT		MAXIMUM SUPPORT SPACING · inches (mm) on center			
			VERTICAL SUPPORTS		HORIZONTAL SUPPORTS	
	PSF	(kg/m²)	WOOD -	METAL -	WOOD OR - CONCRETE	METAL
flat expanded metal	.27	(1.5)	16 (406)	12 (305)	0	0
	.37	(1.8)	16 (406)	16 (406)	16 (406)	13½ (343)
flat rib metal	.30	(1.5)	16 (406)	16 (406)	16 (406)	12 (305)
	.37	(1.8)	19 (483)	19 (483)	19 (483)	19 (483)
3/8" ( ) rib metal	.37	(1.8)	24 (610)	24 (610)	24 (610)	19 (483)
	.44	(2.1)	24 (610)	24 (610)	24 (610)	24 (610)
sheet metal	.50	(2.4)	24 (610)	24 (610)	24 (610)	24 (610)
wire lath	.27	(1.3)	16 (406)	16 (406)	13½ (343)	13½ (343)
wire fabric w/ paper backing			16 (406)	16 (406)	16 (406)	16 (406)

Metal trim shapes are used to finish off edges and corners of plaster surfaces and to provide grounds and screeds to work against so that the finish plaster is brought to a true thickness and a straight level surface. For this reason, all grounds and screeds should be securely fastened to its support and installed straight, level, and plumb. Wood grounds may be used where a nailing base is required for additional trim.

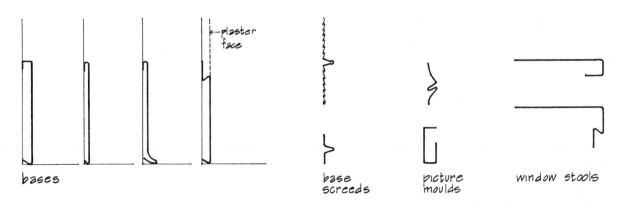

square end

modified square end

quarter round end

casing beads : expanded and solid wing types

expanded wing   flexible   bullnose

corner beads

←plaster face

bases

base screeds

picture moulds

window stools

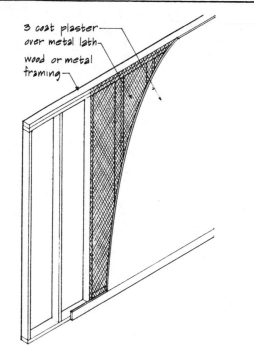

3 coat plaster over metal lath

wood or metal framing

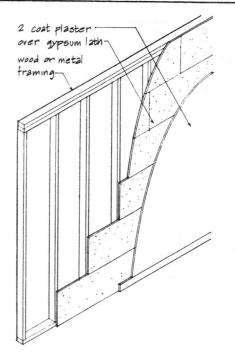

2 coat plaster over gypsum lath

wood or metal framing

PLASTER OVER METAL LATH

- 3 coat plaster is normally used over metal lath although 2 coat plaster may also be used

- the spacing of the wood or metal supports depends on the type and weight of metal lath used
  * see table on 10·3

- metal laid is laid with their long dimension across the supports; rib lath is laid with the ribs across the supports
- lap sides ½"(13) and ends 1" (25)
- no joints should occur at corners

PLASTER OVER GYPSUM LATH

- 2 coat plaster is normally used over gypsum lath

- the spacing of the wood or metal supports depends on the thickness of the gypsum lath:
- support spacing not more 16"(406)o.c. for 3/8"(10)lath
                              24 "(610)o.c. for ½"(13) lath
- lath is laid with the long dimension perpendicular to the supports
- ends of lath should bear on a support member
- internal corners, and corners of wall openings should be reinforced with strips of metal lath

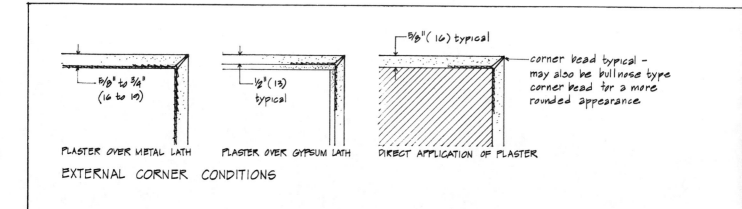

5/8" to 3/4"
(16 to 19)

PLASTER OVER METAL LATH

½"(13)
typical

PLASTER OVER GYPSUM LATH

5/8"(16) typical

corner bead typical - may also be bullnose type corner bead for a more rounded appearance

DIRECT APPLICATION OF PLASTER

EXTERNAL CORNER CONDITIONS

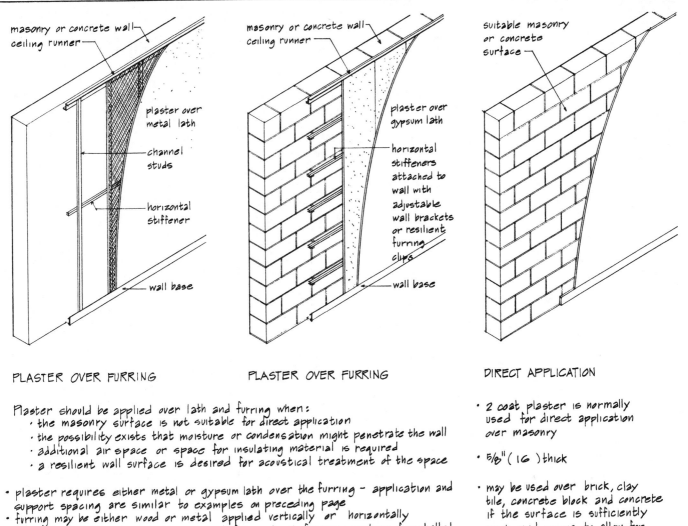

masonry or concrete wall
ceiling runner

plaster over metal lath
channel studs
horizontal stiffener
wall base

masonry or concrete wall
ceiling runner

plaster over gypsum lath
horizontal stiffeners attached to wall with adjustable wall brackets or resilient furring clips
wall base

suitable masonry or concrete surface

PLASTER OVER FURRING

PLASTER OVER FURRING

DIRECT APPLICATION

Plaster should be applied over lath and furring when:
- the masonry surface is not suitable for direct application
- the possibility exists that moisture or condensation might penetrate the wall
- additional air space or space for insulating material is required
- a resilient wall surface is desired for acoustical treatment of the space

- plaster requires either metal or gypsum lath over the furring - application and support spacing are similar to examples on preceding page
- furring may be either wood or metal applied vertically or horizontally
- horizontal stiffeners may be required for vertical furring members if installed away from masonry wall
- furring may be attached to wall with resilient furring clips for acoustical treatment and independent movement between plaster and masonry
- wall brackets are available that adjust to various furring depths

- 2 coat plaster is normally used for direct application over masonry

- 5/8" (16) thick

- may be used over brick, clay tile, concrete block and concrete if the surface is sufficiently rough and porous to allow for absorption and a good bond
- * see additional notes on page 10.2

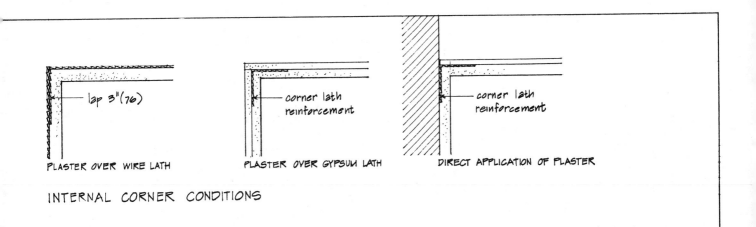

lap 3" (76)

corner lath reinforcement

corner lath reinforcement

PLASTER OVER WIRE LATH

PLASTER OVER GYPSUM LATH

DIRECT APPLICATION OF PLASTER

INTERNAL CORNER CONDITIONS

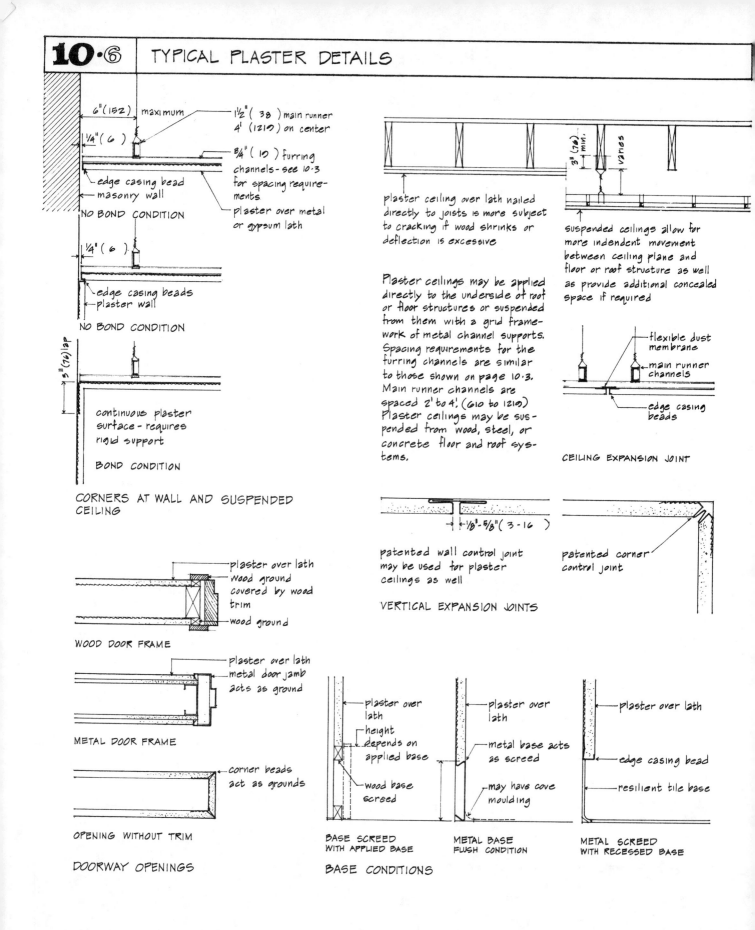

6" (152) maximum

1/4" (6)

1 1/2" (38) main runner
4' (1210) on center

3/4" (10) furring
channels- see 10·3
for spacing require-
ments

edge casing bead
masonry wall

plaster over metal
or gypsum lath

NO BOND CONDITION

1/4" (6)

edge casing beads
plaster wall

NO BOND CONDITION

5" (76) lap

continuous plaster
surface - requires
rigid support

BOND CONDITION

CORNERS AT WALL AND SUSPENDED
CEILING

3" (76) min.

varies

plaster ceiling over lath nailed
directly to joists is more subject
to cracking if wood shrinks or
deflection is excessive

Plaster ceilings may be applied
directly to the underside of roof
or floor structures or suspended
from them with a grid framework of metal channel supports.
Spacing requirements for the
furring channels are similar
to those shown on page 10·3.
Main runner channels are
spaced 2' to 4' (610 to 1210)
Plaster ceilings may be suspended from wood, steel, or
concrete floor and roof systems.

suspended ceilings allow for
more indendent movement
between ceiling plane and
floor or roof structure as well
as provide additional concealed
space if required

flexible dust
membrane

main runner
channels

edge casing
beads

CEILING EXPANSION JOINT

1/8"- 5/8" (3-16)

patented wall control joint
may be used for plaster
ceilings as well

VERTICAL EXPANSION JOINTS

patented corner
control joint

plaster over lath
wood ground
covered by wood
trim
wood ground

WOOD DOOR FRAME

plaster over lath
metal door jamb
acts as ground

METAL DOOR FRAME

corner beads
act as grounds

OPENING WITHOUT TRIM

DOORWAY OPENINGS

plaster over
lath
height
depends on
applied base

wood base
screed

BASE SCREED
WITH APPLIED BASE

plaster over
lath

metal base acts
as screed

may have cove
moulding

METAL BASE
FLUSH CONDITION

plaster over lath

edge casing bead

resilient tile base

METAL SCREED
WITH RECESSED BASE

BASE CONDITIONS

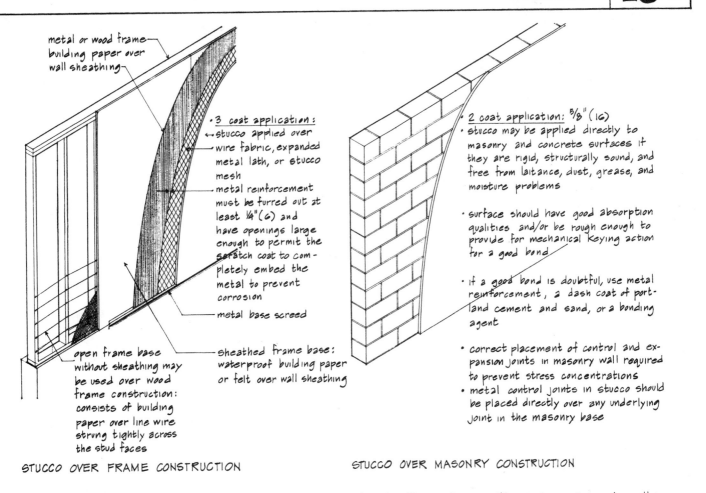

metal or wood frame
building paper over
wall sheathing

· 3 coat application:
← stucco applied over
wire fabric, expanded
metal lath, or stucco
mesh
· metal reinforcement
must be furred out at
least ¼"(6) and
have openings large
enough to permit the
scratch coat to com-
pletely embed the
metal to prevent
corrosion
· metal base screed

· sheathed frame base:
waterproof building paper
or felt over wall sheathing

open frame base
without sheathing may
be used over wood
frame construction:
consists of building
paper over line wire
strung tightly across
the stud faces

· 2 coat application: ⅝" (16)
· stucco may be applied directly to
masonry and concrete surfaces if
they are rigid, structurally sound, and
free from laitance, dust, grease, and
moisture problems

· surface should have good absorption
qualities and/or be rough enough to
provide for mechanical keying action
for a good bond

· if a good bond is doubtful, use metal
reinforcement, a dash coat of portland cement and sand, or a bonding
agent

· correct placement of control and expansion joints in masonry wall required
to prevent stress concentrations
· metal control joints in stucco should
be placed directly over any underlying
joint in the masonry base

STUCCO OVER FRAME CONSTRUCTION   STUCCO OVER MASONRY CONSTRUCTION

Stucco or exterior plaster is normally used for exterior wall and soffit surfaces although it may be used equally
well for interior walls and ceilings. It is similar to gypsum plaster in materials and application except that portland
cement or an epoxy formulation is used instead of gypsum to produce a weather-, fire-, and fungus-resistant surface.

Like gypsum plaster, stucco is a thin, hard, and brittle material that requires a sturdy, rigid, unyielding base. Since
stucco is normally applied over exterior structural walls, it is susceptible to cracking due to structural movement of
the base support, and stresses caused by variations in temperature and humidity levels. Control and relief joints
are therefore required to eliminate or minimize any cracking.

A variety of textures is possible, from smooth, troweled finishes to floated, sandy or pebbled surfaces. A range of
colors may be attained through the use of colored sand, stone chips, and pigment.

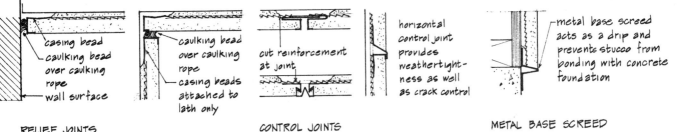

casing bead
caulking bead
over caulking
rope
wall surface

caulking bead
over caulking
rope
casing beads
attached to
lath only

cut reinforcement
at joint

horizontal
control joint
provides
weathertight-
ness as well
as crack control

metal base screed
acts as a drip and
prevents stucco from
bonding with concrete
foundation

RELIEF JOINTS   CONTROL JOINTS   METAL BASE SCREED

Relief joints permit unrestrained move-   Control joints relieve stresses due to shrinkage and/or structural movement
ment of the stucco membrane and are   of the base support. When applied over building paper backing and metal rein-
required at internal corners or where   forcement, stucco should have control joints no more than 18' (5.486) apart
the stucco abuts a structural element.   forming panels not larger than 150 SF (14 m²)

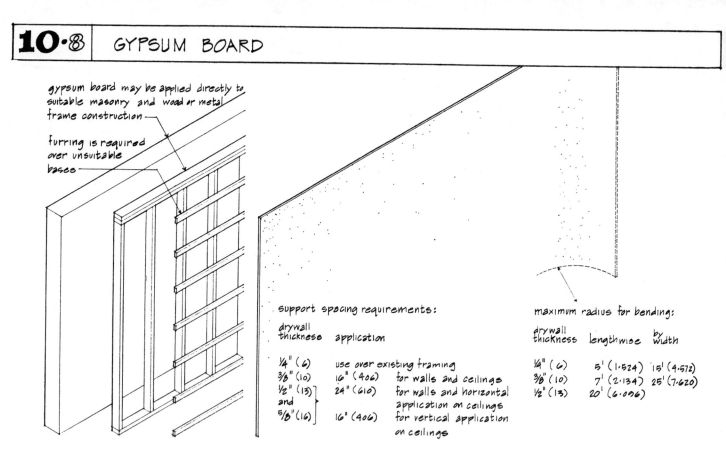

gypsum board may be applied directly to suitable masonry and wood or metal frame construction

furring is required over unsuitable bases

support spacing requirements:

drywall thickness		application	
¼" (6)		use over existing framing	
⅜" (10)	16" (406)	for walls and ceilings	
½" (13) and	24" (610)	for walls and horizontal application on ceilings	
⅝" (16)	16" (406)	for vertical application on ceilings	

maximum radius for bending:

drywall thickness	lengthwise	by width
¼" (6)	5' (1·524)	15' (4·572)
⅜" (10)	7' (2·134)	25' (7·620)
½" (13)	20' (6·096)	

Gypsum board consists of a gypsum core surfaced and edged with various cover materials to satisfy specific performance, application, location and appearance requirements. It has good fire-resistance and dimensional stability. The various types, sizes, and uses of gypsum board are listed below.

Gypsum wallboard is commonly referred to as "drywall" because of its low moisture content and little or no water is used in its application to interior wall and ceiling surfaces. It may be fairly easily erected to form a smooth surface, monolithic in appearance, and finished by painting or applying a paper, vinyl, or fabric wall covering.

TYPE & EDGE	THICKNESS	SIZES	USE OR DESCRIPTION
• regular wallboard tapered	¼" · ⅜" · ½" (6) (10) (13)	4' × 8'·10'·12'·14' (1·210) × (2·438)(3·048)(3·658)(4·267)	surface layer for interior walls and ceilings
• insulating tapered	⅜"·½" (10) (13)	4' × 8'·9'·10'·12' (1·210) × (2·438)(2·743)(3·048)(3·658)	backed with aluminum foil which serves as reflective insulation and a vapor barrier
• moisture-resistant tapered	½"·⅝" (13) (16)	4' × 8'·12' (1·210) × (2·438)(3·658)	base for ceramic or other non-absorbent tile in high moisture areas
• waterproof square	½"·⅝" (13) (16)	4' × 11' (1·210) × (3·353)	similar to above but vinyl-surfaced for use in areas subject to direct wetting – may be fire rated
• fire-resistant (type x) tapered	½"·⅝" (13) (16)	4' × 8'·9'·10'·12' (1·210) × (1·210)(2·743)(3·048)(3·658)	core has glass fiber and other additives for use in fire-resistance rated construction – available with foil backing
• pre-decorated square or beveled	⅜"·½"·⅝" (10) (13) (16)	4' × 8'·9'·10' (1·210) × (1·210)(2·743)(3·048)	vinyl and paper surfaced in various colors, patterns and textures
• backing board square or t&g	⅜"·½"·⅝" (10) (13) (16)	2' or 4' × 8' (610) or (1·210) × (2·438)	base for multi-ply construction – available in regular, fire-resistant, and insulating types
• gypsum sheathing square or t&g	½" (13)	2' or 4' × 8'·9' (610) or (1·210) × (2·438)(2·743)	base for exterior wall finish in wood or metal frame construction – serves as a wind brace and is fire and weather-resistant

• maximum allowable deflection for ceilings = 1/240 span

• furring may be of wood : 1½" (38) face dimension - 2 x 2 (51×51) preferred
or metal: drywall, cold-rolled, or resilient channels

• spacing requirements similar to those for frame construction

• joints at interior corners and between edges and ends should be reinforced with tape and joint compound to produce smooth, monolithic appearance

• horizontal application : length of gypsum board perpendicular to framing
• vertical application : length of gypsum board parallel to framing

Gypsum board may be applied directly to wood or metal frame construction if the spacing of the support members is appropriate for the thickness of gypsum board used (see table on preceding page), and if the face of the frame forms a flat and level plane. The frame must also be structurally sound and rigid enough to prevent the gypsum board from buckling or cracking.

If the spacing of the support members is inadequate or if the frame is not sufficiently flat, the gypsum board should be applied over wood or metal furring.

Gypsum board may be applied to above grade masonry or concrete walls if the surface is dry, smooth, free from oil and other parting materials, and if the plane of the wall is flat and level. Exterior and below-grade masonry or concrete walls require furring before the application of gypsum board to eliminate the capillary transfer of water and minimize condensation on interior wall surfaces.

Besides the reasons mentioned above, furring may also be used to:

Gypsum board may be attached to its supports with nails, screws, or adhesives, or with nails and adhesives.

2 ply gypsum board construction is used when sturdier construction, greater fire-resistance, or improved acoustical isolation is desired.

External corners and exposed edges should be protected against damage by wood trim or metal corner beads and edge trim. Metal trim pieces require finishing with a joint compound.

• improve the thermal insulating properties of exterior walls
• provide additional wall depth to accomodate mechanical equipment
• allow for the use of resilient channels to improve acoustical isolation or isolate the gypsum board from structural movement

corner bead   edge trims

• metal trim pieces

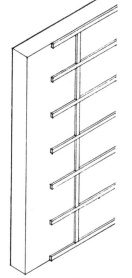

Plywood may be used for interior paneling of walls and ceilings as well as exterior siding depending on its grade, thickness, and finish.

* see 10·20

Plywood may be applied directly to wood or metal framing and furring. Furring is required over masonry walls and may also be used when improved thermal insulation properties, greater acoustical isolation, or additional wall depth is desired.

Application is made normally with nails or screws although water-resistant adhesive may be used for additional rigidity.

The final appearance of a plywood wall surface depends on:
- its surface color, grain or "figure", and finish (see facing page)
- the treatment of the joints between the plywood panels and at corners

- masonry wall base with furring
  (1x2 nominal)
  (25×51)

- wood or metal framing with or without furring
  plywood furring strips minimize the effect of shrinkage of wood framing members on the plywood joints

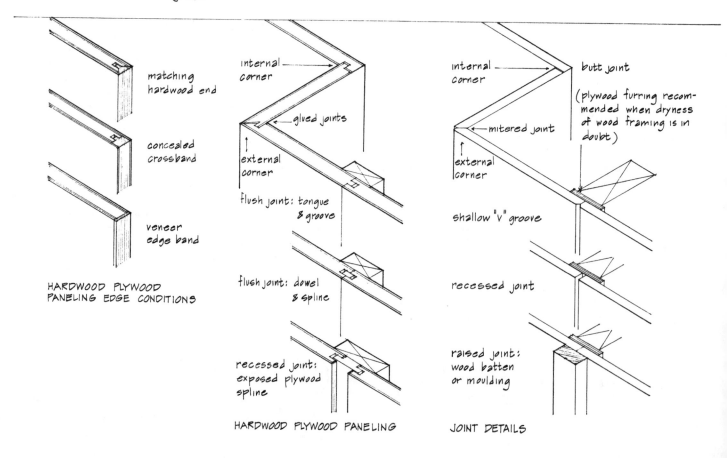

matching hardwood end

concealed crossband

veneer edge band

HARDWOOD PLYWOOD PANELING EDGE CONDITIONS

internal corner

glued joints

external corner

flush joint: tongue & groove

flush joint: dowel & spline

recessed joint: exposed plywood spline

HARDWOOD PLYWOOD PANELING

internal corner

butt joint

(plywood furring recommended when dryness of wood framing is in doubt)

mitered joint

external corner

shallow "v" groove

recessed joint

raised joint: wood batten or moulding

JOINT DETAILS

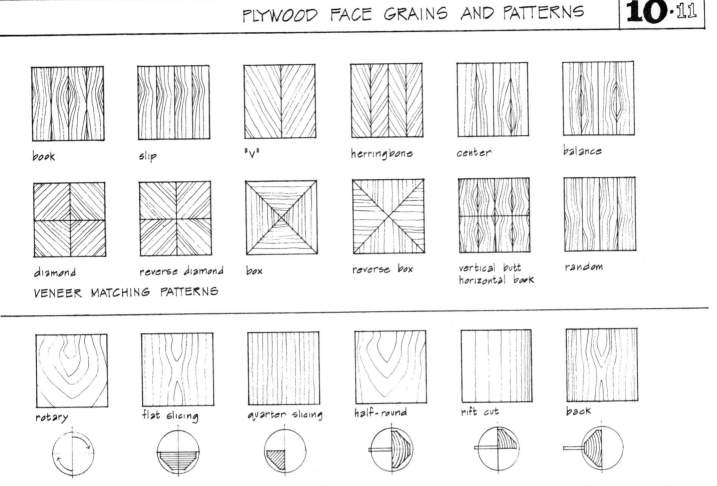

book   slip   "V"   herringbone   center   balance

diamond   reverse diamond   box   reverse box   vertical butt horizontal book   random

VENEER MATCHING PATTERNS

rotary   flat slicing   quarter slicing   half-round   rift cut   back

WOOD GRAIN FIGURES: Various wood grain figure patterns may be produced by varying the way in which the wood veneer is cut from the log.

If the plywood paneling surface is to be painted, the surface must be sanded and without blemishes. If the surface is to have a natural finish, face veneers are used. The final appearance of the plywood paneling in the latter case depends on the species of wood used for the veneer, its grain figure, and the pattern developed by the way in which the panels are matched or arranged.

TYPES OF HARDWOOD PLYWOOD	
technical	fully waterproof bond
type I (exterior)	fully waterproof bond/ weather and fungus resistant
type II (interior)	water resistant bond
type III (interior)	moisture resistant bond

SIZES	WIDTHS	LENGTHS	THICKNESSES
	18" (457)	4' (1·219)	1/8" to 1"
	24" (610)	5' (1·524)	(3 to 25)
	32" (813)	6' (1·829)	in 1/16" (2) and
	36" (914)	7' (2·134)	1/8" (3)
	48" (1219)	8' (2·438)	increments
		10' (3·048)	

GRADES OF HARDWOOD PLYWOOD

premium grade	1	with very slight imperfections
good grade	1	suitable for natural finishes /has no sharp contrasts
sound grade	2	suitable for painted finishes
utility grade	3	may have open defects but are limited in size/no species selected/ no matching
backing grade	4	may have many flaws/no species selected/ no matching

CERAMIC TILE BASES AND APPLICATIONS:

① over water resistant gypsum board, plywood, or plaster, applied with waterproof organic adhesive

② over frame construction, set with cement mortar over metal or gypsum lath

③ over sound, dimensionally stable masonry or concrete walls, set with cement mortar, thin set mortar, or organic adhesive

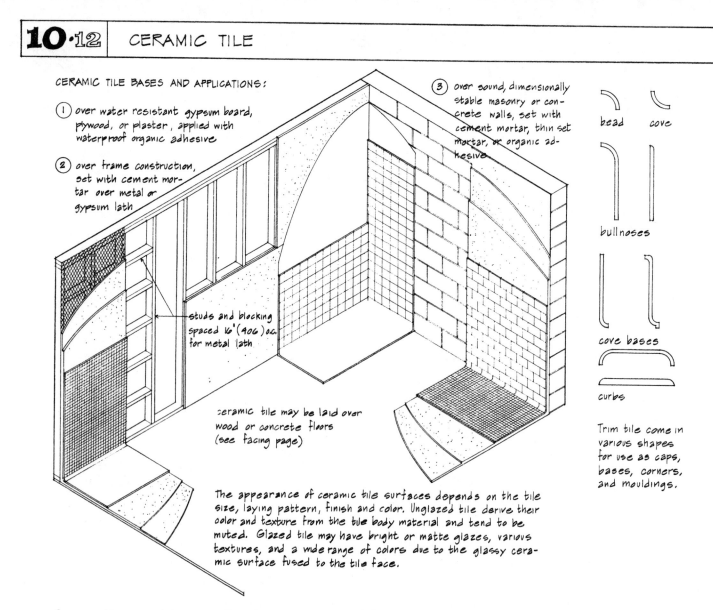

bead   cove

bullnoses

cove bases

curbs

Trim tile come in various shapes for use as caps, bases, corners, and mouldings.

studs and blocking spaced 16" (406) o.c. for metal lath

ceramic tile may be laid over wood or concrete floors (see facing page)

The appearance of ceramic tile surfaces depends on the tile size, laying pattern, finish and color. Unglazed tile derive their color and texture from the tile body material and tend to be muted. Glazed tile may have bright or matte glazes, various textures, and a wide range of colors due to the glassy ceramic surface fused to the tile face.

Ceramic tile are relatively small surfacing units made of fired clay and other ceramic materials. It provides a permanent, durable, waterproof, and easily cleanable surface for interior walls and ceilings. Glazed weatherproof tile and paving tile may be used for exterior surfaces. The types of ceramic tile differ according to material composition, manufacturing process, finish, and degree of vitrification (a measure of tile's density and absorptivity).

CERAMIC TILE TYPE	SIZES	THICK	USE
glazed wall tile	4¼" × 4¼" (108 × 108) 4¼" × 6" (108 × 152) 6" × 6" (152 × 152)	5/16" (8)	interior tiles: for interior walls/non-vitreous exterior tiles: weatherproof and frostproof / for both exterior and interior walls, and (with dull or matte finish) for light or moderate duty floors/semi-vitreous
ceramic mosaic tile	1" × 1" (25 × 25) 1" × 2" (25 × 51) 2" × 2" (51 × 51)	¼" (6) unglazed	porcelain type: resistant to freezing and abrasion of foot wear/ for floors and walls / bright colors/ vitreous natural clay type: muted colors/semi-vitreous
quarry tile and pavers	2¾" × 6" (70 × 152) 4" × 4" (102 × 102) 4" × 6" (102 × 152) 6" × 6" (152 × 152) 6" × 9" (152 × 229) 9" × 9" (229 × 229)	½" and (13) ¾" (19)	quarry tile: unglazed floor tile of natural clay/impervious to moisture, dirt and stains/resistant to freezing and abrasion pavers: similar to ceramic mosaic tile/weatherproof/ suitable for heavy duty floor service/ vitreous or semi-vitreous

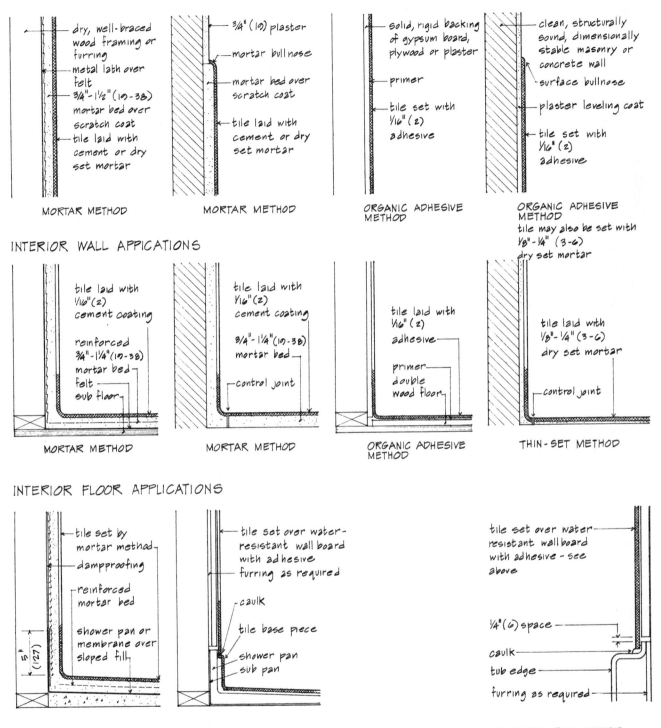

MORTAR METHOD

- dry, well-braced wood framing or furring
- metal lath over felt
- 3/4"-1 1/2" (19-38) mortar bed over scratch coat
- tile laid with cement or dry set mortar

MORTAR METHOD

- 3/4" (19) plaster
- mortar bullnose
- mortar bed over scratch coat
- tile laid with cement or dry set mortar

ORGANIC ADHESIVE METHOD

- solid, rigid backing of gypsum board, plywood or plaster
- primer
- tile set with 1/16" (2) adhesive

ORGANIC ADHESIVE METHOD

- clean, structurally sound, dimensionally stable masonry or concrete wall
- surface bullnose
- plaster leveling coat
- tile set with 1/16" (2) adhesive

tile may also be set with 1/8"-1/4" (3-6) dry set mortar

INTERIOR WALL APPICATIONS

MORTAR METHOD

- tile laid with 1/16" (2) cement coating
- reinforced 3/4"-1 1/4" (19-38) mortar bed
- felt
- sub floor

MORTAR METHOD

- tile laid with 1/16" (2) cement coating
- 3/4"-1 1/4" (19-38) mortar bed
- control joint

ORGANIC ADHESIVE METHOD

- tile laid with 1/16" (2) adhesive
- primer
- double wood floor

THIN-SET METHOD

- tile laid with 1/8"-1/4" (3-6) dry set mortar
- control joint

INTERIOR FLOOR APPLICATIONS

TILE SHOWERS

- tile set by mortar method
- dampproofing
- reinforced mortar bed
- shower pan or membrane over sloped fill
- 5" (127)

- tile set over water-resistant wall board with adhesive
- furring as required
- caulk
- tile base piece
- shower pan
- sub pan

TILE TUB ENCLOSURE

- tile set over water-resistant wallboard with adhesive - see above
- 1/4" (6) space
- caulk
- tub edge
- furring as required

Wood flooring provides a durable, wear-resistant, easily-maintained floor surface with desirable appearance and comfort qualities. It is manufactured under rigid regulations controlling kiln-drying, moisture content, and grading as set by the various flooring manufacturers' associations. Durable, hard, close-grained species of both hardwood (eg. red and white oak, maple, beech, birch, pecan) and softwood (eg. southern pine, Douglas fir, western larch, western hemlock) are used for wood flooring. Of these, oak, southern pine, and Douglas fir are the most commonly used. All heartwood grade of redwood is highly decay-resistant and is therefore used for porch and exterior flooring.

The various species used for wood flooring are graded but not according to the same standards. The following is an outline of the grading standards for oak which are based primarily on appearance. Note that color is not a consideration.

OAK FLOORING GRADES ACCORDING TO NATIONAL OAK FLOORING MANUFACTURERS ASSOCIATION (NOFMA)

TYPE OF WOOD	GRADE	DESCRIPTION	LENGTH OF STRIPS
plain-sawed or quarter sawed	clear	face virtually free of defects; 3/8" (10) bright sap permissible	2' (610) and up 4'3" (1295) average
	select	face may contain small streaks, burls, pin worm hole, slight working imperfections, small bight knots, averaging not more than one every 3' (914)	2' (610) and up 3'9" (1143) average
plain-sawed	nº 1 common	may have varying wood characteristics such as heavy streaks and checks, wormholes, knots, and minor imperfections in working should lay a sound floor without cutting	2' (610) and up 3' (914) average
	nº 2 common	may contain sound natural variations and defects of all types - should lay a service-able floor	1'3" (381) and up 2'6" (762) average

There are three basic types of wood flooring: strip, plank, and block.

STRIP FLOORING   The standard pattern is the most widely used. It has a hollow back to bear firmly on both edges and allow for slight irregularities in the subfloor surface. It may be applied over wood subfloors and sleepers with blind nailing.

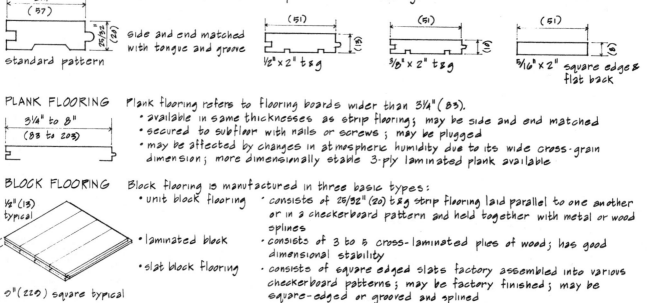

standard pattern

side and end matched with tongue and groove

½" x 2" t&g   3/8" x 2" t&g   5/16" x 2" square edge & flat back

PLANK FLOORING   Plank flooring refers to flooring boards wider than 3¼" (83).
- available in same thicknesses as strip flooring; may be side and end matched
- secured to subfloor with nails or screws; may be plugged
- may be affected by changes in atmospheric humidity due to its wide cross-grain dimension; more dimensionally stable 3-ply laminated plank available

3¼" to 8"
(83 to 203)

BLOCK FLOORING   Block flooring is manufactured in three basic types:
- unit block flooring   · consists of 25/32" (20) t&g strip flooring laid parallel to one another or in a checkerboard pattern and held together with metal or wood splines
- laminated block   · consists of 3 to 5 cross-laminated plies of wood; has good dimensional stability
- slat block flooring   · consists of square edged slats factory assembled into various checkerboard patterns; may be factory finished; may be square-edged or grooved and splined

½" (13) typical

9" (229) square typical

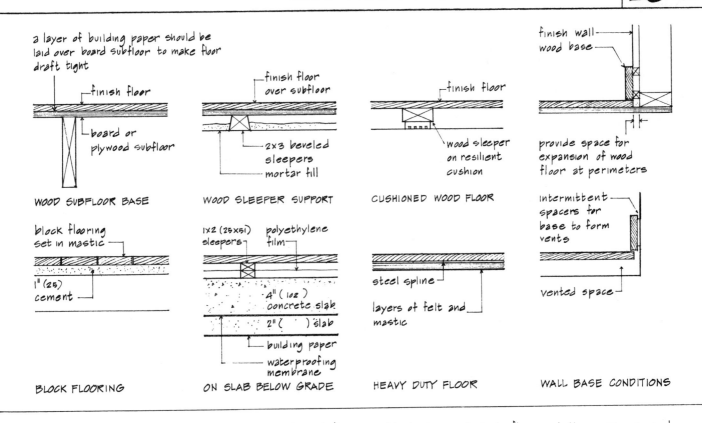

a layer of building paper should be laid over board subfloor to make floor draft tight

finish floor

board or plywood subfloor

WOOD SUBFLOOR BASE

finish floor over subfloor

2x3 beveled sleepers

mortar fill

WOOD SLEEPER SUPPORT

finish floor

wood sleeper on resilient cushion

CUSHIONED WOOD FLOOR

finish wall
wood base

provide space for expansion of wood floor at perimeters

WALL BASE CONDITIONS

block flooring set in mastic

1" (25) cement

BLOCK FLOORING

1x2 (25x51) sleepers

polyethylene film

4" (102) concrete slab

2" ( ) slab

building paper

waterproofing membrane

ON SLAB BELOW GRADE

steel spline

layers of felt and mastic

HEAVY DUTY FLOOR

intermittent spacers for base to form vents

vented space

The above illustrates various applications of wood flooring. Wood strip and plank flooring both require a wood subfloor or spaced wood sleepers as a base. Board or plywood subfloors, integral parts of a wood floor system, may be laid over other floor systems as well to accomodate wood flooring. Wood sleepers are normally required over concrete floor slabs and surfaces to receive either a wood subfloor or the finish wood flooring. This is especially important when wood flooring is applied over concrete slabs on or below grade to protect the wood from dampness.

Wood block flooring is usually installed with mastic, requiring a clean, dry, smooth, flat surface. This surface may be a plywood subfloor with underlayment or a concrete slab or plank floor which may require a cement leveling coat before application of the block flooring.

As a material, wood is susceptible to changes in humidity since it may shrink or swell as its moisture content changes. Manufactured wood flooring usually has a moisture content of 6% to 8% which should be maintained before and during installation. Space for expansion should always be provided along the wood flooring's perimeter. Wood flooring in hot, humid climates should be treated against decay, fungus, and insects.

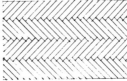

Various decorative geometric patterns may be produced with wood flooring, particularly in the case of block flooring. These patterns, the color and grain of the wood species used, and the type of finishing applied to the flooring all contribute to the end appearance.

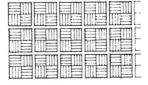

Resilient flooring provides an economical, dense, non-absorbent flooring surface with relatively good durability and ease of maintenance. Its degree of resilience enables it to withstand permant indentation while contributing to its quietness. It may provide comfort underfoot depending on its resilience, its backing, and the hardness of the supporting substrate.

RESILIENT FLOORING TYPE	COMPONENTS	SIZES	THICKNESS	PERMISSIBLE FLOOR LOCATIONS
vinyl sheet	vinyl resins w/ asbestos back	6' (1·820) wide	.065" - .095" (2±)	below grade/on grade/suspended
vinyl tile	vinyl resins	9"x9" (229 x 229) 12"x12" (305 x 305)	1/16" 3/32" 1/8" (2-) (2±) (3)	below grade/on grade/suspended
vinyl asbestos tile	vinyl resins w/ asbestos fibers	9"x9" (229 x 229) 12"x12" (305 x 305)	1/16" 3/32" 1/8" (2-) (2±) (3)	below grade/on grade/suspended
cork tile	raw cork and resins	9"x9" (229 x 229)	1/8" 3/16" 1/4" (3) (5) (6)	suspended
cork tile w/ vinyl coating	raw cork and vinyl resins	9"x9" (229 x 229) 12"x12" (305 x 305)	1/8" 3/16" (3) (5)	suspended
rubber tile	rubber compound	9"x9" (229 x 229) 12"x12" (305 x 305)	3/32" 1/8" 3/16" (2±) (3) (5)	below grade/on grade/suspended
linoleum (sheet and tile)	cork, wood, and oleoresins	6' (1·820) wide or 9"x9" (229 x 229)	1/8" (3)	suspended
asphalt tile	asphalt compounds, resins	9"x9" (229 x 229)	1/8" 3/16" (3) (5)	below grade/on grade/suspended

Vinyl and asphalt resilient floorings may be applied to concrete slabs on or below grade because of their resistance to moisture and alkalies which may occur in those locations. Besides their resistance to moisture and alkalies, the various resilient flooring types may be evaluated according to their resilience (a measure of their quietness, comfort underfoot, and resistance to indentation), grease resistance, durability, and ease of maintenance.

Resilient flooring may be laid over either wood or concrete substrates. The base surface must be clean, dry, flat, and smooth since any irregularities would show through the thin flooring material. In wood floor construction, underlayment is required as a base surface. This may be a single layer of combined subfloor/underlayment plywood or a separate layer of underlayment (plywood or hardboard) laid over a board or plywood subfloor.

Over concrete slabs and surfaces, either a cement topping (thick enough to prevent its cracking) or a thinner coat of mastic underlayment may be used to provide a smooth working base for the resilient flooring.

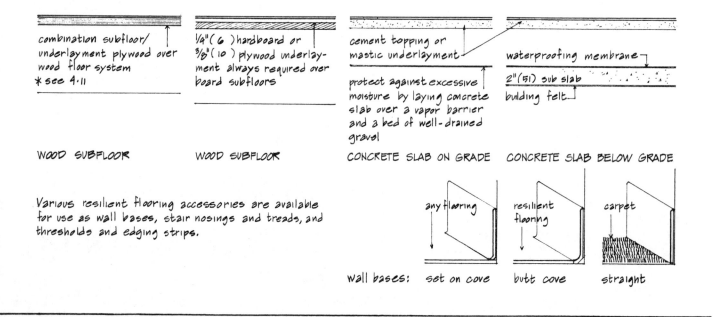

combination subfloor/ underlayment plywood over wood floor system * see 4·11

WOOD SUBFLOOR

1/4" (6) hardboard or 3/8" (10) plywood underlayment always required over board subfloors

WOOD SUBFLOOR

cement topping or mastic underlayment

protect against excessive moisture by laying concrete slab over a vapor barrier and a bed of well-drained gravel

CONCRETE SLAB ON GRADE

waterproofing membrane
2" (51) sub slab
building felt

CONCRETE SLAB BELOW GRADE

Various resilient flooring accessories are available for use as wall bases, stair nosings and treads, and thresholds and edging strips.

any flooring

resilient flooring

carpet

wall bases: set on cove   butt cove   straight

FLOORS: Terrazzo is a ground and polished concrete topping consisting of marble chips or other colored coarse aggregate in a cement or resinous binder. It provides a dense, hard-wearing, smooth surface whose mottled coloring is controlled by the colors of the aggregate and the binder. The terrazzo topping may be bonded to a concrete slab or laid over a wood, steel deck, or concrete floor system. Metal divider strips are used to control cracking and define patterns.

Brick, slate, and flagstone flooring provide durable, textured surfaces. They may be laid in regular or irregular patterns. Consideration should be given to their weight and the dead load they will impose on the supporting floor construction.

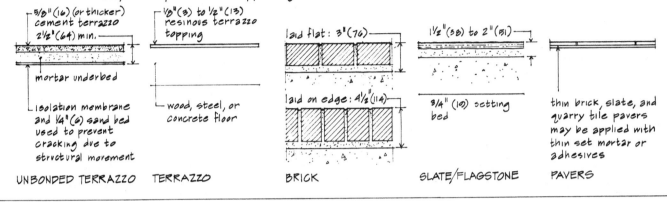

UNBONDED TERRAZZO   TERRAZZO   BRICK   SLATE/FLAGSTONE   PAVERS

WALLS: Exterior wood siding (see 10.20) may also be used for interior wall finishes.
Spaced wood strips may be applied over furring to give a wall a linear texture and pattern or to conceal absorbent acoustical material

Concrete, concrete block, brick, and stone walls may be left exposed where acoustical treatment of the space and smooth, sanitary surfaces are not critical.

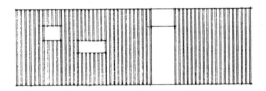

CEILINGS Wood paneling, siding, flooring, and strips all may be used as finish ceiling materials.

Spaced aluminum or stainless steel bars or channels may be used to form a suspended ceiling plane. Light fixtures, air diffusers, and other equipment are usually integrated into the linear pattern. Acoustical material may be supported above the ceiling in the plenum space

Suspended metal louver ceilings provide a continuous, textured ceiling plane that reflects and diffuses light from overhead fixtures while eliminating glare.

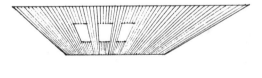

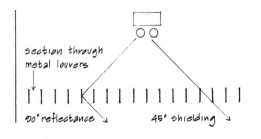

section through metal louvers

90° reflectance   45° shielding

Although used primarily for warmth and comfort underfoot, carpeting may also be used on both walls and ceilings to provide additional texture and acoustically absorbent surfaces in a space.

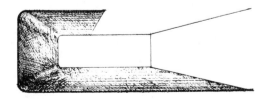

Acoustical ceilings provide integral acoustical treatment along with a finish ceiling surface. They are usually in the form of tiles that may be applied directly to or suspended from the underside of roof or floor constructions.

Acoustical tiles may be of wood or mineral fiber with perforated, patterned, textured, or fissured surfaces that allow sound to penetrate into the fiber voids within the tile. These light, low density tiles are fragile and subject to abrasion and impact damage. They are usually factory-painted or coated to improve their moisture and abrasion-resistance qualities. If repainting is required, only nonbridging paint should be used to avoid closing the surface voids and reducing the tile's acoustical value.

Perforated metal- or cement asbestos-clad tiles containing batt or blanket insulation are also available.

Acoustical tiles are available with square-cut, beveled, rabbeted, or tongue-and-grooved edges. They are usually manufactured according to 1'(305), 2'(610), and 2'6"(762) modules.

Factors to consider in the selection of acoustical tile include:

- acoustical value — consult manufacturer's data
- fire-resistance rating — mineral fiber and metal or cement asbestos-clad tiles are incombustible
  - wood fiber tiles may be treated to be flame retardant
- method of application — see below and facing page
- tile size and modular implications — integration with ceiling light fixtures, mechanical outlets, etc.
  - integration with overall form and dimensions of space
- light reflectance value — consult manufacturer's data
- appearance — surface texture, pattern, and color
- edge conditions — flush or articulated

ACOUSTICAL CEILING APPLICATIONS:

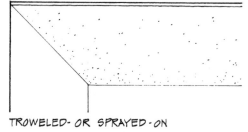

SET WITH ADHESIVES

- solid backing such as concrete, plaster, or gypsum board is required

- tile is set with special acoustical tile adhesive that allows a true flat plane to be maintained even though there may be slight irregularities in the base surface

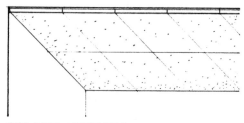

TROWELED- OR SPRAYED-ON

- acoustical material of granular aggregate mixed with a gypsum or cement binder may be troweled on to a base surface to provide an incombustible, acoustical finish

- acoustical material of mineral fibers mixed with a special binder may be sprayed on to a concrete base or metal lath to provide a monolithic, incombustible surface with both acoustical and thermal insulation value
- especially suitable for curved surface applications

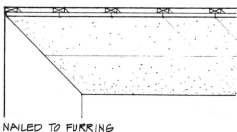

NAILED TO FURRING

- 1x3 (25x76) furring strips at 12" (305) on center are used when the ceiling base surface is not flat enough or otherwise unsuitable for the adhesive application of tile
- line the back side of the tiles with building paper to provide a draft-tight ceiling surface
- cross-furring strips and shims may be required to provide a flat, level base

Acoustical tile ceilings may be suspended to provide a plenum space for mechanical ductwork, electrical conduit, plumbing, and recessed light fixtures. The depth of the plenum may vary according to the space requirements of the utilities and the required floor to ceiling height of the interior. Ceiling systems that integrate the functions of lighting, air distribution, fire protection, and acoustical control to minimize the depth of the ceiling construction are available.

Although the form of suspension systems varies between manufacturers, they all consist basically of a grid of metal channels, runners, and splines. This grid may be exposed, semi-concealed, or completely concealed. In most suspension systems, the acoustical tiles are removeable to provide convenient access into the plenum space.

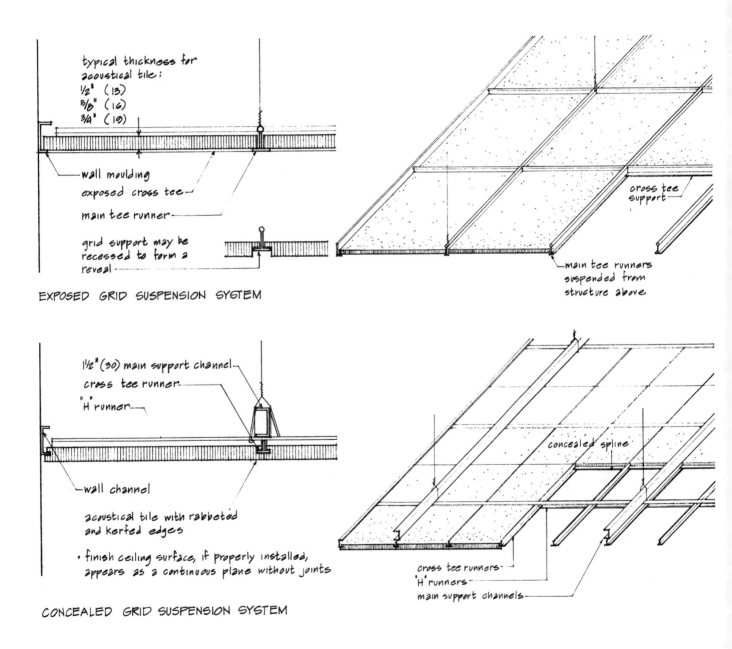

typical thickness for
acoustical tile:
½" (13)
⅝" (16)
¾" (19)

wall moulding
exposed cross tee
main tee runner

grid support may be
recessed to form a
reveal

cross tee
support

main tee runners
suspended from
structure above

EXPOSED GRID SUSPENSION SYSTEM

1½" (30) main support channel
cross tee runner
"H" runner

wall channel

acoustical tile with rabbeted
and kerfed edges

• finish ceiling surface, if properly installed,
appears as a continuous plane without joints

concealed spline

cross tee runners
"H" runners
main support channels

CONCEALED GRID SUSPENSION SYSTEM

plywood siding patterns: may be painted, stained, or left natural wood color to weather

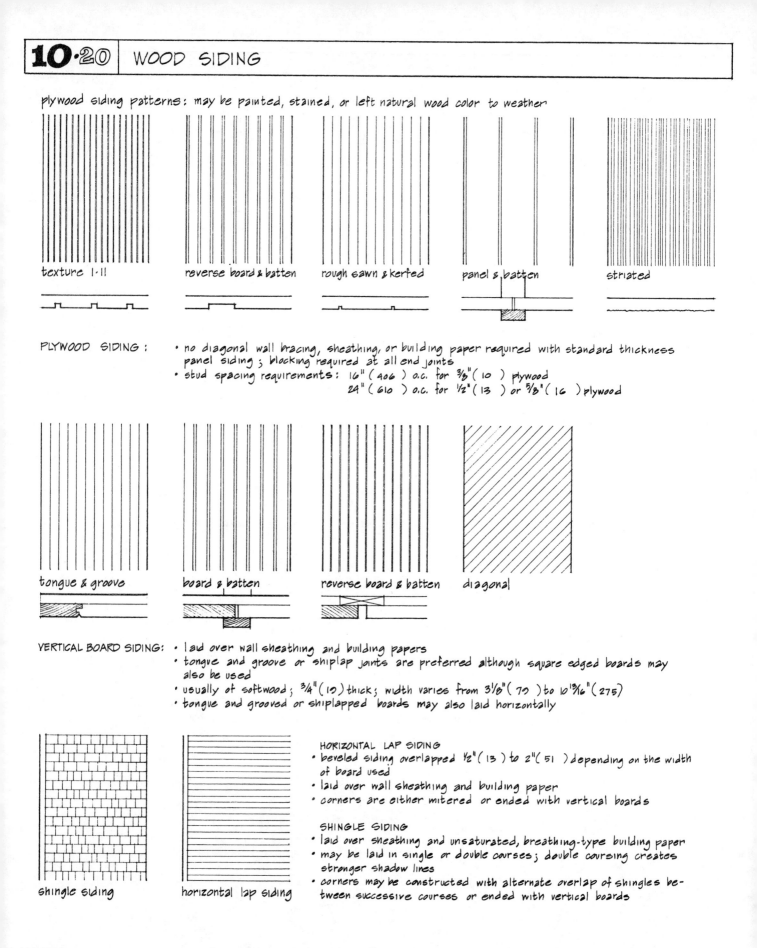

texture 1·11   reverse board & batten   rough sawn & kerfed   panel & batten   striated

PLYWOOD SIDING :
- no diagonal wall bracing, sheathing, or building paper required with standard thickness panel siding; blocking required at all end joints
- stud spacing requirements: 16" (406) o.c. for ⅜" (10) plywood
  24" (610) o.c. for ½" (13) or ⅝" (16) plywood

tongue & groove   board & batten   reverse board & batten   diagonal

VERTICAL BOARD SIDING:
- laid over wall sheathing and building papers
- tongue and groove or shiplap joints are preferred although square edged boards may also be used
- usually of softwood; ¾" (19) thick; width varies from 3⅛" (79) to 10¹³⁄₁₆" (275)
- tongue and grooved or shiplapped boards may also laid horizontally

HORIZONTAL LAP SIDING
- beveled siding overlapped ½" (13) to 2" (51) depending on the width of board used
- laid over wall sheathing and building paper
- corners are either mitered or ended with vertical boards

SHINGLE SIDING
- laid over sheathing and unsaturated, breathing-type building paper
- may be laid in single or double courses; double coursing creates stronger shadow lines
- corners may be constructed with alternate overlap of shingles between successive courses or ended with vertical boards

shingle siding   horizontal lap siding

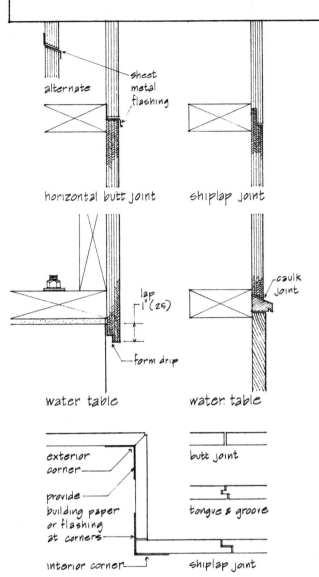

alternate

sheet metal flashing

horizontal butt joint   **shiplap joint**

lap 1"(25)

form drip

water table   **water table**

exterior corner

provide building paper or flashing at corners

interior corner

butt joint

tongue & groove

shiplap joint

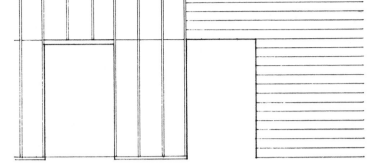

Both panel and board siding wall finishes have exposed joints. These joints may be subtly visible as with flush or "V" joints, or they may be accentuated as with batten joints. Due care should be taken in the determination of wall lengths and heights, and the sizing and placement of window and door openings, so that they are visually correlated to the visible wall joints and unnecessary cutting of material is avoided.

To the left are illustrated exterior plywood siding joint types.

- all exposed butt joints, and exterior and interior corners should be caulked
- allow: 1/8" (3) between square edged panels
  1/16" (2) between shiplapped or tongue and groove panels

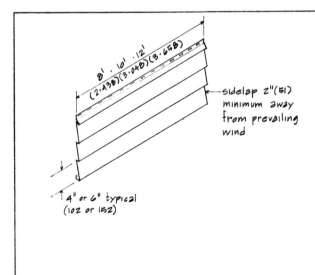

8' 10' 12'
(2.438)(3.048)(3.658)

sidelap 2"(51) minimum away from prevailing wind

4" or 6" typical (102 or 152)

Aluminum siding is formed to simulate horizontal lap or vertical board siding. It has a factory-baked-on paint finish in various colors and may have a smooth, stipple, or embossed wood grain texture.

Aluminum siding may be used over existing construction or new work. When used in new construction, it should be backed with insulating wall board to increase the wall's thermal insulation value and protect the aluminum from denting under impact.

The aluminum panels are crimped to interlock. The nailing holes at the top are slotted to allow for expansion and contraction. Corner and side trim pieces finish the edges and also allow for expansion.

Since the aluminum is impervious to water vapor, it should be vented at its base.

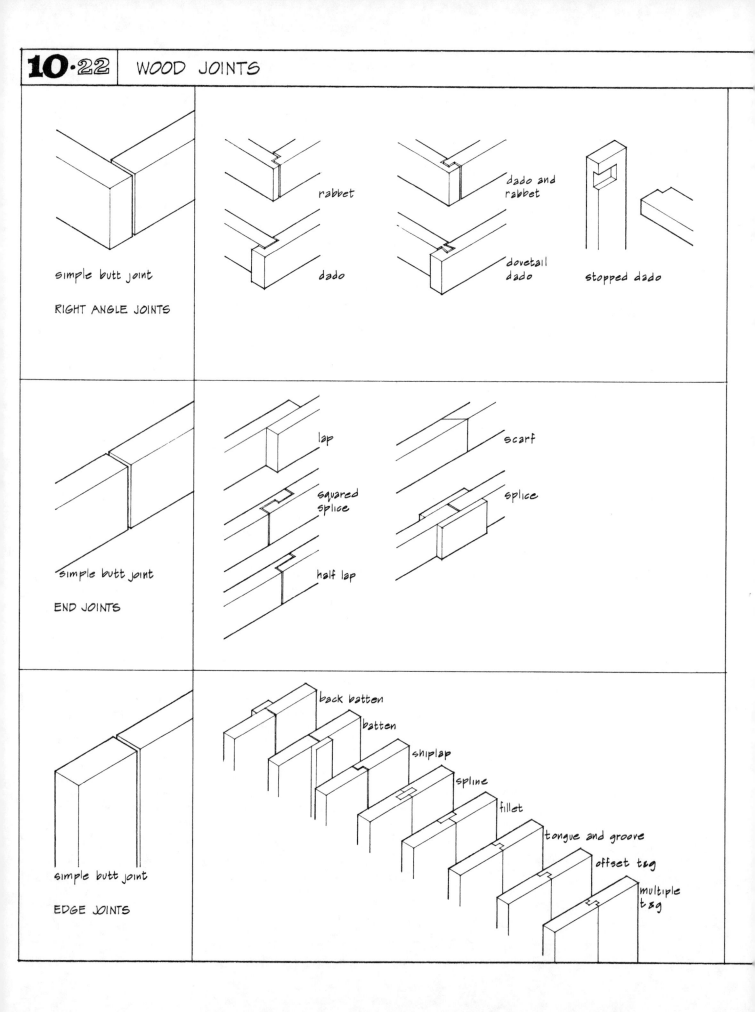

simple butt joint

RIGHT ANGLE JOINTS

rabbet

dado

dado and rabbet

dovetail dado

stopped dado

simple butt joint

END JOINTS

lap

squared splice

half lap

scarf

splice

simple butt joint

EDGE JOINTS

back batten

batten

shiplap

spline

fillet

tongue and groove

offset t&g

multiple t&g

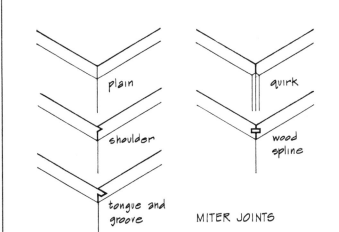

plain

shoulder

tongue and groove

quirk

wood spline

MITER JOINTS

box joint

through multiple dovetail

stopped lap

lap or half blind

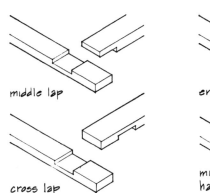

middle lap

cross lap

LAP JOINTS

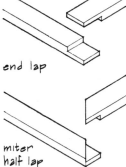

end lap

miter half lap

The strength and rigidity of ordinary wood framing are more important than its appearance since it is normally covered with a finish surface. In finish trim and furniture work, however, a wood joint's appearance becomes just as important as its strength. Small scale work requires more sophisticated and more refined joints which will present a cleaner appearance.

Wood joints are usually inconspicuous if they remain tight. If they open due to wood shrinkage or structural movement, they may become easily noticeable.

In designing and constructing a wood joint, it is important to understand the nature of the forces (compressive, tensile, shear) working on the joint, and to comprehend their relationship with the direction of the wood grain.

* see 12·2

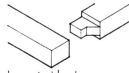

ship

half blind

haunch blind

MORTISE AND TENON JOINTS

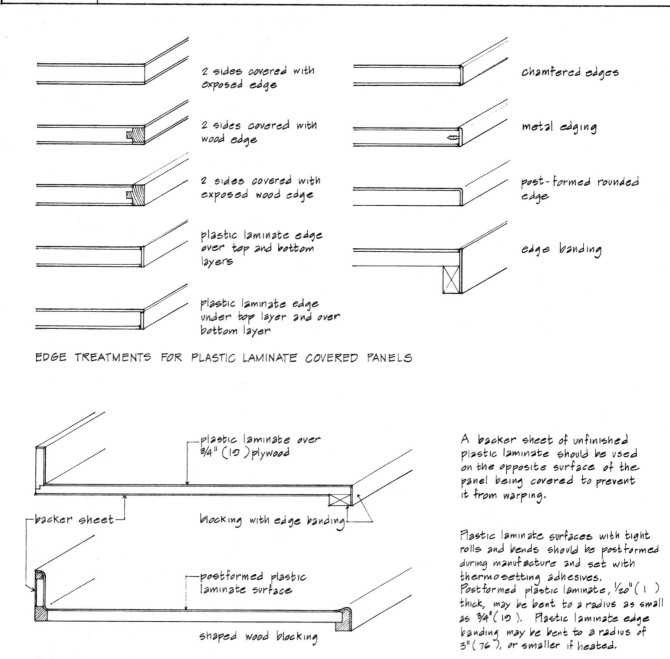

2 sides covered with exposed edge

2 sides covered with wood edge

2 sides covered with exposed wood edge

plastic laminate edge over top and bottom layers

plastic laminate edge under top layer and over bottom layer

chamfered edges

metal edging

post-formed rounded edge

edge banding

EDGE TREATMENTS FOR PLASTIC LAMINATE COVERED PANELS

plastic laminate over 3/4" (19) plywood

backer sheet

blocking with edge banding

postformed plastic laminate surface

shaped wood blocking

PLASTIC LAMINATE COUNTER TOPS

A backer sheet of unfinished plastic laminate should be used on the opposite surface of the panel being covered to prevent it from warping.

Plastic laminate surfaces with tight rolls and bends should be postformed during manufacture and set with thermosetting adhesives. Postformed plastic laminate, 1/20" (1) thick, may be bent to a radius as small as 3/4" (19). Plastic laminate edge banding may be bent to a radius of 3" (76), or smaller if heated.

Plastic laminates provide a hard, durable, heat and water resistant surface covering for walls, countertops, doors and furniture. They may be bonded to finish plywood, hardboard, particle board and other common core materials with contact adhesive in the field or thermosetting adhesives under pressure in the shop.

Plastic laminates consist of layers of different materials (kraft paper, foil, cover overlay sheet of printed paper, wood veneer or fabric) impregnated with phenolic and melamine plastics and cured under intense heat and pressure.

- available in thicknesses: 1/32" to 1/16" (1 to 2)
  widths   : 24" to 60" (610 to 1524)
  lengths   : 60" to 144" (1524 to 3658)

- finishes: gloss, satin, low glare, textured in a wide range of colors and patterns

This chapter discusses those characteristics of mechanical and electrical systems which affect human health, safety, and comfort, as well as building form and construction. The intent is not to provide a design manual but to outline those factors that must be considered for these systems' successful operation and integration into the total building system.

Heating, ventilating, and air conditioning systems condition the interior spaces of a building for the environmental comfort of the occupants. Water supply is essential for human consumption, sanitation, and comfort. The efficient disposal of fluid waste and organic matter is critical to maintain sanitary conditions within a building and in the surrounding area. Electrical systems furnish light, heat, and power to run a building's machines.

The environmental comfort factors that may be controlled by mechanical (heating, ventilating, and air conditioning) systems include:

- the temperature of the surrounding air
- the mean radiant temperature of the surrounding surfaces
- the relative humidity of the air
- air motion
- dust
- odors

The first four are of primary importance in determining thermal comfort. They may be controlled not only by a building's mechanical system but also by:

- a building's site location and orientation   (*see chapter 1)
- a building's materials and construction assembly which can control heat, air, and water vapor flow

---

Balancing heat loss and heat gain to arrive at a comfortable temperature is a basic first step in achieving thermal comfort. The human body loses heat by:

- radiation:
  - transmission of heat energy through the air from a warm body surface to cooler surfaces
  - light colors reflect while dark colors absorb heat — poor reflectors make good radiators
  - radiated heat cannot go around corners and is not affected by air motion

- convection
  - transmission of heat from warm body surfaces to the surrounding air
  - high temperature differentials and increased air motion induce more heat transmission by convection

- evaporation
  - transmission of heat through the evaporation process of moisture into water vapor
  - an important factor when high temperatures, humidity, and human activity levels exist
  - heat loss by evaporation increases with air motion

- conduction
  - transmission of heat from the warm body directly to a cooler body
  - has little effect on actual heat loss

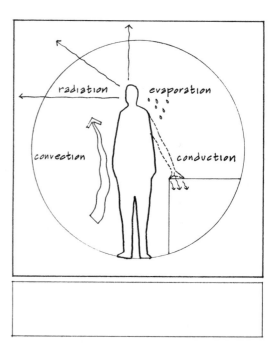

Sources of heat include:

- solar radiation through a building's wall and roof constructions

- building equipment:
  - mechanical heating systems
  - lights
  - other equipment such as ranges

- human activity: amount of heat gain depends on the metabolism rate and level of activity

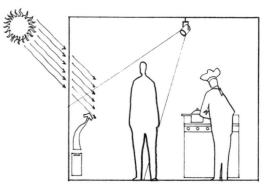

The following relationships between the four primary thermal comfort factors describe recommended comfort zones.

AIR TEMPERATURE AND MEAN RADIANT TEMPERATURE (MRT)

- the higher the mean radiant temperatures of the surrounding surfaces, the cooler the air temperature should be
- MRT has about 40% more direct effect on comfort than air temperature
- in cold weather, the MRT of the interior surfaces of exterior walls should not be more than 5°F (3°C) below the indoor air temperature

AIR TEMPERATURE AND RELATIVE HUMIDITY (RH)

- the higher the relative humidity of a space, the lower the air temperature should be
- the relative humidity level is not critical within the normal temperature range - more critical at high temperatures
- low humidity levels (<20%) may cause undesirable conditions such as static electricity or shrinkage of wood
- high humidity levels (>60%) may cause condensation problems

AIR TEMPERATURE AND AIR MOTION (V)

- the cooler the moving air stream is than the room air temperature, the less velocity it should have
- should range between 10 and 50 feet per minute (FPM) (3 to 15 m/minute)
- higher velocities may cause drafty conditions
- air motion is helpful in hot, humid weather for cooling by evaporation

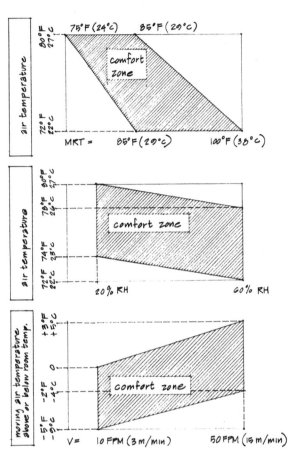

Air temperature requirements are also affected by the age group of the building's occupants, the type of clothing they wear (color and weight), and the level of their activity.

The objective of an air conditioning system is to adjust the above factors according to outdoor and indoor conditions and the level of human activity so that "comfort zone" conditions exist within a space. Below are listed the ways in which thermal comfort factors may be controlled by an air conditioning system.

- air temperature
  - controlled by the supply of warm or cool air to a space through various media: air, water, electricity

- mean radiant temperature
  - surface temperatures may be controlled by:
  - radiant heat panels: hot water, electrical resistance heating, warm air
  - "washing" a surface with warm air

- relative humidity
  - controlled by the introduction of water vapor, or its removal by ventilation

- air motion
  - controlled by mechanical ventilation

Factors to consider in the selection, design, and installation of an air conditioning system include:

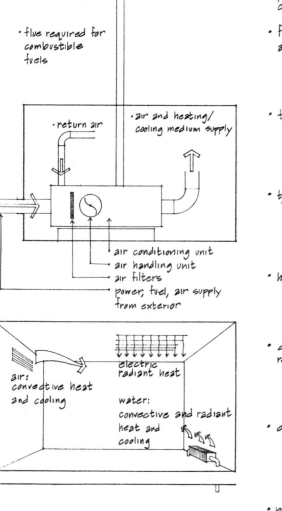

- flue required for combustible fuels

- return air
- air and heating/cooling medium supply

- air conditioning unit
- air handling unit
- air filters
- power, fuel, air supply from exterior

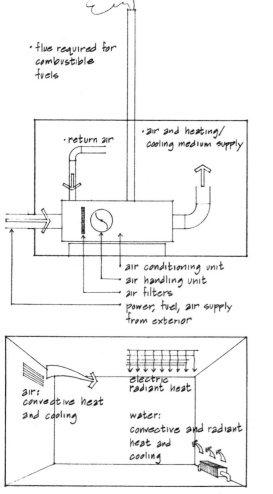

air: convective heat and cooling

electric radiant heat

water: convective and radiant heat and cooling

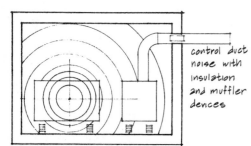

control duct noise with insulation and muffler devices

isolate noise
- by distance (location)
- with mass (enclosure)
- by use of vibration control devices (installation)

- performance, efficiency, and cost of the system used to control the thermal comfort factors

- fuel and power sources required and the means for their delivery and storage:
  - electricity
  - gas
  - oil or coal

- type, size, and location of heating equipment:
  - except for electric heat pumps and resistance heaters, heating is a combustion process requiring a power source, fuel, ventilation and exhaust to the outdoors, fresh air, and possibly a water supply

- type, size, and location of cooling equipment:
  - the cooling process uses a refrigerant that alternately absorbs and gives off heat as it cycles through evaporation and condensing processes — uses air, water, or both as the exchange medium

- heating or cooling medium used:
  - air · heating or cooling by convection/radiation
  - water · heating or cooling by convection/radiation
  - electricity · heating by radiation and convection

- distribution and return systems: size, space, and layout requirements:
  - air · ducts or plenum space
  - water · piping
  - electricity · wiring

- outlets: size, type, and location
  - air · grills, registers, diffusers
  - water · fin or fan coil units
  - electricity · radiant heat panels, infrared heaters

- provision for:
  - the control of humidity
  - ventilation and the supply of fresh air
  - the filtering of supplied air

- noise and vibration control
  - provision for the acoustical isolation of the mechanical equipment within an insulated space
  - provision for the baffing and absorption of noise that may travel through an air duct system

- flexibility of the system in serving zones of a building which have different demands for heating or cooling

- space requirements for the air conditioning equipment and the distribution system

Below are listed the basic types of air conditioning systems. They all utilize the components outlined on the previous page in various combinations to suit specific installation requirements.

- ALL AIR SYSTEMS

  single duct systems:
  · forced warm or cool air is delivered at a constant temperature from the air conditioning unit through a low velocity duct system to the served spaces
  · the variable air flow system uses dampers at the terminal outlets to control the air flow according to the requirements of the space
  · the terminal reheat system is more flexible since it supplies air at about 55°F (12°c) to terminal units equipped with hot water reheat coils to compensate for changing space requirements

  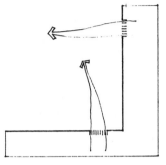

  double duct systems:
  · warm and cool air is delivered through separate duct systems to terminal mixing units which contain thermostatically controlled dampers
  · the mixing units may serve individual or zones of spaces
  · this is usually a high velocity system to reduce duct sizes and installation space

- ALL WATER SYSTEMS

  · hot or chilled water is delivered to the served spaces through piping which requires less installation space than air ducts
  · heat is convected or absorbed in the served space through fan-coil units which blow air over the hot or cold coils into the space
  · ventilation must be supplied through a separate duct system or a direct connection to the outside
  · 2 pipe system: either hot or chilled water may be circulated
  · 4 pipe system: both hot and chilled water is circulated on separate circuits to provide simultaneous heating and cooling to different zones of a building

  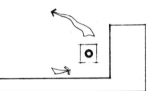
  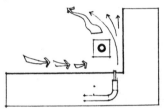

- AIR·WATER SYSTEMS are similar to all water systems except that a high velocity air duct system supplies air to the served spaces through fin-coil units and thereby inducing room airflow over the hot or cold coils.

- REFRIGERANT SYSTEMS (UNITARY AIR CONDITIONERS)

  · refrigerant systems are pre-assembled, self-contained air conditioning units used for rooftop or through-wall installations
  · a number of these units may be located to serve specific zones of a building directly without ductwork (or a supply duct system may be used to distribute the conditioned air to the served spaces from a centrally located unit)
  · cooling is provided by air-cooled condensers or chiller units which require an outdoor location
  · heating is provided by gas or oil furnaces, electric resistance heaters, or heat pumps

  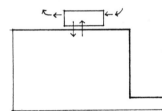

- HEAT PUMPS are electrically-powered heating and cooling units. For cooling, the normal refrigeration cooling cycle is used to absorb and transfer excess indoor heat to the outdoors. For heating, heat energy is drawn from the outdoor air by reversing the cooling cycle and switching the heat exchange functions of the condenser and evaporator. Heat pumps are most efficient in mild climates where heating and cooling loads are almost equal. In freezing temperatures, a heat pump requires an electric resistance heater to keep the outdoor coils from icing.

  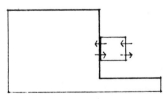

- ELECTRICAL SYSTEMS

  · radiant heat is supplied by electric resistance heating cables embedded in ceiling panels or floor slabs - a concealed heating system
  · other locations for electric resistance heating elements include baseboard units, wall or ceiling fixtures, in furnaces or boilers, within ductwork
  · electrical wiring requires a minimum amount of installation space

  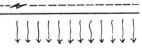

Air conditioning systems are engineered to provide environmental comfort for a building's occupants by controlling the indoor thermal comfort factors in response to outdoor conditions, building heat gain or loss, and the occupants' usage of the building spaces. How efficiently an air conditioning system will work depends on the accuracy of the engineering analysis and the successful integration of the system into the building structure.

All building machinery and equipment occupy significant space within a building. Some also require space or a domain around them for access, service, and maintenance. If this machinery and equipment take up 10% to 15% of a building's area, as they sometimes do, then it becomes necessary to consider the implications of their placement within the building. Factors to consider in the placement of air conditioning equipment and distribution systems include:

- location and method of supply of power, fuel, fresh air, and water (system may require direct access to the outdoors)
- space, enclosure, and construction requirements for the heating and cooling equipment plant (fire code requirements; noise and vibration control requirements)
- accessibility requirements for service and maintenance
- type and layout pattern of the distribution system used for the heating and cooling media
- type of installation: concealed within the building construction or exposed to view

Machinery and equipment may be located in a building in a number of ways:

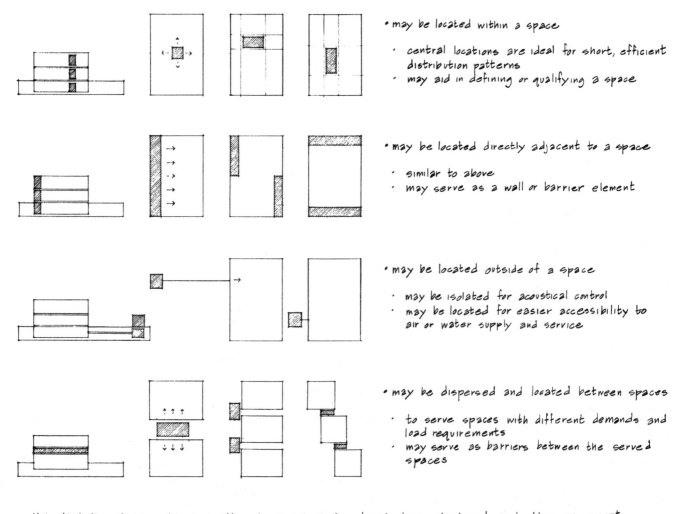

- may be located within a space
  - central locations are ideal for short, efficient distribution patterns
  - may aid in defining or qualifying a space

- may be located directly adjacent to a space
  - similar to above
  - may serve as a wall or barrier element

- may be located outside of a space
  - may be isolated for acoustical control
  - may be located for easier accessibility to air or water supply and service

- may be dispersed and located between spaces
  - to serve spaces with different demands and load requirements
  - may serve as barriers between the served spaces

Note that the above is also applicable at varying scales to plumbing, electrical, and other equipment systems.

As indicated on the previous page, the air conditioning plant may be centralized in one location or dispersed throughout a building. Some equipment plants require both indoor and outdoor components. Others may be self-contained units which may be located on exterior walls or rooftops.

The distribution pattern of the system through which the heating or cooling medium is supplied to the served spaces is directly related to the location(s) of the air conditioning plant(s) and the service outlets.

Air duct systems require more installation space than either pipes carrying hot or chilled water or wiring for electric resistance heating. For this reason, duct-work must be carefully laid out to be properly integrated with a building's structure, form, and spaces, as well as with other systems (ie. water, drainage, electrical). If the ductwork is to be left exposed, it becomes even more important that the layout have a visually coherent order and be coordinated with the physical elements of the space (ie. structural elements, surface patterns, light fixtures).

Concealed ductwork usually have vertical components housed in shaft spaces while horizontal runs may be underground, in basement or crawl spaces, or within floor or roof construction assemblies.

Horizontal distribution patterns may be generally classified as radial, perimeter, or lateral in layout.

- radial pattern: · minimum length of run
  · used in clear spaces which are free of obstacles

- perimeter loop: · effective against perimeter heat loss or gain
  · used often with concrete ground slabs

- lateral: · greatest length of run
  · wide, uniform, flexible distribution patterns possible
  · exposed ductwork usually utilizes a lateral pattern layout

Whenever possible, ductwork should have short, direct runs with a minimum number of turns and offsets to minimize friction loss. Ductwork should also be insulated against heat loss and sound transmission.

Supply and return air may also be distributed through floor-ceiling plenum spaces or the cores or cells of precast concrete floor and roof systems.

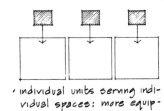

· individual units serving individual spaces: more equipment and less distribution runs

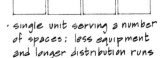

· single unit serving a number of spaces: less equipment and longer distribution runs

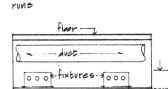

· careful integration between systems' paths may help to conserve space

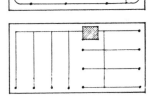

· main vertical feeder:
· less floor area used
· greater building height

· main horizontal feeder
· more floor area used
· lower building height

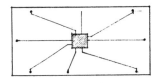
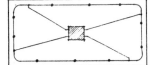
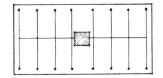
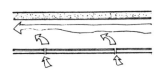
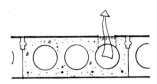
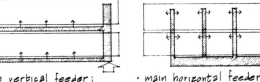

The location of heating and cooling outlets depends on the size and proportions of the space, its areas of heat loss or gain, its wall, ceiling, and floor construction and finish, and the activity patterns of its occupants. The type of outlet used depends on its placement within the space, its heating or cooling capacity, dimensions, and appearance. Below are illustrated various types of outlets according to location and heating or cooling medium used.

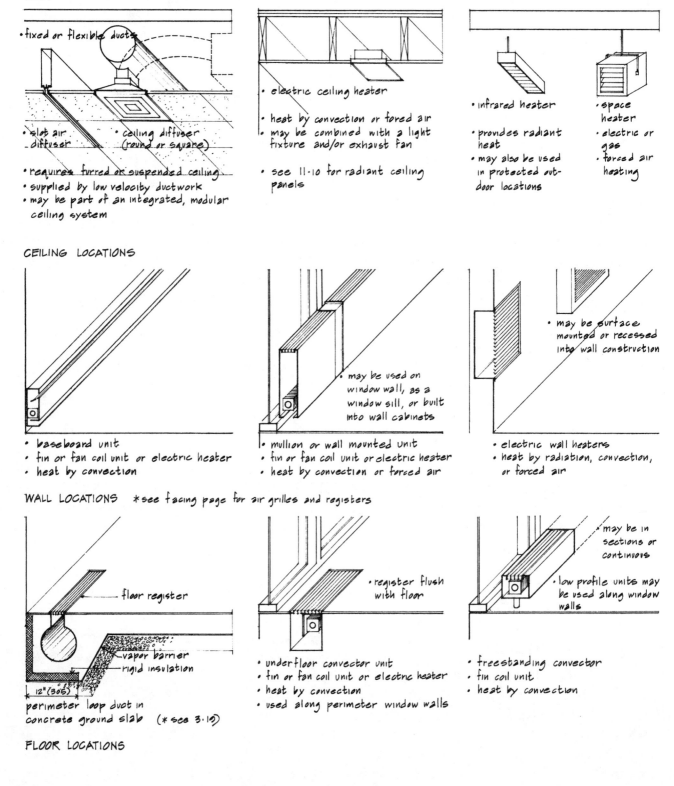

• fixed or flexible ducts

• slab air diffuser   • ceiling diffuser (round or square)

• requires furred or suspended ceiling
• supplied by low velocity ductwork
• may be part of an integrated, modular ceiling system

• electric ceiling heater

• heat by convection or forced air
• may be combined with a light fixture and/or exhaust fan

• see 11·10 for radiant ceiling panels

• infrared heater   • space heater
• provides radiant   • electric or gas
  heat   • forced air
• may also be used   heating
  in protected out-
  door locations

CEILING LOCATIONS

• baseboard unit
• fin or fan coil unit or electric heater
• heat by convection

• may be used on window wall, as a window sill, or built into wall cabinets

• mullion or wall mounted unit
• fin or fan coil unit or electric heater
• heat by convection or forced air

• may be surface mounted or recessed into wall construction

• electric wall heaters
• heat by radiation, convection, or forced air

WALL LOCATIONS   *see facing page for air grilles and registers

floor register
vapor barrier
rigid insulation
12" (305)
perimeter loop duct in concrete ground slab   (* see 3·19)

• register flush with floor

• underfloor convector unit
• fin or fan coil unit or electric heater
• heat by convection
• used along perimeter window walls

• may be in sections or continuous
• low profile units may be used along window walls

• freestanding convector
• fin coil unit
• heat by convection

FLOOR LOCATIONS

Air for the heating, cooling, and ventilation of a space is supplied through grilles, registers, and diffusers. They should be evaluated in terms of their air flow capacity and velocity, pressure drop, noise factor, and appearance.

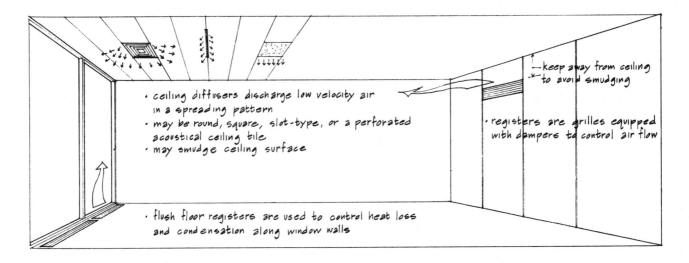

- ceiling diffusers discharge low velocity air in a spreading pattern
- may be round, square, slot-type, or a perforated acoustical ceiling tile
- may smudge ceiling surface

- keep away from ceiling to avoid smudging

- registers are grilles equipped with dampers to control air flow

- flush floor registers are used to control heat loss and condensation along window walls

Air supply outlets should be located to distribute warm or cool air to the occupied areas of a space comfortably, without noticeable drafts, and without stratification. The throw distance and spread or diffusion pattern of the air supply outlet should be considered along with any obstructions within the space that might interfere with the air distribution.

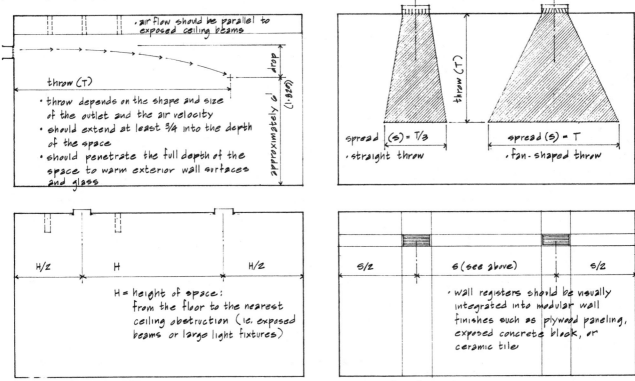

- air flow should be parallel to exposed ceiling beams

throw (T)

approximately 6' drop (1·800)

- throw depends on the shape and size of the outlet and the air velocity
- should extend at least 3/4 into the depth of the space
- should penetrate the full depth of the space to warm exterior wall surfaces and glass

spread (s) = T/3
- straight throw

spread (s) = T
- fan-shaped throw

H/2   H   H/2

H = height of space: from the floor to the nearest ceiling obstruction (ie. exposed beams or large light fixtures)

s/2   s (see above)   s/2

- wall registers should be visually integrated into modular wall finishes such as plywood paneling, exposed concrete block, or ceramic tile

- spacing of ceiling diffusers

- spacing of wall registers

Radiant panel heating systems utilize heated ceilings, floors, and sometimes walls as radiating surfaces. The heat source may be pipes carrying hot water or electric resistance heating cables embedded within the ceiling, wall, or floor construction.

The radiant heat supplied travels direct paths:
· it cannot go around corners and may therefore be obstructed by physical elements within the space such as furniture
· it cannot counteract cold downdrafts along exterior glass areas
· it is not affected by air motion

Because radiant panel heating systems cannot respond quickly to changing temperature demands, they may be supplemented by perimeter convector units. For complete air conditioning, separate ventilation, humidity control and cooling systems are required.

Floor installations are effective in warming concrete ground slabs. In general, however, ceiling installations are preferred because the ceiling construction usually has less thermal capacity and thus faster heat response. Ceiling panels may also be heated to a higher surface temperature than floor slabs.

Note that the installations below are completely concealed except for balancing valves or thermostats.

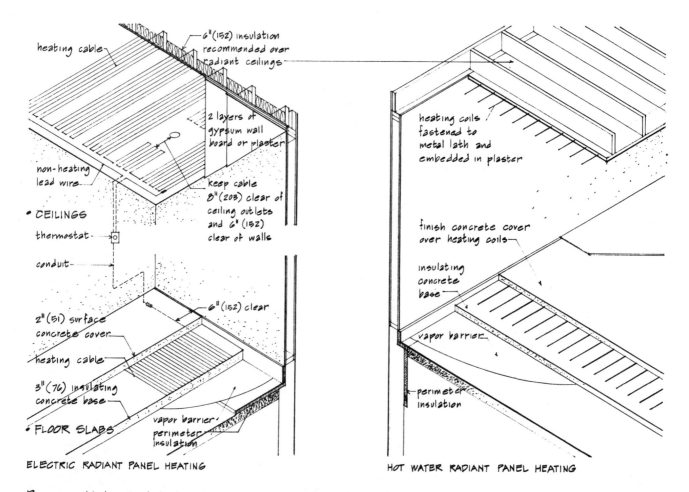

heating cable
6" (152) insulation recommended over radiant ceilings
2 layers of gypsum wall board or plaster
non-heating lead wire
keep cable 8" (203) clear of ceiling outlets and 6" (152) clear of walls
· CEILINGS
thermostat
conduit
2" (51) surface concrete cover
6" (152) clear
heating cable
3" (76) insulating concrete base
vapor barrier
perimeter insulation
· FLOOR SLABS

ELECTRIC RADIANT PANEL HEATING

heating coils fastened to metal lath and embedded in plaster
finish concrete cover over heating coils
insulating concrete base
vapor barrier
perimeter insulation

HOT WATER RADIANT PANEL HEATING

Pre-assembled radiant heat ceiling panels are commercially available. They may be used with modular suspended ceiling systems or to heat specific areas of a space.

Water may be utilized or controlled in a building for the following reasons:

- consumed : by drinking, cooking, washing, etc.   (must be potable)
- circulated : by heating and cooling systems   (should be soft or neutral)
- static (in storage) : for fire protection systems   (no special requirements)
- controlled : to maintain desirable relative humidity levels

Water must be supplied to a building in the correct quantity, and at the proper flow rate, pressure, and temperature, to satisfy the above requirements. For human consumption, water must be palatable and free of harmful bacteria. To avoid the clogging or corroding of pipes and equipment, water may have to be treated for hardness and excessive acidity.

If water is supplied by a municipal or public system, there can be no direct control over the quantity, rate, or quality of water supplied until it reaches the building site. If a public water supply system is not available, then either rainwater storage tanks or drilled wells are required. Well water, if the source is deep enough, is usually pure, cool, and free of discoloration and taste or odor problems.

Factors to consider in the selection of a well location include:
- the quality of water to be supplied: should be checked by the local health department
- the amount of water that can be had from the source
- the required depth and cost of the well
- the proximity of areas containing pollutants (see below)

For water sources less than 25' (7.620) below grade, shallow-well pumps may be used.
- (shallow-well jet, rotary, or reciprocating piston types)
For water source more than 25' (7.620) below grade, deep-well pumps have to be used.
- (deep-well jet, turbine, submersible, or reciprocating types)

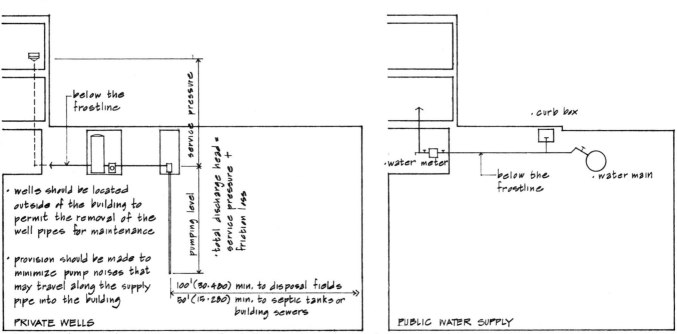

- wells should be located outside of the building to permit the removal of the well pipes for maintenance

- provision should be made to minimize pump noises that may travel along the supply pipe into the building

PRIVATE WELLS

100' (30.480) min. to disposal fields
50' (15.280) min. to septic tanks or building sewers

PUBLIC WATER SUPPLY

* check applicable codes which govern well installations and water supply

Water supply systems work under pressure. The service pressure of a water supply system must be great enough to absorb pressure losses due to vertical travel and friction as the water flows through pipes and fittings, and still satisfy the pressure requirements of each building fixture. Public water systems usually supply water at about 50 psi (35154 kg/m²). This pressure is the approximate upper limit for most private well systems.

Upfeed distribution from the service connection is usually feasible for low-rise buildings (4 to 6 stories in height) if water is suppled
at 50 psi (35154 kg/m²). For taller buildings, or where the service
water pressure is insufficient to maintain adequate fixture service,
water is pumped up to an elevated or rooftop storage tank for
gravity downfeed. (Part of this water is often used as a reserve
system for fire protection systems.)

Hot water is supplied from gas-fired or electric heaters and
circulated in tall buildings by the natural rising action of hot
water. In long, low buildings, pumps are required for hot water
circulation and distribution. Hot water storage tanks may be required for large installations and widespread fixture groupings.
For safety, temperature relief valves are required for all water
heaters.

There must be sufficient pressure at each fixture to ensure their
satisfactory operation. Fixture pressure requirements vary from
5 to 30 psi (3515 to 21092 kg/m²). Too much pressure is as undesirable as insufficient pressure. Water supply pipes are therefore sized to use up the pressure differential between the service pressure (allowing for pressure loss due to vertical lift) and
the pressure requirement for each fixture.

The amount of pressure lost due to friction depends on the size of
the supply pipe, the actual distance of the water flow, and the
number of fittings (valves, tees, elbows) through which the water
passes.

Pipe supports should be adequately spaced to carry the weight
of the pipe as well as the water being distributed through it.
· vertically : at least every story
· horizontally: between 6'-10' (1.820-3.048)
Adjustable hangers are available to ensure proper pitch along
horizontal runs for drainage purposes.

Water "hammer" noise may result when water is shut off abruptly.
To absorb this shock as well as the expansion of hot water, air
chambers or manufactured shock absorbers are required.

In tall buildings, special joints are required to allow for the expansion of long pipe runs carrying hot water.

Cold water pipes should be insulated and covered with a vapor
barrier to prevent surface condensation and unnecessary heat
flow into the water from the warmer surrounding air. Likewise,
hot water pipes should be insulated against heat loss and should
not be closer than 6" (152) to parallel cold water lines to prevent heat interchange.

Water pipes in exterior walls and unheated buildings can freeze
and break during cold weather. In cold climates, pipes should be
on the warm side of insulation. Provision should be made for their
drainage by pitching all pipes to a low point in the system where
a drainage faucet is located (preferably close to a storm drainage line).

Water pipes may be of galvanized steel, galvanized wrought iron,
copper, or plastic. They should be rust and corrosion-resistant.

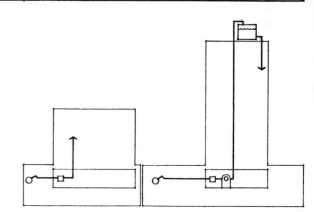

+ fixture pressure requirement
+ pressure loss due to vertical lift
+ pressure loss due to friction in piping
—————————————————————————————
= water service pressure

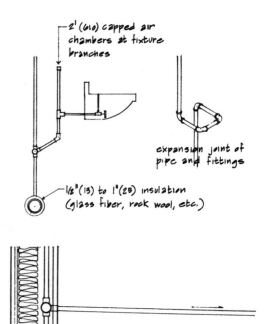

· larger pipes cause
  less friction loss

· every pipe fitting
  causes friction loss

2' (610) capped air
chambers at fixture
branches

expansion joint of
pipe and fittings

½" (13) to 1" (25) insulation
(glass fiber, rock wool, etc.)

The water supply system can usually be accomodated within floor and wall construction spaces without problems. It should be coordinated with the building structure and other systems such as the parallel and bulkier drainage and vent system. (see 11·14) If access is required, piping may be run in furred spaces containing removable panels.

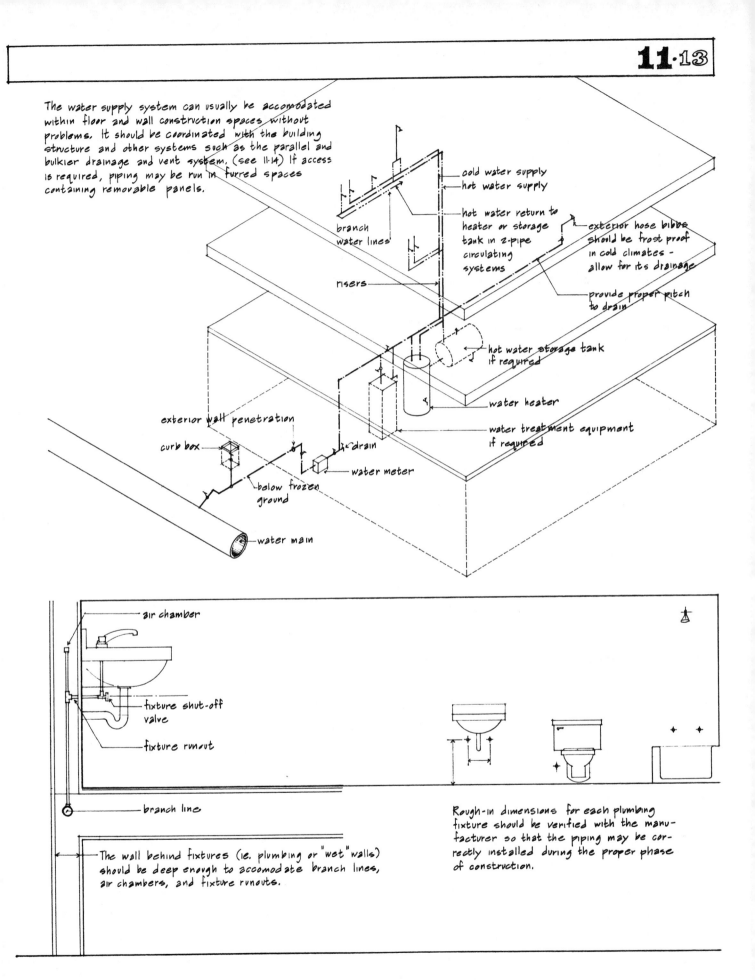

branch water lines'

cold water supply

hot water supply

hot water return to heater or storage tank in 2-pipe circulating systems

exterior hose bibbe should be frost proof in cold climates - allow for its drainage

risers

provide proper pitch to drain

hot water storage tank if required

water heater

water treatment equipment if required

exterior wall penetration

curb box

drain

water meter

below frozen ground

water main

air chamber

fixture shut-off valve

fixture runout

branch line

The wall behind fixtures (ie. plumbing or "wet" walls) should be deep enough to accomodate branch lines, air chambers, and fixture runouts.

Rough-in dimensions for each plumbing fixture should be verified with the manufacturer so that the piping may be correctly installed during the proper phase of construction.

Fluid waste and organic matter accumulated during the occupancy or use of a building is subject to rapid decomposition and must be disposed of as quickly as possible for sanitation and comfort. Whereas a water supply system operates from pressure, a sanitary drainage system depends upon gravity flow and thus requires larger pipes and more installation space than do supply systems. The layout of a sanitary drainage system should be as straight-forward and direct as possible with properly sloped horizontal runs and angular connections.

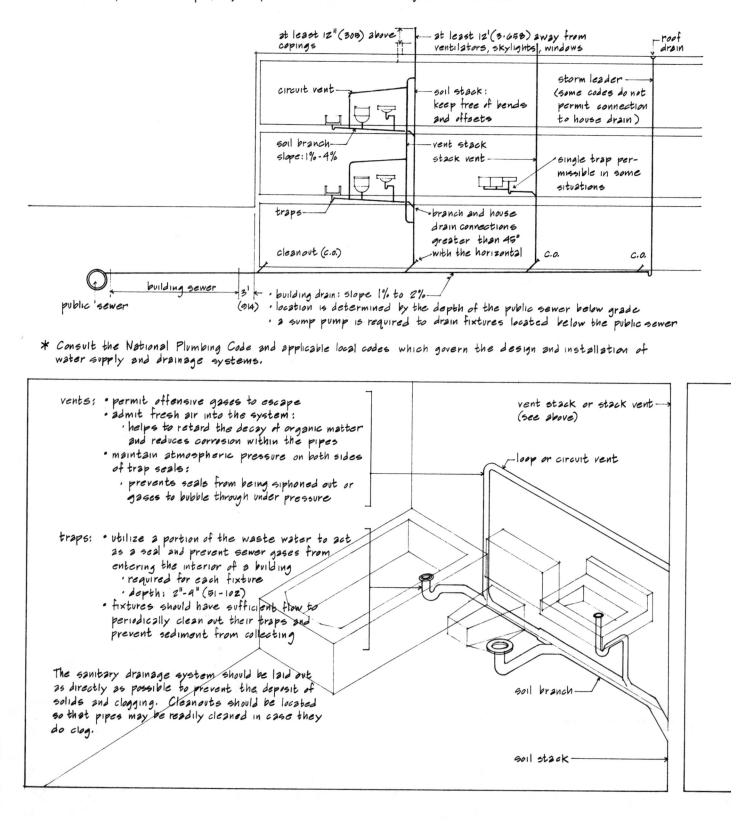

at least 12" (305) above copings

at least 12' (3.658) away from ventilators, skylights, windows

roof drain

circuit vent

soil stack: keep free of bends and offsets

storm leader — (some codes do not permit connection to house drain)

soil branch— slope: 1%-4%

vent stack
stack vent —

single trap permissible in some situations

traps—

branch and house drain connections greater than 45° with the horizontal

cleanout (c.o.)

c.o.   c.o.

building sewer

public sewer

3' (914)

· building drain: slope 1% to 2%—
· location is determined by the depth of the public sewer below grade
· a sump pump is required to drain fixtures located below the public sewer

* Consult the National Plumbing Code and applicable local codes which govern the design and installation of water supply and drainage systems.

vents: · permit offensive gases to escape
        · admit fresh air into the system:
              · helps to retard the decay of organic matter and reduces corrosion within the pipes
        · maintain atmospheric pressure on both sides of trap seals:
              · prevents seals from being siphoned out or gases to bubble through under pressure

vent stack or stack vent (see above)

loop or circuit vent

traps: · utilize a portion of the waste water to act as a seal and prevent sewer gases from entering the interior of a building
              · required for each fixture
              · depth: 2"-4" (51-102)
        · fixtures should have sufficient flow to periodically clean out their traps and prevent sediment from collecting

soil branch—

The sanitary drainage system should be laid out as directly as possible to prevent the deposit of solids and clogging. Cleanouts should be located so that pipes may be readily cleaned in case they do clog.

soil stack —

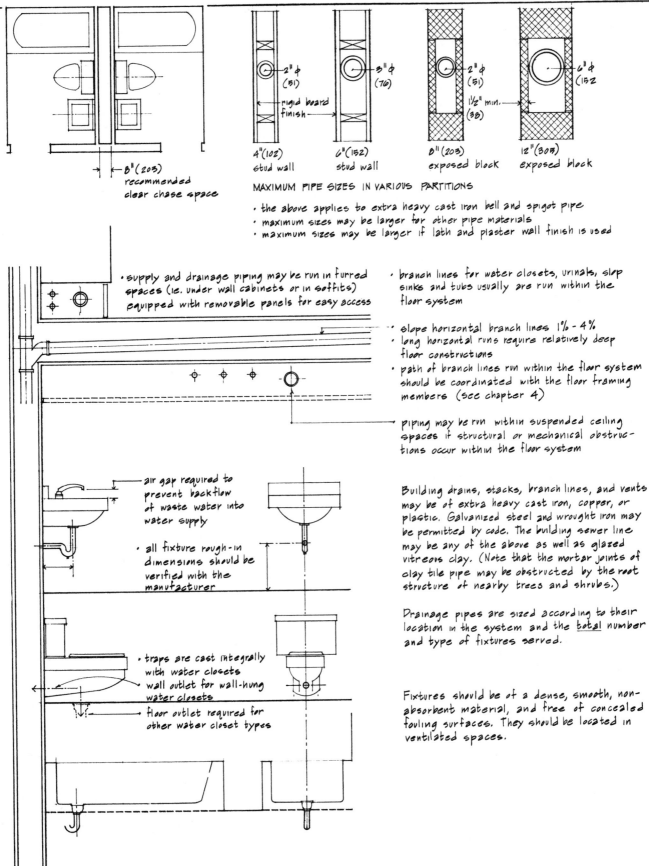

8"(203)
recommended
clear chase space

4"(102) stud wall	6"(152) stud wall	8"(203) exposed block	12"(305) exposed block
2"φ (51)	3"φ (76)	2"φ (51)	6"φ (152)

rigid board finish

1½" min. (38)

MAXIMUM PIPE SIZES IN VARIOUS PARTITIONS

- the above applies to extra heavy cast iron bell and spigot pipe
- maximum sizes may be larger for other pipe materials
- maximum sizes may be larger if lath and plaster wall finish is used

- supply and drainage piping may be run in furred spaces (ie. under wall cabinets or in soffits) equipped with removable panels for easy access

- branch lines for water closets, urinals, slop sinks and tubs usually are run within the floor system

- slope horizontal branch lines 1% - 4%
- long horizontal runs require relatively deep floor constructions
- path of branch lines run within the floor system should be coordinated with the floor framing members (see chapter 4)

- piping may be run within suspended ceiling spaces if structural or mechanical obstructions occur within the floor system

- air gap required to prevent backflow of waste water into water supply

- all fixture rough-in dimensions should be verified with the manufacturer

- traps are cast integrally with water closets
- wall outlet for wall-hung water closets
- floor outlet required for other water closet types

Building drains, stacks, branch lines, and vents may be of extra heavy cast iron, copper, or plastic. Galvanized steel and wrought iron may be permitted by code. The building sewer line may be any of the above as well as glazed vitreous clay. (Note that the mortar joints of clay tile pipe may be obstructed by the root structure of nearby trees and shrubs.)

Drainage pipes are sized according to their location in the system and the <u>total</u> number and type of fixtures served.

Fixtures should be of a dense, smooth, non-absorbent material, and free of concealed fouling surfaces. They should be located in ventilated spaces.

Building sewage wastes are usually deposited into a public sewer system for treatment and disposal. When this is not possible, a private sewage disposal system is required. Its type and size depends on:

- the number of people served
- the type and permeability of the soil
- the site topography
- the elevation of the water table (ground water)
- the proximity of wells and streams

A private sewage disposal system always requires a septic tank.

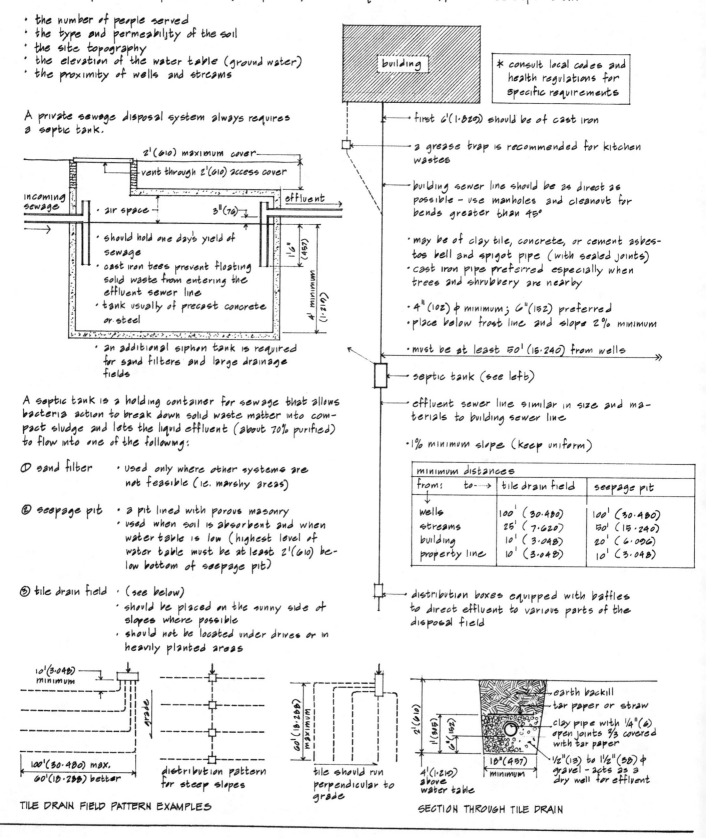

building

* consult local codes and health regulations for specific requirements

- 2'(610) maximum cover
- vent through 2'(610) access cover

incoming sewage

effluent

· air space ·

3"(76)

1'6" (457)

4' minimum (1·210)

- should hold one day's yield of sewage
- cast iron tees prevent floating solid waste from entering the effluent sewer line
- tank usually of precast concrete or steel

- an additional siphon tank is required for sand filters and large drainage fields

- first 6'(1·820) should be of cast iron
- a grease trap is recommended for kitchen wastes
- building sewer line should be as direct as possible - use manholes and cleanout for bends greater than 45°
- may be of clay tile, concrete, or cement asbestos bell and spigot pipe (with sealed joints)
- cast iron pipe preferred especially when trees and shrubbery are nearby
- 4"(102) ⌀ minimum; 6"(152) preferred
- place below frost line and slope 2% minimum
- must be at least 50'(15·240) from wells
- septic tank (see left)
- effluent sewer line similar in size and materials to building sewer line
- 1% minimum slope (keep uniform)

A septic tank is a holding container for sewage that allows bacteria action to break down solid waste matter into compact sludge and lets the liquid effluent (about 70% purified) to flow into one of the following:

① sand filter — · used only where other systems are not feasible (ie. marshy areas)

② seepage pit — · a pit lined with porous masonry
· used when soil is absorbent and when water table is low (highest level of water table must be at least 2'(610) below bottom of seepage pit)

③ tile drain field — · (see below)
· should be placed on the sunny side of slopes where possible
· should not be located under drives or in heavily planted areas

minimum distances		
from: to—→	tile drain field	seepage pit
↓		
wells	100' (30·480)	100' (30·480)
streams	25' (7·620)	50' (15·240)
building	10' (3·048)	20' (6·096)
property line	10' (3·048)	10' (3·048)

- distribution boxes equipped with baffles to direct effluent to various parts of the disposal field

10'(3·048) minimum

grade

100'(30·480) max.
60'(18·288) better

distribution pattern for steep slopes

60'(18·288) maximum

tile should run perpendicular to grade

earth backfill
tar paper or straw
clay pipe with 1/4"(6) open joints 2/3 covered with tar paper
1/2"(13) to 1 1/2"(38) ⌀ gravel - acts as a dry well for effluent

2'(610)
1'(305)
6"(152)
18"(457) minimum

4'(1·210) above water table

TILE DRAIN FIELD PATTERN EXAMPLES

SECTION THROUGH TILE DRAIN

Electrical energy provides power for light, heat, and the operation of appliances, services, and equipment within a building. The electrical system that controls and distributes this power to the points of utilization must be safe, reliable, and efficient in the utilization of its power supply.

This schematic diagram illustrates several voltage systems that may be furnished by a power company according to the type and size of a building's load requirements.

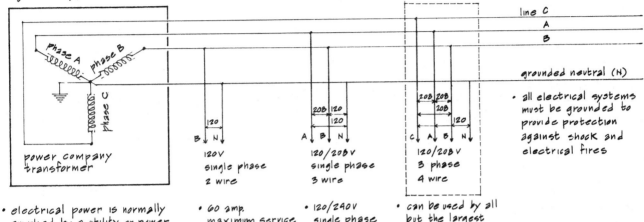

power company transformer

120V
single phase
2 wire

120/208V
single phase
3 wire

120/208V
3 phase
4 wire

line C
A
B

grounded neutral (N)

- all electrical systems must be grounded to provide protection against shock and electrical fires

- electrical power is normally supplied by a utility or power company
- generator sets or batteries may be used for alternative or emergency power required by code (ie. hospitals, public buildings)

- 60 amp. maximum service

- 120/240V single phase 3 wire service more common for residences

- can be used by all but the largest installations which require higher voltages

Electrical energy flows through a conductor because of a difference in electrical charge between two points in the circuit. This potential energy is measured in volts. The actual amount of electrical energy flow is measured in amperes. The power required to keep an electric current flowing is measured in watts. (wattage = amperage x voltage)

Just as pressure is lost due to friction as water flows through a piping system, the flow of electrical current is impeded by resistance, measured in ohms, as it travels through its conductor.

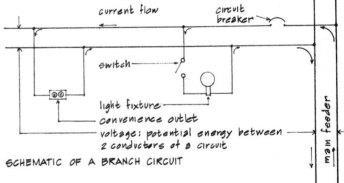

current flow   circuit breaker
switch
light fixture
convenience outlet
voltage: potential energy between 2 conductors of a circuit
main feeder

SCHEMATIC OF A BRANCH CIRCUIT

The basic components of a building's electrical system include:

- service connection   - from the power company
- service switch   - for control, protection, and metering of the power supply
- main switchboard   - for control and protection of the main feeder lines
- panelboards   - for control and protection of branch circuits
- service outlets   - lights, appliances, convenience receptacles, motors, etc.
- switches and controls - for the control of service outlets
- wiring and conduit   - to distribute electrical power between all of the above

All equipment used should meet the Underwriters Laboratories (UL) standards.
Consult the National Electric Code as well as local applicable codes for specific requirements in the design and installation of an electrical system.

The power company should be notified of the estimated total electrical load requirements for a building during the planning phase to confirm service availability, and coordinate the location of the service connection, service switch, and switchboard. In large installations, a transformer may be used to switch from the supply voltage to the service voltage. To reduce cost, maintenance, and noise and heat problems, transformers are usually placed outdoors.

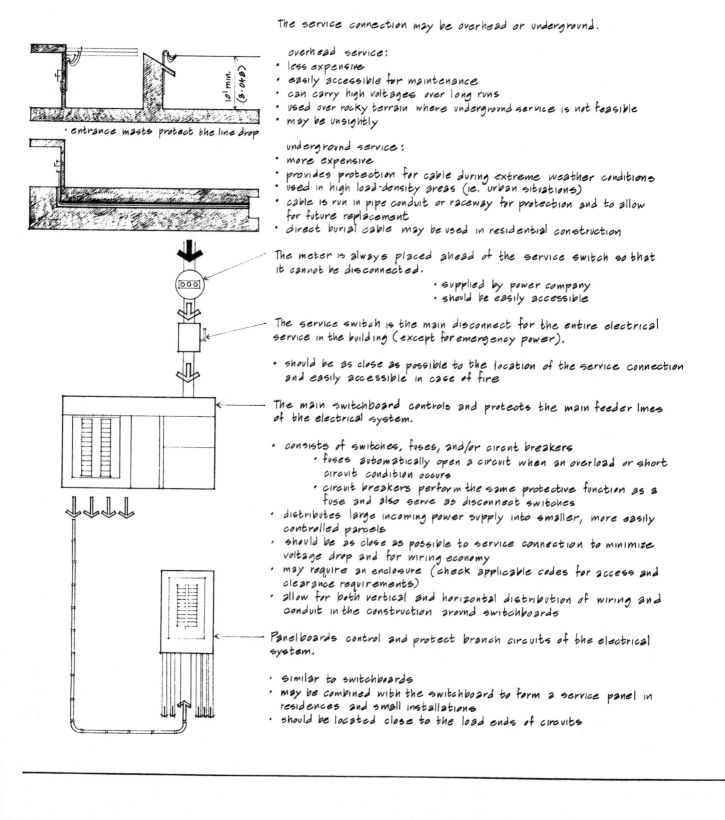

· entrance masts protect the line drop

The service connection may be overhead or underground.

overhead service:
· less expensive
· easily accessible for maintenance
· can carry high voltages over long runs
· used over rocky terrain where underground service is not feasible
· may be unsightly

underground service:
· more expensive
· provides protection for cable during extreme weather conditions
· used in high load-density areas (ie. urban situations)
· cable is run in pipe conduit or raceway for protection and to allow for future replacement
· direct burial cable may be used in residential construction

The meter is always placed ahead of the service switch so that it cannot be disconnected.

· supplied by power company
· should be easily accessible

The service switch is the main disconnect for the entire electrical service in the building (except for emergency power).

· should be as close as possible to the location of the service connection and easily accessible in case of fire

The main switchboard controls and protects the main feeder lines of the electrical system.

· consists of switches, fuses, and/or circuit breakers
    · fuses automatically open a circuit when an overload or short circuit condition occurs
    · circuit breakers perform the same protective function as a fuse and also serve as disconnect switches
· distributes large incoming power supply into smaller, more easily controlled parcels
· should be as close as possible to service connection to minimize voltage drop and for wiring economy
· may require an enclosure (check applicable codes for access and clearance requirements)
· allow for both vertical and horizontal distribution of wiring and conduit in the construction around switchboards

Panelboards control and protect branch circuits of the electrical system.

· similar to switchboards
· may be combined with the switchboard to form a service panel in residences and small installations
· should be located close to the load ends of circuits

Once the service connection, service switch, and main switchboard are sized and located, and the electrical power requirements for the various areas of the building are determined, wiring circuits must laid out to distribute the electrical power to the points of utilization. Panelboards, fed by the main switchboard, distribute their power supply into branch circuits. These branch panels may serve similar types of circuits (eg. lighting panels, receptacle panels, etc.) or specific areas of a building such as kitchens or laboratories.

Branch circuits are the final distribution points of the electrical system.

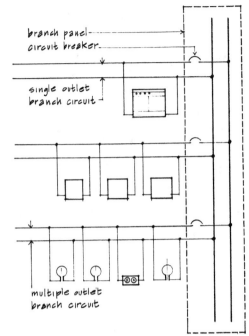

branch panel circuit breaker

single outlet branch circuit

multiple outlet branch circuit

- sized according to load
- allow for flexibility and expansion of load requirements (15% - 25%)
- types • single outlet   designed and sized to serve a specific piece of equipment
  • multiple outlet   serving 2 or more appliances (20 to 50 amp capacity)
  • multiple outlet   serving 2 or more general purpose outlets (10 to 50 amp capacity)
- continuous loading should not exceed 80% of the circuit's rating
  (eg. allowing for 25% future expansion, a typical 20 amp general purpose circuit should have a continuous load rating of 12 amps, enough to handle 1200 watts of power or serve 8 convenience receptacles (rated at 1.5 amps each)
- should not exceed 100 feet (30.480) in length to avoid excessive voltage drop (analogous to friction loss in water pipes)
- all branch circuits should be grounded to provide protection against shock

Low voltage switching is used when a central switching point is desired from which all switching may take place.

- low voltage (6 to 24 v) switches control relays which do the actual switching at the service outlets
- advantages: 120 v branch circuits are shortened
  low voltage wiring may be run without conduit
  useful in alteration and rehabilitation work

Separate wiring circuits are required for sound and signal equipment. (intercom systems, alarm systems, etc.)

- telephone systems:
  • small installations should have the telephone outlets located and prewired during construction
  • large installations require service connections, terminal enclosures, riser spaces, etc., similar to electrical systems
  • usually designed, furnished, and installed by the telephone company except for built-in or fixed equipment such as cabinet enclosures, shaft spaces, and conduit

- TV/fm cable systems
  • signal may be received from an outdoor antenna, a commercial cable company, or a closed circuit system
  • if several outlets are required, a 120 v outlet is supplied to serve an amplifier
  • a co-axial cable in a non-metallic conduit or raceway transmits the amplified signal to the various outlets

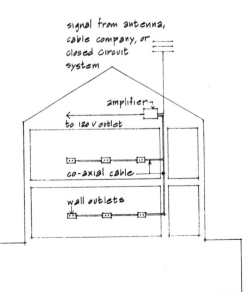

signal from antenna, cable company, or closed circuit system

amplifier

to 120 v outlet

co-axial cable

wall outlets

Metals, offering little resistance to the flow of electric current, make good conductors. Copper and aluminum are the most often used. The various forms of conductors (wire, cable, and busbars) are sized according to their safe current carrying capacity and the maximum operating temperature of their insulation. They are typed and identified according to voltage class, number and size of conductors, and type of insulation.

A conductor is covered with insulation to prevent its contact with other conductors or metal and protect it against heat, moisture, and corrosion. Materials with high resistance to electric current flow, such as rubber, porcelain, glass, and some synthetics, are commonly used to insulate wiring and their connections.

Metallic conduit provides:
• protection for the wiring against physical damage and corrosion
• protection for the surroundings against fire hazards
• a continuous grounded enclosure for the wiring (all connections must be of metal)
• support for the wiring

Types: rigid steel, thin-wall metallic tubing, flexible metal, and non-metallic (all should be corrosion-resistant)
Conduit fittings include: straight and angular couplings, elbows, junction and outlet boxes

Being relatively small, conduit can be easily accomodated in most construction systems. Conduit should be adequately supported and laid out as directly as possible. Codes generally restrict the radius and number of bends a run of conduit may have between junction or outlet boxes. Coordination with the buildings mechanical and plumbing systems is required to avoid conflicting paths.

Electrical conductors may also be run within cellular steel deck or concrete floor systems for convenient access to floor and ceiling outlets.

Special conduit, raceways, troughs, and fittings are available for exposed installations. As with exposed mechanical systems, the layout should have a visually coherent order and be coordinated with the physical elements of the space.

Light fixtures, wall switches, and convenience receptacles are usually the most visible parts of an electrical system. Switches and receptacles should be located for convenience, easy access, and in coordination with visible surface patterns. Wall plates for these devices may be of metal, insulating plastic, or glass, and are available in various colors and finishes.

A receptacle outlet designed to serve a specific type of appliance will have a specific configuration so that only attachment plugs from that type of appliance will fit the receptacle. Waterproof receptacles should be used outdoors and in areas subject to wetting.

Load requirements for light fixtures and electrically powered equipment are specified by their manufacturer. The design load for a branch circuit containing receptacle outlets, however, depends on the number of receptacles served by the circuit and how they are used. Consult local applicable codes for the required number and spacing of convenience receptacles. The following may be used as a guide:

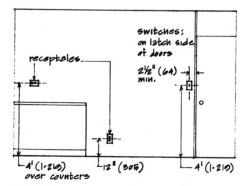

switches:
on latch side of doors

2½" (64) min.

receptacles

4' (1.210) over counters   12" (305)   4' (1.210)

RECEPTACLE AND SWITCH HEIGHTS

residences: 1 every 12' (3.658) along walls in living areas
             1 every 4' (1.010) along countertops in kitchens
             2 in bathroom (not combined with light fixture)

offices: 1 every 10' (3.048) along walls or
             1 every 40 SF (4 m²) of floor area for the first 10,
             1 every 100 SF (9 m²) thereafter

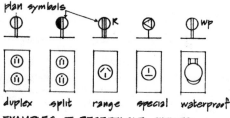

plan symbols

duplex   split   range   special   waterproof

EXAMPLES OF RECEPTACLE OUTLETS

The perception of a space is affected by the nature of the light through which it is seen and the nature of the surfaces off of which the light is reflected.

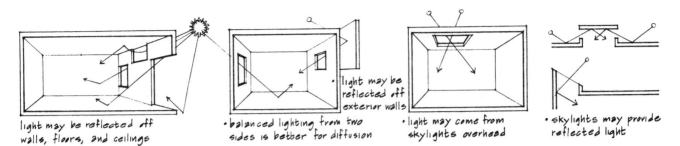

light may be reflected off walls, floors, and ceilings

• balanced lighting from two sides is better for diffusion

• light may be reflected off exterior walls

• light may come from skylights overhead

• skylights may provide reflected light

Natural light from the sun may be harsh, sparkling, hazy, subdued; its quality changes with the time of day and varies with the weather and the seasons. How it penetrates interior spaces depends on the type, size, placement, and orientation of the building's window openings. In contrast to this, artificial light is generally static and unchanging (except when its brightness is manipulated with a dimmer control or its source is moved as with track lighting.)

The primary purpose of an artificial lighting system is to provide sufficient illumination for the performance of visual tasks. As a reference, recommended illumination levels (measured in foot-candles) for various categories of tasks are listed to the right.

task difficulty	(e.g.)	footcandle (Fc) level
• casual	(dining)	20
• ordinary	(reading)	50
• moderate	(drafting)	100
• difficult	(sewing)	200
• severe	(surgery)	>400

• 1 footcandle = 1 lumen/sq.ft = 10.76 lux

(1 lux = 1 lumen/m²)

Illumination level recommendations specify only the quantity of light to be supplied. How this light is supplied affects how a space is perceived or how an object is seen and is just as important as the lighting level. The quality of lighting varies according to the brightness ratios in the space, the light's diffusion, and its color.

Contrast between the object viewed and its immediate surroundings is required for its form, shape, and texture to be seen. As the brightness level increases, the need for contrast decreases. When the contrast in brightness becomes excessive within the field of vision, glare results and causes discomfort for the viewer. Excessive brightness ratios may occur between a light source and its surrounding surfaces or between surfaces in the space.

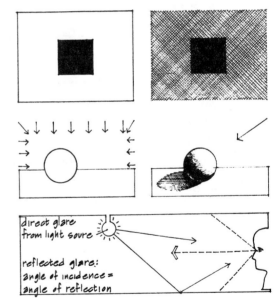

Diffused light, coming from many directions, from multiple sources as well as reflecting surfaces, produces almost uniform illumination with few shadows. Directional light, on the other hand, produces brightness variations and shadows which are necessary for the perception of form and texture. Both types of light complement each other and may be desirable depending on the form and use of the space.

direct glare from light source

reflected glare: angle of incidence = angle of reflection

The perceived color of an object is the result of its ability to modify (ie. reflect or absorb) the color of the light falling on it. The study of this relationship between color and light is beyond the scope of this book but is important for interior design and critical in task areas such as merchandising display. Since white light is normally used for illumination, however, the following may be noted:

• at the same brightness level, light hues appear brighter (ie. reflect more light) than dark colors which absorb light
• warm colors tend to be more washed out (ie. lose their saturation) at high illumination levels than cool colors
• variations in a color's value rather than hue is more important in the definition of form and space

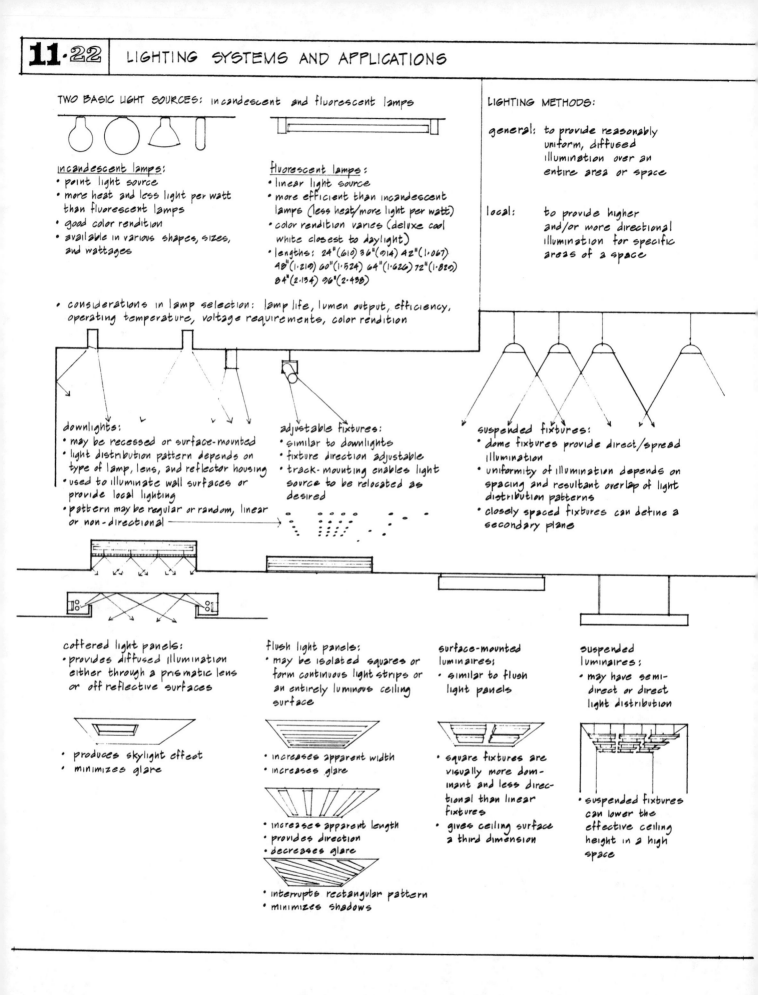

TWO BASIC LIGHT SOURCES: incandescent and fluorescent lamps

LIGHTING METHODS:

general: to provide reasonably uniform, diffused illumination over an entire area or space

local: to provide higher and/or more directional illumination for specific areas of a space

incandescent lamps:
• point light source
• more heat and less light per watt than fluorescent lamps
• good color rendition
• available in various shapes, sizes, and wattages

fluorescent lamps:
• linear light source
• more efficient than incandescent lamps (less heat/more light per watt)
• color rendition varies (deluxe cool white closest to daylight)
• lengths: 24"(610) 36"(914) 42"(1·067) 48"(1·219) 60"(1·524) 64"(1·626) 72"(1·820) 84"(2·134) 96"(2·438)

• considerations in lamp selection: lamp life, lumen output, efficiency, operating temperature, voltage requirements, color rendition

downlights:
• may be recessed or surface-mounted
• light distribution pattern depends on type of lamp, lens, and reflector housing
• used to illuminate wall surfaces or provide local lighting
• pattern may be regular or random, linear or non-directional

adjustable fixtures:
• similar to downlights
• fixture direction adjustable
• track-mounting enables light source to be relocated as desired

suspended fixtures:
• dome fixtures provide direct/spread illumination
• uniformity of illumination depends on spacing and resultant overlap of light distribution patterns
• closely spaced fixtures can define a secondary plane

coffered light panels:
• provides diffused illumination either through a prismatic lens or off reflective surfaces

• produces skylight effect
• minimizes glare

flush light panels:
• may be isolated squares or form continuous light strips or an entirely luminous ceiling surface

• increases apparent width
• increases glare

• increases apparent length
• provides direction
• decreases glare

• interrupts rectangular pattern
• minimizes shadows

surface-mounted luminaires:
• similar to flush light panels

• square fixtures are visually more dom- inant and less direc- tional than linear fixtures
• gives ceiling surface a third dimension

suspended luminaires:
• may have semi- direct or direct light distribution

• suspended fixtures can lower the effective ceiling height in a high space

LIGHT DISTRIBUTION PATTERNS: *depends on the type of light fixture, lens and/or reflector housing*

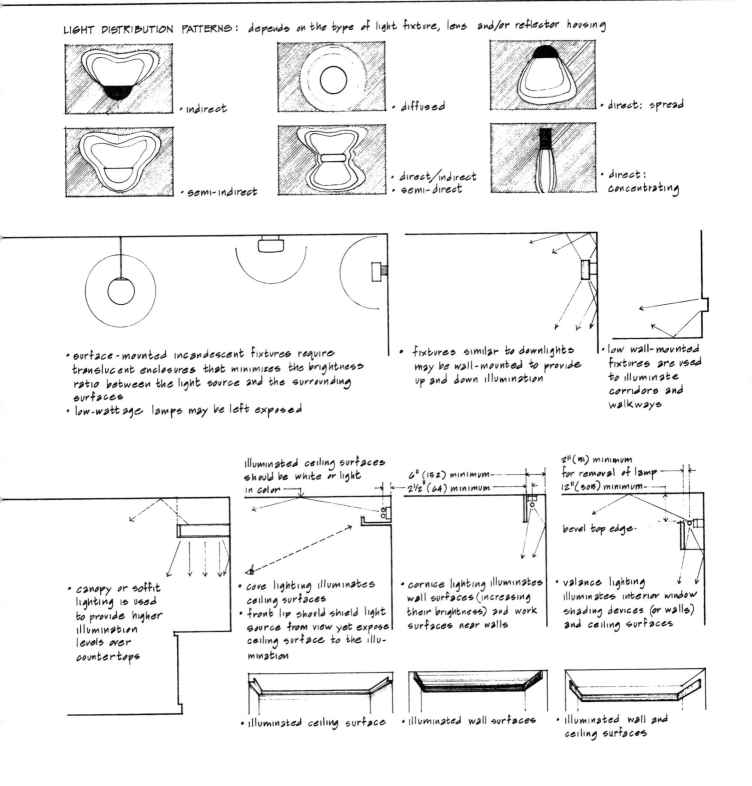

• indirect

• diffused

• direct: spread

• semi-indirect

• direct/indirect
• semi-direct

• direct: concentrating

• surface-mounted incandescent fixtures require translucent enclosures that minimizes the brightness ratio between the light source and the surrounding surfaces
• low-wattage lamps may be left exposed

• fixtures similar to downlights may be wall-mounted to provide up and down illumination

• low wall-mounted fixtures are used to illuminate corridors and walkways

• canopy or soffit lighting is used to provide higher illumination levels over countertops

illuminated ceiling surfaces should be white or light in color

• cove lighting illuminates ceiling surfaces
• front lip should shield light source from view yet expose ceiling surface to the illumination

• illuminated ceiling surface

6" (152) minimum——
2½" (64) minimum——

• cornice lighting illuminates wall surfaces (increasing their brightness) and work surfaces near walls

• illuminated wall surfaces

2" (51) minimum for removal of lamp——
12" (305) minimum——

bevel top edge—

• valance lighting illuminates interior window shading devices (or walls) and ceiling surfaces

• illuminated wall and ceiling surfaces

Solar energy systems absorb, transfer, and store heat energy from solar radiation for building heating and cooling. They normally consist of the following components:

- an insulated, heat-absorbent surface
- a circulation and distribution system for the heat transfer medium
- a heat storage facility

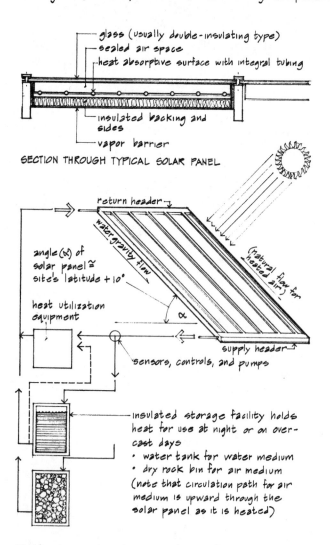

glass (usually double-insulating type)
sealed air space
heat absorptive surface with integral tubing

insulated backing and sides

vapor barrier

SECTION THROUGH TYPICAL SOLAR PANEL

return header

water-gravity flow

(natural flow for heated air)

angle (α) of solar panel ≈ site's latitude + 10°

heat utilization equipment

α

sensors, controls, and pumps

supply header

insulated storage facility holds heat for use at night or on overcast days
- water tank for water medium
- dry rock bin for air medium
(note that circulation path for air medium is upward through the solar panel as it is heated)

The solar collector panel is the solar energy system's prime component. It consists of:

- a flat metal plate to absorb the sun's radiant heat (aluminum, copper, or steel — sometimes coated to increase its heat-absorptive qualities)
- tubing or duct space integral with the collector plate to carry the heat transfer medium (water or air)
- a glass-covered, sealed air space to increase the panel's heat retention
- a well-insulated backing

Solar collector panels should be oriented to best take advantage of the sun's radiation, and located so as not to be shaded by nearby structures, terrain, or trees.

The collector surface area required depends on the heat exchange efficiency of the collector and the heat transfer medium, and the building's heating and cooling load. Current recommendations range from 1/3 to 1/2 of the building's net floor area.

The heat transfer medium (water or air) carries the collected heat energy from the solar panel to the heat utilization equipment or to a storage facility for later use.

water medium:
- requires piping for circulation and distribution
- usually contains an anti-freeze solution
- corrosion-retarding additive required for aluminum piping

air medium:
- requires ductwork and larger installation space
- heat-transfer coefficient less than that of water requiring larger collector surfaces
- panel construction is simpler and not subject to problems of freezing, leakage, and corrosion

The heating and cooling components of the solar energy system are similar to those of conventional systems.
- for heating: air-water or all-air system
- for cooling: a heat pump or absorption cooling unit is required
- an auxiliary heat source is recommended for back-up use

- solar panels may form a single plane or a series of parallel planes
- locating the panels away from the building requires a longer and less efficient distribution run for the transfer medium

For a solar energy system to be efficient, the building itself must be thermally efficient and well-insulated. Its siting, orientation, and window openings should take advantage of the sun's winter and summer sun angles.

Solar collector panels normally are integral parts of a building's roof or wall surfaces, and therefore strongly influence the building's overall form.

NOTES ON MATERIALS

This chapter outlines major building materials, their physical properties, capabilities, and liabilities. Building materials are characterized by distinct properties of strength, stiffness and elasticity, density or hardness, resistance to wear caused by physical or chemical action, fire resistance, and thermal conductivity.

The most effective structural materials are those which combine elasticity with stiffness. Elasticity is the ability of a material to deform under stress (bend, stretch, or compress) and return to its original shape. Every material has its elastic limit beyond which it will permanently deform or break. Those materials that have low elastic limits are termed brittle. The stiffness of a material is a measure of the force required to pull or push a material to its elastic limit.

Most building materials are manufactured in standard sizes. These "stock" sizes may vary slightly between manufacturers and should be verified during the design and planning phase of the building to avoid unnecessary cutting and waste of material during construction. For the same reason, the modular characteristics of building materials such as masonry units and plywood should be considered in determining a building's dimensions.

Following the discussion of building materials, an outline of the various methods of fastenings and finishing materials is included for reference use.

As a construction material, wood offers, in addition to its strength, durability, light weight, and easy workability, natural beauty and warmth to sight and touch. Although it has become necessary to employ conservation measures to ensure a continued supply, wood is still used in construction in many and varied forms.

Their are two major classes of wood: softwood and hardwood. These terms do not indicate the relative hardness, softness, or strength of a wood. Softwoods are the evergreens, and are used for general construction. Hardwoods comes from deciduous or broadleaf trees, and are generally used for flooring, stairs, paneling, furniture, and interior trim.

The manner in which a tree grows affects its strength, its susceptibility to expansion and contraction, and its effectiveness as an insulator. Tree growth also affects how pieces of sawn wood (lumber) may be joined to form structure and enclosure.

Grain direction is the major determining factor in the use of wood as a structural material. Tensile and compressive forces are best handled by wood in a direction parallel to its grain. Generally speaking, a given piece of wood will withstand 1/3 more force in compression than in tension parallel to its grain. The allowable compressive force perpendicular to its grain is only about 1/5 to 1/2 of the allowable compressive force parallel to the grain. Tensile forces perpendicular to the grain will cause wood to split.

Wood's shear strength is greater across its grain than parallel to the grain, and is therefore more susceptible to horizontal shear than vertical shear.

The manner in which wood is cut from a log affects its strength as well as its appearance.

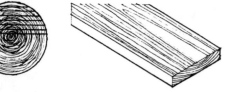

plainsawn lumber:
• may have a variety of noticeable grain patterns
• tends to twist and cup, and wear unevenly
• tends to have raised grain
• surface appearance and strength less affected by knots
• shrinks and swells less in thickness, more in width

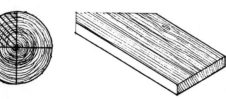

quartersawn lumber:
• has more even grain patterns
• wears evenly with less raised grain and warpage
• less affected by surface checks
• shrinks and swells less in width, more in thickness
• more costly and more waste in cutting

Below a certain moisture content level, wood expands when it absorbs moisture and shrinks when it loses moisture. To increase its strength, stability, and resistance to fungi, decay, and insects, wood should be carefully seasoned before use, either through air-drying (a lengthy process) or through the use of kilns. It is impossible to completely seal a piece of wood to prevent changes in its moisture content, so the possibility of it shrinking and swelling must always be taken into account when detailing and constructing wood joints both in large and small scale work.

Shrinkage tangential to the wood grain is usually twice as much as radial shrinkage. Vertical grain shrinks uniformly while plainsawn cuts near the log's perimeter will cup away from the center.

Thermal expansion of wood is generally much less than that due to moisture so the moisture content of wood is the controlling factor.

Wood "defects" affect the grading, appearance, and use of the wood. They may affect the wood's strength depending on their number, size, and location. Defects include natural characteristics of wood such as knots, shakes, and pitch pockets, as well as manufacturing characteristics such as splits, checking, and warp.

Wood is decay-resistant when its moisture content is under 20%. If installed and maintained within this moisture content range, wood will usually not rot.

Decay-resistant species include redwood, cedar, bald cypress, black locust, and black walnut. Termite-resistant species include redwood, eastern red cedar, and bald cypress.

Preservative treatments are available to protect wood from decay or insect attack. Of these, pressure treatment with the following is the most effective, especially when the wood is in contact with the ground:

- water-borne salt solutions leave the wood clean, odorless and readily paintable

- oil-borne solutions may color the wood

- creosote treatments, used especially in marine or salt water installations, leaves a colored, oily surface

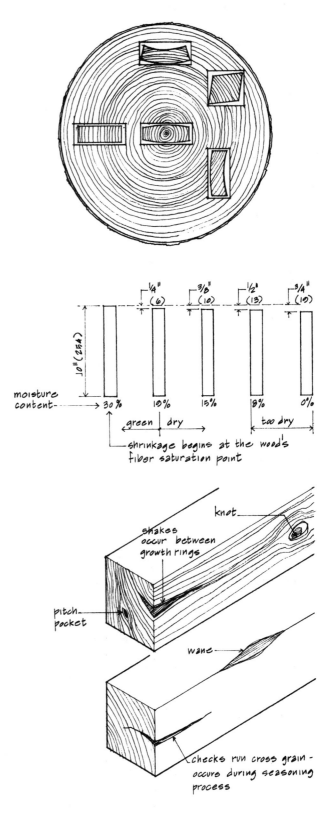

moisture content → 30% | 10% | 15% | 8% | 0%

green ─ dry   too dry

shrinkage begins at the wood's fiber saturation point

knot

shakes occur between growth rings

pitch pocket

wane

checks run cross grain - occurs during seasoning process

nominal thickness or width	minimum dressed thickness or width for surfaced dry softwood (19% m.c. or less)	note: lumber is measured in "board-feet" one board-foot = 1" × 12" × one foot of length
1" (25)	3/4" (19)	Lumber is specified according to its nominal dimensions. The nominal size is the lumber's rough, unfinished size. The dressed finished size is actually smaller due to the seasoning and surfacing of the lumber before use.
2" (51)	1½" (38)	
3" (76)	2½" (64)	
4" (102)	3½" (89)	
5" (127)	4½" (114)	The "face" dimension is the finished width of a piece that is exposed to view after installation.
6" (152)	5½" (140)	
8" (203)	7¼" (184)	
10" (254)	9¼" (235)	Lumber is usually available in lengths from 6' to 24' (1.820 to 7.315) in 2' (610) multiples.
12" (305)	11¼" (286)	
14" (356)	13¼" (337)	
16" (406)	15¼" (387)	

Because of its diversity of application and its use for remanufacturing purposes, hardwood is graded according to the amount of clear usable lumber in a piece that may be cut into smaller pieces of a certain grade and size. Softwood lumber classifications include the following:

YARD LUMBER : • boards: • 1" to 1½" thick ; 2" and wider
                                    • graded for appearance rather than strength
                                    • used as siding, subflooring, interior trim

> refer to table above for metric equivalents

          • dimension lumber: 2" to 4" thick; 2" and wider
                                    • graded for strength (stress graded) rather than appearance
                                    • used for general construction

                                    • light framing   2" to 4" wide
                                    • joists and planks   6" and wider
                                    • decking   4" and wider (select and commercial grades)

          • timbers: • 5" × 5" and larger
                                    • graded for strength and serviceability
                                    • often stocked in green, undressed condition
                                    • may be classified as "structural lumber" along with joists and planks

"Factory and shop lumber" is used primarily for remanufacturing purposes (eg. doors, windows, millwork)

Lumber may be structurally graded as follows: (in descending order - according to stress grade)

         • light framing: construction, standard, utility grades
         • structural light framing, joists, planks: select structural, nº 1, 2, 3 grades
           (some species may also have an appearance grade for exposed work)
         • timber: select structural, nº 1 grades

         • working stress values can be assigned to each of the grades according to species of wood

Lumber may be appearance graded as follows:

         • select   A, B (or "B and better") · for natural finishes
                     C, D   · for paint finishes
         • common: for general construction and utility purposes

Plywood is a laminated panel of wood veneers laid with their grain direction at right angles to one another and bonded together under high pressure with either a water-resistant or waterproof adhesive. The cross lamination of plies takes advantage of the more desirable physical properties of wood and gives plywood added strength and stiffness in two directions. Plywood panels, however, are still stronger and stiffer along their face grain.

Plywood has relatively high shear strength in all directions for loads perpendicular to its face. It also has good nail retention strength. For these reasons, plywood makes an excellent sheathing material for wall, floor, and roof frame constructions.

The two main types of plywood are:

- exterior grade plywood:
  - made with waterproof adhesive
  - C grade face or better
  - for permanent exterior use

- interior grade plywood:
  - made with water-resistant adhesives
  - D grade face or better

Plywood may also be graded according to its face veneers:

- N   all heartwood or all sapwood - for natural finish
- A   smooth paint grade
- B   solid smooth surface
- C   sheathing grade - lowest grade for exterior plywood
- D   lowest grade for interior plywood

Engineered grades of plywood are used for wall and roof sheathing, subflooring, and underlayment. Most construction plywood is stamped with a grade-trademark containing the following information
- type   (interior or exterior)
- grade (of face and back veneers)
- group (of wood species)

thicknesses:
- odd number of plies
- grain direction same for face and back plies (longitudinal)

3 ply: ¼" (6)
       5/16" (8)
       3/8" (10)

5 ply: ½" (13)
       5/8" (16)
       ¾" (19)

7 ply: 7/8" (22)
       1" (25)
       1⅛" (29)
       1¼" (32)

8' (2.438) standard and up available (3.658)

4' (1.219) standard
5' (1.524) available

Structural I & II, Standard, and C-C exterior engineered grades have identification index numbers that refer to the maximum recommended spacing for the panel supports.

32/16 ──left hand number for roof supports
       ←right hand number for floor supports
       (numbers are inches)
       * see 4·11 and 6·9

Laminated timbers are engineered, stress-rated structural members built up of several layers of wood securely bonded with waterproof or water-resistant adhesives. The grain of the laminations [less than 2"(51) thick] are approximately parallel longitudinally. Several grades of lumber may be used, the higher grades in areas of highest stress, the lower grades in areas of lower stress.

For large structural members, laminated timber is preferable to solid timber in terms of finished dressed appearance, weather resistance, controlled moisture content, and size availability. Being factory-made, they are consistent in size, appearance, and strength, and more dimensionally stable than solid timber.

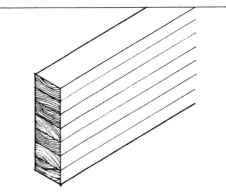

* see 4·13 for typical sizes and spans

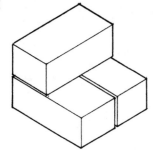

Masonry refers to man-made units which are formed and hardened into modular building units. This modular aspect (ie. uniform size and proportional relationships) distinguishes masonry from most of the other construction materials discussed in this chapter.

Masonry units are formed from shapeless material and hardened in either of two ways:

① through heat:
- brick
- structural clay tile | made from various types of clay
- terra cotta

② through chemical action:
- gypsum block
- concrete block | made from a mixture of cement or gypsum, aggregate,
- concrete brick | and water

Since masonry units are relatively weak (as compared to other structural materials) and the mortar used to bond them together is even weaker still, masonry units must be laid up in such a way as to enable the entire masonry mass to act as an entity. Continuous planes of mortar should be avoided. (see 5·18 for masonry wall structural requirements)

Masonry is structurally effective in compression. The following are minimum compressive strength values for various masonry unit types:

- brick
  - 2500 psi   type SW   (severe weather) for use below
    $(1757 \times 10^3 \, kg/m^2)$ grade and where exposed to freezing

  - 2200 psi   type MW   (medium weather)
    $(1546 \times 10^3 \, kg/m^2)$ for exterior walls above grade

  - 1250 psi   type NW   (no weather)
    $(878 \times 10^3 \, kg/m^2)$ for interior use

- concrete block
  - 600 psi   hollow load-bearing units
    $(422 \times 10^3 \, kg/m^2)$

  - 1600 psi   solid load-bearing units
    $(1125 \times 10^3 \, kg/m^2)$

  - 3000 psi   concrete brick units
    $(2110 \times 10^3 \, kg/m^2)$

mortar consists of:

- portland and/or masonry cements
- aggregate
- water
- lime is used in portland cement-lime mortars

The mortar used to bond the masonry units together can also be graded according to compressive strength and use

- type M
  - 2500 psi   · for basements and reinforced masonry
    $(1758 \times 10^3 \, kg/m^2)$ (foundations, piers, pilasters)

  S
  - 1800 psi   · for interior load-bearing walls and
    $(1266 \times 10^3 \, kg/m^2)$ exterior walls

  N
  - 750 psi   · for interior walls and masonry veneers
    $(527 \times 10^3 \, kg/m^2)$

It should be noted that the compressive strength of a masonry wall assembly is much less than the values given above since the quality of the masonry units, mortar, and workmanship may vary. As a guide, use the following values:

- 250 psi $(176 \times 10^3 \, kg/m^2)$ for solid brick walls
- 175 psi $(123 \times 10^3 \, kg/m^2)$ for concrete block walls
- 140 psi $(98 \times 10^3 \, kg/m^2)$ for cavity walls

The appearance of the various masonry units depends on the raw materials used and the method of manufacture. Brick faces can vary in color, texture, and pattern. Concrete block can vary in tones of gray, and surface patterns and textures.

BRICK SIZES

nominal dimensions of modular brick

actual dimensions of modular brick	thickness in. (mm)	height in. (mm)	length in. (mm)	modular coursing (c) = course
with 3/8" (10) mortar joints	3 5/8" (92)	2 1/4" (57)	7 5/8" (194)	3c = 8" (203)
with 1/2" (13) mortar joints	3 1/2" (89)	2 3/16" (56)	7 1/2" (191)	3c = 8" (203)
nominal dimensions of other brick types:				
• double	4" (102)	5 1/3" (135)	8" (203)	3c = 16" (406)
• economy	4" (102)	4" (102)	8" (203)	1c = 4" (102)
• roman	4" (102)	2" (51)	12" (305)	2c = 4" (102)
• norman	4" (102)	2 3/3" (68)	12" (305)	3c = 8" (203)
• "SCR" brick	6" (152)	2 3/3" (68)	12" (305)	3c = 8" (203)

The actual size of brick units varies due to shrinkage during the manufacturing process. Their nominal dimensions include the thickness of the mortar joints which vary from 1/4" (6) to 1/2" (13).

* see 5.35 for bonding patterns

CONCRETE BLOCK

may have 2 or three cores

actual dimensions of the basic concrete block unit

corner block   jamb block   partition block

Concrete block is manufactured in many shapes to satisfy various construction conditions. Their availability varies between localities and manufacturers.

The basic concrete block unit has nominal modular dimensions of 8" x 8" x 16" (203 x 203 x 406). Half-length and half-height units are available for most unit types.

The three basic types of concrete block are:

• solid load-bearing units (75% or more net area)
• hollow load-bearing units
• hollow non-load-bearing units

Aggregates used in concrete block include:

• sand and gravel: block characteristics
  • light gray color
  • fine face texture
  • high compressive strength
  • low absorption
  • dense and durable

• cinder: block characteristics
  • dark gray color
  • medium to coarse face texture
  • high insulation and fire-resistant properties
  • good acoustical value (porous)
  • nailable

* 5.25 for bonding patterns

Stone is an aggregate or combination of minerals, each of each is composed of inorganic chemical substances. To qualify as a construction material, stone should have the following qualities:

- strength
  - most types of stone have more than adequate compressive strength - their shear strength is usually about 1/10 of their compressive strength
- hardness
  - important when stone is used for flooring, paving, stairs, etc.
- durability
  - resistance to weathering effects of rain, wind, heat, and frost action is necessary for exterior stonework
- workability
  - required for stone to be quarried, cut, and shaped - depends on stone's hardness and grain texture

- a stone's porosity affects its ability to withstand frost action and staining
- appearance factors include color, grain, and texture

Almost all stone is adversely affected by sudden changes in temperature and should not be used where fire-resistance is required.

Stone may be classified according to geological origin into the following types:

- igneous
  - cooled molten matter
  - eg. granite
- sedimentary
  - deposited by the action of water
  - eg. limestone
- metamorphic
  - formed under intense pressure and heat
  - eg. marble and slate

As a structural load-bearing wall material, stone is similar to modular unit masonry. Although stone is not necessarily uniform in size, it is laid up with mortar and used in compression, similar in principle to brick and concrete block walls.

Stone is used in construction in the following forms:

- rubble (fieldstone)
  - used primarily as a wall material
- dimension
  - cut stone is the most widely used form; has many applications
- flagstone
  - flat slabs used for flooring and horizontal surfacing
- crushed rock
  - used primarily as aggregate in concrete products

Types of stonework include:

- rubble work
  - rough, uncut stonework
- ashlar
  - cut stone facing
- trim
  - cut stone for copings, sills, lintels, etc.

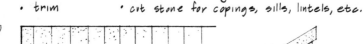

Concrete has wide application in the construction field because it combines many of the advantages of wood, steel, and masonry. It is inherently strong in compression; to handle tensile forces, it can encase and bond with steel reinforcement. It is capable of being formed into almost any shape with a variety of surface finishes, textures, and patterns. It provides fireproof construction.

Concrete's liabilities include its weight and the forming or molding process required before it can be placed to set and harden.

Concrete is a mixture of:

① cement
- normal portland cement, types I and IA — for general construction
- modified portland, types II and II A — to combat water with sulfate content
- air-entraining portland — for improved resistance to frost action
- white portland — for a white or light-colored finish
- high-early-strength — used when high strength is desired within 3 days after placement

② water
- should be clean, free of oil, alkali, sulfates; general criteria: should be potable

③ aggregate
- fine and coarse aggregate used
- should be clean, durable, and free of organic matter

The characteristics of concrete vary according to the characteristics of the ingredients listed above and the proportions of their mix. The quality of a concrete product is affected by the mix as well as the manner in which the concrete is placed, finished, and cured.

The potential strength of concrete is determined by its water: cement ratio. Theoretically, the strength of concrete will increase as the amount of water used per unit of cement decreases. Concrete is normally specified according to the compressive strength it will develop within 28 days after placement. (7 day for high-early-strength concrete.

The water:cement ratio also affects the concrete's workability during placement, as well as its durability, weather-resistance, and water-tightness after set.

The most economical mix occurs when the fine and coarse aggregates are evenly graded so that a minimum amount of cement paste is required to surround all of the aggregate and fill the spaces in between. The proportion of fine to coarse aggregate and the maximum size of coarse aggregate that may be used depend on the method of placement, the thickness and reinforcement of the concrete section, and the finish requirements.

Lightweight aggregate, such as expanded shale, cinder, and vermiculite, may be used in lieu of the regular stone aggregate to reduce the concrete's weight and increase its thermal insulating value, fire-resistance, and nailability. At the same time, they may decrease the concrete's strength.

Admixtures may be added to the concrete mix to improve its workability, entrain air, make the concrete more impervious, or to accelerate or retard the hardening process.

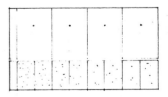

Concrete may be finished in a number of ways. Troweling produces a smooth, dense surface. Surfaces may be textured by brooming, raking, or sandblasting to expose the aggregate. The formwork itself, which naturally leaves an impression on the concrete after its removal, may be used to produce desired textures and patterns. Concrete may also be painted or have a finish applied to it such as stucco.

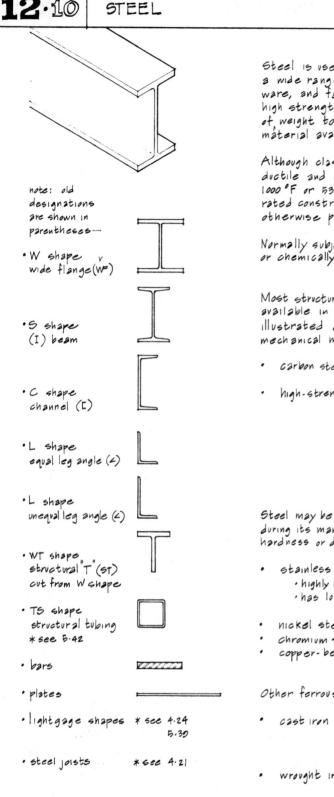

note: old
designations
are shown in
parentheses—

• W shape
  wide flange (WF)

• S shape
  (I) beam

• C shape
  channel (Ľ)

• L shape
  equal leg angle (∠)

• L shape
  unequal leg angle (∠)

• WT shape
  structural "T" (ST)
  cut from W shape

• TS shape
  structural tubing
  * see 5·42

• bars

• plates

• lightgage shapes * see 4·24
                      5·30

• steel joists   * see 4·21

Steel is used for heavy and light structural framing as well as a wide range of building products such as windows, doors, hardware, and fastenings. As a structural material, steel combines high strength and stiffness with elasticity. Measured in terms of weight to volume, it is probably the strongest low-cost material available.

Although classified as an incombustible material, steel becomes ductile and loses its strength under high heat conditions (over 1000°F or 538°C). When used in buildings requiring fire-resistance rated construction, structural steel must be coated, covered, or otherwise protected with fire-resistant materials.

Normally subject to corrosion, steel must be painted, galvanized, or chemically treated for protection against oxidation.

Most structural steel is medium carbon grade steel which is available in plate and bar forms, and in the structural shapes illustrated on the left. They may be fastened by welding or mechanical means.

• carbon steel: yield point = 34,000 psi (25.3×10^6 kg/m²)

• high-strength low-alloy steel:

  • yield point = 50,000 psi (35.2×10^6 kg/m²)
  • high strength is achieved through small alloy additions rather than heat treatment
  • "USS Cor-Ten" steel has excellent atmospheric corrosion resistance due to a tight oxide coating it forms on its surface — may be left bare

Steel may be heat-treated or altered with additives (to form alloys) during its manufacture to develop special properties of strength, hardness or ductility, expansion, corrosion-resistance, or workability.

• stainless steel (alloy of steel, nickel, and chromium)
  • highly resistant to corrosion, heat, and oxidation
  • has low heat conductivity but high thermal expansion

• nickel steel   • stronger than regular carbon steel
• chromium steel   • very hard and corrosion resistant
• copper-bearing steel • corrosion-resistant

Other ferrous metals used in building construction include:

• cast iron   • high carbon content
               • brittle but strong in compression
               • used for piping and ornamental work

• wrought iron • extremely low carbon content
                • resistant to progressive corrosion
                • soft, malleable, tough
                • used for piping, hardware, and ornamental work

Aluminum, copper, and lead are nonferrous metals commonly used in building construction.

ALUMINUM

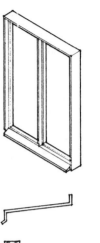

Aluminum is a relatively soft yet strong, lightweight, and workable metal. It is corrosion-resistant due to the transparent film of natural oxide it forms on its surface. This oxide coating can be thickened to increase its corrosion-resistance by an electrical and chemical process known as anodizing.

Naturally light in color (making it an excellent reflective material), aluminum may be dyed a number of warm, bright colors during the anodizing process. It may also have enamel or lacquer finishes applied to it.

Aluminum is widely used in extruded and sheet forms for secondary building elements such as windows, doors, roofing, flashing, reflective insulation, trim and hardware. Because of its excellent electrical conductivity, it is also used for electrical cable.

In architectural work, aluminum is normally used in alloy form. These alloys alter aluminum's strength and hardness while reducing its workability and corrosion-resistance. For use in structural framing, high-strength aluminum alloys are available in shapes similar to those of structural and lightgage steel. Aluminum forms may be welded, bonded with adhesives, or mechanically fastened.

Care must be taken to insulate aluminum from contact with other metals to prevent galvanic action. It should also be protected from alkaline materials such as wet concrete, mortar or plaster.

COPPER

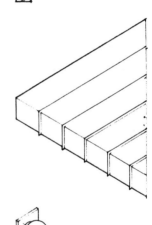

Copper is used in construction where corrosion-resistance, impact-resistance, ductility, or high electrical and thermal conductivity is required. It is most commonly used in sheet form for roofing and flashing. Its color and resistance to air and salt water corrosion make copper an excellent outdoor material.

Copper will corrode aluminum, steel, stainless steel, and zinc. It should be fastened, attached, or supported with copper or carefully selected brass fittings. Contact with red cedar in the presence of moisture (as in roof construction) will cause premature deterioration of copper.

BRASS · an alloy of copper and zinc
· used for doors, windows, hardware, fastenings, and plumbing
· often termed bronze (eg. architectural or statuary bronze)

LEAD

Lead is a soft, malleable, plastic, corrosion-resistant material used most often for roofing and flashing. Although the heaviest of the common metals, its pliability makes it desirable for application over uneven surfaces. Lead is also used for fastenings and piping.

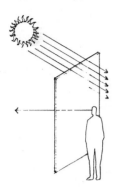

Glass is a chemically inert, transparent, hard, brittle material. It is used in building construction in various forms. Foamed or cellular glass is used as rigid, vaporproof thermal insulation. Glass fibers are used in textiles and for material reinforcement. In spun form, glass fibers form glass wool used for acoustical and thermal insulation. Glass block is used to control light transmission, glare, and solar radiation.

Glass is used most commonly used to glaze a building's window, sash, and skylight openings. The three basic types of glass are:

① sheet glass:
- 2 surfaces are never parallel and therefore never distortion-free
- thickness: from 1/16" (2) to 7/16" (11)

- maximum size
  - single strength (ss) 3/32" (2+) thick   40" x 50" (1.016 x 1.270)
  - double strength (ds) 1/8" (3)   60" x 80" (1.524 x 2.032)
  - high strength (hs) 3/16 (5)   120" x 84" (3.048 x 2.134)
    - 1/4" (6)   120" x 84" (3.048 x 2.134)
    - 3/8" (10)   60" x 84" (1.524 x 2.134)
    - 7/16" (11)   60" x 84" (1.524 x 2.134)

② float glass
- better quality surface than sheet glass with less distortion
- thicknesses: 1/8" (3) 3/16" (5) 1/4" (6)

- maximum size: 122" x 200" (3.099 x 5.080)

③ plate glass
- provides virtually clear, undistorted vision
- thicknesses: from 1/8" (3) to 1" (25)

- maximum size:
  - 1/8" (3) thick   130" x 80" (3.302 x 2.032)
  - 1/4" (6)   130" x 240" (3.302 x 6.096)
  - 3/8" (10)   125" x 281" (3.175 x 7.137)
  - 1/2" (13)   125" x 281" (3.175 x 7.137)

Variations of the above include:

- heat-absorbing glass
  - tinted sheet or plate glass that absorbs a significant amount of solar radiation, reduces heat build-up within a building, and controls glare
  - tint may be bronze, gray, or blue-green

- tempered glass
  - heat-strengthened for increased resistance to impact and thermal stresses
  - 3 to 5 times as strong as plate glass
  - pulverizes into pebble-sized pieces when broken

- safety-laminated glass
  - consists of a thin sheet of tough, transparent plastic laminated between 2 layers of sheet or plate glass
  - used where glass is susceptible to impact; fractured glass particles tend to adhere to adhesive plastic sheet
  - may be tinted to control light, glare, and heat

- wired glass
  - wire mesh is inserted into rolled glass during manufacture
  - has high impact-resistance, and will remain intact even after breakage; considered a fire-resistant material
  - used to glaze openings susceptible to fire hazards

- insulating glass
  - consists of 2 layers of glass separated by a hermetically-sealed air space to provide thermal insulation and restrict condensation
  - sheet glass with a glass edge used with 3/16" (5) airspace
  - plate glass with a metal edge used with 1/4" (6) or 1/2" (13) air space

The purpose of a finish is to protect, preserve, or visually enhance the surface to which it is applied. Finishes include paint, stains, sealers, and laminated surface coverings such as plastic laminates and vinyl or fabric wall coverings.

Paint generally refers to an opaque or clear film-forming material that acts as a shield or barrier between the building material and those elements or conditions that may adversely affect or deteriorate it. Depending on its end use, the paint film must resist deterioration due to sunlight, heat, temperature variations, water or moisture vapor, mildew and decay, chemicals, and physical abrasion. Paint may also serve to make surfaces more sanitary, improve heating and lighting effects, and promote human comfort and safety.

When using paint, the psychological effects of color and surface texture must be considered. Certain colors may be stimulating while others are relaxing. White and light colors reflect light, brighten spaces, and increase visibility and the apparent size of form and space. Dark colors can inhibit the perception of form and may be used for contrast. Flat paint finishes soften and distribute illumination evenly. Glossy finishes reflect light and can cause glare, but they also provide smooth, easily-cleaned, non-absorptive surfaces.

Most paints are carefully formulated to meet specific application and use requirements and are ready-mixed for application except for thinning, stirring, or the addition of an activator or catalyst. It is always advisable therefore to follow the paint manufacturer's recommendations in the application and use of a paint or other protective coating.

Considerations in the selection and use of a paint include:

- surface preparation
  - the foundation of any paint system must be properly prepared to ensure proper adhesion of the paint film to its surface
- type of paint
  - paint must be compatible with the material to which it is applied
  - specifications include the paint vehicle, finish, color, exposure, and manufacturer and/or trade name
- film thickness
  - the dry film thickness (DFT) is more important than the number of coats
  - multiple thin coats are generally more effective than a single thick coat
  - a minimum of 2 coats is required to produce 5 mil DFT
- coverage
  - a paint's coverage can be estimated by its percentage of volume solids:
  - ie. · paint with 100% volume solids: 1 gallon will cover 1600 SF (149 m²) @ 1 mil DFT
    (no thinner)   or   800 SF (74 m²) @ 2 mil DFT
                                          or   400 SF (37 m²) @ 4 mil DFT
    · paint with 50% volume solids: 1 gallon will cover 800 SF (74 m²) @ 1 mil DFT
    (50% thinner)   400 SF (37 m²) @ 2 mil DFT
- method of application
  - depending on the type of paint and the material to which it is being applied, coatings may be brushed, rolled, or sprayed on
- drying
  - the time and conditions necessary for a paint to dry must be checked

Paint generally consists of: · pigment
  - finely ground solids that provide the paint's covering or hiding power and its color

· vehicle
  - liquid medium to carry the pigment in suspension during application
  - consists of binders and solvents

    · binders serve to form the paint film and cause it to adhere to the surface being painted
    · binders are largely responsible for the protective quality and durability of the paint film or protective coating

    · solvents or thinners act as drying agents
    · depending on the type of solvent used, a paint may dry or harden by oxidation, evaporation, chemical action, or by thermosetting action at elevated temperatures

Paints may be classified according to:

- material to which it is applied — wood, metal, masonry, concrete, plaster, etc.
- surface finish/texture — gloss, semi-gloss, eggshell, satin, flat
- color — depends on the type of paint and its manufacturer
- exposure — exterior or interior
- application — prime, sealing, or top coat

- characteristics:
  - pigmented coatings   paints and enamels
  - clear coatings   varnishes, lacquers, shellac, sealers
  - rust inhibitive coatings   zinc-pigmented coatings
  - heat resistant coatings   zinc, silicone alkyd, or asphalt-base coatings
  - bituminous coatings   asphalt or tar coatings that form non-permeable barriers against water and oxygen to protect submerged ferrous metals and to waterproof masonry surfaces
  - cement mortar coatings   mixture of portland cement, lime, and water used to dampproof masonry materials and protect exposed steel
  - plastic and synthetic rubber coatings
  - coatings resistant to mildew, mold, fumes, marine environments, etc.

Paints may also be classified according to its vehicle or binder:

- alkyds
  - oil-modified resins that harden by oxidation and evaporation
  - the most common paint vehicle
  - faster drying and harder than ordinary oil paints
  - oil content extends the drying time, lowers the gloss, and improves the paint's wetting properties and elasticity to resist blistering
  - have good drying properties, durability and water-resistance for exterior exposures, and good color retention

- asphalts
  - coatings with a vehicle of both petroleum and natural asphalts are used to protect wood, steel, masonry, concrete, and as a roof coating
  - have good water-resistance but thermoplastic in nature
  - addition of aluminum flakes helps to reflect the sun's rays
  - addition of epoxy resins minimizes the cold flow and maximizes the chemical-resistance of asphalt

- chlorinated rubber
  - used in coatings highly-resistant to alkalies, acids, chemicals, and water
  - may be removed by coal tar solvents
  - has limited resistance to prolonged heat exposures
  - used in swimming pools, water treatment plants, etc.

- epoxy-catalyzed
  - two-component coatings consisting of a pigmented primer or enamel and an activator or catalyst
  - mixed just prior to use - has limited "pot life"
  - produces by chemical action a dense, hard film similar to baked enamel
  - has excellent resistance to solvents, chemicals, physical abrasion, traffic wear, and cleaning materials
  - has good adhesion properties, color retention, and stain-resistance
  - has good durability for exterior exposure but may chalk

Paint classification by vehicle or binder (cont'd)

- epoxy esters
  - similar to catalyzed epoxy coatings but modified by oils to produce a tough, hard film that hardens by oxidation
  - not as hard or chemically resistant as catalyzed epoxies but easier to apply and has no pot-life restrictions
  - packaged as a conventional paint

- latex emulsions
  - latex binder types are synthetic materials such as acrylics, vinyl-acetate acrylics, polyvinyl acetate, and styrene butadiene
  - latex paints have the following advantages over oil or alkyd paints:
    - ease of application, quick drying and recoating, freedom from solvent odor, minimal fire hazard
  - latex paints have good color retention, adhesion to surfaces, flexibility, and are blister and peel resistant

- oils
  - declining in use - usually used in alkyd paints and to modify other paint vehicles
  - oil types:
    - fish oil — inexpensive but inferior to most other oils
    - linseed oil
      - raw — relatively slow drying
      - boiled — hardens more quickly
      - bodied — has less moisture permeability
    - oiticica oil — similar to tung oil
    - soybean oil — has good flexibility and non-yellowing characteristics - slow-drying
    - safflower oil — has excellent non-yellowing characteristics
    - tung oil — has better water and weather resistance than most oils

- oleoresins
  - vehicles composed primarily of oil but modified by resins
  - harder, more durable, dries faster, and produces a higher gloss than oil paints

- phenolics
  - vehicles of phenolic resins modified by oils
  - have good resistance to water and chemicals but may be softened by solvents
  - hardens and yellows with age and therefore difficult to recoat

- silicone alkyds
  - may be modified by oils or mineral spirits
  - should consist of at least 25% silicone resin to produce a coating with excellent color and gloss retention
  - recommended for heat-resistant applications

- urethanes
  - polymers with characteristics similar to epoxy coatings
  - unmodified urethanes:
    - have excellent flexibility and resistance to water, chemicals, and physical abrasion
    - cures by evaporation of solvent and reaction with moisture in the air (requires 30% - 90% relative humidity)
    - may be pigmented or clear
    - has limited pot-life
  - oil-modified urethanes are clear, air-drying coatings that are harder than epoxy esters with excellent abrasion resistance

- vinyls
  - plasticized copolymers of vinyl chloride and vinyl acetate
  - dries rapidly - applied by spray
  - have low gloss, excellent flexibility, and good weathering properties
  - inert to water and most chemicals but susceptible to heat and solvents

- zinc-pigmented coatings
  - coatings with 85% - 95% zinc content dispersed in various vehicles to protect steel from galvanic action

Stains are non-protective finishes that are used to impart color to wood surfaces without obscuring or concealing the natural wood grain. They may be pigmented to either accentuate or even out the color differences in wood grain.

Basic types of stains include:

- penetrating oil stain
  - oil-soluble dyes in coal tar and petroleum solvents
  - provides good coloring but may fade in sunlight
  - tends to bleed into finish coat
  - may be applied by sponge, spray, or dipping

- water stain
  - water-soluble synthetic dyes
  - has deep, even penetration
  - most permanent type of stain/ non-fading and non-bleeding
  - tends to raise wood grain
  - may be applied by brush, sponge, spray, or dipping

- spirit stain
  - dyes in an alcohol vehicle
  - produces the brightest, strongest colors but susceptible to fading
  - has high penetration but tends to bleed and raise wood grain
  - used for refinishing and repair work and to even out color differences
  - applied by spray

- non-grain-raising stain
  - light-fast dyes in an alcohol vehicle
  - has moderate penetration/ not as permanent as water stains
  - does not run, bleed or raise wood grain
  - applied by spray

- pigment wiping stain
  - similar to oil stains
  - applied by brush or cloth and then wiped off after a setting period
  - does not raise wood grain/ has good light resistance and color uniformity
  - not as transparent as other stains

Clear coatings are used to visually enhance and protect surfaces without obscuring their natural appearance.

- varnish
  - consists of resins dissolved in a drying oil with driers and solvents
  - resins may be natural to produce oleoresinous varnish, or synthetic such as alkyd, acrylic, epoxy, phenolic, or vinyl resins
  - produces a clear, protective coating with a glossy finish

  - often-used as a vehicle for a class of pigmented coatings, generally termed "enamels," that provide quick drying and a smooth, level finish
  - enamels provide a hard, tough film, resistant to rough usage and washing
  - may have a glossy, semi-glossy, or flat finish
  - baked enamels are factory-applied, thermosetting coatings based on synthetic resins that produce hard, durable films that are alkali and acid resistant

- shellac
  - consists of refined lac resin dissolved in denatured alcohol
  - may be its natural color (orange) or bleached (white)
  - easy to apply and fast-drying / finish may be discolored by sunlight or softened and bleached by alkaline water
  - used as a clear finish for wood work, to seal knots and pitch stains in wood before painting, and to seal bituminous coatings before painting

- lacquer
  - nitrocellulose with resins, plasticizers, and volatile solvents
  - lacquers are fast-drying and produce a thin, tough film
  - not as sunlight and moisture resistant as premium varnish
  - may be clear or pigmented (lacquer enamel)
  - may have a glossy, flat, or transparent water-white finish

All materials to receive paint or other coating must be properly prepared and primed to ensure adhesion of the film coating to their surfaces and maximize the life of the coating. In general, surfaces should be clean and dry. All contaminants such as dirt, grease, moisture, and mildew should be removed; all surface defects such as cracks, holes, and loose knots should be repaired; all sharp edges, surface rust, metal burrs, and powdered masonry should be eliminated. The following are general recommendations for various materials.

- **aluminum**
  - any corrosion should be removed by wire brushing
  - any oil or other foreign matter should be removed by solvents or steam cleaning
  - unweathered aluminum may require surface-etching treatment before painting
  - prime with a zinc-chromate coating

- **brick**
  - dirt, loose or excess mortar, efflorescence, and other foreign matter should be removed by brush, air, or steam cleaning
  - should weather for one month before finishing with a latex material
  - may be sealed with a latex primer-sealer, a clear resin (phenolic, alkyd, or epoxy), or a clear silicone water-repellant

- **concrete**
  - should be free of dirt, loose or excess mortar, form oils, or curing compounds
  - should weather for one month before finishing with a latex material
  - porous surfaces may require a block filler or a cement grout/latex primer
  - grouted or chalky surfaces may require an alkali-resistant primer such as a clear phenolic or alkyd resin coating
  - may also be sealed with a clear silicone water-repellant

- **concrete block**
  - should be free of dirt, loose or excess mortar, and be thoroughly dry
  - porous surfaces may require a block filler or a cement grout/latex primer if the acoustical value of a rough surface is not important

- **concrete floors**
  - should be free of dirt, wax, grease and oils, and should be etched with a muriatic-acid solution to improve adhesion of the floor finish
  - prime with an alkali- and moisture- resistant coating such as a butadiene-styrene sealer

- **galvanized iron**
  - all grease, residue and corrosion should be removed by solvent or chemical washes
  - may be primed with a zinc dust/zinc oxide coating, or a latex or portland cement paint
  - if weathered, should be treated as a ferrous metal

- **gypsum board**
  - should be clean and dry; prime with a latex emulsion to avoid raising the surface fibers

- **old paint surfaces**
  - should be clean and dry; surface should be roughened to provide a "tooth" for the new paint film by sanding or washing with a detergent solution

- **plaster and stucco**
  - should be allowed about 30 days to dry thoroughly and be completely cured
  - soft surfaces should be treated (ie. with a vinegar/water solution) to provide a hard, paintable surface
  - may be primed with a latex or alkyd base primer-sealer; highly-alkaline or fresh plaster should be primed with an alkali-resistant latex or alkyd coating

- **steel**
  - should be free of dust, surface rust, metal burrs, and foreign matter
  - may be cleaned by solvents, hand or power tooling, wire brushing, flame-cleaning, sandblasting, or pickling with acids
  - should be primed with a rust-inhibitive coating

- **wood**
  - should be clean, dry, well-seasoned lumber
  - knots and pitch stains should be sanded and sealed before full prime coat
  - surfaces to be painted should be primed or sealed to stabilize the moisture content of the wood and prevent the absorption of succeeding coats; stains and some paints may be self-priming; all surface defects should be repaired; and all nail holes, cracks, and other small holes should be filled after the full prime coat

The following is a general outline of common paint types available to coat various material surfaces. There is no one best paint for any surface. The paint selected depends on the desired appearance and durability, conditions of service, method of application, curing time, cost, etc. It should also be noted that not all materials require painting. Depending on their exposure to weather, physical wear, and other deteriorating conditions, some materials should remain unpainted. Once a surface is painted, it requires maintenance and periodic repainting.

EXTERIOR SURFACES

MATERIAL	FINISH	TOP COATS	PRIME COAT
WOOD:			
• wood, plywood, hardboard	gloss gloss semi-gloss flat	exterior oil paint exterior alkyd paint/enamel exterior latex paint exterior alkyd or latex paint	mildew-resistant alkyd primer (acrylic emulsion for plywood surfaces) ↓
• wood, plywood, shingles, rough-sawn lumber	flat stain flat stain flat stain flat stain	semi-transparent oil base stain solid-color oil base stain weathering, semi-transparent oil base stain latex base stain	self-priming ↓
• wood floors • for clear finishes • for preservation • redwood	gloss clear gloss clear flat stain	alkyd enamel phenolic base varnish chloro-phenolic wood preservative semi-transparent alkyd stain	self-priming oil stain and filler self-priming self-priming
MASONRY:			
• brick, concrete, stucco	semi-gloss flat clear	exterior latex paint exterior latex paint silicone water-repellant	alkali-resistant alkyd or latex primer sealer none
• concrete block	semi-gloss flat	exterior latex paint exterior latex paint	synthetic rubber latex block filler synthetic rubber latex block filler
• concrete floors	gloss	alkyd floor enamel	alkali-resistant butadiene-styrene primer-sealer
METAL:			
• aluminum, steel, galvanized iron	gloss gloss semi-gloss flat	exterior oleoresinous paint exterior alkyd enamel exterior latex paint exterior latex paint	aluminum: zinc chromate primer galvanized iron: zinc dust/zinc oxide primer steel: red lead or zinc chromate primer

• for high temperatures
  up to 400°F (204°C)
  500°F (260°C)
  700°F (371°C)
	aluminum
	flat gray
	aluminum
		oleoresinous aluminum paint
		zinc dust/zinc oxide paint
		silicone alkyd aluminum paint
			self-priming
			self-priming

• for corrosive conditions	gloss flat gloss flat aluminum	chlorinated rubber base enamel vinyl base enamel catalyzed epoxy or epoxy ester base enamel zinc rich coating silicone alkyd aluminum paint	organic or epoxy zinc-pigmented primers ↓ self-priming

INTERIOR SURFACES

MATERIAL	FINISH	TOP COATINGS	PRIME COAT
WOOD:			
• wood, plywood	gloss gloss semi-gloss eggshell flat	catalyzed epoxy enamel alkyd enamel alkyd or latex enamel alkyd enamel alkyd or latex wall paint	self-priming enamel undercoater ↓ ↓

• wood flooring	gloss
	clear gloss
	clear gloss
	clear gloss
	clear dull
		alkyd floor enamel
		alkyd base varnish
		oil-modified polyurethane varnish
		heavy-duty polyurethane varnish
		oil-modified polyurethane satin
		varnish
			self-priming
			  • wood stain optional
			  • use paste filler for open
			    grain woods
			polyurethane gloss varnish

PLASTER:			
• plaster, gypsum, drywall	gloss gloss semi-gloss eggshell flat	catalyzed epoxy enamel alkyd enamel alkyd or latex enamel alkyd enamel alkyd or latex wall paint	self-priming alkyd primer (use latex primer for gypsum and plaster board)
MASONRY:			
• brick	gloss semi-gloss flat	alkyd enamel alkyd or latex enamel alkyd or latex wall paint	alkali-resistant alkyd primer- sealer ↓
• concrete block	gloss flat	catalyzed epoxy enamel latex wall paint	latex block filler ↓
METAL			

• aluminum,
galvanized iron,
steel
	gloss
	gloss
	semi-gloss
	flat
		catalyzed epoxy enamel
		alkyd enamel
		alkyd or latex enamel
		alkyd or latex wall paint
			catalyzed epoxy primer
			aluminum: zinc chromate primer
			galvanized iron: zinc dust/zinc oxide
			                    primer
			steel: red lead or zinc chromate
			         primer

• for aluminum:	aluminum aluminum	oleoresinous aluminum paint silicone alkyd aluminum paint	self-priming self-priming

Metal fastenings are the most common means of securing pieces of material to one another in building construction. Basic types of fastenings include nails, screws, and bolts.

NAILS

A nail consists of a metal shaft or shank, pointed at one end and formed into or attached to a head at the other.

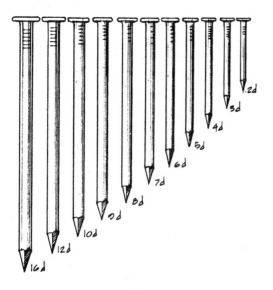

2d
3d
4d
5d
6d
7d
8d
9d
10d
12d
16d

common nails · for general construction (2d to 60d)

box nails · for light construction (2d to 40d)

casing nails · for interior trim (2d to 40d)

finishing nails · for furniture and cabinetry (2d to 20d)

wire brad nails · for light work and trim (3/16" to 3")
(5 to 76)

cut nails · for flooring (2d to 20d)

double-headed · for temporary construction

masonry nails · for driving into concrete, masonry, and soft stone

roofing nails · several types available to secure specific roofing materials - may have neoprene or lead washers to seal the nail holes

material:
· nails are usually of mild steel
· may also be of aluminum, copper, brass, zinc, stainless steel, or monel metal for increased corrosion-resistance
· nails may also be coated with zinc, tin, copper, brass, nickel, or chromium
· heat-treated, high-carbon steel nails are used for greater strength in masonry applications
· the type of metal used should be checked for compatibility with the materials being secured to avoid loss of holding power and prevent staining or discoloration of the materials' surfaces

length and diameter of the shank:
· nail lengths are designated by the term "penny" represented by the symbol (d)
· nails range in length from 2d [about 1"(25)] to 60d [about 6"(152)]
· nails larger than 20d may be referred to as "spikes"
· rule of thumb: use a nail whose length is 3 times the thickness of the board being secured

· large diameter nails are used for heavy work while lighter nails are used for finish work
· thinner nails are used for hardwood than for softwood

form of the shank:
· most nails have plain cylindrical shafts
· for greater gripping strength, nail shafts may be serrated, barbed, annularly or helically threaded, fluted or twisted
· nail shafts may be zinc- or cement- coated for greater resistance to withdrawal

nail heads:
· nails may have flat, tapered, cupped, hooked, or slotted heads
· flat heads provide the largest amount of surface contact area and gripping power and are used when exposure of the head is acceptable
· the heads of nails which are to be countersunk for concealment are only slightly larger than the shaft and may be tapered or cupped
· double-headed nails are used for easy removal in temporary construction (ie. scaffolding, concrete formwork)

nail points:
· most nails have diamond points
· sharp-pointed nails have greater holding strength but may tend to split some woods
· use blunt-pointed nails for easily-split wood
· nails may also have needle, truncated, or chisel points

SCREWS

Because of their threaded shafts, screws have greater holding power than nails with plain, serrated, or barbed shafts, and are normally easily removable. The more threads they have per inch, the greater their gripping strength. Screws are classified by:

- use   - wood, machine, sheet metal, set screws, etc.
- type of head   - flat, round, oval forms
                 - slotted, phillips, allen type heads
- finish   - primarily steel and brass
                 - as in the case of nails, other metals such as aluminum or bronze may also be used
                 - screws may also be plated
- length   - available up to 5" (127) in length, in 1/8" (3) and 1/4" (6) increments
- diameter   - ranges from 0 to 24 gauge

Wood screws should be long enough so that 1/2 to 2/3 of its length penetrates the base material and be about 1/8" (3) less than the combined thickness of the boards being joined. Holes for screws should be pre-drilled equal to the base diameter of the threads. Fine-threaded screws are generally used for hardwoods while coarse-threaded ones are used for soft woods.

flat   round   oval

wood screws   machine screw   sheet metal screw

regular slotted head   phillips head   allen or socket head (used primarily with set screws)

BOLTS

Bolts are round sections of metal, headed at one end and threaded at the other. They are normally used in frame construction for wood and metal connections. They may also be used to anchor sill and base plates to masonry or concrete walls, foundations, and footings.

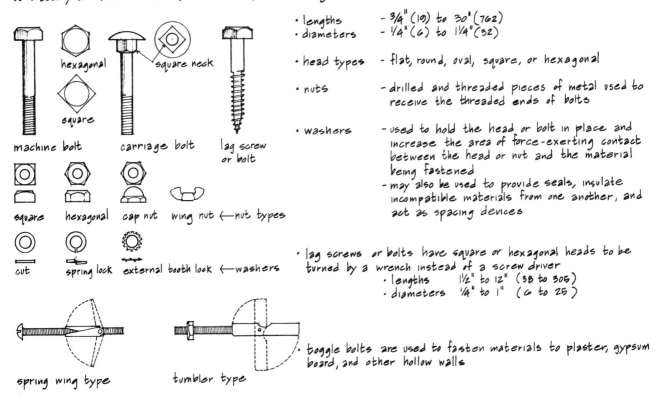

hexagonal   square neck

square

machine bolt   carriage bolt   lag screw or bolt

square   hexagonal   cap nut   wing nut ←nut types

cut   spring lock   external tooth lock ←washers

spring wing type   tumbler type

- lengths   - 3/4" (19) to 30" (762)
- diameters   - 1/4" (6) to 1 1/4" (32)

- head types   - flat, round, oval, square, or hexagonal

- nuts   - drilled and threaded pieces of metal used to receive the threaded ends of bolts

- washers   - used to hold the head or bolt in place and increase the area of force-exerting contact between the head or nut and the material being fastened
                 - may also be used to provide seals, insulate incompatible materials from one another, and act as spacing devices

- lag screws or bolts have square or hexagonal heads to be turned by a wrench instead of a screw driver
  - lengths   1 1/2" to 12" (38 to 305)
  - diameters   1/4" to 1" (6 to 25)

- toggle bolts are used to fasten materials to plaster, gypsum board, and other hollow walls

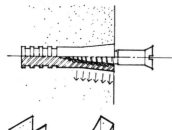

Expansion shield devices
· used to secure materials to plaster, gypsum board, masonry, or concrete bases
· upon the insertion and turning of a screw or bolt, the shield expands in size (diameter) and thus exerts pressure on the base material

Metal framing connectors
· used to join wood framing members to wood, masonry, or metal supports
· may eliminate the need for toenailing or the use of heavy spikes or bolts
· typical types include post anchors and caps, joist and beam hangers, and plywood clips

Heavy timber connectors
· used to distribute a load over a large area of the timber in heavy frame construction and trusswork
· split-rings are used for wood-to-wood connections and shear plates for wood-to-metal connections

Rivets
· used for permanent fastenings

ADHESIVES

Adhesives are means of tightly securing two surfaces together. Numerous types of adhesives are commercially available, many of them being tailor-made for use with specific materials and under specified conditions. They may be in solid, liquid, powder, or film form. Some require catalysts to activate their adhesive qualities. It is always advisable to follow the manufacturer's recommendations in the use of an adhesive. Important considerations in the selection of an adhesive include

· strength — adhesives are usually strongest in resisting tensile and shear stresses and weakest in resisting cleavage or splitting stresses

· curing or setting time — ranges from immediate bonding to setting times of up to several days
· setting temperature range — some adhesives will set at room temperature while others require baking at elevated temperatures

· method of bonding — some adhesives bond on contact while others require clamping or higher pressures

· characteristics — adhesive's resistance to water, heat, sunlight, chemicals, as well as its aging properties

Common types of adhesives include:

· animal or fish glues — primarily for indoor use where temperature and humidity do not vary greatly
— may be weakened when exposed to heat or moisture

· white glue — polyvinyl glue
— sets quickly and does not stain; slightly resilient

· epoxy resin — extremely strong
— may be use to secure porous as well as non-porous materials such as metal and concrete may dissolve some plastics
— unlike other adhesives, epoxy glues will set at low temperatures and under wet conditions

· resorcin resin — strong, waterproof, and durable for outdoor use ; flammable
— dark color may show through paint

· contact cement — forms a bond on contact; does not require clamps
— generally used to secure large surface materials such as paneling and countertops
— surfaces must be carefully pre-fit

Caulking compounds are used to fill joints and cracks in a building's surfaces such as around door and window openings. They should have good adhesion to the surfaces to which they are applied and remain flexible over a wide range of temperatures. They should dry on the exterior to form a tough, elastic surface while remaining tacky on the inside. They should be non-staining when used in exposed areas.

Glazing compounds are similar to caulking compounds except that they are used to seal glass in sash or window openings.

Joint sealants are used to provide weatherproof joints where movement in a building might occur (ie. at control or expansion joints * see 5·22/5·28/8·20). They should therefore have better adhesive qualities and greater elasticity than caulking compounds.

- putty   - a mixture of linseed oil and finely ground calcium carbonate
          - used to glaze wooden sash and fill small cracks and crevices in wood surfaces before painting
          - dries and becomes brittle with age
          - has no appreciable elongation value

- mastic-type compounds
          - oxidizing type: composed of drying and non-drying oils, a drier, solvent, stabilizer and fillers
          - forms a dry film on its surface: suitable for use in exposed areas where painting over the compound might be desirable
          - capable of elongations of up to 10%

          - non-oxidizing type: asphalt and polybutene compounds
          - does not form a surface film: used in concealed locations (ie. under flashing and in lapped joints)
          - capable of elongations of up to 50%

- elastomeric-type compounds
          - capable of elongations of 100% or more
          - types include   silicone mastics
                             butyl, neoprene, and hypalon rubbers
                             vinyl chloride polymers
                             polysulfide polymers
                             butadiene-styrene co-polymers

Joint sealants are normally applied over a back-up material that controls the depth of the joint, serves as a bond break to ensure free movement of the joint, and prevents moisture from penetrating the joint. Types of back-up materials include:

- non-tarred oakum
- sponge rubber
- neoprene or butyl cord or tubing
- fiberglas insulation
- polyurethane or polyethylene foam

* oil-, tar-, and asphalt-impregnated materials and moisture-absorbing materials should not be used as back-up materials

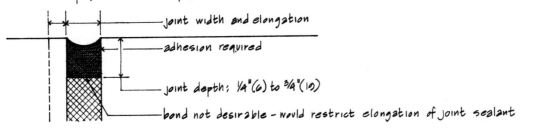

joint width and elongation

adhesion required

joint depth: 1/4"(6) to 3/4"(10)

bond not desirable - would restrict elongation of joint sealant

APPENDIX

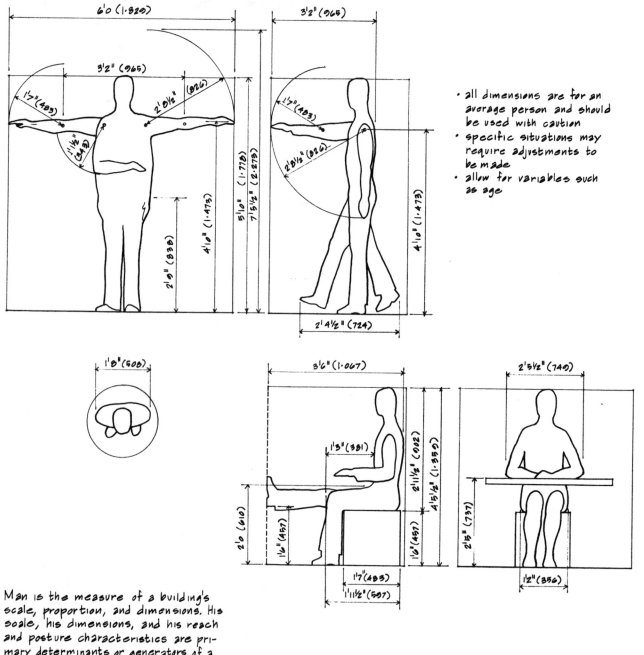

- all dimensions are for an average person and should be used with caution
- specific situations may require adjustments to be made
- allow for variables such as age

Man is the measure of a building's scale, proportion, and dimensions. His scale, his dimensions, and his reach and posture characteristics are primary determinants or generators of a building's form, size, and spatial layout.

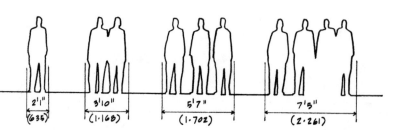

Planning for the handicapped involves the design of facilities that are:

- **accessible** to those confined to the wheel chair and the ambulatory
  - avoid changes in level and the use of stairs
  - use ramps only where necessary

- **identifiable** to the blind requires the use of:
  - raised lettering
  - textured hardware surfaces to indicate hazardous openings
  - audible warning signals

- **usable** · circulation spaces should be adequate for movement
  - all public facilities should have fixtures designed for use by the handicapped

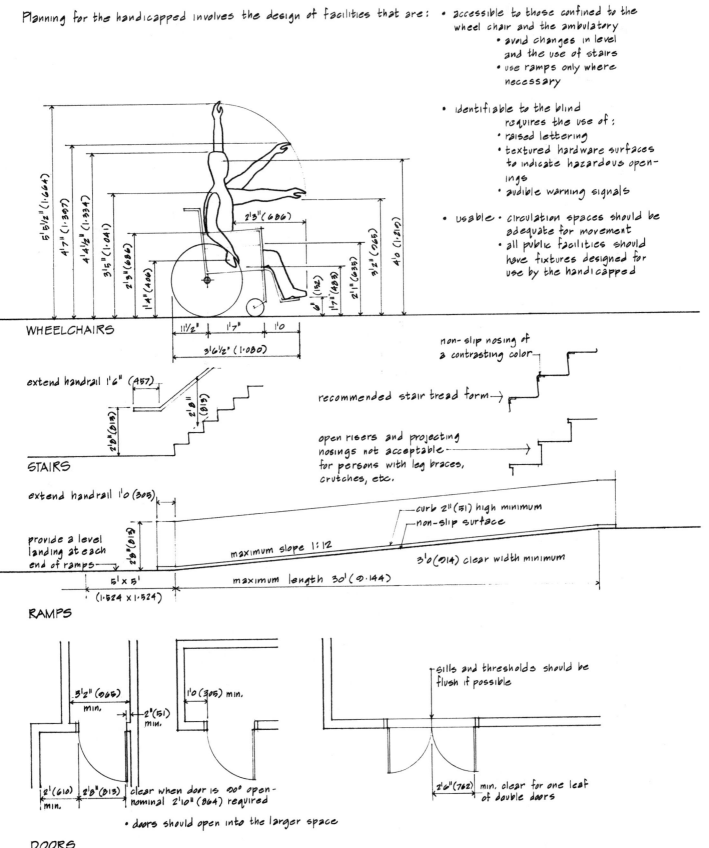

WHEELCHAIRS

5'5½" (1.664)
4'7" (1.307)
4'4½" (1.334)
3'5" (1.041)
2'3" (686)
1'4" (406)
2'3" (686)
3'2" (965)
4'0 (1.219)
2'1" (635)
1'7" (483)
6" (152)

11½" 1'7" 1'0
3'6½" (1.080)

STAIRS

extend handrail 1'6" (457)
2'0" (615)
2'0" (615)

non-slip nosing of a contrasting color
recommended stair tread form →
open risers and projecting nosings not acceptable for persons with leg braces, crutches, etc.

RAMPS

extend handrail 1'0 (305)
provide a level landing at each end of ramps
2'0" (615)
maximum slope 1:12
curb 2" (51) high minimum
non-slip surface
3'0 (914) clear width minimum
5' x 5' (1.524 x 1.524)
maximum length 30' (9.144)

DOORS

3'2" (965) min.
1'0 (305) min.
2"(51) min.
2'(610) min.
2'8" (813)
clear when door is 90° open— nominal 2'10" (864) required

sills and thresholds should be flush if possible
2'6" (762) min. clear for one leaf of double doors

- doors should open into the larger space

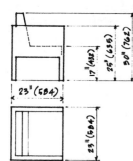

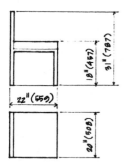

ARM CHAIR

17" (432) 25" (636) 30" (762)

23" (584)

23" (584)

SIDE CHAIR

18" (457) 31" (787)

22" (559)

22" (558)

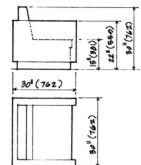

LOUNGE CHAIR

15" (381) 22" (559) 30" (762)

30" (762)

30" (762)

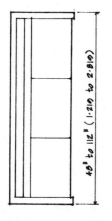

SOFA

48" to 112" (1.219 to 2.819)

BEDS

39" (991) 54" (1.372) queen 60" (1.524)
king 72" (1.829)
king 76" (1.930)

80" (2.032) 84" (2.134)

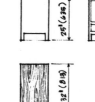

NIGHT TABLE

15" (381) 25" (636) 32" (813)

HIGH CHEST

18" (457) 42" (1.067) 36" (914)

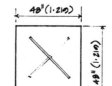

LOW TABLES

17" (432) 48" (1.219) 48" (1.219)

45" (1.143) 17" (432) 23" (584)

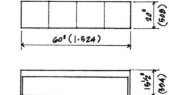

STOOL   BENCH

18" (457) 18" (457) 29" (737)

20" (508) 60" (1.524) 15½" (394)

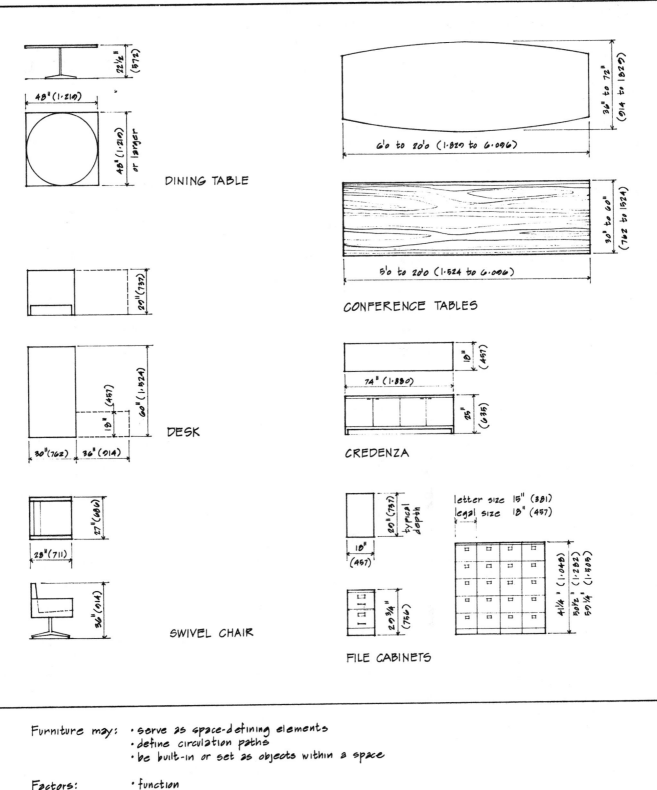

22½" (572)

48" (1·210)

48" (1·210) or larger

DINING TABLE

36" to 72" (914 to 1826)

6'0 to 20'0 (1·829 to 6·096)

30" to 60" (762 to 1524)

5'0 to 20'0 (1·524 to 6·096)

CONFERENCE TABLES

29" (737)

DESK

60" (1·524)

18" (457)

30" (762)   36" (914)

18" (457)

74" (1·880)

25" (635)

CREDENZA

27" (686)

28" (711)

36" (914)

SWIVEL CHAIR

29" (737)

typical depth

18" (457)

letter size 15" (381)
legal size 18" (457)

20¾" (756)

41¼" (1·048)

50½" (1·282)

59¼" (1·505)

FILE CABINETS

Furniture may:
• serve as space-defining elements
• define circulation paths
• be built-in or set as objects within a space

Factors:
• function
• comfort
• scale
• color
• style

* all dimensions are typical - verify with manufacturer

MINIMUM UNIFORMLY DISTRIBUTED LIVE LOADS	lbs/sq.ft.	kg/m²
ASSEMBLY FACILITIES		
· theaters with fixed seats	60	293
· movable seat facilities (auditoriums, gyms, etc.)	100	488
· corridors and lobbies	100	488
· stages	150	732
LIBRARIES · reading rooms	60	293
· book stacks	150	732
MANUFACTURING FACILITIES	125	610
OFFICES · office spaces	80	391
· lobbies	100	488
RESIDENTIAL FACILITIES		
· private dwellings, apartment units, hotel rooms	40	195
· public rooms	100	488
· corridors	60	293
SCHOOLS · classrooms	40	195
· corridors	100	488
SIDEWALKS AND VEHICULAR DRIVES	250	1221
STAIRS, FIRE ESCAPES, EXITWAYS	100	488
STORAGE WAREHOUSES · light	125	610
· heavy	250	1221
STORES · retail: first floor	100	488
upper floors	75	366
· wholesale	125	610
ROOF LOADS		
minimum, not including wind or earthquake loads	20	98
roof-gardens	100	488

Live loads to be assumed in the design of a building should be the maximum expected to be produced by the intended use or occupancy, but never less than the above. Always verify live load requirements with local applicable building codes.

In some instances, concentrated load conditions will take precedence (eg. office floors with heavy equipment or parking garages).

AVERAGE WEIGHTS OF MATERIALS	lbs/cu.ft.	kg/m³
SOIL, SAND AND GRAVEL		
cinder	45	720.8
clay, damp	110	
clay, dry	63	1009.2
earth, dry and loose	76	1217.4
earth, moist and packed	96	1537.8
sand and gravel, dry and loose	105	1682.1
sand and gravel, wet	120	1922.4
WOOD		
cedar	22	352.4
Douglas fir	32	512.6
hemlock	29	464.5
maple	42	672.8
oak, red	41	656.8
oak, white	46	736.8
pine, southern	29	464.5
redwood	26	416.5
spruce	27	432.5
METAL		
aluminum	165	2643.3
brass, red	546	8746.9
bronze, statuary	509	8154.2
copper	556	8907.1
iron, cast	450	7209.0
iron, wrought	485	7769.7
lead	710	11374.2
monel metal	556	8907.1
nickel	565	9051.3
stainless steel	510	8170.2
steel, rolled	490	7849.8
tin	459	7351.2
zinc	440	7048.8
CONCRETE		
stone, plain	144	2306.8
stone, reinforced	150	2403.0
cinder	100	1602.0
lightweight: haydite	85-100	1361.6 - 1602.0
vermiculite	25-60	400.5 - 961.1
STONE		
granite	175	2803.5
limestone	165	2643.3
marble	165	2643.3
sandstone	147	2354.0
slate	175	2803.5
WATER max. density @ 4°c	62	993.1
ice	56	897.0
snow	8	128.1

AVERAGE WEIGHTS OF MATERIALS

	lbs/ft²	kg/m²
FLOOR AND ROOF CONSTRUCTION:		
concrete, reinforced, per 1" (25)		
· stone	12.5	61
· slag	11.5	56
· lightweight	6-10	29-49
concrete, plain, per 1" (25)		
· stone	12	59
· slag	11	54
· lightweight	3-9	15-44
concrete, precast hollow core plank, 6" (152)		
· stone	40	195
· lightweight	30	146
· cinder plank 2" (51)	15	73
· gypsum plank 2" (51)	12	59
steel deck	2-4	10-20
FLOOR FINISHES		
cement finish/topping, 1" (25)	12	59
marble	30	146
terrazzo, 1" (25)	13	63
tile, ceramic or quarry, 3/4" (19)	10	49
wood: · hardwood 25/32" (20)	4	20
· softwood 3/4" (19)	2.5	12
· wood block 3" (76)	15	73
vinyl asbestos tile, 1/8" (3)	1.33	7
CEILINGS		
acoustical fiber tile, 3/4" (19)	1	5
acoustic plaster on gypsum lath base	10	49
channel suspended system	1	5
ROOFING		
built-up (5-ply felt and gravel)	6	29
copper or tin		
corrugated asbestos	4	20
corrugated iron (galvanized)	1.5	7
Fiberglas	0.5	2
lead, 1/8" (3)	8	39
monel metal	1.5	7
shingles: · asphalt	3	15
· asbestos cement	3	15
· slate, 1/4" (6)	10	49
· wood	2	10
tile: · cement	16	78
· clay	14	68

	lbs/ft²	kg/m²
WALLS AND PARTITIONS		
brick, per 4" (102) of thickness	35	171
concrete block:		
· stone and gravel aggregate		
· 4" (102)	34	166
· 6" (152)	50	244
· 8" (203)	58	283
· 12" (305)	90	439
· lightweight aggregate		
· 4" (102)	22	107
· 6" (152)	31	151
· 8" (203)	38	186
· 12" (305)	55	269
glass block, 4" (102)	18	88
gypsum board, 1/2" (13)	2	10
metal lath	0.5	2
metal studs, with lath and plaster	18	88
plaster, 1" (25)		
· cement	10	49
· gypsum	5	24
plywood, 1/2" (13)	1.5	7
stone · granite 4" (102)	59	288
· limestone 6" (152)	55	269
· marble 1" (25)	13	63
· sandstone 4" (102)	49	239
· slate 1" (25)	14	68
tile · ceramic mosaic, 1/4" (6)	2.5	12
· glazed wall tile, 3/8" (10)	3	15
tile, structural clay		
· 4" (102)	18	88
· 6" (152)	28	137
· 8" (203)	34	166
· 10" (254)	40	195
wood studs, 2x4 with lath and plaster	16	78
INSULATION		
batt or blanket, per 1" (25)	0.4	2
fiber board	2.0	10
foamed board, per 1" (25)	0.2	1
loose	0.5	2
poured in place	2.0	10
rigid	1.5	7
GLASS		
insulating glass, with 1/8" (3) plate	3.25	16
plate, 1/4"	3.30	16
sheet (DS) 1/8" (3)	1.60	8
(HS) 1/4" (6)	3.25	16
wire glass, 1/4" (6)	3.50	17

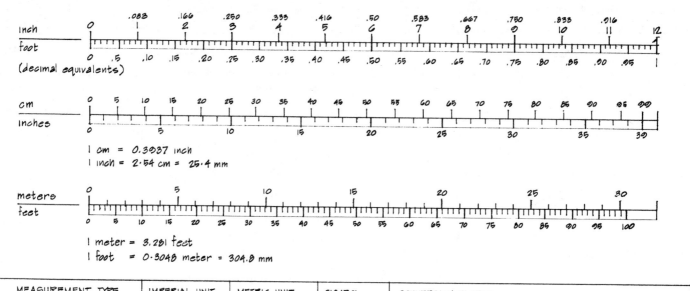

1 cm = 0.3937 inch
1 inch = 2.54 cm = 25.4 mm

1 meter = 3.281 feet
1 foot = 0.3048 meter = 304.8 mm

MEASUREMENT TYPE	IMPERIAL UNIT	METRIC UNIT	SYMBOL	CONVERSION FACTOR
LENGTH	mile	kilometer	km	1 mile = 1·609 km
	yard	meter	m	1 yard = 0·9144 m = 914·4 mm
	foot	meter	m	1 foot = 0·3048 m
		millimeter	mm	= 304·8 mm
	inch	millimeter	mm	1 inch = 25·40 mm
AREA	square mile	sq. kilometer	km²	1 mile² = 2·590 km²
		hectare	ha	= 259·0 ha $\quad$ [1 ha = 10,000 m²]
	acre	hectare	ha	1 acre = 0·4047 ha
		square meter	m²	= 4046·9 m²
	square yard	square meter	m²	1 yard² = 0·8361 m²
	square foot	square meter	m²	1 foot² = 0·0929 m²
		sq. centimeter	cm²	= 929·03 cm²
	square inch	sq. centimeter	cm²	1 inch² = 6·452 cm² = 645·2 mm²
VOLUME	cubic yard	cubic meter	m³	1 yd³ = 0·7646 m³
	cubic foot	cubic meter	m³	1 ft³ = 0·02832 m³
		liter	liter	= 28·32 liter $\quad$ [1000 liter = 1 m³
		cubic decimeter	dm³	= 28·32 dm³ $\quad$ 1 liter = 1 dm³]
	cubic inch	cubic millimeter	mm³	1 in³ = 16390 mm³
		cubic centimeter	cm³	= 16·39 cm³
		milliliter	ml	= 16·39 ml
		liter	liter	= 0·01639 liter
MASS	ton	kilogram	kg	1 ton = 1016·05 kg
	kip (1000 lbs)	kilogram	kg	1 kip = 453·50 kg
	pound	kilogram	kg	1 lb = 0·4536 kg
	ounce	gram	g	1 oz = 28·35 g
CAPACITY	quart	liter	liter	1 qt. = 1·137 liter
	pint	liter	liter	1 pt. = 0·568 liter
	fluid ounce	cubic centimeter	cm³	1 fl.oz. = 28·413 cm³

MEASUREMENT TYPE	IMPERIAL UNIT	METRIC UNIT	SYMBOL	CONVERSION FACTOR
MASS PER UNIT AREA	pound/square foot	kilogram/square meter	kg/m^2	$1\ lb/ft^2 = 4.882\ kg/m^2$
	pound/square inch	kilogram/square meter	kg/m^2	$1\ lb/in^2 = 703.07\ kg/m^2$
	ounce/square foot	gram/square meter	g/m^2	$1\ oz/ft^2 = 305.15\ g/m^2$
DENSITY	pound/cubic foot	kilogram/cubic meter	kg/m^3	$1\ lb/ft^3 = 16.02\ kg/m^3$
	pound/cubic inch	gram/cubic centimeter	g/cm^3	$1\ lb/in^3 = 27.68\ g/cm^3$
		megagram/cubic meter	Mg/m^3	$= 27.68\ Mg/m^3$
VOLUME RATE OF FLOW	cubic feet/minute	liter/second	liter/s	$1\ ft^3/min = 0.4791\ liter/s$
	cubic feet/second	cubic meter/second	m^3/s	$1\ ft^3/sec = 0.02832\ m^3/s$
	cubic inch/second	milliliter/second	ml/s	$1\ in^3/sec = 16.39\ ml/s$
	gallon/hour	liter/hour	liter/h	$1\ gal/hr = 4.5461\ liter/h$
	gallon/minute	liter/second	liter/s	$1\ gal/min = 0.07577\ liter/s$
	gallon/second	liter/second	liter/s	$1\ gal/sec = 4.5461\ liter/s$
FUEL CAPACITY	gallon/mile	liter/kilometer	liter/km	$1\ gpm = 2.825\ liter/km$
	miles/gallon	kilometers/litre	km/liter	$1\ mpg = 0.354\ km/liter$
VELOCITY	miles/hour	kilometer/hour	km/h	$1\ mph = 1.609\ km/h$
	feet/minute	meter/minute	m/min	$1\ fpm = 0.3048\ m/min = 0.0051\ m/s$
	feet/second	meter/second	m/s	$1\ fps = 0.3048\ m/s$
	inch/second	millimeter/second	mm/s	$1\ in/sec = 25.4\ mm/s$
TEMPERATURE	°Fahrenheit	degree Celsius	°C	$t°C = 0.5556\ (t°F - 32)$
				$= 5/9\ (t°F - 32)$
• temperature interval	°Fahrenheit	degree Celsium	°C	$1\ deg F = 0.5556\ deg C$
HEAT	BTU	joule	J	$1\ Btu = 1055\ J$
		kilojoule	kJ	$1\ Btu = 1.055\ kJ$
• heat flow rate	BTU/hour	watt	W	$1\ Btu/hr = 0.2931\ W$
		kilowatt	kW	$1\ Btu/hr = 0.0002931\ kW$
• density of heat flow rate	$BTU/ft^2 \cdot hour$	$watt/meter^2$	W/m^2	$1\ Btu/ft^2 \cdot hr = 3.155\ W/m^2$
• thermal conductivity	BTU·inch/ $ft^2 \cdot hour \cdot deg F$	watt/meter·deg C	W/m°C	$1\ Btu \cdot in/ft^2 \cdot hr \cdot deg F$ $= 0.1442\ W/m°C$
• thermal conductance	$BTU/ft^2 \cdot hour \cdot deg F$	$watt/meter^2 \cdot deg C$	$W/m^2°C$	$1\ Btu/ft^2 \cdot hr \cdot deg F$ $= 5.678\ W/m^2°C$
• refrigeration	ton	watt	W	$1\ ton = 3510\ W$
POWER	horsepower	watt	W	$1\ hp = 745.7\ W$
		kilowatt	kW	$0.7457\ kW$
LIGHTING	foot-candle	lux	lux	$1\ ft\text{-}candle = 10.76\ lux\ [1\ lux = 1\ lumen/m^2]$
	lumen/square foot	lux	lux	$1\ lumen/ft^2 = 10.76\ lux$

FACTOR	MULTIPLES/SUBMULTIPLES · PREFIXES · SYMBOLS		
thousand million	10^9	giga	G
one million	10^6	mega	M
one thousand	10^3	kilo	k
one hundred	10^2	hecto	h
ten	10^1	deca	da
one-tenth	10^{-1}	deci	d
one-hundredth	10^{-2}	centi	c
one-thousandth	10^{-3}	milli	m
one-millionth	10^{-6}	micro	u

Fire codes specify:
- the required means of egress for a building's occupants in case of fire
- the fire-resistance ratings of materials and construction required for a building depending on its:
  - location (fire district)
  - use and occupancy
  - size (volume, height, and area per floor)
- fire-protection systems required for hazardous uses or large occupancies

The purpose of these requirements is to control the spread of fire and allow sufficient time for the occupants of a burning building to exit safely before the structure weakens to the extent that it becomes dangerous. The following is an outline of the principles involved in fire protection. Consult the local applicable code in force for specific requirements. (see bibliography for list of building codes)

A means of egress requires adequate access to protected fire exits leading to safe discharge points.

- exit access
  - passages leading to an exit should be as direct as possible, unobstructed with projections, and well-lit (emergency power may be required)
  - exits should be clearly marked

- exits
  - fire exits must provide a protected means of evacuation from the building to safe discharge points to the exterior
  - typical fire-rating requirements for exit enclosures (floor, wall, ceiling, stair construction)
    - one-hour fire-rating for buildings up to 3 stories in height
    - two-hour fire-rating for buildings 4 or more stories in height
  - for most occupancies, a minimum of two exits is required to provide a margin of safety in case one exit is blocked
  - exits should be located as remote from each other as possible without creating deadend passageways
  - maximum travel distances to any one exit is usually specified by code according to a building's use, occupancy, and fire hazard
  - required width:
    - basic unit width = 22" (559)
    - number of persons allowed per unit width depends on a building's use and occupancy:
      - places of assembly   100
      - offices, schools, stores   60
      - residential buildings   45
  - fire stairs: maximum riser = 7½" (191); minimum tread = 10" (254)

- exit discharge
  - exits should discharge to a safe place of refuge outside of the building at ground level

Most codes classify a building according to the following construction categories:
- wood frame or unprotected noncombustible
- ordinary
- heavy timber
- protected noncombustible
- fire-resistant

A building's maximum size (height and area per floor) is limited by its construction, use, occupancy, and location. The size limitation may in some cases be exceeded if the building is equipped with a fire sprinkler system or if it is divided into fire areas not exceeding the size limitation. These fire areas must be separated by fire-rated walls or barriers. The integrity of these fire walls must be maintained through the use of protected openings such as fire-rated windows and skylight assemblies, automatically closing fire doors, and ducts or shaft spaces equipped with fire dampers.

Fire doors are classified according to their location:

class	fire-rating	location
A	3 hour fire-rating	- fire walls separating buildings or fire areas within a building
B	1½ hour	- vertical enclosures of fire stairs and elevators
C	¾ hour	- corridors and partitions
D	1½ hour	- exterior walls subject to severe fire exposure
E	¾ hour	- exterior walls subject to moderate fire exposure

Almost all materials suffer damage from fire. Even noncombustible materials such as steel may be weakened by by high temperatures caused by fire. "Fire-resistant" is therefore a more accurate term than "fireproof". Fire-resistant construction refers to methods of:
- controlling the spread of fire
- increasing the length of exposure to fire a material can withstand without damage
- reducing a material's flammability

Materials used to provide fire protection for a building's construction must be inflammable and able to withstand very high temperatures without disintegrating. They should also be low conductors of heat to insulate the protected material from the heat generated by the fire. Materials commonly used to provide fire-resistant protection include concrete (often with lightweight aggregate), gypsum concrete, gypsum board and plaster, and mineral fiber products. Wood may be chemically treated to reduce its flammability.

The following is a sampling of fire-resistance ratings for typical wall, floor, and roof constructions. Consult the Underwriters' Laboratories, Inc. Building Materials List for complete specifications.

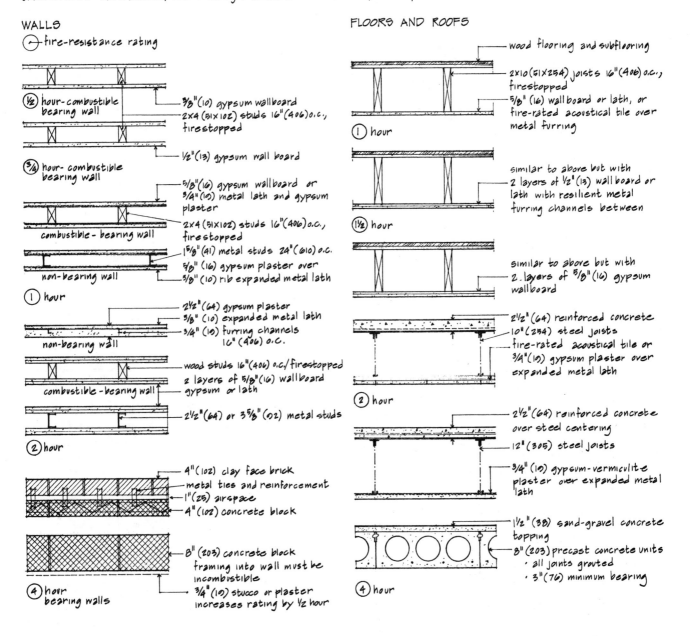

WALLS
⌒ fire-resistance rating

½ hour - combustible bearing wall
- 3/8" (10) gypsum wallboard
- 2x4 (51x102) studs 16" (406) o.c., firestopped
- ½" (13) gypsum wall board

¾ hour - combustible bearing wall
- 5/8" (16) gypsum wallboard or 3/4" (19) metal lath and gypsum plaster
- 2x4 (51x102) studs 16" (406) o.c., firestopped

combustible - bearing wall
- 1 5/8" (41) metal studs 24" (610) o.c.

non-bearing wall
- 5/8" (16) gypsum plaster over
- 3/8" (10) rib expanded metal lath

1 hour
non-bearing wall
- 2½" (64) gypsum plaster
- 5/8" (10) expanded metal lath
- 3/4" (19) furring channels 16" (406) o.c.

combustible - bearing wall
- wood studs 16" (406) o.c./firestopped
- 2 layers of 5/8" (16) wallboard gypsum or lath
- 2½" (64) or 3 5/8" (92) metal studs

2 hour
- 4" (102) clay face brick
- metal ties and reinforcement
- 1" (25) airspace
- 4" (102) concrete block

4 hour bearing walls
- 8" (203) concrete block framing into wall must be incombustible
- 3/4" (19) stucco or plaster increases rating by ½ hour

FLOORS AND ROOFS
- wood flooring and subflooring
- 2x10 (51x254) joists 16" (406) o.c., firestopped

1 hour
- 5/8" (16) wallboard or lath, or fire-rated acoustical tile over metal furring

1½ hour
- similar to above but with 2 layers of ½" (13) wallboard or lath with resilient metal furring channels between

- similar to above but with 2 layers of 5/8" (16) gypsum wallboard

2 hour
- 2½" (64) reinforced concrete
- 10" (254) steel joists
- fire-rated acoustical tile or 3/4" (19) gypsum plaster over expanded metal lath

- 2½" (64) reinforced concrete over steel centering
- 12" (305) steel joists
- 3/4" (19) gypsum-vermiculite plaster over expanded metal lath

4 hour
- 1½" (38) sand-gravel concrete topping
- 8" (203) precast concrete units
  - all joints grouted
  - 3" (76) minimum bearing

Acoustics may be defined as the science of sound, including its production, transmission, and control of its effects. Sound requires a source for its production, a path for its transmission, and a receiver. It may be defined by the frequency, velocity, and magnitude of its energy waves. Sound waves generated by a vibrating object radiate outward from the source equally in all directions until they hit a surface that either reflects or absorbs them.

The acoustical design of spaces involves the reinforcement of desirable sounds and the control of undesirable noise. A room's acoustics is dependent on its shape, form, volume, and the nature of its surfaces.

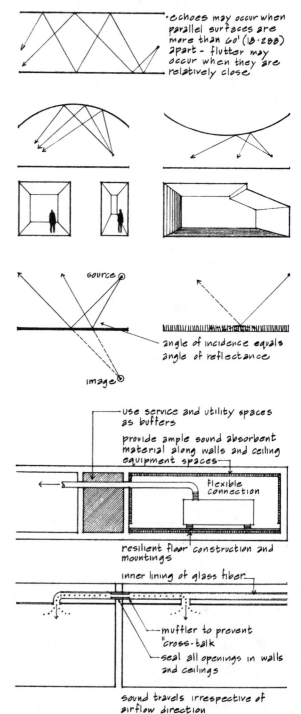

- room form
  - parallel surfaces cause sound to reflect back and forth across a space
  - may cause excessive reverberation and undesirable echoes or flutter

  - concave surfaces focus sound
  - may cause undesirable "hot spots" of sound

  - convex surfaces diffuse sound
  - diffused sound is desirable in listening areas

  - high cubical and long narrowly proportioned spaces may require splayed surfaces to diffuse reflected sounds and absorbent surface to control reverberation

- nature of the surfaces

  - hard surfaces reflect sound while soft, porous surfaces tend to absorb sound energy
  - the area and disposition of hard and soft surfaces within a space depends on the level of sound, reverberation time, and resonance required for the intended use of the space

· echoes may occur when parallel surfaces are more than 60' (18·288) apart - flutter may occur when they are relatively close

source

image

angle of incidence equals angle of reflectance

Undesirable noise should be controlled at its source. Noise sources within a building include:

- mechanical equipment and supply systems
  - select quiet equipment
  - use resilient mountings and flexible bellows to isolate equipment vibrations from the building structure and supply system
  - control noise transmission through ductwork by:
    - lining the ducts internally with glass-fiber
    - installing sound attenuating mufflers
    - using smooth duct turns
  - minimize "cross-talk" through ducts by maximizing the distance between diffusers in adjacent spaces
- water supply and drainage systems
  - use expansion valves and flexible loop connections to prevent pipe rattling and noise transmission along the pipes
  - seal pipe penetrations through walls and floors with flexible packing

- use service and utility spaces as buffers
- provide ample sound absorbent material along walls and ceiling equipment spaces
- flexible connection
- resilient floor construction and mountings
- inner lining of glass fiber
- muffler to prevent "cross-talk"
- seal all openings in walls and ceilings

sound travels irrespective of airflow direction

When control of a noise source does not reduce the undesirable sound to an acceptable level, then its transmission through the air or a building's structure must be controlled by sound absorption and/or isolation.

- sound absorption is achieved through the use of fibrous materials or panel resonators

    - fibrous materials: absorptive efficiency depends on their thickness, density, porosity, exposure, and method of mounting
    - panel resonators: consists of a thin membrane material (eg. plywood) mounted in front of a sealed air space (effective for low-frequency sounds)
    - all sound-absorbent devices absorb sound by converting acoustical energy into heat energy within the structure of the absorbent material
    - many sound-absorbent products are commercially available such as acoustical ceiling tile
    - other materials and products that are effective sound absorbers include carpeting, heavy drapes, and upholstered furnishings

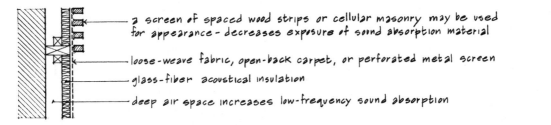

a screen of spaced wood strips or cellular masonry may be used for appearance - decreases exposure of sound absorption material

loose-weave fabric, open-back carpet, or perforated metal screen

glass-fiber acoustical insulation

deep air space increases low-frequency sound absorption

- sound isolation involves increasing a path's resistance to both air-borne and structure-borne sound

    - the required reduction in noise level from one space to another depends on the level of the sound source and the level of that sound's intrusion that may be acceptable to the listener
    - the perceived or apparent sound level in a space is dependent on:
        - the transmission loss through the wall, ceiling, or floor construction
        - the absorptive qualities of the receiving space (non-reverberent or highly-absorbent spaces enhance transmission loss and increase noise reduction)
        - the level of background or masking sound (which increases the threshold of audibility of other sounds in its presence)

- a wall or floor construction set in vibration by the energy waves from a sound source will itself become a sound source
- transmission loss through a wall or floor construction depends on the frequency of the sound, and the construction's mass, resilience or stiffness, and area

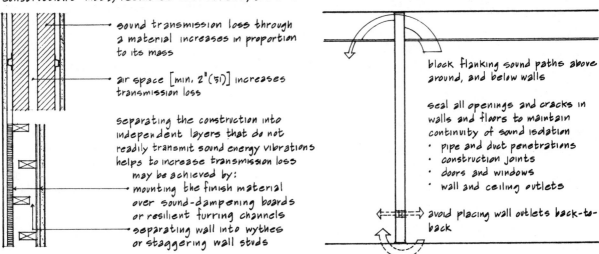

sound transmission loss through a material increases in proportion to its mass

air space [min. 2"(51)] increases transmission loss

separating the construction into independent layers that do not readily transmit sound energy vibrations helps to increase transmission loss may be achieved by:
- mounting the finish material over sound-dampening boards or resilient furring channels
- separating wall into wythes or staggering wall studs

block flanking sound paths above around, and below walls

seal all openings and cracks in walls and floors to maintain continuity of sound isolation
- pipe and duct penetrations
- construction joints
- doors and windows
- wall and ceiling outlets

avoid placing wall outlets back-to-back

These symbols are some of the abstract conventions commonly used in architectural construction drawings.

EARTH
- earth
- rock
- gravel fill

CONCRETE
- structural
- lightweight
- block
- block

BRICK
- common brick
- face brick
- fire brick
- plaster, sand, cement grout

STONE
- cut stone
- rubble
- cast stone
- marble
- slate

METAL
- iron/steel
- aluminum
- brass/bronze
- sheet metal/all metals at small scale
- structural

WOOD
- finish
- rough
- plywood (large scale)
- plywood (small scale)
- wood stud walls

INSULATION
- loose or batt
- rigid
- rigid insulation — small scale
- STRUCTURAL CLAY TILE

MISCELLANEOUS
- resilient flooring
- acoustical tile
- waterproofing/flashing
- glass (large scale)
- glass (small scale)

• PLAN AND SECTION INDICATIONS

GLAZING

CONCRETE/PLASTER

STONE
- ashlar
- rubble

MASONRY
- brick
- block
- running bond
- stack bond
- ceramic tile

WOOD
- shingles
- panel

METAL
- metal

Within the limitations of the scale of the drawing, a material's scale, texture, and pattern should be drawn as accurately as possible.

• ELEVATION INDICATIONS

BIBLIOGRAPHY

ARCHITECTURE AND DESIGN

Architecture as Space	Bruno Zevi, Horizon
Art and Visual Perception	Rudolph Arnheim, Univ. of California Press, 1964
Art of Color	Johannes Itten, Van Nostrand Reinhold, 1973
The Arts in Modern American Civilization	John A. Kouwenhoven, Norton, 1967
Design with Climate	Victor Olgyay, Princeton University Press, 1963
Experiencing Architecture	Steen Eiler Rasmussen, MIT Press, 1962
Interior Design	Friedmann/Pile/Wilson, Elsevier, 1971
Introduction to Modern Architecture	J. M. Richards, Pelican, 1956
The Place of Houses	Moore/Allen/Lyndon, Holt·Reinhardt·Winston, 1974
Shelter	Shelter Publications, Random House, 1973
Towards a New Architecture	Le Corbusier, Architectural Press, 1927

BUILDING CONSTRUCTION · STRUCTURE · MECHANICAL SYSTEMS

Architectural Graphic Standards	Ramsey and Sleeper, Wiley, 1970
Building Construction Handbook	Frederick S. Merritt, McGraw-Hill, 1965
Concepts in Architectural Acoustics	M. David Egan, McGraw-Hill, 1972
Concepts in Thermal Comfort	M. David Egan, Prentice-Hall, 1975
Construction: Principles, Methods, Materials	Schmid/Olin/Lewis, Interstate, 1972
Dwelling House Construction	Albert Dietz, MIT Press, 1974
Materials and Methods of Architectural Construction	Parker/Gay/McGuire, Wiley, 1966
Materials and Methods of Contemporary Construction	Hornbostel/Hornung, Prentice-Hall, 1974
Mechanical and Electrical Equipment for Buildings	McGuinness/Stein, Wiley, 1971
Simplified Design of Reinforced Concrete	Parker, Wiley, 1968
Simplified Design of Roof Trusses for Architects and Builders	Parker, Wiley, 1953
Simplified Design of Structural Steel	Parker, Wiley, 1974
Simplified Design of Structural Timber	Parker, Wiley, 1967
Structure and Form in Modern Architecture	Curt Siegel, Reinhold, 1962
Structure in Architecture	Salvadori/Heller, Prentice-Hall, 1963
Structure: the Essence of Architecture	Forrest Wilson, Van Nostrand Reinhold, 1972

BUILDING CODES AND STANDARDS

ASTM Standards and Specifications	American Society for Testing and Materials
Basic Building Code	Building Officials Conference of America
Minimum Property Standards	Federal Housing Administration
National Building Code	American Insurance Association
National Electric Code	National Fire Protection Association
National Plumbing Code	American Standards Association
Southern Standard Building Code	Southern Building Code Congress
Underwriters' Laboratories, Inc., Building Materials List	Underwriters' Laboratories, Inc.
Uniform Building Code	International Conference of Building Officials
Uniform Heating and Cooling Comfort Code	Western Plumbing Officials Association
Uniform Plumbing Code	Western Plumbing Officials Association

trade associations

Trade associations are valuable sources of product information and construction standards

Acoustical and Insulating Materials Association	205 W. Touhy Ave., Park Ridge, Illinois	60068
Adhesive Manufacturers Association of America	441 Lexington Ave., New York, N.Y.	10017
Air-Conditioning and Refrigeration Institute	1815 N. Fort Meyer Drive, Arlington, Virginia	22209
Aluminum Association	750 Third Ave., New York, N.Y.	10017
American Association of Nurserymen	Suite 835, Southern Bldg., Washington, D.C.	20005
American Concrete Institute	P.O. Box 4754, Redford Sta., Detroit, Michigan	48219
American Concrete Pipe Association	1501 Wilson Blvd., Arlington, Virginia	22209
American Forest Institute	1619 Massachusetts Ave., N.W., Washington D.C.	20036
American Hardboard Association	Suite 2236, 20 N. Wacker Dr., Chicago, Illinois	60606
American Hardware Manufacturers Association	2130 Keith Bldg., Cleveland, Ohio	44115
American Home Lighting Institute	230 N. Michigan Ave., Chicago, Illinois	60601
American Institute of Architects	1785 Massachusetts Ave., N.W., Washington, D.C.	20036
American Institute of Planners	Rm. 800, 917 15th St., N.W., Washington, D.C.	20005
American Institute of Steel Construction, Inc.	101 Park Ave., New York, N.Y.	10017
American Institute of Timber Construction	333 W. Hampden Ave., Englewood, Colorado	80110
American Insurance Association	85 John St., New York, N.Y.	10038
American Iron and Steel Institute	150 E. 42nd St., New York, N.Y.	10017
American National Standards Institute	1430 Broadway, New York, N.Y.	10018
American Paper Institute	260 Madison Ave., New York, N.Y.	10016
American Plywood Institute	1119 A St., Tacoma, Washington	98401
American Savings and Loan Institute	111 E. Wacker Dr., Chicago, Illinois	60601
American Society for Testing and Materials	1916 Race St., Philadelphia, Pennsylvania	19103
American Society of Civil Engineers	345 E. 47th St., New York, N.Y.	10017
American Society of Heating, Refrigerating, and Air-conditioning Engineers, Inc.	345 E. 47th St., New York, N.Y.	10017
American Society of Landscape Architects	1425 H St., N.W., Washington, D.C.	20005
American Society of Mechanical Engineers	345 E. 47th St., New York, N.Y.	10017
American Society of Planning Officials	1313 E. 60th St., Chicago, Illinois	60637
American Society of Sanitary Engineering	228 Standard Bldg., Cleveland, Ohio	44113
American Walnut Manufacturers Association	Rm. 1729, 666 N. Lake Shore Dr., Chicago, Illinois	60611
American Wood-Preservers Association	1012 14th St., N.W., Washington, D.C.	20005
Architectural Aluminum Manufacturers Association	410 N. Michigan Ave., Chicago, Illinois	60611
Architectural Woodwork Institute	5055 S. Chesterfield Rd., Arlington, Virginia	22206
Asphalt and Vinyl Asbestos Tile Institute	101 Park Ave., New York, N.Y.	10017
Asphalt Institute	Asphalt Institute Bldg., College Park, Maryland	20740
Asphalt Roofing Manufacturers Association	757 Third Ave., New York, N.Y.	10017
Associated General Contractors of America, Inc.	1957 E St., N.W., Washington, D.C.	20006
Batelle Memorial Institute	505 King Ave., Columbus, Ohio	43201
Building Officials and Code Administrators Int'l.	1313 E. 60th St., Chicago, Illinois	60637
Building Research Institute	2101 Constitution Ave., N.W., Washington D.C.	20418
California Redwood Association	617 Montgomery St., San Francisco, California	94111
Cast Iron Soil Pipe Institute	2029 K St., N.W., Washington, D.C.	60521
Clay Products Association	507 York Rd., Elmhurst, Illinois	60126
Concrete Reinforcing Steel Institute	228 N. LaSalle St., Chicago, Illinois	60601
Construction Specifications Institute, Inc.	1717 Massachusetts Ave., N.W., Washington D.C.	20036
Copper Institute	50 Broadway, New York, N.Y.	10004
Division of Building Research of Canada	Montreal Road, Ottawa 7, Canada	
Electric Heating Association, Inc.	437 Madison Ave., New York, N.Y.	10022
Expanded Shale, Clay, and Slate Institute	1041 National Press Bldg., Washington, D.C.	20004
Facing Tile Institute	111 E. Wacker Dr., Chicago, Illinois	60601
Federal Housing Administration	451 7th St., S.W., Washington, D.C.	20411
Fine Hardwoods Association	666 N. Lake Shore Dr., Chicago, Illinois	60611
Flat Glass Marketing Association	1325 Topeka Ave., Topeka, Kansas	66612
Forest Products Laboratory	U.S. Dept. of Agriculture, Madison, Wisconsin	53705
Gypsum Association	201 N. Wells St., Chicago, Illinois	60606
Hardwood Plywood Manufacturers Association	Box 6246, 2310 S. Walter Reed Dr., Arlington, Virginia	22206
Home Ventilating Institute	230 N. Michigan Ave., Chicago, Illinois	60601
IIT Research Institute	10 W. 35th St., Chicago, Illinois	60616
Illuminating Engineering Society	345 E. 47th St., New York, N.Y.	10017

International Conference of Building Officials	50 S. Los Robles, Pasadena, California	91101
Iron League of Chicago, Inc.	228 N. LaSalle St., Chicago, Illinois	60601
Maple Flooring Manufacturers Association	424 Washington Ave., Oshkosh, Wisconsin	54901
Marble Institute of America	1984 Chain Bridge Rd., McLean, Virginia	22101
Metal Lath Association	221 N. LaSalle St., Chicago, Illinois	60601
National Association of Home Builders	1625 L St., N.W., Washington, D.C.	20036
National Builders' Hardware Association	1200 Ave. of the Americas, New York, N.Y.	10019
National Bureau of Standards	U.S. Dept. of Commerce, Washington, D.C.	20234
National Concrete Masonry Association	1800 N. Kent St., Arlington, Virginia	22209
National Electrical Manufacturers Association	155 E. 44th St., New York, N.Y.	10017
National Fire Protection Association	60 Batterymarch St., Boston, Massachusetts	02110
National Forest Products Association	1619 Massachusetts Ave., N.W., Washington D.C.	20036
National Hardwood Lumber Association	59 E. Van Buren St., Chicago, Illinois	60605
National Kitchen Cabinet Association	Suite 248, 334 E. Broadway, Louisville, Kentucky	40202
National Mineral Wool Insulation Association, Inc.	211 E. 51st St., New York, N.Y.	10022
National Oak Flooring Manufacturers Association	814 Sterick Bldg., Memphis, Tennessee	38103
National Paint, Varnish and Lacquer Association	1500 Rhode Island Ave., N.W., Washington, D.C.	20005
National Particleboard Association	2306 Perkins Place, Silver Spring, Maryland	20910
National Safety Council	425 N. Michigan Ave., Chicago, Illinois	60611
National Slate Association	455 W. 23rd St., New York, N.Y.	10011
National Society of Professional Engineers	2029 K St., N.W., Washington, D.C.	20006
National Terrazzo and Mosaic Association, Inc.	716 Church St., Alexandria, Virginia	22314
National Woodwork Manufacturers Association, Inc.	400 W. Madison St., Chicago, Illinois	60606
Northeastern Lumber Manufacturers Association, Inc.	11-17 South St., Glen Falls, New York	12801
Perlite Institute, Inc.	45 W. 45th St., New York, N.Y.	10036
Plastic Pipe Institute	250 Park Ave., New York, N.Y.	10017
Plywood Fabricator Service, Inc.	1119 A St., Tacoma, Washington	98401
Ponderosa Pine Woodwork Association	30 S. LaSalle St., Chicago, Illinois	60603
Porcelain Enamel Institute, Inc.	1000 L St., N.W., Washington, D.C.	20036
Portland Cement Association	Old Orchard Road, Skokie, Illinois	60076
Red Cedar Shingle and Handsplit Shake Bureau	5510 White Bldg., Seattle, Washington	98101
Society of American Registered Architects	111 E. Wacker Drive, Chicago, Illinois	60601
Society of American Wood Preservers, Inc.	Suite 1004, 1501 Wilson Blvd., Arlington, Virginia	22209
Society of the Plastics Industry, Inc.	250 Park Ave., New York, N.Y.	10017
Southern Building Code Congress	1116 Brown-Marx Bldg., Birmingham, Alabama	35203
Southern Cypress Manufacturers Association	1614 Berwick Rd., Jacksonville, Florida	32207
Southern Forest Products Association	3525 Causeway Blvd., New Orleans, Louisiana	70150
Southern Hardwood Lumber Manufacturers Association	805 Sterick Bldg., Memphis, Tennessee	38103
Stanford Research Institute	Menlo Park, California	94025
Steel Door Institute	2130 Keith Bldg., Cleveland, Ohio	44115
Steel Joist Institute	2001 Jefferson Davis Hwy., Arlington, Virginia	22202
Steel Window Institute	2130 Keith Bldg., Cleveland, Ohio	44115
Structural Clay Products Institute	1750 Old Meadow Rd., McLean, Virginia	22101
Stucco Manufacturers Association, Inc.	15926 Kittridge, Van Nuys, California	91406
Superintendent of Documents	U.S. Government Printing Office, Wash., D.C.	20402
Tile Council of America, Inc.	360 Lexington Avenue, New York, N.Y.	10017
Underwriters' Laboratories, Inc.	207 E. Ohio St., Chicago, Illinois	60611
United States Savings and Loan League	111 E. Wacker Dr., Chicago, Illinois	60601
Urban Land Institute	1200 18th St., N.W., Washington, D.C.	20036
Vermiculite Institute	141 W. Jackson Blvd., Chicago, Illinois	60604
Western Red and Northern White Cedar Association	P.O. Box 2786, New Brighton, Minnesota	55112
Western Red Cedar Lumber Association	700 Yeon Bldg., Portland, Oregon	97204
Western Wood Products Association	1500 Yeon Bldg., Portland, Oregon	97204
Wire Reinforcement Institute	5034 Wisconsin Ave., N.W., Washington, D.C.	20016

INDEX